HARFLEUR TO HAMBURG

D. J. B. TRIM
BRENDAN SIMMS
(Editors)

Harfleur to Hamburg

Five Centuries of English and British Violence in Europe

OXFORD
UNIVERSITY PRESS

OXFORD
UNIVERSITY PRESS

Oxford University Press is a department of the
University of Oxford. It furthers the University's objective
of excellence in research, scholarship, and education
by publishing worldwide.

Oxford New York

Auckland   Cape Town   Dar es Salaam   Hong Kong   Karachi
Kuala Lumpur   Madrid   Melbourne   Mexico City   Nairobi
New Delhi   Shanghai   Taipei   Toronto

With offices in

Argentina   Austria   Brazil   Chile   Czech Republic   France   Greece
Guatemala   Hungary   Italy   Japan   Poland   Portugal   Singapore
South Korea   Switzerland   Thailand   Turkey   Ukraine   Vietnam

Oxford is a registered trade mark of Oxford University Press
in the UK and certain other countries.

Published in the United States of America by
Oxford University Press
198 Madison Avenue, New York, NY 10016

Copyright © D. J. B. Trim, Brendan Simms and the contributors, 2024

All rights reserved. No part of this publication may be reproduced,
stored in a retrieval system, or transmitted, in any form or by any means,
without the prior permission in writing of Oxford University Press,
or as expressly permitted by law, by license, or under terms agreed with
the appropriate reproduction rights organization. Inquiries concerning
reproduction outside the scope of the above should be sent to the
Rights Department, Oxford University Press, at the address above.

You must not circulate this work in any other form
and you must impose this same condition on any acquirer.
Library of Congress Cataloging-in-Publication Data is available

ISBN: 9780197784204

Printed in the United Kingdom
by Bell and Bain Ltd, Glasgow

CONTENTS

1. Introduction   1
   D. J. B. Trim and Brendan Simms

2. Strategy, Piety, and Chivalry: Violence and Restraint   15
   Under Henry V in 1415
   Clifford J. Rogers

3. Thomas Howard and the Character of English   41
   Violence during the Reign of Henry VIII
   Neil Murphy

4. English Atrocities in the Reign of Elizabeth I and   57
   Their Context
   D. J. B. Trim

5. State of Emergency: The English Subjection of Early   73
   Modern Ireland
   David Edwards

6. Violence in Scotland: The British Army and Government   93
   after Culloden
   Murray Pittock

7. 'Alas Poor Danes!': The Bombardment of   115
   Copenhagen, 1807
   Brendan Simms

v

8.	British-Army Violence against Civilians in the Peninsular War	135
	Charles Esdaile	
9.	'You Have Not Had A Sufficient Number Killed and Wounded': The Baltic Campaigns of the 'Crimean' War, 1854–56	155
	Andrew Lambert	
10.	The Blockade in the First World War	185
	Mary Elisabeth Cox	
11.	Legitimising Violence in the British Attack on the French Fleet At Mers-El-Kébir	201
	Karine Varley	
12.	Operation Gomorrah: Ruthlessness and the British Air War, 1943	219
	Richard Overy	

Notes	237
About the Contributors	301
Index	305

1

INTRODUCTION

D. J. B. Trim and Brendan Simms

Britain today, and the Anglo-British state historically, is and has been widely regarded as an upholder of international norms—including the law of nations and international law, as well as uncodified but influential value systems—at least in its relations with Western states. As a 'normative power', it has often sought to defend and export values and norms based on ideas of representative government and individual liberty, a historical legacy which informs its contemporary stance as a promoter of the 'Liberal International Order'.[1] This has often been contrasted with the ruthless, even extreme, violence perpetrated in colonial contexts; historians have emphasised the extent to which actions carried out in Ireland, and to some extent Scotland and Wales, were generally within the colonial framework, rather than a European one. What is often missed is the extent to which England and then Great Britain inflicted extreme violence on its European neighbours, even when still using the rhetoric of neighbourliness and friendship; with the exception of the Crusades, virtually all of England's enemies pre-1600 were European in any case. This history of English and British ruthlessness in Europe, occurring in and alongside wars in defence of persecuted peoples, complicates simple notions of England as either a champion of the 'standards of civilisation' or, to borrow the admittedly ironic title of Boyd Hilton's celebrated book, a 'mad, bad, and dangerous people'.[2]

The eleven case studies that follow examine English and British violence from roughly the siege of Harfleur in 1415 to the fire-bombing of Hamburg in 1943. The emphasis will not be on crimes carried out by individuals, but on ruthless violence—whether 'legal' or 'illegal'—sponsored by the state, whether directed by statesmen and politicians—such as the decisions to bombard Copenhagen in 1807 and Mers-el-Kébir in 1940 and to devastate Germany by bombing in World War II—or by instruments of the state such as military commanders. In other words, we are chiefly concerned with actions that were top-down and directed, and perpetrated for specific geopolitical and/or strategic reasons, many of them at or well beyond the bounds of what was sanctioned by the prevailing international norms of the time, which of course shifted across the 500 years in question, so that the casualties inflicted at Copenhagen in 1807, which were regarded by contemporaries as terrible, pale into insignificance in comparison to those inflicted by the strategic bombing of Germany. But we also look at the military culture that existed around such actions, which at times impelled military actors towards acts of violence. We look at how these actions were conceived, executed, and perceived, not only by their authors, but by the English/British public, by theorists of international law, and, in some cases, by the victims.

The term 'English and British violence' is awkward, but the key thing to bear in mind is that our use of the term refers to the state, and not the people ('English' or 'British' violence could be actually perpetrated by foreign soldiers under English or British command). Foreigners, of course, often refer to Britain and the British simply as *Angleterre* or *Anglais/Engländer*. For us, 'English and British' violence is that perpetrated by the state based in London, which was England until 1707 and Great Britain from then until 1801, when it became the United Kingdom. There is continuity in the Anglo-British state, with English input being dominant, due to England's greater size, population, and wealth, and for states based in London—even after the union with Scotland—both the Irish and the Scottish highlanders were seen as verging on uncivilized, and requiring strong action to

INTRODUCTION

bring them fully into the Anglo-British polity. If 'English violence' is anachronistic after 1707—or, in light of Murray Pittock's arguments in Chapter 6, after c.1750—'British violence' would be anachronistic before then, hence our use of 'English and British'. A book subtitle '500 Years of Violence Perpetrated by the State Whose Capital was Located in London' would be clumsy, but readers will take the point.

We do not, to be clear, regard the English or British as peoples, or the Anglo-British state, as being unusually violent, though at times it was probably unusually effective in its deployment of ruthless violence. Neither do we suggest that English/British statesmen and commanders were necessarily ruthless without justification. At times they undoubtedly were part of a wider culture of military atrocity and/or were reacting to the actions of other polities and their statesmen and generals or admirals. But the fact that at times, in strategic interest, they disapproved of extreme violence (see Chapters 2, 8 and 9 by Clifford Rogers, Charles Esdaile and Andrew Lambert), thereby to some extent—though, as Esdaile shows, not entirely—foreclosing atrocities, highlights the extent to which violence was often state-directed and strategic.

Contributions to Scholarship

The book intersects with several areas of scholarship. The first and most obvious is the history of international relations, in particular the relations of the Anglo-British state with what was initially called Christendom before becoming 'Europe'. While Brexit has given this history a new relevance, the book does not engage directly in that heated debate. It does, however, inevitably cast light on the place of Europe in English/British statecraft. The book exposes as flawed claims that, in geopolitical terms, England always looked to the oceans, and not to the continent. However, as Lambert suggests in Chapter 9, there was a perception 'that Europe was a strategic risk, to be managed', and this sense may have helped feed strategic ruthlessness. Further, essays also show that, despite the undoubted cultural importance of Europe and European connections for English elites, they brought a merciless sensibility to political and military interactions with European polities and nation-states;

3

despite cultural or confessional commonalities, there was an ongoing English readiness to apply ruthlessness in treatment of continental cities, civilians, and defeated enemies. Thus, the volume complicates Europhobic, Eurosceptic, and pro-European approaches alike, albeit in different ways.

Second, the volume engages with a recent emphasis on the Anglo-British state as a 'warfare state' and the levels of violence it was willing to deploy in colonial settings.[3] This historiography is mostly focused on the twentieth century, but there is a broader context, including the 'fiscal-military state' concepts of seventeenth- and eighteenth-century British historiography and the place of war-making in English state development.[4] The willingness to be ruthless, sometimes in defiance of widely agreed Christian/civilised norms, in Europe, has yet to be explored. Separating the violence inflicted by the Anglo-British state (not just by English and British soldiers as individuals) into European and colonial categories has created a dichotomy that historically is often a false one. English statesmen undoubtedly differentiated up to a point between Europe (seen initially as Christian, then as civilised) and the wider world (un-Christian and, in the nineteenth and twentieth centuries, deemed as beyond the bounds of civilisation).[5] Yet as most chapters demonstrate, there was also a willingness to behave brutally in Europe among statesmen and senior military and naval commanders of England-Great Britain-United Kingdom—and it should be stressed that, while commanders inflicted ruthless violence, as several chapters show, they usually did so with the explicit blessing of statesmen and politicians. As a result, this book argues that, in spite of a recent trend in scholarship to locate English violence in Ireland and Scotland in a colonial context, it should be primarily understood as taking place within a European framework of strategic violence.[6] This is something British imperial and colonial historians as well as historians of Anglo-British relations with Europe need to take on board.

Third, the book contributes to the growing body of scholarship on the history of violence, which has produced much exciting work, but currently is disproportionately focused on the twentieth century. The *longue durée* approach of the volume in and of itself offers the potential of new perspectives. But in addition, the nature of English

INTRODUCTION

violence in Europe is of interest. The ruthlessness referred to above is all the more marked because it often was calculated. It certainly was not simply the default stance of the English in Europe, yet, even as ideas of 'civilisation' reduced the incidence of brutal violence in the nineteenth century (Chapter 9 by Andrew Lambert), arguably it was always there as an option, ready to be deployed when it was thought necessary. Modes of behaviour practised in northern France and on the Scottish border under Henry VIII were perpetuated under other Tudor rulers and applied with particular brutality to Ireland in the sixteenth and seventeenth centuries (Chapter 3 by Neil Murphy and Chapter 5 by David Edwards) and then were repeated in Scotland in the eighteenth (Chapter 6 by Murray Pittock). There is clear evidence of continuity of practice in the sixteenth and seventeenth centuries, but there is little evidence of specific borrowing in the eighteenth; though Pittock quotes an English general's idea of 'reviving laws once used against the Irish', this seems to have been more general than particular. Nevertheless, the comparability of practice may suggest an existing toolbox that soldiers could make use of when it was thought necessary. And we can go further: the fact that the attack on Copenhagen in 1807 (Chapter 7 by Brendan Simms) was raised in the discussions that led to the destruction of the French fleet at Mers-el-Kébir in 1940 suggests that at times ruthlessness—and Churchill used 'ruthlessly' to describe British action at Mers-el-Kébir—was more than a handed-down mentality (Chapter 11 by Karine Varley); it could reflect and be based on a conscious awareness of past practice.[7]

Three chapters (Chapter 2 by Clifford Rogers, Chapter 3 by Murphy, and Chapter 4 by David Trim) explore the particular factors in England's relationship with the continental powers and in the common European martial culture of the fifteenth and sixteenth centuries, which helped to tap English wellsprings of violence. The volume sheds light on debates about whether or to what extent England was influenced by a putative 'civilising process' in early modern Europe—Chapter 8 (Charles Esdaile) shows that violence remained common among soldiers and the class from which they were drawn; this suggests that the rise of politeness as an English cultural value applied only in domestic relations and only among

5

the middle and upper orders.[8] While traditional chivalric values are examined in Chapter 2 (Rogers), two other chapters remind us that they continued to motivate military and naval officers in the nineteenth and twentieth centuries (Chapters 9 and 11 by Lambert and Varley), at least when dealing with Europeans.

But it is clear from the majority of chapters that, while adherence to a code of honour was real, it only went so far. Arguably, when courtesy and kindness were used internationally, they were often understood, by English and British statesmen and commanders, to be largely pragmatic devices to win over populations who were not seen as so alienated (or so alien) that extreme violence was warranted (e.g., see the limits put on plundering by Henry IV in Scotland in 1400 and Henry V on the march from Harfleur to Calais in 1415, or Henry V's prohibition on holding women or children for ransom or killing unarmed men: Chapter 2 by Rogers). Striking is the way that, in the nineteenth and twentieth centuries, Britain justified actions that breached international norms by appealing to a higher morality – defeating Napoleon or Hitler was portrayed as so important, for the preservation of a just and moral international order, that the ends justified the means (Chapters 7, 11, and 12, by Simms, Varley, and Richard Overy). Finally, this volume also sheds light on the role of religious conflict in generating callous conduct (Chapters 4–6, by Trim, Edwards, and Pittock), though religion intersected with geopolitics and grand strategy in effecting strategic violence.

A fourth area of scholarship that the following essays collectively intersect with, and contribute to, is the history of strategy. Increasingly debates about grand strategy, strategy, and 'operational art' blur these categories, and blur, too, policy and methodology. Given that 'strategies of attrition' are well recognized in war studies and strategic studies, can ruthlessness be regarded as a strategy? Under Henry VIII it seems to have been (Chapter 3 by Murphy). In the nineteenth and twentieth centuries, Britain used ruthlessness strategically, not least in the maritime sphere (Chapter 7 by Simms, Chapter 10 by Mary Cox, and Chapter 11 by Varley), including as a previously unrecognized factor in British 'offshore balancing' (Chapters 7 and 9). But perhaps premeditated brutality is better understood as a methodology that can help achieve strategy as more

INTRODUCTION

classically understood (Chapters 2, 6 and 12, and cf. Chapters 7, 10–11), rather than a strategy itself. Karine Varley's comment on Mers-el-Kébir (Chapter 11) is striking: 'The use of violence was calculated and was chosen as much for its political effect as for its military value'.

Fifthly, the chapters illuminate how Britain claimed and underpinned her growing 'ordering' role in Europe. To be sure, this historically rested in part on her 'soft power', her alliances and her commitment to the 'rules-based' international order, but it also required the repeated infliction of often extreme and sometimes catastrophic violence. This was the case during the English, and later British, state-building project in Ireland and Scotland (Chapters 5 and 6), which was seen as a vital precondition of Britain's security and influence in Europe. It was also evident throughout the numerous attempts to maintain the European balance of power and the British maritime supremacy on which it depended (Chapters 7, 9–12). Sometimes this violence was merely implicit, for example when Britain threatened to attack St. Petersburg during the Crimean War (Chapter 9), and sometimes it was terrifying explicit, for example during the bombardment of Copenhagen (Chapter 7) or the 'devastation' of Germany in World War II (Chapter 12). The entire European balance, in short, often rested on Anglo-British structural violence.

Collectively the essays suggest that medieval, early modern, and nineteenth- and twentieth-century statesmen and military or naval commanders consciously weighed the advantages and disadvantages of harsh treatment of 'enemies' in Europe, against peer competitors. If there was not a strategy of ruthlessness, there was at times certainly a policy of brutality in the service of what would now be called strategic ends. There were indeed wars or campaigns in which violent conduct was uncommon; one only has to contrast the Royal Navy's Baltic campaign during the Crimean War, where the British self-consciously conducted themselves in a different way to the way they waged war against 'uncivilised' peoples (Chapter 9 by Lambert), with the campaigns against Denmark almost half a century earlier (Chapter 7 by Simms). There were times when extreme violence was neither top down, nor deployed strategically (Chapter 8 by

Esdaile). However, such examples only serve to throw into relief the episodes of intense ruthless, strategic violence in Europe. The essays thus bring into focus questions that are increasingly important in present-day strategic studies and international relations, as well as in military history.

Themes

Our volume explores how violence was conceived: how it was embedded in wider policy (Chapters 3, 7 and 12) and the extent to which there was willingness to contemplate civilian damage and casualties. The essays show that there was often a high-level intention to inflict such damage with the goal of breaking the enemy will or eliminating an enemy or a particular force (Chapters 2–3, 5–7, 10, and 12). They also highlight the status of the victim: Chapters 2–6 bring out the crucial importance of being (or being perceived or portrayed as) 'rebels' and engaged in 'rebellion' in medieval and early modern Europe. This licensed all kinds of ruthless actions that would now be seen as atrocities but would not have been seen as illegitimate by medieval and early modern standards, because there were then few restraints on action against rebels.[9] However, Chapters 3 and 4 show that conduct was carried out that would have been regarded as extreme even by the standards of the sixteenth century. Continental European practice shaped English practice: Chapter 4 shows the wider context of atrocities in early modern warfare. At the same time, however, when not sanctioned or directed by commanders, soldiers might be punished for freelance looting or killing (Chapters 2, 3, and 8). Strategic violence might be coercive, intended to break the will to resist (Chapters 2–7, 10–11), expropriatory (Chapters 2–3), or annihilatory (Chapter 12).

There is, of course, an alternative history to be addressed. What the examples of Chapters 8 and 9 underscore, by the very choice of British commanders to try to avoid extreme violence or atrocities, is how they were very often a strategic choice. British commanders in the Peninsular War strategically sought to avoid extreme violence, as a way of rallying support among the Portuguese and Spanish populations—though as Chapter 8 illustrates, atrocities were so

INTRODUCTION

endemic to early modern warfare that, even when not strategic in purpose, they could still happen. But Britain was sometimes able to achieve strategic effect without extreme violence. Culture played a role here. After 1815, the horrors of total war on land, including the treatment of civilians in besieged cities (as at Copenhagen in 1807: Chapter 7; and, though against British commanders' wishes, in Spain: Chapter 8), prompted a reaction (Chapter 9). As Britain relied on naval rather than military power, it had little occasion for violence in Western Europe, extreme or otherwise: it did not deploy troops in Western Europe for a century. Furthermore, Britain's relatively limited aims in the conflicts of the era, in essence maintaining a stable European state system, and protecting wider economic interests, could be secured by focussed naval-economic warfare. Chapter 9 by Lambert, on the largely ignored Baltic campaigns of the 'Crimean' War, 1854–56, highlights how maritime strategy secured strategic aims at minimum cost in human life, relying on limited violence directed against professional military forces, economic pressure, and deterrence to coerce the enemy. There were no examples of civilians being terrorized or brutalized. The loss of life among British and Russian combatants, and Russian and Finnish civilians, was very low, little more than 100 in total in 1854. Lethal violence was used against civilians in the Baltic only once, at Kokkola, when British personnel engaged trained local militias.

As this shows, another theme is the shift in how violence was perceived by contemporaries. In the fifteenth-through-seventeenth centuries, English authorities and commanders, operating in Wales, Ireland, Scotland, France, and the Low Countries regarded ruthlessness as part of the normal conduct of war (Chapter 2, Wales and France; Chapter 3, France and Scotland; Chapter 4, Low Countries; Chapter 5, Ireland). As a reflection of what is sometimes seen as a civilising process, in mid-eighteenth-century Scotland (Chapter 6), there seems to have been some recognition among perpetrators and their political masters that the violence being undertaken was extreme, but they justified it on political grounds. Atrocities are not necessarily strategic in purpose, yet they may still happen. The British government during the Napoleonic Wars (Chapter 7) likewise recognized that its conduct towards the Danes

9

would be regarded as uncivilized by some other European states, but the geopolitical and strategic benefits were held to outweigh the negative publicity. What is striking about Copenhagen in 1807 is that there was widespread pushback from the British public. This had to be overcome as well as negative perceptions in the wider European audience. In contrast, the decision to destroy the French fleet at Mers-el-Kébir was, as far as one can tell, applauded as unfortunately necessary by the British public and accepted in the same sense by neutral powers (Chapter 11). The blockade of Germany attracted both positive and negative feedback, but there were no doubts about its necessity or legitimacy among those responsible (Chapter 10). The strategic bombing campaign seems to have been accepted by those perpetrating it in an entirely positive light, as necessary and justified, and they identified continuity with colonial practice of bombing recalcitrant indigenous peoples in the British Empire (Chapter 12); but there was, even at the time, a limited opposition among the British public on ethical grounds, and negative perceptions have, understandably, only grown since the end of World War II.

Soldiers, sailors, and airmen were almost all men, and there was a sexual dimension to strategic violence against civilians. This was especially true in early modern France and Ireland. In the Hundred Years' War, English commanders, who at least nominally subscribed to the chivalric ethos, attempted to restrain sexual violence, and also executed troops for illegitimate, i.e. self-directed, plundering (Chapter 2); but there can be little doubt that rape occurred. In sixteenth-century France, there was far less restraint (Chapter 3), while in early modern Ireland, rape seems to have been regarded as a tactic, part of the toolkit of ruthless measures (Chapter 5). A different form of sexual violence was the castration of Jacobite prisoners in the aftermath of Culloden (Chapter 6), which was a form of demasculinization. By the Napoleonic Wars, British generals sought—probably unsuccessfully—to restrain sexual violence against Portuguese and Spanish women, but this was not least because the British forces on the Iberian Peninsula were operating among allied populations (Chapter 8). The nature of the remaining campaigns and actions considered in this book meant sexual violence against enemy civilians was not an option, but meanwhile British

INTRODUCTION

troops in colonial contexts in the nineteenth and twentieth centuries were guilty of sexual violence as part of atrocities.

An obvious question is the extent to which English/British actions were distinctive. It is notable that English actions did not particularly stand out in the early modern period. The assumption, noted above, that strategic violence was part of the normal conduct of war was widely accepted—in this sense, English violence in the fifteenth-through-seventeenth centuries (Chapters 2–5) existed within a broader European normative framework of violence. That said, the chivalric restraint sometimes (though not always) exercised in France by Henry V (Chapter 2) notably was largely absent in the reign of Henry VIII, under whom extreme violence was often calculated and approved at the highest level of the English state, and thus was strategic (Chapter 3); restraint was also entirely absent in Ireland (Chapter 5). Early modern English practice was often unusually ruthless, and perceived to be so by other Europeans.[10] Moreover, even if the violence inflicted was not exceptional in kind, it frequently was in degree. It is notable that a distinction was drawn between violence directed from above, which was legitimate, and the autonomous violence of ordinary soldiers, which could draw punishments (Chapters 2–3). Atrocities and extreme violence in eighteenth-century Scotland (Chapter 6) were unusual in a European context marked by restraint in warfare against civilians and, as Murray Pittock shows, ruthlessness was pushed by the field commanders on reluctant civil authorities. There was unhappiness in British political society as a result of the attack on Copenhagen (Chapter 7); the French had taken actions against cities and civilians in Spain, but they were not seen as justifying British attacks on civilians. There was doubt as to whether British action against Copenhagen was legitimate, and while the language of norms did not exist then, there must be some question as to whether it can be regarded as normative, since French conduct against Spanish civilians during the Peninsular War was widely regarded as extreme and illegitimate and would not have normatized conduct at Copenhagen.

British violence in the Peninsular War, in contrast (Chapter 8) is very different from the examples of the preceding 400 years, since there were attempts to restrain it by commanders, for whom, again,

11

violence was only legitimate when sanctioned—if not directed—by higher military authorities, a key point. Over the next century, British naval actions, in the Baltic in the mid-nineteenth century (Chapter 9), and against Germany in World War I (Chapter 10), can be said to have taken place within a normative framework, in which courses of action were generally regarded by statesmen, generals, and admirals—and not only in Britain—as consistent with international norms and the laws of war. In contrast again, however, as Karine Varley points out in Chapter 11, the attack on Mers-el-Kébir 'contravened the accepted use of military violence in war'. And also in World War II, despite German bombing of civilians—in Poland, the Netherlands, France and in Britain itself—the direct targeting of civilians by British bombers was not within the existing norms of war, so that, as Richard Overy shows, the Air Ministry made efforts to obscure, through use of deliberately abstract language, what was actually happening and even occluded it in internal discussions (Chapter 12). Thus, the volume highlights how normative frameworks evolve and develop—and were ignored by British politicians and commanders when it suited them for strategic purposes.

* * *

Taken together, our volume suggests that England—and later Britain—was neither uniquely violent, nor unusually restrained in its use of state violence within Europe and the European state system. The distinction between colonial and European violence may have existed in theory, but in practice largely collapsed in the face of 'necessity'. That said, England and then Britain's use of violence for strategic aims, at least in the cases examined here, was rarely gratuitous and generally highly effective. The objectives set were usually, though not always, reached; paradoxically, these often involved the vindication of international law (or of a higher international morality), as the London government and often many others saw it, through violent means. Sometimes, such actions involved appeal to previous acts of violence as precedent. It is therefore not too much to speak of a tradition of calculated Anglo-British state violence. This played a significant role in the evolution

INTRODUCTION

of England—an important but not a dominant state in late medieval Europe—into the mid-twentieth century European ordering power of Britain, whose aircraft ranged across the skies of the continent at will, in order to restore, at least in the West, the international legal order. Viewed historically therefore, the relationship between law and violence in the Anglo-British engagement in Europe appears less contradictory than symbiotic.

2

STRATEGY, PIETY, AND CHIVALRY
VIOLENCE AND RESTRAINT UNDER HENRY V IN 1415

Clifford J. Rogers

Introduction

The subject of this volume, of course, is English violence in Europe, as a context for assessing British use of violence in colonial situations—including the control of Ireland and Scotland. On a per capita basis, I think the Hundred Years War must be the high-point—or low-point—of that exercise. For a hundred and sixteen years, soldiers enlisted or authorized by the English crown regularly sailed across the Channel for the purpose of committing violence within France, and repeatedly the result was to bring the kingdom of France low in a way it never had been before, and never would be again. No part of the kingdom was spared. In the area around Paris itself in 1359, for example, due to the direct and indirect consequences of English violence, an eyewitness wrote that 'it is very doubtful that this country, which used to be very fertile for wheat and wine, won't be entirely wasted and dead this year, or that there will be anyone to take care of the vines and pick the grapes, or anywhere to put the wine, since the casks in the villages are all burned, as are the villages themselves'.[1] Historian Guy Bois titled

15

the section of his book on Late Medieval Normandy dealing with the end of the Hundred Years War 'Hiroshima in Normandy'.[2] That may seem over the top, at first, but less so after one reads the eyewitness accounts of the French countryside in the war zones 'left entirely uninhabited,' so that 'of a hundred people only one remains',[3] or 'absolutely deserted, uncultivated, abandoned, squalid, emptied of all the country folk, [and] filled up with thickets and brambles'.[4] The desolation of the countryside was mainly the result of the 'little wars' between garrisons, who had driven off the peasants even more by exactions imposed both on friendly and enemy villages under threat of violence than by the actual use of destructive force. The walled towns, thanks to their fortifications, were in general somewhat better off, but they could not prosper if their surrounding areas were laid waste. Moreover, across the course of the war, hundreds, if not thousands, of them endured the intense suffering of a prolonged siege or a brutal sacking. In 1346 alone, the army under Edward III's direct command—one of three English armies in operation that year—destroyed Barfleur, Cherbourg, St-Lô, Torigny, Liseux, Caen, Gisors, Louviers, Pontoise, Poix, Poissy, Valognes, Longueville, Pont-de-l'Arche, Poissy, Le Crotoy, Étaples, and Wissant, to name only some of what the contemporary chronicler Jean le Bel called 'the large towns, rich beyond measure', before adding that he 'wouldn't know how to name the mid-sized ones, nor the common little villages, which were infinite'.[5] Even the citizens of towns or cities that were spared from destruction could die by the thousands from hunger or disease during a long siege, for example that of Rouen in 1418–19. Then there were the battles, which—despite being small in scale compared to modern conflicts—could be very lethal. At Agincourt, for example, probably more Frenchmen died on the field, even in absolute numbers, than at Solferino in 1859 and Sedan in 1870 combined. The rate of combat death for the aristocracy was astoundingly high: a higher proportion of French noblemen were killed on that St. Crispin's Day than the proportion of French citizens killed in all of World War One.[6] Nor was it just the aristocracy, or just the supporters of the Valois monarchy, who suffered catastrophic damage in battle. At 'la Male Jornade' of 1450, which for the citizens of Bordeaux truly was 'The Bad Day', more than 15% of the adult male population of the city may have been killed, which, in proportion to national populations, would be roughly 100 times higher than British losses on the first day of the Somme, or 300 times higher than the American dead at Antietam.[7]

The introduction of this volume notes that while Britain has often been seen as an upholder of international law globally, especially where relations with Western powers are concerned, England also has inflicted extreme violence on its European adversaries, including with actions 'at or well beyond the bounds of what was sanctioned by the prevailing international norms of the time'. Certainly, as we've already seen, English violence during the Hundred Years War was in some ways 'extreme', even if we exclude the very substantial amount of harm done by individuals—be they soldiers, criminals, or both—for their own ends, separate from violence 'sponsored by the state... for specific geopolitical and/or strategic reasons'. But was the high level of destruction wrought 'at...the bounds of what was sanctioned by the prevailing international norms', or was it 'well beyond' those limits? Or, alternately, could the English crown during the war reasonably claim to be acting as 'an upholder of international norms', erring on the side of restraint more than its adversaries did?[8] How did the exercise of violence against France compare to the use of force by the crown within the British Isles in the same period? How did the level of violence employed reflect tensions between what was expedient in war and what was understood to be admirable, or at least licit, in the state's application of violence—or did that dilemma not really apply?

The invasion of France by Henry V in 1415 initiated a new phase of the war, driven by a new strategic vision. Thanks in part to its extremely dramatic and important climax (the battle of Agincourt), we have exceptionally rich documentation of this campaign. Both those considerations make the year's operations an ideal topic for a case study approach to the questions just outlined. But because 1415 marks a turning point for some of the issues this book is meant to address, I will start with a significant amount of background and generalization about medieval warfare. Without that it is not really possible to appreciate or understand how or why English violence on the Continent in this new phase of the war was distinctive, and indeed consequential for the future development of British—and European—ideas about the exercise and the limitation of military violence.

Devastation and the War to 1396

When Henry V came to the throne in 1413, he was clearly already planning to break the truce agreed in 1396 and to resume the war.[9] When he considered how best to do so, taking into account both what was licit and what was wise, his thinking was framed both by his own experience of war—for though still young in 1415, he was already a veteran, more than a decade past his first battlefield command role—and by his knowledge and understanding of the course of the war to that point. Both of those subjects, therefore, need to be briefly reviewed here. Although contemporary sources and modern textbooks sometimes suggest that the war broke out in 1337 because Edward III claimed the throne of France, that is incorrect: in fact, he did not do that until several years into the struggle, and for him the claim was in any case largely a diplomatic chit. With fairly solid justification, he proclaimed himself the rightful king of France, but all along he was willing to give up the title in exchange for what he really wanted, which was sovereign rule over his paternal inheritance, the duchy of Aquitaine, along with an end to French interference in Scotland. Of course, even those 'limited' aims were a lot to ask of the French monarchy, and initially Philip VI had no thought of bowing to the demands of the ruler of a kingdom much smaller and weaker than his own, with only around a quarter of the population and wealth of France. Nonetheless, to the shock of all Europe, by 1360 Edward achieved a complete strategic victory with the Treaty of Brétigny, by which the French agreed to surrender around a third of the realm to him in full sovereignty, and to end their support for Scottish independence.[10]

How had Edward and his very able lieutenants accomplished this astounding result? In short, by effective application of all the main categories of medieval warfare—by devastating thousands of square miles of the French countryside in great *chevauchées* (mounted ravaging expeditions), by capturing or destroying hundreds of castles

STRATEGY, PIETY, AND CHIVALRY

and walled towns, by winning a dozen battles on land and sea, and by establishing or authorizing innumerable garrisons to inflict ongoing damage in almost every region of the county. Every military operation the English undertook involved the direct infliction of harm on the enemy population at large. The strategic purposes for the use of devastation in Edward's campaigns—or the campaigns of medieval warfare in general—can be summed up by five Ps: Profit, Provocation, Pressure, Punishment and Prostration. The devastation of enemy territory was a means to all these purposes. From Edward III's perspective, he allowed and encouraged his men to collect plunder partly because profit, for himself as well as his men, was an end in itself, but mainly because it contributed to the four other Ps. Ravaging enemy territory—including both pillaging and more wanton destruction, such as burning houses and mills, where the enemy's loss did not create an identical English gain—was intended to provoke the French to do battle: English strategy throughout the war was consistently battle-seeking, and the French were consistently hesitant to give battle, so provocation was necessary. In addition, devastation created political and moral pressure on the opposing king to make peace, if he could not protect his people by direct military action. As well as pressing the enemy to do what an attacker did want, devastation could punish the enemy nation for doing what he did not like. Lastly, as documentary evidence clearly shows, devastation was explicitly intended to weaken the enemy's economic and fiscal resources by draining or diverting the nation's stored wealth and destroying the means of production.[11] In the short term, that could contribute to provocation, pressure, or punishment, pushing the enemy to do what Edward wanted (fight a battle and ultimately make peace on English terms), but in the longer term, it could also prostrate the enemy, impoverishing him to the point where even if he was still willing to continue fighting, he would not be able to.

By 1356, English *chevauchées* and sieges had provoked Jean II into doing battle at Poitiers, where he was captured, creating irresistible pressure on him to make a peace deal. He did so, but the Dauphin and the Estates General initially rejected the surrender of a large part of France to English sovereignty. Nonetheless, the punishment inflicted in the 1359–60 campaign, and the recognition that the nearly prostrate French government could not prevent the English from continuing and escalating the devastation of the kingdom, led to the Treaty of Brétigny and a peace of victory for England.[12]

To accept such a damaging treaty—by far the greatest humiliation the kingdom had ever suffered, or (with the debatable exception of the Treaty of Troyes in 1420) that it ever would suffer in the future— was a maneuver of desperation, and as soon as the French saw the opportunity to abrogate the deal, they did it: in 1369 under Charles the Wise, who earned his sobriquet by a prudent, battle-avoiding, and damage-mitigating strategy that enabled him to recover practically all of the territory ceded at Brétigny, though not to conquer the hard core of the English position in Gascony. After Charles V and Edward III passed from the scene, the government of Charles VI made more aggressive attempts to carry the war into Guienne and even into England, with an immense amphibious force collected in preparation for an invasion in 1386, but those efforts failed, leading to an expensive military stalemate that was in no one's interest. Yet the two sides were unable to make peace, because doing so would require one king or the other to make a concession that was even worse than sustaining the burden of the stalemate: to give up the claim to sovereignty over Aquitaine. In a rather elegant diplomatic maneuver that dodged the second problem while resolving the first, the two realms negotiated a 28-year status quo armistice in 1396.[13]

Prince Henry's Military Experience

As we will see, when Henry V resumed the war in 1415, he initiated a very major shift in England's military strategy for the Hundred Years War—that is, in how he used violence in France as a tool towards achieving his political ends. The change in approach was partly the result of a change in goals, and, although our ability to know what was inside the mind of a medieval king or commander is limited, we can draw a logical inference that both those changes reflected, to a substantial degree, the experiences and lessons of the warfare inside the British Isles that began just as young Prince Henry was reaching an age to understand politics and war.

20

STRATEGY, PIETY, AND CHIVALRY

It is completely unsurprising that during the operations that ended with the deposition of Richard II, the self-proclaimed Henry IV kept violence to an absolute minimum. Pillaging would have turned the country against him and caused his rebellion to fail, while the rallying of the country to his banner practically left Richard prostrate, without even the need to provoke a battle. Likewise, the first military operation that the future Henry V himself participated in was the response to the Percy rebellion that ended at the battle of Shrewsbury in 1403: it too was conducted with only a minimum of violence against property and against people, aside from during the bloody culminating battle. Before that, neither army viewed the land it moved through as enemy territory, which meant that burning and plundering would have been neither legally permissible nor strategically beneficial.

The relatively low level of devastation of the countryside, though not the lack of battle, was typical for a civil war in this period.[14] Quite untypical, however, was the comparably low level of violence in Henry IV's next campaign: an invasion of Scotland in 1400. There was some ground for considering the Scottish war also to be a form of civil war. The official English position for more than a century had been that the Scots were contumacious rebels, who deserved punishment for supporting a king who failed to pay the homage he owed to his rightful overlord, the king of England. But ever since the start of the war with France, enforcing that claim to overlordship had not been a priority. The two royal invasions of Scotland in this period, in 1356 and 1385, had been punitive expeditions, intended to restore peace by demonstrating to the Scots the pain of war. They involved intense devastation inflicted for purposes of pressure and punishment, with no real prospect of provoking the outclassed Scots to do battle, and with the Scottish economy being too underdeveloped to be prostrated by ravaging, and too poor to promise much profit. The campaign of 1400 was different; Henry's use of violence, as even the Scottish chroniclers admit, was remarkably restrained.

This reflected a shift in strategy arising from particular circumstances. The daughter of the Scottish earl of March had just been dishonored by King Robert III, so the 'gretly wrangit' earl joined Henry IV's army, promising to do homage to the English king.

21

This opened the possibility of establishing a buffer zone protectorate in the south-east between Berwick and Edinburgh. Thus, when the English army marched north as far as Leith, Henry proclaimed his desire to avoid the effusion of blood and, meeting practically no resistance, granted protection to the castles and villages in his path that requested it, so that there was very little plundering or burning. The campaign was not successful: no other Scottish magnates joined Henry, supplies fell short, and when the English army fell back south of the border after two weeks, March could not hold his earldom. But Henry did at least retain the loyalty of March himself, who made major contributions to Henry's decisive battlefield victories over the Scots at Homildon Hill in 1402 and the Percy rebels at Shrewsbury in 1403, and then in 1411 helped negotiate an Anglo-Scottish truce. In any case, the operation demonstrated that for the fifteenth-century English monarchy, the use of devastation as an instrument of war was a choice, not a necessity.[15]

The context of the rest of Henry's military experience prior to his accession and the resumption of the French war fell in between domestic and foreign, as he oversaw a counterinsurgency war against the *soi-disant* prince of Wales, Owain Glyndŵr. When the Welsh rebellion began in 1400, Glyndŵr's men 'burned on all sides the towns wherein the English dwelt amongst them, pillaging them and driving out the English': treating them, in other words, as foreign enemies. Henry IV could have responded in kind, but instead, as the Welsh chronicler Adam of Usk put it, once Glyndŵr was 'subdued and driven away', 'with others who yielded peacefully the king dealt gently', hoping to succeed more with politics than with force.[16]

When the rebellion refused to die down, however, King Henry returned the following year, and this time the punishment stick came out: 'the English, invading those parts with a strong power, and utterly laying them waste and ravaging them with fire, famine, and the sword, left them a desert, not even sparing children or churches, nor the monastery of Strata-Florida … and they carried away into England more than a thousand children of both sexes to be their servants'.[17] This strategy of punishing devastation proved even less successful than the moderation exercised a little earlier in Scotland: instead of being extinguished by fear, it seems the rebellion was

STRATEGY, PIETY, AND CHIVALRY

enflamed by anger. Owain matched and exceeded this escalation, committing 'deeds of unheard-of cruelty with fire and sword'. According to Thomas Walsingham, the 'inhuman' barbarity of the Welsh rebels extended to mutilating slain Englishmen by cutting off their noses and penises, then stuffing them respectively into their anuses and mouths.[18]

Meanwhile Glyndŵr's strength rose so much that he felt able not only to launch destructive counter-strikes into England, but even to mount conventional operations with full-scale armies, sacking towns and capturing castles. When the tide turned against him in 1405, it was not because of stepped-up campaigns of destruction, but because his army was defeated in battle by Prince Henry's household troops, with much slaughter of his men, an action followed by Prince Henry's consolidation of that success through a campaign of sieges supported by thorough logistical planning and facilitated by the use of newly developed 'great bombards', capable of demolishing at least second-rate fortifications in relatively short order.[19]

The 1415 Campaign

When Henry V re-opened the French war, he seems to have had the same core objective as Edward III: to secure full sovereignty over a good-sized chunk of his ancestral possessions in France, in exchange for renouncing his claim to the rest. He also had some of the same advantages and disadvantages in means as Edward. His advantages included well-disciplined and veteran troops, both longbowmen and men-at-arms; subordinate commanders of high quality; and his own high military talents, deployed against enemy forces that were inferior in cohesion and boldness. But on the other hand, England's economic and demographic resources were far inferior to France's— even when France was riven by civil war and ruled by the mentally ill Charles VI. Despite having ends and means similar to his role-model great-grandfather, however, when King Henry developed his strategy to use his advantages to achieve his goals, he only partially adopted the strategy that had brought Edward success in 1360 (and failure from 1369–77). Like Edward, he pursued a battle-seeking strategy, trying first to draw the French into a fight to save Harfleur,

23

then when that failed, by trailing himself and his army as bait across the length of northern France, which did finally bring on battle at Agincourt. But there was this large difference: it seems that from the start he envisioned using the freedom of maneuver that a battlefield victory would give him to conduct a conquest of Normandy based on sieges and occupation, rather than a war of destructive *chevauchées*. The new strategy could give him *de facto* what he wanted even if he could not get the French to accept his acquisitions. That was a major advantage over a renewed attempt to extort from them both the surrender of territory and treaty recognition of his sovereignty over it.[20]

Immediately after disembarking in France, King Henry gave clear proof of this change of approach, when he issued a set of ordinances of war—essentially what today would be called 'rules of engagement'—and had copies delivered to every captain in the army, to be read aloud to every soldier.[21] The rules were composed in English rather than Anglo-Norman or Latin, so the men could be expected to understand them—and therefore at least possibly to obey them. Although the language of the document was an innovation, the issuing of ordinances for an army was not. We know that Edward III too had issued ordinances when his forces landed in Normandy in 1346, and we have full copies of the ordinances issued in 1385 both for Richard II's army and for the Franco-Scottish force preparing to invade England. Anne Curry has studied these texts carefully, and her core conclusion is that they are all similar, which fits with Maurice Keen's brilliant analysis of the general consistency the medieval Law of Arms displayed across large stretches of geography and time.[22] Those similarities are certainly there, and indeed many of the clauses of Henry's ordinances are essentially translations, sometimes expanded or elaborated, of Richard's document. But there are also a few key innovations in the 1415 ordinances that go right to the heart of our topic.

Just a few years before 1415, English soldiers under Henry's brother, the duke of Clarence, had landed in Normandy as allies of the Armagnac faction in the ongoing French civil war, and 'spread themselves over the...country, destroying or plundering everything they could find'.[23] They also took many prisoners: probably meaning

STRATEGY, PIETY, AND CHIVALRY

that they seized for ransom any lay men they encountered, as was standard practice in the warfare of the time.[24] Their French allies were pleased rather than dismayed by this destruction within France; they had just been doing the same in their attacks on the duke of Burgundy, and formally proclaimed that they had 'committed no offense' thereby, since they had the right to do so as lords of the blood-royal.[25] So long as the English refrained from raping or killing women, killing or abducting members of the clergy, or burning or robbing churches, whatever devastation they committed—including robbing priests of their personal property, or slaying peasants they overtook in the fields—would have been allowed under Richard II's 1385 ordinances.[26] To stay on the right side of the explicit provisions of the Franco-Scottish ordinances issued the same year, they would not even have had to refrain from killing unarmed priests, or seizing nuns and holding them for ransom.[27]

Henry V's ordinances, however, were significantly more stringent in terms of protection for enemy non-combatants. They spelled out that boys under the age of fourteen should not be taken prisoner, unless they were the sons of lords. Women and members of the clergy, likewise, were to be spared from abduction or any violence.[28] As in Richard II's ordinance, the penalty for rape, or killing a woman or cleric, or pillaging the property of a church, was death—much stricter than the 1385 Franco-Scottish ordinance, according to which the penalty could be as low as loss of an ear for an archer, or loss of horse and arms for a man-at-arms. Even burning buildings, except by specific command of the king, was forbidden, again under penalty of death.[29] Considering that Henry V is reported to have quipped that 'war without fire is as worthless as sausages without mustard', that last-mentioned provision was so surprising that at first I wondered if I was misunderstanding the Middle English, but that is in fact what the text states—including in the Latin version—and the provision is confirmed by the eyewitness author of the *Gesta Henrici Quinti*.[30] The latter source adds that for the march across France, another clause was added to forbid even taking prisoner unarmed men who offered no resistance.[31] That too is a surprising restriction, considering that there is abundant evidence that it was standard practice in the wars of this period for adult males—even of low status—to be seized and compelled under threat of harsh imprisonment or worse to pay ransoms that were, relative to their economic resources, very substantial.[32] That was the fate of farmers seized by English troops in the first days of the campaign, though it is not clear if this was allowed by King Henry or done contrary to his intent. He had told the prisoners 'that he had entered his land, country, and realm to restore them to the liberty and freedom St. Louis had maintained his people in, and ordered them to return to their labors'.[33] The English garrisons of Lancastrian Normandy, a few years after 1415, certainly did not refrain from the practice.[34]

We've already seen that maximizing destruction served the purposes of the five Ps: profit, provocation, pressure, prostration, and sometimes punishment. By implication, any change that reduced the harm done to the population also reduced the strategic effectiveness of devastation. Why, then, might a prince prefer a policy providing more protection to the people, particularly the population of the agricultural countryside? In the context of the Agincourt campaign, the reasons can be summarized under the heading of six more Ps: Preservation of the army, Preservation of hostages, Preservation of taxpayers, Pacification, Propaganda, and Piety.

To explain these, I will initially skip past the siege of Harfleur, the first main phase of the campaign, though I will return to it later. When Henry marched out of the captured city on his way to Calais, the factors encouraging a high level of destruction were, relative to previous campaigns of the Hundred Years War, weakened. Providing profit for the troops is always helpful, but it is less important when the soldiers have been paid for months in advance.[35] As to provocation: from intelligence Henry had received, the French were already getting ready to fight a battle, and if he had not yet given them enough encouragement to do so by invading their territory and capturing Harfleur, he had added to the scales by challenging the Dauphin to personal combat, then in effect announcing where he would march to and when he would leave, and finally and most importantly, by setting off with an army that was quite small—only 6,000 men, less than half the size of Edward III's at Crécy—and that moreover was unbalanced, being dangerously weak in men-at-arms.[36] Political pressure on the French court developed through

STRATEGY, PIETY, AND CHIVALRY

devastation was less important because, as already mentioned, Henry had in mind following up a battle with a campaign to conquer and occupy territory, rather than one to extort its surrender. Punishment was not relevant, as the areas through which he would pass had done nothing special to merit it. And prostration through economic and fiscal destruction was beyond his reach: his army was too small and especially too weak in cavalry to thoroughly devastate the countryside, and unlike Edward III in 1346 or the Black Prince in 1355, he would be passing through an area now accustomed to war, with fortifications in good repair.

The same weakness in men-at-arms that was itself a provocation, and that made prostration impractical, made it imperative to keep his forces concentrated, in a way that had not been necessary for Edward III. Henry's force was barely strong enough to risk battle with a French army; indeed, most of his advisors thought it was not strong enough to fight even when concentrated.[37] He could not afford to weaken it further, and, since even at the beginning of the march the local French superiority in cavalry was of the order of five to one, any troops breaking away from the main body, either to seek profit or to do general damage to the enemy by setting fires, would be very vulnerable to being isolated and picked off. Henry's troops had packed enough food for an eight days' march, just enough to reach Calais without needing to do much foraging, but that proved insufficient, and so he supplemented his supplies by summoning local officials to bring bread to him, threatening to burn their villages and vineyards if they did not.[38] A threat is only effective if it is credible both in itself (you will do what you say if you don't get what you want) and as an implied promise (that you *won't* do what you threaten if you do get what you want). A farmstead, manor, or village preserved intact was a hostage that could be threatened to secure obedience; one already burnt down had no value.

A burnt village also could generate no revenues to support its lord or its king in making war. That indeed was the very point of much of the destruction wrought by Edward III or the Black Prince, falling under the heading of 'prostration'. But at least in the first phase of the march, Henry was moving through Normandy, which he intended to occupy and retain as his own duchy in the not-too-

27

distant future; the more its productive potential was preserved, the greater the value of the property he planned to possess. As the English told the townsfolk of Harfleur, 'our king does not want to lay waste his own country'.[39]

To be productive, a conquered area needs not only intact barns, mills, vines, fruit-trees, and farmsteads, it also needs people, preferably peasants prepared to pay *patises* [protection money] or taxes without too much resistance. As Henry had seen in Wales, indiscriminate violence could provoke the population to fury, making an area difficult to control and practically impossible to profit from. As modern theorists since Jomini have emphasized, counterinsurgency efforts need to be firm, and even harsh, in punishments for resistance, but if they are perceived as capricious or unjust, the value of the threat of punishment is undermined by the unreliability of the promise of security in exchange for obedience.[40] Maximum fear deriving from maximum harm may work to compel a population to buy an invader off and get him to depart, but it does not work if the objective is eventually to rule the land in peace. It is not actually necessary to win both the hearts and minds of a population you wish to control—just the minds will suffice—but it is important to avoid angering people so much that hatred in their hearts overrides the plans for self-preservation in their minds.

The restraint shown by Henry's army on the march thus sent a message about the reliability of his promises (to spare as well as to destroy) to the people of the areas he passed through, preparing for their later pacification, but it also sent messages to Normans far from his army's march, and to people at home in England. Among Henry's greatest concerns, as we can see in many of his documents as well as in chronicle accounts, was to be perceived as a just king, and also as a pious one. The famous episode of the hanging of a soldier who, early in the march, stole a copper-gilt pyx from a church, was meant not just as a deterrent message to the other soldiers, but also as a communication of Henry's justice and piety to audiences in France at large, at the Council of Constance, in the Empire (where Henry was angling for an alliance), and at home, where allegations of injustice or 'tyranny' had been the main cause of Richard II's downfall, and where some harbored doubts about the justice of the war, or

STRATEGY, PIETY, AND CHIVALRY

about the relatively brutal way it had been prosecuted during the fourteenth century.[41]

Here it is worth referring to the most influential treatise on the laws of war of that time, completed just after Richard II's war ordinances: Honorat Bouvet's *The Tree of Battles*. This text offered a reluctant admission that it was legitimate to target the common people of an enemy realm, and their property, if they incurred culpability by supporting their king's war effort—which of course, for all practical purposes, was always the case. But that was a question of law, and Bouvet extended his discussion past the law to speak of honor, saying that a soldier who captures and demands heavy ransoms 'without pity or mercy' from 'poor laborers who cultivate lands and vineyards, and, under God, give sustenance to all by their toil,' 'is not a gentleman, but a tyrant, and no knight....If I *wanted* to decide that there was honour or valour in attacking a poor innocent who has nothing more in mind than to eat his dry bread alongside his sheep in the fields', Bouvet continued, '...I could not do it'.[42] The same logic applied all the more to inflicting harm on women and children, who generally (as the medieval mind perceived it) did not have either the physical capacity or the economic autonomy to contribute to the enemy war effort.[43] By making clergy, women, and children off-limits for violence or abduction—and by at least attempting to enforce those ordinances against his own soldiers—Henry was building his reputation for justice and honor, while minimizing the effectiveness of any accusation that his war in France was tyrannical, unjust, or un-Christian.[44]

When a king (or politician) displays his own justice and piety, it is always difficult to know if he does so purely because it benefits him to *appear* just and pious, or whether it is also because of a genuine desire to *be* just and pious. After the battle, according to the well-informed chronicler of Ruisseauville abbey (right next door to the battlefield), Henry told French leaders that they had been defeated because God and Mary and St. George had fought against them, because they had advanced into battle filled with pride (a sin) after their soldiers had raped married women and maidens, and robbed the countryside and the churches: 'when you act like that, God will never aid you'. On the other hand, Henry is reported to have declared, none of his men

HARFLEUR TO HAMBURG

'ever mounted [sic] a woman, or robbed anyone [of the church?] or any church, that we know of, or set any fires in France—[or] if they have done, certainly we have done justice to them for it'.[45] For a genuinely pious king, this would be perfectly reasonable logic and a good reason to enforce discipline during the march—and a reason to be willing to seek battle with confidence (in divine favor), despite any numerical disadvantage. The action lines up with the justification. That admittedly does not prove that the justification was the true motivation, since for reasons already noted, the restraint of violence embodied in Henry's ordinances would have made sense for purely practical reasons. Nonetheless, it would be unduly cynical to presume the justification was insincere.[46]

The strength of piety as an independent motivating factor can best be determined in a case where expediency and religious morality point in *different* directions, rather than (as generally in 1415) lining up to point at the same path. I find telling one of Henry's lesser-known ordinances, dating to 1421. 'Not a few of our soldiers of our garrisons, and their servants,' he wrote, 'not fearing God or man, hold, as we are informed, women in concubinage and (what is worse) in adulterous relations and in other illicit embraces ... provoking divine anger, to our and our commonwealth's harm'.[47] So he ordered the practice to stop, on pain of a month in jail. This seems to me a clear case of putting moral and religious concerns ahead of practical expediency: the order can't have been good for morale. And if in one case he was more motivated by piety than expediency, it makes it credible that in other cases where he also declared religious justifications for his actions, they should be taken seriously. That in turn indicates that his desire to spare the poor and weak—as much as possible without too badly undermining his war effort— was likewise motivated in part by the desire to *be* a good Christian king, not just to be seen as one. I highlight this one instance because it connects to the discussion of other ordinances in this chapter, but in fact, as a recent biographer puts it, evidence of Henry's piety 'is to be discerned in almost every aspect of his life... the more one looks, the more one sees the signs of his deep religious conviction'.[48]

So overall, in his treatment of the people of the countryside, as reflected both in his ordinances and in his actions during his campaigns—as described in French as well as English chronicle sources—Henry V did both uphold and strengthen the international laws and norms favoring restraint; the violence he inflicted in that context was, for the time, the opposite of extreme. But what about in the other two main modes of medieval warfare, siege and battle— that is, violence directed at the defenders of fortifications, and violence directed at armies in the field?

The Siege of Harfleur

Although Henry sought to limit the exercise of violence against the people of the countryside during the short march from the shore to the town of Harfleur, he opened the siege itself with an extreme threat: should the defenders—meaning the townsfolk as well as the garrison—fail to surrender the town to him, they should expect to suffer according to the law of Deuteronomy (20:10-14) when he captured the place by storm. In other words, all the men would be killed, and everything of value in the town would be plundered; the women and children might be held for ransom, and at best would be left in poverty.[49] When, predictably, the town did not open its gates, he soon ordered that it be bombarded by his artillery. The guns were not only directed at the town walls, but also used to throw immense stones *over* the walls, so that 'really fine buildings, almost as far as the middle of the town, were either totally demolished or threatened with inevitable collapse'. The purpose was to 'scourge' the defenders: to inflict pain on them to motivate them to surrender more quickly.[50] Of course, shooting blindly into the middle of the town did not allow for discriminating between combatants and non-combatants, or ecclesiastical versus other property. An English chronicler notes the results: not only the destruction of beautiful buildings, but also the crushing and dismembering of people.[51]

These threats and actions may seem to reflect a very different policy than the ordinances, with the latter's emphasis on protecting church property and defenseless people, but actually the principles at work had not changed. The ordinances excepted from non-combatant protections anyone who offered active resistance: a priest taken in arms, for example, could legitimately be captured and held for ransom. Once Henry's surrender offer had been delivered and refused, the English considered that everyone inside the fortress was in a state of active resistance—and indeed, even worse, in a state of active rebellion against Henry's rightful authority as duke of Normandy and king of France. But that additional factor was gilding the lily; the idea that the canonical protections for 'the poor laboring folk' or for women ought to rule out indiscriminate bombardment of a fortified town under siege would have been so far outside contemporary norms that it would likely never have even occurred to anyone involved. Rather, whatever struck 'fear into the besieged to make them surrender the town sooner' was considered a contribution to the 'greater good'.[52] Similarly, if the town had been taken by assault, it would have gone without saying that it would then be too late for the adult male defenders to surrender and claim protection as non-resisters. They would have to be 'punished' for their refusal to surrender. That would put the fear of complete disaster into the next town that considered resisting Henry to the bitter end.[53]

But Harfleur was not taken by assault; it agreed to surrender precisely to avoid a brutal sack. As mentioned earlier, the ability to threaten effectively requires also the ability to promise reliably: hence it was vital as a matter of strategy, as well as a concern of chivalry, that a commander ensure his troops adhered to the terms of a negotiated surrender. From a strategic perspective, however, in the first instance the incentive was to deal with defenders who had put up a prolonged resistance as harshly as the agreed terms allowed. That would encourage the next place attacked to surrender more quickly in return for more favorable terms. In the case of Harfleur, however, Henry did not do that.

The surrender was, formally, unconditional—Henry had just rejected a late offer for the town to surrender if he would spare the lives and goods of the defenders. But there was at least an implicit, and possibly an explicit, understanding that most of the defenders would not be killed or physically harmed, with the exception of 30 leading defenders, whose lives the king could take or not, as he chose.[54] If not communicated in advance more clearly, which it may have been, that understanding was at least strongly suggested

STRATEGY, PIETY, AND CHIVALRY

by the date the king insisted the surrender take place: the feast of St. Maurice, a military commander martyred (in part) because he refused to participate in the slaughter of fellow Christians. Once the surrender agreement was sealed, 'the English said to the good folk of Harfleur, "have no fear, don't worry, no harm will come to you"'.[55] In the event, moreover, Henry went beyond just sparing the defenders in life and limb, treating them better than they expected.[56] After the unconditional surrender, Henry told the leaders of the defenders that 'because they had submitted themselves to his mercy, even though tardily, they should not depart entirely without mercy.'[57] Not even the leaders of the garrison were executed (as they might have been), and in general the men-at-arms and wealthy bourgeois taken prisoner were not held indefinitely or pending heavy ransoms (as they probably expected).[58] Instead, most were released on parole to arrange their ransoms, which, judging by the absence of complaint, were kept at reasonable levels. Although all the property of the defenders fell to the king by the terms of the surrender, Henry left untouched the goods—other than real estate—of anyone who even at this late stage was willing to do fealty to him. Among those who refused to swear loyalty to Henry, the poorer men, instead of being treated as 'taken in arms', were released without ransom, along with the clerics, women, and children. Indeed, they were not merely released: they were given food and drink, and escorted under guard to protect them from assault by English or French miscreants. Women and churchmen were allowed to go in their best clothes and with whatever goods they could carry without packing them into a bundle. Very unusually, the women were even provided with a small cash allowance for their journey. English soldiers were, moreover, forbidden from searching the clerics, or the women's bosoms or under their head-coverings, despite the obvious financial loss that in practice meant for Henry and his men.[59]

In all this, despite differences in context and in application, we see largely the same impulses at work as we did in the field campaign. Again the application of violence against the French king's subjects during the siege tried to provoke the French into giving battle to save the town.[60] It also created pressure on the defenders to surrender earlier, and punished the townsfolk for their obstinacy, satisfying

Henry's sense of justice.[61] The fall of the city brought profit—from the king's perspective, more than a sack would have, though from the soldiers' viewpoint, less—and contributed to the further prostration of the already weak French government, though in 1415 this was mainly through political rather than economic damage.[62] And again, tempering violence provided pragmatic political advantages, either at the moment or in anticipation. The king's mercy was ostentatiously public, creating the opportunity for propaganda that would aid the pacification of the rest of Normandy. The poor townsmen preserved from death or ruin amounted to a pool of potential taxpayers as the rest of the duchy came under English control. 'The king... does not wish to lay waste his own country', the townsfolk were told.[63] The pair of promises kept—that the defenders who refused to submit promptly would be punished for their contumacy, and the implicit one that even a belated surrender would ameliorate that punishment—would help Henry in future siege situations, setting a precedent encouraging immediate surrenders, but also discouraging those who *did* resist from continuing the struggle to the bitter end. And piety played a part too; prior to processing to the port's parish church, where they gave thanks to God for their success, the English reassured the people of the town: 'We won't do to you what was done at Soissons [during the brutal sack by the Armagnacs in 1414]; we are good Christians'.[64]

Agincourt

In the High Middle Ages (c. 1000–1300), in battles where knights fought knights, the death toll was often very low. At Brémule in 1119, only three knights out of 900 engaged were killed; as Orderic Vitalis explains, 'they were all clad in mail and spared each other on both sides, out of fear of God and fellowship in arms; they were more concerned to capture than to kill the fugitives. As Christian soldiers [the victors] did not thirst for the blood of their brothers, but rejoiced in a just victory given by God'. Besides, each soldier had a strong personal incentive to capture rather than kill when that was possible, because prisoners could be ransomed for substantial sums, to the personal profit of the captor.[65]

STRATEGY, PIETY, AND CHIVALRY

At Agincourt, the outcome was utterly different. Out of around 11,000 well-armed French troops engaged, the dead probably totaled 5,000–6,000.[66] That was far higher in number and in proportion even than the bloody French defeats at Crécy and Poitiers earlier in the war. A significant number of those slain, moreover, were killed by the English *after* they had surrendered and become prisoners of war. These simple facts led John Keegan to describe the battle as 'a story of slaughter-yard behaviour and of outright atrocity'.[67]

At the level of individual perspective, slaughter (in the sense of 'killing in a brutal fashion') is part of the essential nature of battle. But did the leap in lethality at Agincourt result from an escalation of violence, the brutalizing effect of a long-running war, a reduced willingness to show Christian or chivalric mercy to the defeated? If so, did that imply a change in the norms and laws of war, or a failure of the English to adhere to unchanged rules—a failure that would be hypocritical, given Henry's oft-professed piety and desire to avoid the effusion of Christian blood?

The short answer to both questions is 'no'. The laws and norms of war were remarkably stable over the period of the Hundred Years War. They were influenced by canon law—which was itself, in military matters, largely unchanged since the days of Gratian—but were primarily a form of 'common law': shaped by tradition and precedent that created a general understanding of the rules shared by most men-at-arms.[68] The English soldiers at Agincourt were not bloodthirsty, nor was their commander. After the battle, many of them felt such pity for the fate of the French that they wept with compassion for their suffering, not just for the loss of ransoms their deaths entailed.[69] Archer and king alike would have been overjoyed to end the battle with 4,000 fewer French dead and 4,000 more French prisoners. But that was not an option they had.

For most of the duration of the battle—as was completely usual for English armies in royal battles since 1333—English soldiers were strictly forbidden from taking prisoners until the battle was fully won, because they were badly outnumbered, and could not afford the distraction of taking surrenders or guarding captives while fighting for their lives. Thus, as was a recognized option under the laws of war then prevailing, they raised a red banner to signify *guerre*

35

mortelle, meaning no prisoners would be taken during the battle.[70] But to explain the exceptionally high death rate at Agincourt, that scenario is a necessary but far from a sufficient cause. Most of the rest of the explanation lies in specific tactical circumstances that can only be briefly summarized here. The initial French decision to array most of their men-at-arms in two dense and deep phalanxes interacted with the specific terrain, and with the formidable power of the English longbow, to set up a medieval Cannae: a battle where the attacking formation suffered a double envelopment, causing the advancing soldiers to compress to the point where individuals could not fight effectively, and then to compress further so that large numbers were crushed by crowd pressure until there was a tall mound of dead and dying men roughly 250 yards long and six feet high. A man knocked out by a poll-axe swing to the head, or pierced through the thigh with an arrow, would in a normal battle have had a good chance of being made prisoner after the fighting was over, or escaping while it still continued, but here was more likely to be trampled and suffocated to death.[71]

Once the two main lines of French men-at-arms had been defeated in this way and it seemed that the battle had ended with an English victory, Henry's soldiers did start making prisoners, pulling still-breathing men-at-arms out of the 'mound of pity and blood'.[72] Soon, however, Henry ordered that the prisoners were to be put to death. A company of archers was put to the work of seeing that the orders were carried out, against the reluctance of at least some of the captors, whether inspired merely by cupidity (as Le Fèvre emphasizes), or also, as seems inherently likely, by concern that to slay in cold blood men who had lawfully surrendered would be cruel, unchivalrous, unchristian, or even unlawful.[73]

Such worries, which are of high relevance to the topic of this volume, would not have been unwarranted. When in 1342, Louis of Spain wanted to put to death two English prisoners, as revenge for their participation in a defeat he had suffered earlier, there was general agreement that it was shocking for a worthy knight to consent to 'such cruelty as to put to death knights captured while fighting their lords' wars': to do so would bring 'great blame' and 'eternal reproach'.[74] The generally accepted authorities on the laws

36

STRATEGY, PIETY, AND CHIVALRY

of war, Honorat Bouvet and Christine di Pizan, concurred that 'so soon as a man has surrendered, and is in prison, mercy should be shown to him' and 'he should not be killed'; even though classical Roman law did permit doing so, 'among Christians, where law is based on mercy and pity, it is not proper ... [but rather] denounced and reproved'. [75] Indeed, a captor had an obligation to protect his prisoner against any threat.

Nonetheless, though not unwarranted, these concerns ultimately would not have been, and were not, judged as valid by most observers at the time. First, according to the law of arms and canon law, the prisoner's right to mercy only solidified once he was 'out of battle' (Bouvet) and 'in prison' (di Pizan). [76] At Agincourt, Henry ordered the executions when and *because* he observed French preparations for a renewed attack in his front (and possibly also his rear), which led him to conclude that the battle was not over. [77] Hence, the prisoners were not yet 'out of battle'; rather, there was still a risk that in the chaos of a renewed battle they might escape or take up arms against their captors 'with the result of...damage, or mischief' to their captors. That case created an exception to the general rule forbidding the killing of prisoners, according to Bouvet and John of Legnano. [78] Third, even though it might not be permissible for a captor to slay his prisoner at his own will, [79] it could remain licit for a sovereign to order a captive's execution, especially if otherwise 'great harm might come to him and his own land'. [80] That was precisely what worried the English: as the Chaplain says, the prisoners were killed 'lest they should be our ruin in the coming battle'. [81]

In such a situation, precedent—which was part of the law of arms—as well as written law justified the king's decision. At Aljubarrota in 1385, a similar sequence of events had led to the same result. The Castilian vanguard was operating well ahead of the rest of the army and was thoroughly defeated by a Portuguese army. As soon as that combat was resolved, many knights and esquires were taken prisoner, gave their oaths, were disarmed, and thought they were safe. But at the approach of the main Castilian force, by the advice of the English in the Portuguese army, and in accordance with a pre-battle decree, 'it was ordered, on pain of being killed without mercy, that each person who had a prisoner kill him, no matter how worthy, puissant, noble or rich he might be'. 'It is better to kill than to be killed,' said those responsible for the order; 'if we don't kill them, they will free themselves when we are fighting, and kill us. No one should trust his enemy.' The killing of prisoners was deemed 'exceedingly pitiful' and a 'great misfortune', but the chroniclers made no criticism of the action on chivalric or legal grounds.[82] The same goes, somewhat more surprisingly, for Constable Bertran du Guesclin's command to kill most of the prisoners taken by the French at the battle of Chizé in 1373, which is reported with seeming approval by the constable's biggest booster, the poet Cuvelier, even though it was done in cold blood after the battle was clearly over.[83]

Likewise, none of the near-contemporary chronicle accounts of Agincourt, including those written by French authors, criticize Henry's action in 1415. Indeed, none of them, including those written by English authors, chose to actively defend it.[84] Apparently no defense was needed because no accusation was levelled, and no accusation was levelled because Henry's order, lamentable though it might be, was considered under the circumstances to be self-evidently licit, and indeed *sans reproche*. As Craig Taylor, a leading expert on chivalry, rightly concludes, 'the order to kill the prisoners was neither unlawful nor unchivalric'.[85]

Conclusion

Thus, the more 'extreme' violence we see Henry directing at Harfleur and at Agincourt does not undermine the core argument of this chapter. The English in France in 1415 exercised an unusual-for-the-time level of restraint in their exercise of violence. This was partly because keeping his men on a tight leash minimized his losses during the campaign and set valuable strategic precedents. It also helped the king with his broader international agenda, and suited his genuine (though distinctly medieval) commitment to what he saw as Christian kingship. In his own words, he hoped to minimize the sufferings of the common people in order 'to acquire the approbation of God and the praise of the world', though he had a 'duty' to prosecute the war if that was what it took to achieve his God-given rights.[86] The king's policies in 1415 were broadcast to the world for

STRATEGY, PIETY, AND CHIVALRY

propaganda reasons, and remembered—including with the copying of his military ordinances—because Henry was widely seen as one of the greatest conquerors and most admirable kings of all time, equal to the famous 'Nine Worthies', whose actions were to be emulated by those who desired success and high reputations of their own.[87] Had he not been so successful (in 1415 and for the rest of his short reign), the enhanced protections for non-combatants he introduced in his military ordinances might have been abandoned, or at least restricted to the particular contexts where they did not conflict with military expediency. Instead, they were largely retained.[88] Until the time of Henry V, there was a substantial gap between the common-law expectations of the law of arms and the customs and mores of soldiers, on the one hand, and the higher standards advocated by non-combatant writers on the other. Henry V's ordinances, his actions to enforce them, and his successors' desire to emulate them, bent the arc of history in the direction of justice, at least a little.

3

THOMAS HOWARD AND THE CHARACTER OF ENGLISH VIOLENCE DURING THE REIGN OF HENRY VIII

Neil Murphy

The first half of the sixteenth century witnessed a marked upsurge in English violence as Henry VIII sought to use warfare to make his mark on the international stage. Seeking to emulate his predecessors' conquests in France during the Hundred Years' War, Henry mobilised the largest armies ever raised by an English monarch and invaded France on five occasions (1512, 1513, 1522, 1523, and 1544). Yet his wars were not confined to the continent, particularly as the longstanding Franco-Scottish alliance ensured that his northern neighbour was drawn into these conflicts, in addition to which he faced rebellions in England and Ireland. While Henry VIII occasionally took the field in person (at Tournai in 1513 and at Boulogne in 1544), for the most part he left command of his armies to his generals, of whom Thomas Howard, duke of Norfolk, was his most important. Throughout these wars, Howard employed a military strategy which was based on the use of extreme violence against civilian populations. He was responsible for some of the most destructive wars seen anywhere in Europe during the first half of

41

the sixteenth century. By the time of his death in 1554 at the age of 81, he had brought death and misery to tens of thousands of men, women, and children across north-western Europe.

During Henry VIII's first invasion of France in 1512, of which Thomas Howard became effective leader, English soldiers attacked the undefended French town of Saint-Jean-de-Luz and 'brent, robbed, and killed the inhabitauntes' before going on to do the same to the populations of neighbouring villages.[1] In the same year, Thomas's brother, Edward Howard, cut a swathe of devastation through Brittany, burning crops and villages, and killing peasants.[2] During one of these raids, the English 'passed, seven myle into the countrey, brenning and wasting townes and villages', as part of a campaign which recalled the violence of the Hundred Years' War.[3] When Edward was killed during a naval battle outside Brest in April 1513, Thomas took his place and continued to implement this brutal style of war against the population of Brittany. He was kept away from Henry's 1513 invasion of France, when the English king sought to mitigate the violence against the civilian population, and instead fought beside his father at Flodden, a bloody battle which saw the death of James IV and most of his leading nobles. In 1520, he was made governor of Ireland, during which time he burned the lands of rebels. Yet this was low-level activity in comparison to his actions in France and Scotland in 1522–3, when Henry VIII deployed him specifically to attack French civilians.[4] After sacking Morlaix and burning the surrounding towns, villages, and farms, Howard launched a scorched earth campaign in north-eastern France so severe that seventy years later peasants in the region still remembered 1522 as 'the year of the great fires'.[5] Following his appointment in February 1523 as lieutenant-general of the king's army against Scotland, Howard systematically destroyed large tracts of the Scottish borders and turned them into wastelands. He was brought back to France in 1544 to destroy the land and kill or drive out the indigenous population in a campaign that led to the total depopulation of tens of thousands of acres of the Boulonnais, lands which were then colonised by English settlers.[6]

This paper focuses on officially sanctioned English state violence against civilians, rather than the unlicensed pillaging of populations by both enemy and friendly soldiers alike. Certainly, this type of pillaging was endemic during the wars which ravaged Europe during the first half of the sixteenth century, when rulers tried—and frequently failed—to prevent soldiers, who were themselves often starving and months in arrears in wages, from preying on civilians (and which, as we see in Charles Esdaile's chapter later in this volume, continued to be a problem which plagued British armies fighting on the continent in later centuries). While pillaging was undoubtedly destructive for affected communities, the sixteenth-century version of total war, of which Howard was one of the leading proponents, was of a different magnitude. Howard's violence was sanctioned at the highest level and approved by both the king and parliament. Cardinal Wolsey, chancellor of England, spoke of the 'honourable enterprise' done by Howard in Brittany in 1523, which 'dispoyled and destroyed the great towne of Morles [Morlaix]…with all the villages and Countrey adioynyng to the same'.[7] As we shall see, Thomas Howard, like many of the other individuals in this volume, was acting at the extreme end of the accepted contemporary international standards governing warfare.

War in the Countryside

Howard's campaigns, especially those of the 1520s and 1540s, surpassed normal levels of destruction, and they were probably the most brutal launched by any English army since the fourteenth century. In particular, Howard employed extreme violence to achieve the prolonged ruination of the frontiers of France and Scotland. In 1522, Howard sought to destroy and depopulate vast swathes of northeastern France. One of his commanders on the campaign, Sir William Sandys, informed Henry VIII that the army had swept the region clean of settlements and sources of food, while Howard himself told Wolsey that the damage he had inflicted on the land was so great it would not recover for seven years.[8] Howard went on to impose similar levels of destruction on the Scottish borders. Before setting out to sack the town of Jedburgh and burn large parts of Teviotdale in September 1523, Howard declared that 'more distruction shalbe done in brennying corne and throwying downe of howsis then…

has been done in one journey within Scotland thes hundred yeres'.[9] A wide range of contemporary evidence demonstrates that Howard made good on his promises and that his campaigns in France and in Scotland saw exceptional levels of violence directed against civilian populations.

Howard's wars were designed to cause as much harm to civilian populations as possible. The violence was not indiscriminate; rather, it was carefully planned to achieve extensive damage.[10] While raids often took only a matter of hours, the ruination of crops ensured that their effects lasted for weeks, months, or even years. During his invasion of northeastern France in 1522, soldiers spread out across the land to burn crops and villages in a systematic fashion, so that 'all the countreye twelve myle about was of light fyer'.[11] As a result of the careful application of this strategy, Howard burned thousands of acres of countryside and sacked numerous villages, towns, and castles.[12] While there were numerous instances of the direct killing of civilians on Howard's campaigns, it was the burning of crops and food stores which caused the greatest hardship for rural communities. The disproportionate effect the destruction of corn had on the peasantry was paramount in Howard's mind when he ordered scorched earth attacks. As he prepared to invade Scotland in late summer 1523, for instance, he observed that if the Scottish lords met his demands 'the poore people of the borders of Scotland shuld not bee nowe distroyed by brynnung of their corne'.[13]

Destroying the land to create famine conditions was central to English military strategy. Howard timed his attacks to occur at the points of the agricultural year when they would do most damage, particularly following harvest.[14] As he explained to Wolsey during his Scottish expedition of 1523, it was better to attack crops when they were ripe and ready to be gathered than when they were growing.[15] After being instructed to 'distroye the…[Bou]lonoyse [Boulonnais]' in June 1544, Howard advised the privy council to wait until harvest to extend the conflict zone into neighbouring regions as more damage could be caused when 'the corne be rype'.[16] Good to his word, at harvest time, Howard launched highly destructive raids into the territories lying adjacent to the Boulonnais. On 2 September 1544, he informed Henry VIII and his council that a

THOMAS HOWARD AND THE CHARACTER OF ENGLISH VIOLENCE

company of soldiers led by his son 'had made suche an excourse, that the like hath not bene made sythe these warres beganne' and that they had 'burned all the countrie' along the river Somme.[17] One of the French refugees fleeing the warzone records that the English had so completely destroyed the Boulonnais that they were unable to find any sustenance in the land, with the result that many of his companions died.[18]

As well as burning crops, English commanders destroyed the population's sources of food production, including buildings such as mills and storehouses, as well as agricultural equipment such as draught horses and ploughs.[19] As specialist buildings and items were difficult to replace, this strategy ensured that people starved even should grain become available, thus hindering families from returning to their homes. While the English were unable to slaughter the population of Desvres in 1545, as the population had fled, they destroyed the bakeries, breweries, houses, and mills, thus denying the returning population access to food and shelter.[20] The effects of starvation were compounded by exposure to the elements and the impact of disease. As the Welsh soldier Elis Gruffydd, then serving in Howard's army, passed through the village of Neufchâtel in 1544, he saw 'as many as a hundred people, old and young, with not one healthy man among them, but all shivering with ague [a malarial fever], and death in their faces from the scarcity and lack of bread to strengthen them'.[21] To ensure that grain was not brought into the region, the English destroyed enemy ports. In September 1544, Howard attacked Étaples where his soldiers 'made great ravages in the supply of food and burnt three big ships full of wheat and other food as well as more than a dozen small food ships in the haven. They also burnt the town which contained the breweries of the French king which were filled with food in the pipes, hogsheads, barrels and vats, and burnt all the houses which had been built to keep the grains of corn to be baked and brewed, and killed a number of people'.[22] The systematic destruction of crops and livestock, combined with the ruination of the means to produce food, created a man-made famine.[23]

45

Violence against Urban Populations

While rural populations suffered most from the effects of scorched earth, sieges of towns formed a key component of Tudor warfare. If sieges were the most codified aspect of warfare in sixteenth-century Europe, the rules which governed them offered little protection to civilians.[24] Although threats of extreme violence were designed to encourage urban populations to surrender, Howard looked to apply the full severity of the laws of war against the towns he assaulted. In July 1522, Howard took Morlaix by force and gave his soldiers permission to spend two days sacking it.[25] When he returned to France later that year, he sacked numerous towns, including Doullens where he slaughtered the population 'withought sparynge of any'.[26] Besieging the town of Hesdin, Howard declared that he would kill the men, women, and children sheltering in its castle, though the actions of the town's garrison in repelling the army prevented Howard's threatened general slaughter of its civilian population.[27]

While there were few major urban settlements in the Scottish borders, Howard sacked what towns he could. After cutting a swathe of destruction through Teviotdale in September 1523 and destroying thousands of acres of prime agricultural land, Howard captured Jedburgh and had it razed to the ground. The inhabitants 'were all taken, slain and driven into the abbey', which Howard then had burned along with the rest of the town.[28] Henry VIII wrote to Howard on 3 October 1523 to congratulate him for the 'arracing and destruction' of Jedburgh and the burning of the countryside.[29] Two decades later, while Howard was in France besieging the town of Montreuil, Henry VIII sent Edward Seymour, earl of Hertford, to sack Edinburgh. Arriving before the walls of the city, Hertford told Edinburgh's rulers that 'unless they would yelde up the towne frankley without condition, and cause man, woman and childe, to issue into the fieldes, submitting them to his will and pleasure, he woulde put them to the sworde, and their towne to the fire'.[30] When the city refused to surrender and was taken by force, Hertford ordered his soldiers to 'put the inhabitants to the sword' and burn it to the ground.[31] As a result, the sixteenth-century English chronicler, Thomas Lanquet, records that 'the towne was destroyed, and cleane wasted'.[32] Certainly, Henry was keen on the sack of towns as it provided a key way to broadcast his power, in addition to which it caused major economic harm. For example, Howard's sack of Morlaix was so severe that the town lay in ruin for a decade and its previously thriving linen industry was decimated.[33]

Exposure, Stripping, and Sexual Violence

Henry VIII could also display mercy to urban populations, as at Tournai in 1513 and Boulogne in 1544 when he permitted the people to depart. Yet even when populations were spared direct killing or granted their lives following a siege, being deprived of food and shelter and put on the road in a war zone could effectively amount to a death sentence. Exposure to the elements certainly played a key part in the depopulation of the Boulonnais in the 1540s. The autumn and the winter of 1544–5 were especially severe, with heavy rain, extreme cold, and storms, precisely when there were large numbers of refugees on the road. Elis Gruffydd, participating in Thomas Howard's siege of Montreuil in September 1544, observed the refugees as they were driven out of the region. He states that the men, women and children 'fainted while walking because it was so wet that there had not been one dry hour for ten days', noting how they sought shelter in 'the ruins of a church and village which we had burnt a short time before. Many both old and young died there of cold'.[34] One of the refugees recorded that they were unable to find any shelter from the incessant rainfall because of the total destruction of the buildings in the region, while a local chronicler notes that the refugees passed through a land that had been entirely burnt and depopulated, while many drowned in rivers swollen by the heavy rains.[35]

Contemporary descriptions of the refugees who streamed out of the Boulonnais in 1544 also strongly suggest that they were stripped of their clothing during the attacks.[36] Soldiers stripped captives in the aftermath of sieges both as a way to shame the vanquished and to search for concealed valuables.[37] When the English settlement of New Haven in the Boulonnais fell to French King Henry II in 1549,

French troops 'stripped men and women naked, and went as far as searching their secret parts, [to see] if they had any money hidden; and not finding anything, they left some naked, and others with only their shameful parts [covered]'.[38] On the one hand, there was a basic financial incentive to this act because clothes were valuable and could be sold for a profit, yet stripping was also intended to humiliate the victims. Moreover, stripping was also an effective way to kill people without resorting to direct slaughter, especially during a period of bad weather.[39]

There were also strong associations between the stripping of women and the ability to commit sexual violence, particularly in the wake of a siege.[40] The French writer Guillaume Paradin claimed that English soldiers attacked a group of the townspeople of Boulogne and raped some of the women.[41] Certainly, rape was—and continues to be—a common threat for women during periods of warfare, and there are numerous reports of soldiers raping women during the wars that afflicted this region in the mid-sixteenth century, while Jean de Beaugé records rapes taking place during the Anglo-Scottish wars of the 1540s.[42] Contemporary reports on the evacuation of Boulogne mention that large numbers of women were present amongst the civilian population leaving the town.[43] It is significant that the rapes took place in the immediate aftermath of a siege, when customary restraints on soldiers' violence were often lifted. Under normal circumstances, rape was a capital crime, while the codes of conduct issued to the English army in 1544 made the rape of women punishable by death.[44] Nonetheless, soldiers believed that the laws of war gave them the right to rape women after a victorious siege, which made it difficult to restrain their actions.[45] The soldiers attacked the refugees and stole their goods, raped the women in front of their menfolk, and left them exposed to harsh weather in a region that had been destroyed and depopulated.[46] The townspeople's attackers may have been the very soldiers Henry VIII had sent to protect them. Louis Brésin, a monk based in the nearby town of Saint-Omer, writes that the townspeople's goods were taken by the soldiers appointed to escort them, following which they were led to the small town of Rue 'which they had already burnt, together with the neighbouring villages, up to the suburbs of Abbeville'.[47]

THOMAS HOWARD AND THE CHARACTER OF ENGLISH VIOLENCE

As these attacks were made against the express orders of the king, who had granted mercy, Howard instructed Sir Edmund Wyndham 'to hange uppe dyvers that have spoiled some of the said Frenche' from Boulogne.[48] In the eyes of the English crown, there was a significant difference in destruction carried out on the orders of the army command and unlicenced attacks on civilians. Yet while Howard hanged soldiers for unlicensed pillaging in 1544, he began to systematically burn crops and destroy villages from the moment he crossed out of the Calais Pale into the Boulonnais. For Howard, there was no tension between these two policies. As pillaging was against military law codes, soldiers who looted from or molested the population of the Boulonnais without licence had challenged his authority and should be punished accordingly. In contrast, the destruction of the land (and its people) was legitimate because it was carried out on his instructions and sanctioned by the state.

Rebels and the Laws of War

Restraints on soldiers' actions allowed the English to show that they were acting within the accepted parameters of warfare in sixteenth-century Europe. Unlicensed pillaging was unacceptable because it contravened the military law codes issued by the king, while the burning of peasants' houses and crops was justifiable because they were rebels (as we shall also see in David Trim's chapter on atrocities in the reign of Elizabeth). The depopulation which occurred in the war of 1544–6 resulted from Henry VIII's view that the inhabitants of the Boulonnais were a hostile and rebellious people who were supporting his enemy, Francis I. For Henry VIII and his generals, military concerns necessitated the implementation of severe methods of violence against the French, practices which were sanctioned by contemporary laws of war. Before invading France in 1544, Henry VIII issued a summons instructing the populations of the targeted lands to come and take an oath of loyalty to him as their rightful king.[49] Although Henry did not believe that the French would willingly give him their allegiance in 1544, this summons served an important purpose in underpinning his strategy in the Boulonnais because it enabled him to label as rebels all those who failed to come and take an oath of allegiance to him and drive them from the land. It provided the English monarch with grounds to apply harsh methods of warfare against people he deemed to be his own subjects, as well as giving him the pretext to confiscate their goods and property.

While peasants—even those belonging to an enemy ruler—were in theory protected from violence in contemporary military law codes, including those Thomas Howard issued to his soldiers in 1544, in reality these codes offered little security. Any actions civilians took to insulate themselves from soldiers' violence would make them legitimate targets for killing. Any who sheltered in churches—often the strongest building in a village—made themselves legitimate targets for killing. During Howard's 1522 campaign in France, Sir William Sandys burned the priests and villagers of Whitsandbay in the bell-tower of the church they defended against the English, while in 1544 one contemporary chronicler records how 'in many places the poor people were burned in their bell-towers'.[50] Those peasants who sheltered in churches made themselves subject to the same laws of war that governed the conduct of sieges of towns and castles. At one village in the Boulonnais in 1544, the English promised mercy to the peasants who had fortified themselves in their church. Yet as they exited the building, the soldiers slaughtered them. When the village women tried to stop the massacre of their menfolk, they too were killed. At a neighbouring village, peasants sheltering in the church attempted to surrender. Yet the commander refused to accept their surrender and he massacred eighty men as well as an unknown number of women and children.[51] By seeking refuge inside churches and defending them against soldiers, these peasants had relinquished the protection given to them in military codes of conduct.

Instead of seeking refuge in defensible churches, other peasants fled to woods, caves, and other remote spots to try and escape the violence. While they were not barricading themselves in churches and resisting soldiers, even this action put them beyond the laws of war. During the 1544 campaign in France, fears that peasants were helping French soldiers led the English to deliberately depopulate the region. To this end, English soldiers hunted down and drove out villagers who had fled into the woods.[52] Thomas Howard wrote to Henry VIII on 24 July 1544 advising him to launch an attack on

THOMAS HOWARD AND THE CHARACTER OF ENGLISH VIOLENCE

Hardelot castle, stating that its capture would mean that 'the paysones, which kepe the forests and woddes bytwene this and Bullen, beyng wel handeled and serched, shalbe enforced to fle thens', following which the English king agreed to 'the scooring of the cuntry'.[53] During the 1544 campaign, one Tudor soldier recorded how he had 'clensed the Woode' of 'pyllers and robbers', while another wrote of the peasantry 'living like thieves and bandits in the woods and caves and valleys of the country round Boulogne'.[54] States labelled people they wanted to take punitive action against as brigands or criminals because it justified the use of violence against them.[55] In short, the Tudors employed a legal vocabulary which legitimized their use of violence against civilian populations.

Military Strategy and Scorched Earth

The English state undertook this style of savage warfare against civilians to achieve particular strategic objectives. As Clifford Rogers shows, the English used a devastation strategy during the Hundred Years' War to try and provoke the French into giving battle.[56] Similarly, in 1522 Howard cut a swathe of destruction through northern France designed to provoke this French into battle. The English burned the lands of Charles, duke of Vendôme, who was leading the defence of Picardy, because they hoped he would 'revenge the same [i.e., the burnings] by bataille'.[57] Scorched earth was a key strategy for broadcasting the presence of an enemy army in the kingdom. Howard informed Henry VIII on 7 September 1522 that the burnings were so extensive that if the French 'wynk not they shall se plente off sm[oke]'.[58] By highlighting Francis I's inability to protect his own subjects, the burnings undermined his kingship.

Even when not intended to provoke a battle, scorched earth was a highly effective way of seeking to undermine a ruler's authority or provoke rebellion. During his Scottish campaign of 1523, Howard stated that his burning of villages and crops was designed to achieve Henry VIII's aim of causing the Scottish lords to give up the duke of Albany (regent of Scotland) 'orels to dryve theym [the peasantry] to hunger by distroying ther corne that the total ruyne of ther borders shall ensue'.[59] By the 'total ruyne', Howard meant achieving the entire depopulation of some of the most populous parts of the Scottish borders. Howard sought to create a belt of wasteland twelve miles deep across the borders so that 'few or none Scottishmen shall dwell, sow, or kepe catall' within twelve miles of the frontier.[60] The English used scorched earth tactics to depopulate areas by creating starvation conditions. In 1521, Thomas Howard stated that his burnings in Ireland ensured that people in the targeted areas 'shalbe enforced eyther to forsake the cuntrey, or dye for honger this wynter comyng'.[61] Howard's incursions into Scotland so effectively destroyed the borders that by the end of 1523 raiding parties from Berwick had to travel far over the frontier to find goods to take and people to capture as there was nothing left on the borders.[62] To ensure that this region was unable to sustain a population, Howard appointed 600 horsemen from Northumberland to launch further attacks in November 1523, specifically to ensure that the local population did not attempt to return and sow winter cereals.[63] Howard also hunted down Scottish villagers who had fled their villages to hide in remote locations (as we shall see in Murray Pittock's chapter, this strategy continued to be employed by the British after Culloden). In 1523, Howard enlisted 500 men from Northumberland who, knowing the terrain were to prevent the Scots from going to their 'cots as they wer wont to do when their howsis wer brent but shalbe enforced for lak off corne and vitell to abandon the contre and to leve the same wast'.[64]

As we saw above, Howard timed his attacks to take place at harvest. As well as generating famine conditions, burning the crops in September also ensured there was little possibility of peasants obtaining straw to re-thatch their burned houses. The destruction of crops and houses meant that peasants would either die of hunger and exposure during the winter months or else be forced to flee. Howard so completely destroyed parts of the Scottish borders in 1523 that there was 'left neither house fortresse village tree cattail corne or other socour for man', so that any of the former residents of this region who returned would find 'no sustentacion' and be reduced to starvation and begging and have to leave their homes.[65] This situation is confirmed by Thomas Dacre, Howard's second-in-command, who wrote in June 1524 that 'litill of nothing is left upon

THOMAS HOWARD AND THE CHARACTER OF ENGLISH VIOLENCE

the frontiers of Scotland, without it be parte of ald howses' and that there was nothing left to burn.[66]

The English used a similar strategy in France in 1544, destroying and depopulating the Boulonnais to prevent enemy armies from campaigning in the region. On 8 October 1544, Henry VIII remarked to Thomas Howard that the French could not easily campaign in the region because the English had 'so far divaste' the territory.[67] Henry VIII instructed Howard to 'totally ruinate and burn' the Boulonnais, to create a defensive wasteland, which would help ensure 'a gret quiet for our subjectes there this winter, a continuaunce of our possession in Bullonoyes, and no small honour to you'.[68] These tactics were effective, and the privy council observed that the French would be unable to launch a campaign to recover Boulogne, due to 'the greate destruction of that which was upon the grounde'.[69] Certainly, Gruffydd writes that the Boulonnais was made 'barren' through the production of a man-made famine in the region.[70] The English then employed these tactics in Scotland in the 1540s, with Henry VIII's ambassadors informing Charles V in April 1545 that the French could not invade England through Scotland because 'the cuntrey to be so wasted, spoyled, and heryed'.[71]

As we saw, the Tudors justified their killing of traditional non-combatants by claiming that the laws of war did not protect them because of their actions in helping enemy soldiers. Henry VIII's commanders were particularly concerned about the woods of the Boulonnais because they feared attack from those who hid in them, both peasant and soldier. One soldier records that on 26 September 1544 Thomas Howard took a company of soldiers to 'a Wood beyonde the River to chasse certain Frenchemen whiche were there seen the night before'.[72] If the line between soldier and civilian was especially blurred for men (male peasants often had some degree of military training, and in both France and Scotland they could be called upon to fight in national armies), even women and children were seen as enemy agents and thus could be killed. The character of the warfare Tudor soldiers prosecuted in France in 1544 was especially severe and it produced a fear amongst the French that the English were indiscriminately killing civilians. One local chronicler stated that people were fleeing because of

53

a rumour that the English commanders had ordered the killing of men, women, and children.[73] While it is easy to dismiss such reports, the nature of the warfare the English prosecuted meant that soldiers were ordered to kill traditional non-combatants, including women and children. From the perspective of English commanders in France there could be compelling reasons to kill women and children, particularly when they were supporting the enemy's war effort. In 1544, the English ruled that anyone caught bringing victuals into the French town of Ardres was to be killed. When a group of women were caught trying to supply Ardres, English soldiers threatened them with 'having their hair and ears cut off and being sewn in sacks and thrown into the lakes'.[74] Indeed, soon after the English executed five men and twelve women caught trying to supply Ardres and displayed their corpses as examples to others.[75] Similarly, for the Scottish campaign of 1544, Henry VIII instructed Edward Seymour to put 'man, woman, and childe to fyre and swoorde without exception where any resistence shallbe made agaynst you'.[76] Women's and children's customary immunity from violence was removed because they were perceived to be supporting the enemy's war effort.

European and Global Contexts to English Violence

If the destruction of crops and villages was practiced across Europe, the scale and severity with which Thomas Howard employed it deviated from normal standards of behaviour. The Habsburg commanders who fought with Howard during the French campaign of 1522 were shocked by the severity of his scorched earth strategy, while Charles de Bourbon, duke of Vendôme, who led the defence of the region, condemned Howard for waging a 'very fowle warre'.[77] Howard informed Henry VIII that while most of Charles V's commanders were opposed to any burning, he had nonetheless launched a widespread scorched earth programme and made 'somany smokes' in the Boulonnais that the Habsburgs 'think it is to late to forbere to burne'.[78] By pressing ahead with the burning of France, Howard forced the Habsburg commanders into a severe military strategy with which they were uncomfortable.[79]

54

THOMAS HOWARD AND THE CHARACTER OF ENGLISH VIOLENCE

As a result of such actions, the English gained a reputation as European specialists in the use of scorched earth. When Charles V wanted to launch a brutal war against France in 1553, the count of Roeulx observed that the English were the most skilled at burning.[80] Even with years of experience of the wars which repeatedly devastated this part of Europe, Roeulx singled out the English as the most skilful at implementing scorched earth at its most severe. He was in a good position to comment as he had fought with Howard in 1522 and 1544, witnessing first hand his systematic destruction of the countryside. During the conquest of the Boulonnais in 1544, one English soldier was so keen to burn a village that he started to fire the houses before the artillery train had passed through, while Henry Eure was known as 'a verry fre bornner' for his actions in the Scottish borders in the Anglo-Scottish wars of the 1540s, where he had burned such 'a greatt meyney stakkes, and a greatt meyny howsses full of corn...[in] townes and in the fyldes, [that] Scottland shall have a great famen'.[81] While the Italian Wars were marked by atrocities against civilians, the widespread destruction of the countryside, which was the hallmark of English campaigns in north-western Europe, was largely absent.[82]

In the wider historiography of European global expansion from the late fifteenth century, this type of warfare is typically seen as a hallmark of colonial violence. In other words, that the colonial wars England (and later Britain) fought showed 'a disregard for codified international standards of warfare' and were 'informed by a racial ideology that was central to imperialism and which viewed colonial foes as "savage" and "barbaric" and thus not subject to European "standards" of warfare'.[83] This specifically colonial type of violence is believed to have originated in the sixteenth century, and historians have argued the conduct of war the English waged against Native Americans and the Irish—about whom they held a racial ideology—was considerably more brutal than it was against other Europeans.[84] Yet a study of Thomas Howard's military career shows that there was nothing specifically colonial about the style of violence early modern Europeans employed in the New World (of which it is argued that English actions in Ireland were a part). Scorched earth, famine, and massacre were styles of violence the English used at their most severe against fellow Europeans from countries such as France, which were deemed to be at the centre of 'civilization'. A racial ideology was not necessary for this type of violence to occur.

Conclusion

Thomas Howard was the person most responsible for the marked increase in the severity of English state violence against civilians during the reign of Henry VIII, though as we have seen, his actions had Henry VIII's blessing. Howard's campaigns marked the beginning of a highly destructive period of English violence which was aimed squarely at civilian populations. Right through to the end of Tudor rule, English monarchs employed the extensive use of scorched earth to lay waste to entire regions and create famine conditions. It was because the mass implementation of scorched earth was such an effective method of warfare that it re-emerged as a key military strategy and came to be increasingly implemented across various English theatres of conflict throughout the sixteenth century and beyond. The deployment of men across England's various frontiers led to the diffusion of military practices. In 1523, Thomas Howard implemented in Scotland the scorched earth tactics he had used against the French in the previous year. Rather than English warfare on the continent being distinct and less brutal than that used in other theatres of operation, France in particular was a training ground where English soldiers developed skills in scorched earth and border warfare which they went on to implement elsewhere. Continental Europe was the focus for the greatest excesses of English violence against civilians during the reign of Henry VIII. This importation of violence into Britain and Ireland by troops who had served in continental wars was not particular to the reign of Henry VIII but would be seen in other eras, from the Hundred Years' War to Cromwell's Protectorate and beyond.

4

ENGLISH ATROCITIES IN THE REIGN OF ELIZABETH I AND THEIR CONTEXT

D. J. B. Trim

This chapter on ruthless military violence during the reign of Elizabeth I only briefly considers violence directed by the English state. Instead, it has as its focus violence involving English soldiers who in part were not serving the Tudor state. This is because English warfare from 1563 to 1585 was largely an 'underhand' war—as contemporaries described it—of deniable operations.[1] For this reason, under Elizabeth I's rule from late 1558 to early 1603, England can be described as being, for much of her reign, peaceful, and yet also characterized by war. England was openly at war with France briefly in 1560, again in 1562–3, and with Spain from 1585 to 1603. However, there were also hostilities in Ireland during 1569–73 and 1579–83 and again for much of the period 1593–1603. English troops were, moreover, engaged on the continent of Europe, serving in Protestant armies in France and the Netherlands during 1567–70 and for more than thirty years from 1572 until after Elizabeth's death, and for most of that period, English troops were serving with the connivance and compliance of the Elizabethan regime. Thus, though for more than the first half of Elizabeth's reign, England was rarely at war, warfare was an English constant. And

57

in this period, atrocities were frequently committed both by and against English troops.

As already noted, the English state waged war in Ireland in this period (addressed in Chapter 5 by David Edwards), and I briefly consider some state-sanctioned atrocities in Ireland. But English soldiers engaged across the Irish Sea were outnumbered by those across the North Sea and English Channel, aiding the Huguenots, or French Protestants, in the French Wars of Religion, and aiding the Dutch Revolt against Spain. These English troops were sent with the knowledge and covert blessing of the Tudor state but up until 1585 did not serve in a royal English army. Instead, the official English position was that such soldiers were mercenaries, serving without royal sanction and against Elizabeth's wishes. But this was a veil of plausible deniability, which we can pull back to see the reality. One English soldier wrote to the queen, requesting her authority 'as it were but wynckinge at oure doynges' to raise a force to take to Zeeland, which as we will see was one of the chief theatres of operations in the Dutch struggle against the Spanish Monarchy.[2] Another English warrior suggested to the queen in 1572 that she 'permitt some rashe, willful felo, lyke my sellf, against your majesties will,' to attempt the relief of La Rochelle, the besieged Huguenot stronghold, and he declared himself ready

> most willingly ... to digest with settled mynd the infamy, the exile, the shewes of offens, that shuld be published against me, so that I wer the meane whiles sure they shuld be but shewes, and my sellfe sure of your majesties favor ... having commission to doo it openly or suerty of your highnes favor secretly.[3]

That the disavowals of English troops by Elizabeth and her ministers were a pretence was often apparent to the French crown and the Spanish administration in the Netherlands, but they largely went along with English denials in the hope of preventing an open state of war in which fleets and larger armies might be mobilized. Eventually, in 1585, Elizabethan England could no longer achieve its aims by deniable operations and went to war with Spain openly. Yet, for nearly a quarter of a century, thousands of English soldiers served on the Continent, doing Elizabeth's bidding, but nominally against her wishes.

ENGLISH ATROCITIES IN THE REIGN OF ELIZABETH I

This had two consequences. First, it meant that to gauge how English soldiers regarded atrocities, it is necessary to look to men who were not immediately under state scrutiny. Second, however, it meant that English soldiers were themselves at greater jeopardy, if taken prisoner, because they had been formally disavowed by their sovereign. There is also another reason, however: the disruption of the ethics of military service by the Reformation, which put both English soldiers on the continent, and Spanish and Italian soldiers in Ireland, at risk if taken prisoner. The reasons were essentially religious. Complicating this was the fact that the conflicts in which Elizabethan soldiers were involved were rebellions, and massacres of prisoners were often justified in the language of rebellion and the fate due to rebels; but as we will see, religious reasons also underpinned atrocity, not least because heretics were regarded as rebels against God.

The divisions engendered by the Reformation thus led to a climate of atrocities, in which English soldiers joined very willingly. And I suggest that the willingness of English troops to massacre their captured enemies may reflect more than vengefulness against ruthless enemies who were also on the wrong side of the post-Reformation confessional divide. It is an indication of the readiness of English soldiers to embrace physical violence as a calculated act. The actions of soldiers during the reign of Elizabeth—including both massacres by state forces in Ireland and atrocities by troops that were sent to the Continent, but serving under the Dutch—is important partly for the continuity it shows between the period of Henry VIII and that of Oliver Cromwell.

Two points should be noted: first, in this paper I am *not* discussing massacres that occurred in the storming of cities or forts (as opposed to after capitulations), since by the standards of the time these were not atrocities. It was accepted in early modern Europe that the storming of defended walls was so dangerous that if the garrison put the attacking force to the risk of a storm, then they could expect to be killed out of hand and a city or town sacked. Second, I do not consider English violence against civilians, simply because in France and the Netherlands in this period, English soldiers were serving on the same side as those they served among, and there was no officially

59

sanctioned violence against civilians.[4] While individual English soldiers were guilty of illegal acts of violence to the population, this was officially disapproved—there was no English strategic violence against civilian populations in France and the Netherlands in the period covered by this chapter.

* * *

The spring of 1562 saw the outbreak of the first of eight wars of religion in France. The Elizabethan regime was keen to aid the Huguenots but was at this point determined to extract certain territorial concessions from France's Calvinists in exchange for English support. It took time for mutually agreeable terms to be negotiated between the representatives of the English crown and the Huguenot leadership, but while negotiations dragged on in England, across the Channel the Huguenots had seized control of the large Norman port-city of Rouen near the mouth of the Seine and its outport of Havre de Grace—what is today Le Havre; soon after, Dieppe was captured. Since control of ports would be necessary for English aid to be sent to France, there was an incentive to do something to help France's Protestants hold the three Norman ports. Consequently, the Elizabethan regime arranged for Henry Killigrew to recruit a force of 'volunteers' to go to Normandy. Killigrew was a zealous Protestant from the West Country who had lived in France during the reign of Queen Mary and was well connected to both leading Huguenots and leading members of Elizabeth's council. Eventually, Elizabeth and the Huguenots agreed terms and an English expeditionary force was sent to occupy Le Havre, Dieppe, and Rouen. But the first troops to arrive in Normandy were soldiers in Huguenot pay, though recruited from England's Puritan community. These troops were disavowed by their government, despite its complicity in their recruiting. They were the only English soldiers in Normandy from early July to early October when the first troops of a royal English army commanded by the Earl of Warwick started to arrive in Le Havre.[5]

By the start of October, however, Rouen was under close siege by a royal French army and appealing for help. Some 200 English soldiers from Warwick's expeditionary force plus a number of

ENGLISH ATROCITIES IN THE REIGN OF ELIZABETH I

Killigrew's force were sent to join 300 English soldiers in Huguenot pay who were already in Rouen.[6] In breaking through to the city from the coast, a number of English soldiers were captured. Eleven were hanged from trees, with an inscription placed alongside them 'for having come against the will of the Queen of England in the service of the Huguenots'.[7] The very deniability that made Killigrew's force so useful to the English crown in the summer returned to haunt its members in the autumn. Meanwhile, despite the reinforcements from Le Havre, Rouen's position was hopeless and in late October the city fell. With it, more English soldiers, including Henry Killigrew, fell into the hands of the French royal and Catholic army.

The soldiers who were from Elizabeth's army were imprisoned and held until freed by the terms of the capitulation of Le Havre in 1563 and the Treaty of Troyes in 1564.[8] But the soldiers who were from Killigrew's force faced a different fate. Of them, the English ambassador to France grimly reported that 'of th'English they take the French killeth without mercie'.[9] In Orléans, the Huguenot leaders received reports that the French crown's generals had given instructions to take none as prisoners.[10] A week later, the English ambassador reported that a 'great number of English soldiers ... hurt and laid together in a house ... had their throats cut and were thrown into the river'.[11] Those few who *were* taken alive were sent as slaves to France's galley fleet, with a handful of exceptions.[12] Some survived in the galleys until they were finally released in 1569 after they made contact with the English court, and importuning by Elizabeth.[13]

Killigrew survived but only just, and his peril is indicative of the role played by religion. Killigrew was a gentleman—a nobleman in continental European terms. Nobles had long been able to choose which princes they fought for and what armies they served in. Across Christendom, there was a belief that all noblemen—which included the English gentry—had the right to use force, either in defence of their own honour or in the service of a legitimate just cause. This belief was a basic part of the *jus in bello* norms as they had evolved in medieval Europe. There was thus a sense of a universal brotherhood of warriors, one that transcended the differences of

61

language or nation; this sense made it highly probable that nobles taken prisoner as a result of combat would be spared and treated with courtesy before they were ransomed.[14] Yet when Killigrew was captured, he found himself in peril for his life. Killigrew was placed in the hands of a high French military official, the Constable de Montmorency, but the Duke of Guise, a senior French commander at Rouen, declared that Killigrew should be put to death (according to an English summary) because 'he was a vakabonde … that was fled his contrye unknowne to the Queen'. Killigrew was in fact held until the conclusion of the French campaign to expel Warwick's army from Normandy, yet even after two months in captivity, the Constable still 'wolde have had hym [Killigrew] hanged', so he was in danger for some time.[15]

The declaration cited a moment ago that soldiers were hanged 'for having come against the will of the Queen of England in the service of the Huguenots' and Guise's comments about Killigrew's service being 'unknowne to the Queen' partly indicate new concepts of what constituted legitimate military service, based on the rise of the early modern state, in which a sovereign's approval was needed for foreign service. However, there were also confessional factors that underlay the condemnation of English soldiers to the gallows or the galleys and Killigrew's close shave with death. This is clear, because just a few years before, in the 1550s, Killigrew had served in the *French* army against the Spanish, without the approval of his queen, then Queen Mary, whose reign he had fled because of his zealous Protestantism.[16] Killigrew had been welcome in the French army because there was no confessional division between the Habsburg monarchs and the Valois kings and so the traditional, medieval ethics applied. Less than a decade later, the French civil war resulted from religious fault lines and so Killigrew found himself in jeopardy of execution, though in the end he was ransomed.

During the 1570s, more English soldiers served on the Huguenot side in the French Wars of Religion, and some taken prisoner were probably condemned to the galleys, for in 1577 the English ambassador to France, Sir Amias Paulet, had discussions with Henry III and Catherine de Médici about 'fower English prisoners condemnpned to the gallies', in which he emphasizes 'I was the more bold to deale herein, because *they* weare [...] no other but comon mariners', which implies that other English prisoners had not been.[17]

* * *

In 1568 there had been a revolt in the Netherlands against its foreign Habsburg sovereign, Philip II of Spain. The revolt was crushed by a large army commanded by the Duke of Alba, who was ruthless and sanguinary even by the standards of a bloody century. William, Prince of Orange, who had led the Dutch resistance, and his younger brother, Louis of Nassau, retreated to the Nassau family's estates in the German Rhineland, on the frontier with the Netherlands. Many other Netherlanders went into exile, some taking to the sea as privateers, known as the Sea Beggars, and attacked Spanish shipping and coastal districts of the Low Countries for the next four years, while Alba, as governor-general of the Netherlands, won himself an unenviable reputation for harshness.

Then in 1572, a new revolt was sparked by two incursions into the Netherlands. The first was by the Sea Beggars, aided by a force of English infantry, who in April seized the port-cities of Den Brielle, in Holland, and Flushing on the island of Walcheren, at the mouth of the Scheldt in the province of Zeeland.[18] We shall return to this littoral theatre of operations in a moment. In the first week of May, there was a second incursion, into the south of the Netherlands, today's Belgium, from France by a multinational force consisting of Huguenot, English, Welsh, and Dutch exile troops commanded by Louis of Nassau. Louis successfully seized Valenciennes and Mons, and hoped to connect with an army led by his brother, William, invading from Germany, but Louis was surrounded by Spanish troops under the Duke of Alba and cut off.[19] Eventually, Louis surrendered on honourable terms—however, soldiers who were subjects of the Spanish king were exempted from the surrender terms. Louis and his personal household, including English, Welsh, and Huguenot soldiers, safely left Mons, while the Dutch troops were executed.[20]

What, however, of the first incursion? Here atrocities were common. The capture of Flushing sparked resistance to the Spanish across Zeeland and much of the province of Holland, and troops were raised to fight the Spanish. But the rebel forces in Zeeland would have been inadequate were it not for the arrival of a sizeable English and Welsh force raised by great nobles of Elizabeth I and commanded by Sir Humphrey Gilbert, a client of Elizabeth's chief counsellor, Lord Burghley (and also a veteran of the Irish conflicts examined by David Edwards in his chapter).[21] Like Killigrew's force, however, Gilbert's was officially disavowed, putting them in greater jeopardy. The circumstances in which they helped the Dutch were not propitious ones in several ways, including their likely fate if captured. In the campaigns in Zeeland and Holland, as the historian Geoffrey Parker observes, Alba 'hanged all the Dutch troops who came into his hands'.[22] But as Fernando González de León points out, Alba's subordinate generals also 'were known for their severity and even brutality. They asked and gave no quarter, instigated their troops to sack captured cities, exterminate their population and kill prisoners of war'.[23] Alba even hanged messengers sent under flag of truce, in violation of all the normal laws and practices of war.[24]

The Dutch and the English soldiers in their service responded by killing the prisoners they took in turn. The garrison of Flushing regularly executed Spanish prisoners, even hanging them in groups of tens and twenties at a time.[25] They may even have 'used the heads of Spanish prisoners as cannonballs'.[26] English troops, being a significant part of the rebel force at Flushing, would have been party to some of these practices—and in some cases we know explicitly that they committed atrocities.

For example, the Dutch forces from Flushing moved on the city of Bruges, on the other side of the Scheldt, where they called on the Spanish governor to surrender. In refusing, he sardonically asked Sir Humphrey Gilbert to nevertheless keep his army before the city walls of Bruges, since a relieving army of 'divers troupes of horsemen ... & a great number of footmen' would soon arrive— and then, he promised, the English would all be hanged. The enraged Gilbert responded in like terms, 'swearing divers oathes, that hee would put all to the sword, unless they would yeeld'.[27] But the assault on Bruges was repulsed, and the Anglo-Dutch force retreated back to Walcheren island, which prompted the Spanish in Middelburg to make a follow-up attack. Roger Williams, a Welsh soldier who was part of the force at Flushing, later recalled: 'To doe it

ENGLISH ATROCITIES IN THE REIGN OF ELIZABETH I

the more terribly, they [that is, the Spanish] prepared a great number of haulters; giving them to their souldiers with a commandement, to hang all the prisoners they should take'.[28] But the English were not in as bad a state as the Spaniards had suspected and in battle 'gave [them] a full overthrow', after which, as Williams later recalled with satisfaction, 'our men hung a number of them with their owne haulters'.[29] To be clear, this was not a matter of refusing to take prisoners and killing men in hot blood—this happened not infrequently in sixteenth-century (as in twentieth-century) warfare. Rather it was a matter of *accepting* the surrender of enemy troops and *later* executing them in cold blood. This was not accepted as part of warfare. These were atrocities. Added to this is the apparent levity with which Williams recalled the hangings decades later, not least because, a couple of years after, Williams himself had been captured by the Spanish, and survived the experience, which one would have thought might make him more rueful about his and his comrades' contrasting readiness to kill their captives in 1572.[30] To judge from his description of hanging Spaniards with their own ropes, Williams seems to have seen this as poetic justice and as what we might call quasi-retaliatory: the Spanish had not been able to commit their own atrocities, but they had threatened them and then were hoist, not on their own petards, but in their own nooses.

Meanwhile, after the capitulation of Mons, Louis of Nassau made his way north to join William of Orange, but the revolt was soon confined to the province of Zeeland and parts of the province of Holland. In the winter of 1572–3, the north Holland city of Haarlem was besieged, and its mixed German, English, French, Scottish, and Dutch garrison desperately held out, while William frantically tried to break the siege. Eventually the city capitulated to Alba. The garrison yielded on terms of 'mercy'—but mercy in sixteenth-century siege-warfare parlance meant not actual mercy, but mercy at the discretion of the commander of the besieging army. The result was appalling, and regarded as such at the time, at least by those who were not partisan on the Spanish side. Haarlem surrendered on 13 July 1573. The city fathers had paid a fine of 240,000 florins and on the 14 July, they were told, as a Dutch chronicler recorded, 'that all their lives were saved, by the making up of that summe of money'. However, 'The same day that the Spaniards entred, The Scots and Almaines [i.e., Germans] were commanded to carry their armour and weapon to the town house, from whence, they were counducted to the Monasteries ... where the Spaniardes kept them. ... And the same day the Captaines and Ensigne[s] ... were led prisoners.... But whiles the citizens and souldiers were kept in the Church, the Spaniards sackt and spoyled' the city. On 15 July, 'three hundred Walon [that is, French-speaking Netherlandish] souldiers were hanged, and beheaded'. On 16 July several officers were beheaded (note again that the noble class, which supplied captains, was not being exempted), the Calvinist pastor of the town 'was hanged, & 247 souldiers [were] drowned in Harlem Mere'. The Spanish thought it fitting to drown Protestant prisoners who they often assumed to be Anabaptists. On 17 July, the chronicler is vague: 'one part of the soldiours were beheaded.' This was probably several hundred. On 18 July, 'more than 300 soldiours [were] put to the sword'. During 20 to 25 July, various civil leaders and Dutch captains were executed.[31] The massacre became a subject of illustration: a Welsh soldier serving William of Orange, Walter Morgan, produced an illustrated account of his service in the Netherlands. One of the grimmest drawings in his manuscript is a depiction of the outcome at Haarlem, with those awaiting execution praying, headless bodies littering the market place, and other bodies being thrown into Haarlem Meer. A Dutch or German illustrator produced a graphic print, showing some prisoners beheaded, some shot, some hanged, and piles of corpses; it was produced as anti-Spanish propaganda, and had wide circulation, including in Baudart's contemporary history.[32]

Geoffrey Parker, in his authoritative history of the Dutch Revolt, estimates that 2,000 prisoners were killed in cold blood, but says that 'the entire garrison, with the exception of some English and German troops, was executed', and he is followed by the military historian Stephen Turnbull.[33] Some of the Germans *were* spared and enlisted into Alba's army—which, like its Dutch opponents, was not truly a Spanish army, but rather a multinational army, drawn from across Philip II's wide domains and beyond; Alba already had German troops serving him. But there is actually no evidence that

ENGLISH ATROCITIES IN THE REIGN OF ELIZABETH I

English were spared; indeed, there is contrary evidence. A different chronicler wrote that on the 20 July, eighteen captains and 500 soldiers were executed, 'as many Walloons as French, English and Scots'.[34] These were not the last English prisoners slaughtered, for others were killed in the coldest of cold blood. On 11 August, four weeks after Haarlem's surrender, 'about three hundred, what of Englishmen, French, Scottes, and Walons, who till then lay in prison were beheaded'.[35] On 19 August a further batch were killed, when 'Others who were ill or wounded having been guarded in the hospital, were executed'.[36] There probably were not any more English survivors of the siege than would have been killed on 20 July and 11 and 19 August. As Roger Williams writes of Alba, 'he executed the most part of them most cruelly'.[37]

The Dutch and their English auxiliaries responded in kind as and when the fortunes of war gave them the opportunity. In 1574, during the celebrated siege of Leiden, whose garrison included English troops, a Spanish captain, according to one of the English soldiers, flew 'the bloody ensigne', signifying that his company would take no prisoners; the garrison sallied and captured the flag along with a number of prisoners; the latter they hanged, the former they flew in turn from their walls as a symbol to other Spanish troops.[38]

Once the Dutch were successful enough in the field to take sizeable numbers of prisoners, there was an incentive to return to the traditional norms of the laws of war, but it took time for this reversion to take place.[39] Fernando González de León has characterized Spanish brutality as a deliberate policy of the Duke of Alba, but points out that Alba's successor as governor-general of the Netherlands, Don Luis de Requesens, initially insisted to his officers 'that Dutch prisoners be killed and not ransomed'.[40] In 1578, under the next Spanish governor-general, Don Juan of Austria, there seems to have been at least one mass execution of prisoners.[41] In 1579, when the great city of Maastricht fell to Don Juan's successor, the Prince of Parma, there was another mass slaughter of prisoners. As a Dutch soldier reported, the garrison 'capitulated on terms of their lives saved' and were then imprisoned in a number of houses in the city. 'The enemy ... disregarded their promise and massacred them cruelly for three hours'.[42]

67

HARFLEUR TO HAMBURG

In response, the Dutch were still executing soldiers whose surrenders had been accepted into 1580.[43] When the English soldier John Norreys, commanding a force of 800 English and 400 Dutch and Scottish troops, stormed the city of Mechelen in 1580, an English chronicler describes how, after initial resistance 'every one cried Misericorde, and fell pitifully at the feete of the Soldiors, who findyng victorie used not mutche extremitie'. However, not only is there an implication that this was unusual, but also the same chronicler then notes 'the number of all those that were slaine were not aboue twoo hundreth persones'.[44] And this was the outcome when there was 'not mutche extremitie' and 'misericorde' or mercy *was* granted by a force two-thirds of whom were English.

In 1581, Norreys and his English contingent were moved to the northeast of the Netherlands where Norreys commanded a sizeable army against a force consisting mostly of Catholic Dutch who had joined the rebellion against Spain in 1577 but then in 1580 returned to their original allegiance. These 'Malcontents' as both Dutch and English called them were disliked as renegades. One English soldier who served in the campaign, William Blandy, wrote of how they were 'cruell, bloudy, and ... in manners barbarous'. Blandy continued that 'sufferaunce towards so cursed and perverse a generation [was] to be marvailed at'.[45] It appears to be the case that 'Dutch nobles took a more liberal view, and the "malcontents" were judged as lawful mercenaries, or soldiers, in the service of legitimate nobles and potentates,' but it seems likely in light of Blandy's comments that English soldiers took a harder view and sometimes killed rank-and-file prisoners out of hand.[46] Yet we know that officers were held for ransom by both sides.[47] Roger Williams, whom we last saw in Flushing in 1572 but who in the 1580s was one of Norreys's officers, even, on a celebrated occasion, accepted the challenge of a Spanish officer to a formal joust. Their chivalric single combat ended in a draw, and Williams and his Walloon opponent 'betooke themselves to drink freely together' afterwards, parting on good terms.[48]

It has to recognized, however, that the situation was qualitatively different in the late 1570s and early 1580s, when the soldiers in Dutch pay were in the service of the States-General—a recognized, legitimate pan-provincial political institution; troops in its service could not be dismissed as mere traitors or rebels, because they were serving a legitimate and sovereign authority. For that matter, the 'malcontent' southern Netherlandish captains and commanders who served in Parma's army had been on the rebel side only a short time before and were more likely to show clemency. Finally, Parma seems to have decided that his predecessors had been wrong in their policies and promoted instead a return to traditional chivalric ethics, in which nobles were treated with respect. But Parma was also at pains to show mercy to besieged Dutch towns and cities and their garrisons after they capitulated in the hope of conciliating the rebels.[49] The ideological heat was largely drained out of conflict in the Netherlands—though as we will see, not entirely.

* * *

The Spanish (and at times French Catholic) refusal to accept Protestant enemies as lawful enemies had repercussions beyond the continent. A contingent of Italian and Spanish mercenaries that landed at Smerwick in Ireland in 1580 was massacred after surrendering to an English force under the Lord Deputy of Ireland, Lord Grey de Wilton. Like the garrison of Haarlem, the Spaniards and Italians in Smerwick surrendered on terms of 'mercy'. One factor in the decision to show them, in fact, no mercy was the perception that they were allies of Irish rebels against their legitimate sovereign, Queen Elizabeth, so that their service was illegitimate.[50] Further, as a recent study concludes, they were executed on the grounds that they 'were no better than pirates or brigands with no legal standing under the law of nations'—this may again seem to point to the emergence of new concepts of the state and of state sovereignty. But as the same study shows, religious factors were decisive in Grey's interpretation of the Italian and Spanish soldiers' status; and it is inconceivable that the fate of English troops on the continent did not influence Grey in reaching his view, for his force included men who had served with the Huguenots or Orangists, while others (Grey included) had strong personal connections to soldiers serving in France or the Netherlands.[51] Sir Richard Bingham, a veteran of campaigning in the Netherlands in 1573 and 1578, took a leading part in the massacre

HARFLEUR TO HAMBURG

at Smerwick in 1581, and in 1588 was assiduous in slaughtering survivors of Spanish Armada shipwrecks; one historian estimates he killed at least 1,100 survivors.[52]

Bingham is an interesting case. He won himself a horrible reputation in Ireland for his severity; Irish chroniclers wrote, for example, that he 'made a bare, polished garment of the province of Connaught', of which he was governor.[53] Bingham, then, may have been brutal or bloodthirsty by nature. Against that, Angus Konstam has argued that the summary execution of Spanish survivors of Armada wrecks in Ireland was an exceptional policy prompted by fears that their presence might provoke a general rebellion.[54] We come back to the importance, in contemporary understanding of the laws of war, of rebellion, and the status of rebels. However, Spanish sailors and soldiers of the Armada were *not* rebels, and Bingham's practice towards them was probably motivated by more than fear of rebellion, but also by more than bloodlust or brutality, for Irish chroniclers decried his opposition to 'true' religion, and he was a patron of Puritan ministers.[55] For Bingham, Spaniards were also Catholics and thus legitimate targets of massacres. We come back to the confessional factors that underpinned many sixteenth-century revolts and rebellions.

* * *

I want, however, to suggest that even beyond religion there was a ruthless streak in English soldiers' mentality that could come out whenever the chips were down. This was not inevitable. In the expedition to Spain that captured Cadiz in 1596, the Earl of Essex, who was in command, enforced collective self-restraint, which may have reflected the degree to which he subscribed to the chivalric ethos, and the success of the expedition.[56] In contrast, if Sir Humphrey Gilbert before the walls of Bruges, threatening the Spanish that he would 'put all to the sword', was plainly actuated by retaliatory considerations, arising from the Spanish threat of atrocities against his own force, Norreys at Mechelen (despite his men's supposed mercy) had no grievance he was taking reprisal for. In any case, English commanders could go well beyond simple tit-for-tat retaliation.

ENGLISH ATROCITIES IN THE REIGN OF ELIZABETH I

In October 1595, the commander of the English army in the Netherlands, Sir Francis Vere, bombarded a Spanish fort in the north-eastern province of Overijssel into submission. Six weeks earlier, Francis Vere's brother, Robert, had been involved in a cavalry skirmish near Groenlo in the eastern province of Gelderland and had surrendered but then been killed. He fell into the hands of an Italian cornet of horse who, as a contemporary reported, 'cruelly murdered [him] in cold blood'.[57] After the fort surrendered, Sir Francis selected half the garrison and had them executed, likewise in cold blood.[58] If reprisal for his brother might understandably have been on Francis Vere's mind, killing half the garrison went rather beyond what might have been seen as reasonable, even in the sixteenth century. Just over six years later, in January 1602, Ostend, the city commanded by Sir Francis Vere which had a largely English garrison, underwent a famous siege. As a Dutch chronicler relates, during a major Spanish assault, 'no man [of the attacking force] was spared, notwithstanding he cried out, take me prisoner, I am an Ensigne, Lieutenant, or Captaine, one promising an hundred, an other two, three, foure, five, yea sixe hundred crownes to have their lives spared'. One Italian nobleman 'who was very rich ... and promised to give as much for his ransome as his bodie weighed' was slain 'with a poniard' by 'a common soldier', disregarding the prospect of wealth.[59] There was a ruthlessness in the English troops that could be unveiled at moments of stress.

* * *

In conclusion, we have to recognize the context in which English committed atrocities, which include the rise of the early modern state, the fact that the key wars in which Elizabethan soldiers took part were mostly rebellions (or could be seen that way), and the confessional hostilities, indeed hatreds, consequent on the Reformation; and also that, due to these factors, English soldiers were the victims of atrocities themselves as often as they made victims of others. However, English willingness to kill enemies out of hand and to massacre those whose surrender had been accepted suggests that atrocity was part and parcel of the military vocabulary, so to speak, of Elizabethan soldiers, an inheritance from the earlier sixteenth century (as Neil Murphy shows in Chapter 3) and one that was perpetuated in the seventeenth century (as David Edwards shows in Chapter 5). The Elizabethan period fits in many ways into the longer-term history of English and British violence in Europe.

5

STATE OF EMERGENCY
THE ENGLISH SUBJECTION OF EARLY MODERN IRELAND

David Edwards

11 September 1649: following an artillery bombardment, an English parliamentary army, commanded by Oliver Cromwell, stormed the walled town of Drogheda on the east coast of Ireland, where a large royalist garrison of English and Irish troops had assembled against them. The actions of Cromwell's army over the following hours and days shocked contemporaries. Indeed, they have continued to be talked and written about ever since, becoming a standard reference point in discussions of the darker legacy of centuries of English involvement in Ireland.[1] It is not only that the numbers slain by Cromwell's men were unusually high by the standards of Irish warfare, but rather that grim distinctions can be drawn— and were drawn by contemporaries—between the different types of killing sanctioned in the course of the action.[2] According to the best scholarly estimates based on accounts written soon afterwards, nearly 2,800 members of the defending garrison were slain, along with a less easily quantifiable number of unarmed and defenceless civilians: it is reckoned that these may have totalled as many as 800 victims.[3]

While it is not possible to draw a precise distinction, it is clear from the surviving evidence that much of the slaughter was done in cold blood, after the town had been taken and resistance ended. Cromwell himself seems to have gloried in the bloodshed. Writing six days later to the speaker of parliament at Westminster, he credited the encounter as being 'the righteous judgment of God' and praised the virtuous steadfastness of the New Model Army in delivering such a great and holy victory.

Yet even as he wrote, news was spreading that much of the killing he had authorized constituted what would nowadays be termed a war crime, having contravened the accepted rules of war as they were understood in England as well as Ireland.[4] Though many of the royalist garrison had surrendered on promise of quarter, soon after laying down their weapons they were shot, stabbed, and clubbed to death by the parliamentarians into whose protection they had been invited. As the Anglo-Irish magnate and royalist leader James Butler, marquis of Ormond ruefully observed when eyewitness accounts reached him, 'they [the prisoners] were butchered an hour after quarter was given them'.[5]

The slaying of hundreds of civilians was an even greater outrage. Though Cromwell tried to present it as revenge for the 'barbarous' treatment meted out by Irish Catholics to English Protestants in Ulster eight years before—more about that in a moment—he could not deny that in Drogheda his men had killed without limit. The principal source is a pamphlet printed in London just over three weeks later called *Letters from Ireland, Relating the several great Successes it hath pleased God to give unto the Parliaments Forces*. This included in full Cromwell's letter to the speaker announcing Drogheda's capture wherein he admitted that besides the high number of enemy combatants killed on his orders, 'many inhabitants' were also slain— an evasive phrase, and all the more chilling for that.[6] That it caused political discomfort for Parliament's leaders in London is revealed by the removal of any reference to civilian deaths in some of the subsequent republications of Cromwell's triumphant letter that appeared in the following months.[7] But such suppression had only a limited effect. Far beyond the control of the Westminster leadership was what was disseminated by word of mouth by Cromwell's men

STATE OF EMERGENCY

on their return to England from Ireland.[8] One such account by Thomas à Wood, later published by his brother, an Oxford antiquary, told the story of the taking of St Peter's Church, a key building in Drogheda of strategic importance as a vantage-point over the town. Wood's tangible sense of dishonour, even shame, stood in marked contrast to Cromwell's self-righteous bravado. Most whom Wood had helped kill in the church had been civilians desperately seeking sanctuary, women and children, not royalist soldiers. Laying hold of some wriggling youngsters to use as 'bukler[s] of defence'— human shields—the parliamentarians made their way up to the lofts and galleries and into the church tower, killing 'all' within. Then, proceeding down into the vaults where 'the flower and choicest of the women had hid themselves', the troops killed everyone there too.[9] Regarding the total number of civilian casualties, around 800 people, the population of Drogheda most likely numbered about 6,000–7,000 souls before the wars of the 1640s began, and this would have been swollen by an influx of refugees immediately before Cromwell's arrival outside its walls.[10] Whatever the figure, it is safe to conclude that after the storming of the town the *proportion* of defenceless civilians slain was high.

As for Cromwell's insinuation that the civilians' deaths were somehow justifiable as revenge for earlier Irish atrocities against English settlers in Ulster—a supposed 'general massacre'—this merely heaped insult on the injuries and fatalities he inflicted. One of the reasons the royalist forces he attacked in Drogheda had gathered in the town was because its people had *not* participated in the Irish rebellion of 1641, or any attendant slaughter, and had in fact offered support and assistance to the many English who had fled for their lives out of Ulster. Here is not the place to discuss the numbers of English killed in the country between the autumn of 1641 and spring of 1642, a very complex matter which requires careful testing of highly unsatisfactory evidence.[11] What matters is that though many English had been exposed to rebel Irish violence in 1641–2, they had not experienced it in Drogheda. The town had instead been a haven, somewhere that English refugees were protected as the rebellion had taken root, escalated, and spread. By presenting the slaughter he ordered in 1649 as Drogheda's just deserts for what had previously occurred beyond its

75

walls, Cromwell made its townspeople victims twice over, of his utter ignorance (which had been stimulated, of course, by a flood of lurid Irish 'news' reports, often false, that had earlier appeared in print in London) as well as the sheer cruelty of his army.[12]

The capture of Drogheda initiated a series of victories over the following eight months in which Cromwell conquered nearly half the country before the political situation in England compelled his return to London (May 1650).[13] His next major Irish action after Drogheda, the siege and sacking of Wexford in the south-east in October 1649, proved almost as bloody. It has been estimated that his troops slew approximately 2,000 people after being granted entry to the town by one of its Irish Catholic commanders who, fatally, was willing to concede its surrender; he himself was among those slain. Unlike in Drogheda, military prisoners were mostly spared— they were destined for white servitude in Barbados. But otherwise, like Drogheda, the brutality of the New Model Army troops was left unchecked. For several hours, until nightfall, they killed many unarmed civilians as they swarmed through Wexford's narrow streets.[14] A near-contemporary source, published in England a few years after Cromwell's own death, claimed that the civilian fatalities included 200 women, but this can be neither proved nor disproved.[15] What is clear is that many civilians were among those recorded as killed trying to escape the town in rowing-boats over the Slaney river. Moreover, after overcoming the garrison and receiving its surrender, it is evident that the New Model Army forces went on a sustained rampage of pillaging and rapine directed entirely against the ordinary population that lasted the rest of the day and left survivors deeply traumatized as well as impoverished.[16] Though he very likely had lost control of his men, Cromwell was unapologetic for their actions. In another letter to Westminster, he emphasized the alluring wealth of Wexford and insinuated that his army had saved Parliament precious treasure by taking 'a very good booty in this place'.[17]

I

The exceptional violence perpetrated at Drogheda and Wexford was not repeated in the subsequent military engagements that Cromwell personally oversaw in Ireland. Indeed, if his reports are true, he had envisaged the massacres, especially Drogheda, as necessary and justifiable episodes of exemplary severity designed to avoid greater carnage: 'this bitterness will save much [further] effusion of blood'.[18] Yet it is equally important to realize that it was only in Ireland that Cromwell deployed this *ad terrorem* strategy. While the English Civil Wars (1642–5, 1648–9) in which he had risen to power had been grim affairs, nonetheless both sides, royalist and parliamentarian, had exercised restraint to a significant degree. As John Morrill has noted, in England, killings of combatants in cold blood had been rare, killings of civilians in hot blood even rarer. There is no evidence of prisoners being killed at the end of battles; captured officers were ransomed or exchanged and rank-and-file soldiers merely disarmed and sent home, or else offered the opportunity to switch sides. The nearest comparison to Drogheda or Wexford was the siege of Basing House, Hampshire, in 1645, when maybe a third of the defenders were slain in hot blood; of the survivors, having surrendered, all were spared, except six Catholic priests. It is true that in the second Civil War a harder attitude had taken hold, but even at the siege of Colchester (1648), only the three principal officers of the royalist garrison were punished, for having delayed its surrender.[19] No amount of historical revision can undo the fact that once they had crossed the Irish Sea, Cromwell and his forces had abandoned their usual methods. Ireland's status as England's principal outlying dominion afforded its people scant protection: it became instead the great killing-zone where the residual military strength of Stuart royalism was eviscerated, while the assertive Catholicism of the Irish who hosted the royalist forces added ideological encouragement for extreme measures. Indeed, the ethno-sectarian rationale for the violence intensified after Cromwell's departure and culminated in what amounted to a revolutionary remodelling of the country. To the accompaniment of a wave of executions that were conducted with and without trial, the indigenous Catholic elite of Gaelic Irish and Anglo-Irish landowning dynasties that had controlled most of the country for centuries was comprehensively terminated, its lands confiscated and redistributed. A greatly expanded Protestant ascendancy class emerged, destined to remain in place until the late nineteenth century.[20]

In the broad outline of Irish history, the enduring importance of the Cromwellian conquest and subsequent land settlement is undeniable. It marks the country's final and bloody transition from having been (circa 1500) a largely autonomous bi-cultural region of the Atlantic world to somewhere completely subjected to the centralizing power of English civil and military government.[21] After the 1650s, little would remain of the indigenous Gaelic political order that for over a millennium had controlled most of the country, while the surging influence of the Catholic Church, such a major feature of the early seventeenth century, would be heavily suppressed and driven underground. Henceforth Ireland, if not fully 'made English', would at the very least be extensively anglicized, and its economy increasingly tied to the service of an emerging English/British Empire.[22]

II

But as the following pages will show, the Cromwellian era is also significant in Ireland for another reason: it was actually the second time that the English state had had to conquer the country in the early modern period, occurring just a few decades after an earlier and much longer phase of conquest and colonization overseen by the Tudor and Early Stuart monarchy. Beginning in the reign of Henry VIII (1509–47) and continuing almost without a break into the early years of his Stuart successor James VI and I (1603–25), generations of English officers and soldiers had pursued the subjugation of Ireland as an imperial project intended to ensure English domination and control over the wider British Isles and counter the threat of external interference from Europe.[23]

The story of the wars that advanced this new level of English dominance in Ireland has traditionally been confined to the larger conflicts only, namely the Kildare rebellion (1534–5), the Ulster or Shane O'Neill wars (1557–62, 1565–7), the Desmond rebellion (1579–83), and the Nine Years War (1594–1603).[24] It is, though, a more involved tale than that. By omitting all the many other conflicts that irrupted throughout the country at the time, even characterizing them as mere 'little wars', Irish historians have not always grasped the scale and reach of the spiralling violence that accompanied Tudor and Early Stuart expansion.[25] A number of recent new studies have begun to correct this oversight.[26] It is now appreciated that beginning in the 1530s, English power and government extended further outwards from Dublin in direct correlation to the growing regional presence of Crown forces. Captains and soldiers, not judges or tax collectors, led the way; the judges and taxmen emerged later. The larger wars certainly wreaked death and destruction over greater areas, but the numerous little wars were no less impactful because of the frequency with which they were waged.[27] Under the Tudors, between 1546 and 1603 there was not a year when English forces weren't engaged in operations in some part of the country; under the Stuarts, following the Treaty of Mellifont that ended the Nine Years War (30 March 1603), the scale of operations tapered, but did not cease. Native opposition continued to flicker all through the early seventeenth century, necessitating a military response.[28]

However, the importance of the army was never confined to combat or counter-insurgency operations. The English administration of Ireland itself became heavily militarized. This process is best traced from the top. After 1534, the chief qualification for the office of viceroy, other than high English birth, was military experience. Unlike, for instance, the viceroys of the Spanish Habsburg dominions in Sicily or Sardinia, whose functions were essentially ceremonial and conservative, overseeing established systems of government, the English viceroys of Ireland were expected not merely to take charge of the Crown forces symbolically, but to do so actively, at the head of military expeditions intended to introduce or maintain English rule in parts of the country that otherwise would have remained beyond the Crown's reach.[29]

As study of their official papers shows, they regularly performed their numerous administrative tasks while leading such 'hostings' or 'journies', carrying on routine state correspondence, hearing reports and petitions, issuing orders, and signing warrants while far from Dublin, out in the provinces. Accordingly, the English government of Ireland was often government on horseback or by campsite.[30] It was also, of course, heavily intimidating, broadcasting English power and demanding its acceptance through the repeated demonstration of force. The viceroys' letters and reports, especially their journals of service, reveal the high levels of violence and bloodshed that routinely accompanied their outings. Take Henry VIII's most famous viceroy, Sir Anthony St Leger, considered a politically moderate governor by some historians.[31] In late August or early September 1540, he led a 'journey' into the Gaelic lordship of Idrone that bordered the medieval county of Carlow. For ten days, he and his troops engaged in a 'little war', killing whomever they encountered and systematically burning the territory. Having arrived at harvest-time, their actions ensured there would be dearth in the coming year. Only when the land- and crop-burning was completed, and the territory effectively ruined, did Sir Anthony invite the local Kavanagh chieftain to meet him. There was to be no discussion: St Leger instead dictated terms of 'settlement' which declared Kavanagh's customary sovereign rights in the region as extinguished. Meanwhile, as Idrone's fields and woodlands crackled and burned around him and indigenous survivors fled, the more mundane business of English government continued. Having remained in contact with the royal Council in Dublin, with messengers riding back and forth, on his return to the capital St Leger was able to resume the other functions of his office almost seamlessly.[32]

Thus a blended form of English vice-regal rule developed from Henry VIII's time that merged military itinerancy and war-making for part of the year with more sedentary gubernatorial behaviour the rest of the time. A generation later, under Elizabeth I, the interim viceroy Sir William Pelham would travel much further than St Leger at the head of the royal forces, passing through three of Ireland's four provinces in response to growing unrest and rebellion. Absent from Dublin for nearly nine months, from January to September 1580, Pelham's journeying threatened to disrupt the regular functioning of state government.[33] However, as recorded in the diary kept by his secretary, Sir William took measures to ensure his continued oversight of government business. Beginning on 23 February 1580, he made Limerick his temporary headquarters and secondary capital, and brought half the Irish Council and dozens of administrators and clerks to the south-western city to attend on him and keep all the paperwork and treasure flowing.[34] This allowed him to concentrate

STATE OF EMERGENCY

on soldiering, in particular the reduction of the Desmond rebellion, his prime concern. Days before his arrival in the city, Pelham had authorized the first round of raiding and killing in the neighbouring area, and after establishing his command centre in King John's Castle he had had a gibbet constructed in the civic market place for the public dispatch of 'traitors' and 'malefactors' following their capture and trial.[35] Once out of the city, he quickly dispensed with such formalities, and led his troops on a series of marches designed to crush resistance through the general use of summary executions and scorched-earth, systematically depopulating and devastating wide areas of Counties Limerick, Cork, and Kerry. A diary entry for 11 March describes his forces at work. Having already secured the important bridge at Rathkeale and torched the countryside to a distance of five or six miles, Pelham's men then went looking for the local inhabitants. Their blood was up, consumed with 'fury'. The diarist succinctly observes how they committed 'many murders'— an interesting choice of term—and 'spared neither man, woman nor child'. The following day was similar. Having passed to the north of Slievelogher (the Mullaghereirk Mountains), the troops 'spent the day in searching all the woods and bogs ... to the Shannon [river] side.... Many towns and habitations were consumed with fire, and ... about 400 people of the rebels put to the sword'.[36]

The severity shown to native women was not incidental. When Pelham learned that the commander of the Kilmallock garrison Sir George Bourchier had ordered his troops to refrain from killing or otherwise mistreating the local womenfolk he had sent him a letter explicitly ordering him to 'not protect any women'.[37] The text of the letter is not extant: all we have is the brief summary of its content and notice of its dispatch by Pelham's secretary, but even so it is enough to catch a glimpse of something that usually was concealed in official reports, of how violence against women was not merely tolerated in the course of military campaigns, but sanctioned.[38] What is perhaps most significant about this reference is the implication that Bourchier's shielding of local females was out of line: evidently all of Pelham's other officers knew not to offer any such protection, having been informed of the viceroy's policy orally. It is interesting to note in this regard that studies of the poetry of Edmund Spenser, who served in Munster immediately after Pelham's departure, have noted how a brooding ambience of sexual menace lingers all through Book V of *The Faerie Queene*, parts of which were inspired by the poet's wartime experience in the province.[39] Pelham's order to Bourchier clearly indicates that the threat of rape was real, not just a metaphor. To his mind, to spare the women was to lessen the state of terror he was pursuing. As he informed Queen Elizabeth soon afterwards, in order that the people of Munster be restored to obedience, it was necessary that 'the example with terror must light upon some', to which purpose he had authorized his soldiers to behave with abandon, to kill everyone 'wheresoever we found them'.[40] The Gaelic annalists confirm his report: not only had Sir William's troops killed 'men fit for action, but they killed blind and feeble men, women, boys, and girls, sick persons, idiots, and old people'.[41]

All the time this was going on, Pelham remained in contact with his administrators in Limerick, dictating and signing letters, having commissions and other legal documents drafted, even on one occasion issuing orders regarding recent political developments in County Wexford, on the other side of the country.[42] The war he was conducting was just another part of the government that he oversaw, albeit by far the most important part.

Space precludes further discussion of this phenomenon, save to emphasize that Pelham was behaving as he was expected to behave. Under the Tudors and Early Stuarts, those who served as viceroy both before and after him performed a similar balancing act. As figureheads of an expanding civil administration, they had to deal with all manner of political and legal, financial and bureaucratic business, while also, most years, preparing for and taking charge of major army expeditions deep into the interior of the country. As the situation unfolded and English power grew, these came more to resemble formal regal 'progresses', with wider areas having been brought within the government's control and the viceroy's arrival mostly accepted by the local people as a core feature of the new political order. But this emerging English supremacy should not obscure the fact that the royal government remained heavily reliant on military force. By the beginning of the seventeenth century the everyday tasks associated with English rule simply could not have

STATE OF EMERGENCY

been accomplished by the Crown's civil and administrative officers without the protection provided by the extensive network of army garrisons that had been established, fort by fort, since the 1540s to facilitate conquest and secure local acquiescence.[43] It is well known that the division of Ireland into thirty-two separate English-style counties was largely completed during the reign of James VI and I; what is less well known is that by that time, twenty-seven of these counties played host to and were within the operational reach of thirty-eight English garrison outposts.[44] Moreover, to reinforce the menace that the garrisons could pose, many of their commanders were issued with commissions of martial law, which, unlike in England, empowered them to carry out summary executions of anyone below the rank of a senior landowner or titled noble, and to do so on mere suspicion, without trial.[45]

A similar situation lay behind the plantations. In three separate bursts of activity the Crown had sought to increase its grip over broad swathes of the country through government-planned colonization schemes. Starting in the Midlands, in Laois and Offaly (1550), then moving to Munster (1586), and finally to Ulster (1609), thousands of English, Welsh, and later Scottish settlers were encouraged to establish towns, villages, and homesteads on vast tracts of land that the government had declared forfeit and seized from their indigenous owners and occupants.[46] Military coercion had made these schemes a reality. In the case of the Ulster Plantation, an area encompassing 3.6 million statute acres had to be secured and the native inhabitants of the land dispossessed before the new settlers could be put in place. With the authority of martial law, the officers and men of the main royal garrisons in Ulster at Carrickfergus, Loughfoyle, Enniskillen, Ballyshannon, Donegal, and Charlemont had ensured that this was done, with the support of smaller 'wards' that operated more locally in a dozen other garrison points. Moreover, as a first step towards attaining the required level of dispossession, special measures had to be taken to reduce the threat of native resistance by creating what amounted to a state monopoly of violence: the remnants of the private armies of the Gaelic lords were rounded up at gunpoint and transported overseas, mostly to serve as soldiers in Scandinavian kings' armies. In 1614, hearkening back to his ten years in charge of

83

King James's government, the viceroy Sir Arthur Chichester claimed to have had 'above 6,000' native soldiers—'bad members' of the intended new society—removed in this way.[47] Their banishment, once effected, gave the English garrison unprecedented control of the north and enabled the plantation to at least begin and the colonists to arrive with their families and belongings.

Underpinning this new-found English dominance of Ireland was the gory legacy of all the wars, large and small, that had preceded it. The true level of death and destruction incurred in the various conflicts is unknown. It may even be unknowable: notices of killing and burning, raiding and pillaging, though widespread, are for the most part scattered and sketchy, and make informed estimates difficult. Yet historians who have attempted to explore the cumulative impact on Irish society of the Tudor and Early Stuart conquest agree that the toll in both lives and livelihoods was great. Anthony McCormack's study of the Desmond war in Munster has shown how between English commanders like Viceroy Pelham on one side, and the earl of Desmond and his confederates on the other left whole regions of the south were left utterly devastated. With both armies using scorched earth wherever they went—though the Crown forces, it must be said, used it much more systematically—crops were destroyed and successive harvests missed. Famine was the predictable—and intended—result. Totting up the available evidence to establish a basis for a projection, McCormack has suggested that 48,000 people may have perished in Munster between 1579 and 1583 as a result of the war, 'either directly through the fighting or through famine and associated illness'.[48] Extrapolating from this to calculate the demographic impact of the entire Tudor conquest, Hiram Morgan has reckoned that a figure of over 100,000 casualties is not implausible.[49] As I have commented elsewhere, even if such estimates can never be proven, they chime with eye-witness descriptions of the desolation that survive from several of the war-zones, written by English as well as Irish observers.[50] And again, as with Cromwell's heavy impact in 1649, discussed above, it is important to think of the mortality levels inflicted during this earlier era of conquest as a percentage of the general population. Currently Irish historians broadly accept that the inhabitants of the country numbered somewhere between 750,000 and 1 million people in the early sixteenth century, before the conquest began. Viewed as a proportion of the population it would seem, therefore, that the Tudor and Early Stuart conquest of Ireland may rank as one of the bloodiest phases of conflict anywhere in Western Europe prior to the Thirty Years' War.[51]

III

Sometimes Irish people need reminding that historic English violence in the country was neither constant nor inevitable and often sprang from circumstances in which England itself and its rulers faced various challenges and emergencies. Even Oliver Cromwell's campaigns of 1649–50 can be viewed in this light, initially undertaken to prevent Ireland being used as a rallying ground for the new king, Charles II, against Parliament, and the dire prospect that that heralded, of a third English Civil War. For their part, the Tudors' Irish wars clearly stemmed from the prolonged international crisis sparked by Henry VIII's matrimonial problems of the 1530s and its profound implications for the English royal succession. In 1520–1, years before his obsession with Anne Boleyn, King Henry had flirted with the notion of conquering Ireland, but had soon lost interest once the difficulties and expense of pursuing it had been pointed out to him.[52] However, in 1533 his divorce from Catherine of Aragon and rejection of papal authority altered everything. Excommunicated by Clement VII, Henry subsequently led England and its dominions, including the 'lordship of Ireland', into schism.[53] In the ensuing slew of changes that the king was compelled to implement to secure the succession for such children as he might sire by his new queen, Anne, and also to assert full control over his realm and prevent the threat of 'papist' opposition or rebellion, it quickly became apparent that Ireland needed to be taken in hand. The historical rights of the English monarchs to Irish sovereignty—the aforementioned 'lordship'—owed their origins to a papal grant of the mid-twelfth century. That, clearly, might now be revoked in Rome and foreign powers such as the Holy Roman Emperor or the kings of France and Scotland be emboldened to meddle in Irish matters the better to destabilize the isolated Tudor monarchy.[54] The well-known 'Act for the Kingdom of Ireland' of 1541, by which Henry made Ireland a sister kingdom of England and had himself declared its first king, did little to change this. Until his death and all through the reign of his son and successor Edward VI (1547–53), the fear of French and Scottish intervention, with papal support, was constant.[55] The reconciliation with Rome of his daughter Mary I (1553–8) seemed briefly to settle the Irish sovereignty question, when in 1554 Pope Paul IV granted her the title 'Queen of Ireland',[56] but it was reignited a generation later when in 1570 Gregory XIII issued the bull *Regnans in Excelsis* excommunicating Mary's Protestant successor, her half-sister Elizabeth I (1558–1603).[57] The various Catholic assassination plots that Queen Elizabeth endured during the rest of her reign, combined with the growing antagonism of Philip II's Spain, stoked an abiding sense of emergency among her Protestant ministers at Whitehall.[58] This soon informed the framing of Irish policy. In parallel with a more intensive repression of Catholics in England, the pursuit of greater control in Ireland was increasingly animated by suspicion and fear of the Irish as inveterate maintainers of 'popery' who might rise *en masse* against the queen and excite fresh foreign interference, if permitted the opportunity. Only military force could stifle the danger, preferably before it materialized, through decisive and, if necessary, pre-emptive action.[59] The fact that such an approach would inevitably deny the Irish their legal rights post-1541 as equal subjects of the Crown was not discussed. Exigency was what mattered: better to break a few Catholic Irish bones than allow the Protestant English body politic to be weakened.

Recent studies have begun debating the extraordinary levels of violence that accompanied Tudor and Early Stuart military policy, especially the frequency with which campaigns purportedly against rebel Irish lords and their forces tended to target the civilian inhabitants of the regions affected. In part, this was due to English frustration with the rebels for avoiding open combat with royal forces when they ventured into their territories, instead using the landscape as cover to tail the English troops and set ambushes, or pick off stragglers. Yet it is clear that during the reign of Henry VIII the deliberate slaughter of civilians had also become standard practice for the English Crown forces when operating beyond England's shores—so much so, in fact, that it inculcated what Bernard Bailyn and Nicholas Canny have characterized as the 'ruthless philosophy' of English overseas warfare, and Geoffrey Parker, more bluntly, as fighting 'dirty'.[60] The impressive research of Neil Murphy bears this out. Examining Henry VIII's efforts to extend his dominion in north-eastern France by right of conquest, Murphy has revealed how the king commanded the English forces to wage unlimited war against all French people they encountered, killing and destroying at will, in order to make room for an intended influx of colonists. The carnage his armies inflicted was frightful.[61] However, whether such tactics originated in France or in Ireland may require further exploration. As indicated by the behaviour of Sir Anthony St Leger's forces in Idrone, noted above, the deliberate slaughter of peasants and the inducement of famine was already being used in parts of Ireland several years before King Henry commenced the French war in 1544. Indeed, long before that, the very author whose report had previously dissuaded Henry from attempting a full conquest of Ireland, Thomas Howard, earl of Surrey (later duke of Norfolk), had actually written to inform the king of the difficulties the Crown might face there after having himself led a series of similar burn-and-destroy campaigns in outlying areas of the country in the early 1520s.[62]

That said, it is beyond doubt that the French campaigns of 1544–6 took the prosecution of what King Henry himself acknowledged to be 'extreme war' to a new level of intensity, being repeatedly employed throughout the French countryside by much larger forces than those generally used in Ireland.[63] And moreover, as Murphy has suggested, the subsequent redeployment of veterans from the French campaigns to Ireland in the 1550s can only have encouraged the tendency to extreme measures in England's new sister kingdom. Four of the viceroys who headed the Irish government in the mid-Tudor years 1548–65 had previously served in the Boulogne campaigns; in the case of one of them, Thomas Radcliffe, third earl of Sussex (viceroy 1556–65), the waging of war in Ireland would reach its highest pitch since the ruthless suppression of the Kildare Fitzgeralds and their allies in 1534–5. Often burning as he went,

Sussex led three, even four expeditions per year, into regions that hitherto had lain beyond Dublin's reach, pursuing the utter ruination of local populations as a military priority if cooperation and obeisance was not forthcoming.[64] Though unable to vanquish the Tyrone warlord Shane O'Neill, Sussex did manage to break the growing presence in Ulster of the powerful Scottish Gaelic lineage, the MacDonalds of the Glynns in Antrim. The key moment in his assault came in September 1557 when Sussex dispatched a small invasion force from the Ulster mainland to Rathlin Island, where the MacDonalds' tenants and followers had taken refuge. For three entire days, 'till Sunday at night', the Crown forces scoured the island 'spoiling and killing as many as they might come by or get out of the caves, both man, woman, child and beasts'. As in north-eastern France so in north-eastern Ireland: deliberate annihilation of all those deemed enemies, whether combatants or non-combatants.[65] The notion that Sussex only authorized this action because the MacDonalds and their followers were Scottish aliens, not subjects of the English Crown, needs to be balanced by his ready deployment of the same approach against the native Irish inhabitants of O'Neills's country a month later.[66] Similarly, his 1557 instructions to his brother Sir Henry Radcliffe empowered the latter to 'prosecute with sword and fire ... all Irishmen and their countries' in the Midlands should they fail to acquiesce to the presence of English forces.[67]

The repetition of such measures during each of the major campaigns that were undertaken by the Crown in subsequent decades, culminating in the onslaught overseen by Viceroy Mountjoy and Lord President Carew in Ulster and Munster respectively at the close of the Nine Years War (1600–3), has prompted historians to begin examining the extent to which the English conquest of Ireland might best be approached as an early modern genocide.[68] Ever since D.B. Quinn first drew attention to the range of English literary and political texts in circulation during Elizabeth I's reign depicting the Gaelic Irish as wild, savage, backward, and dangerous, and urging their outright repression to preserve English rule and domination, scholars have comprehended these texts as reflecting a general hardening of attitudes as the Irish wars dragged on and conflict intensified.[69] The associated debate about the significance of one particular text, Edmund Spenser's notorious 1596 treatise *A View of the Present State of Ireland*, has compounded the sense that the conquest was ultimately a horror story, with England's most esteemed poet contending that the time for half-measures had passed. Only mass executions, repeated scorched earth, famine, and dispossession would break the back of Irish resistance, he said, and create the *tabula rasa* necessary for the final emergence of a new improved Irish polity, governed by strong Protestant English officers and defined by superior Protestant English standards of order and (yes) civility.[70] But extreme attitudes were nothing new. Versions of what Spenser advocated in 1596 had been advocated long before, by the likes of Robert Cowley in 1536 and Henry Ackworth in 1574, for instance. Yet, if carefully considered, there is surely a clue to be had in the repeated demands of these writers for a more generalized killing.[71] Evidently English military behaviour, awful though it could be, usually stopped short of the levels of slaughter associated with a wholesale genocide.

But what of a more limited form of genocide, something more episodic, defined and contained by particular circumstances? As already seen, from the reign of Henry VIII to that of James VI and I, numerous expeditions set out from Dublin Castle (or from other government centres) with the express purpose of seriously reducing local population groups in order to defeat rebel Irish lords and destroy forever the popular basis of their power and legitimacy. The elimination of the 'meaner sort'—tenants, peasants, labourers, and 'churls'—was central to how the last embers of the Geraldine League conspiracy were snuffed out in 1540; to how the Midlands septs of the O'Mores and O'Connors were driven out of Laois and Offaly and a plantation introduced in 1548–50; how the MacDonalds were brought to their knees in Antrim in 1556–8; how the FitzMaurice rising was curbed and then defeated in Munster in 1569–73; how the twin rebellions of the earl of Desmond and Viscount Baltinglass were extinguished in the early 1580s; how O'Rourke was driven out of north Connacht in 1589–90; and how, ultimately, the countrywide confederation led by Hugh O'Neill, earl of Tyrone and Red Hugh O'Donnell was made to collapse, exhausted, in 1601–3, following the defeat at Kinsale. Besides all the land-burnings and the killings of defenceless people that characterized these campaigns, they have one other important factor in common: they each happened to coincide with a wider state of emergency—or perceived emergency—in which the very existence of English monarchy was challenged by powerful outside forces and England itself exposed to danger.

The Geraldine League had sought foreign intervention against Henry VIII, and even offered to recognize the Stewart King of Scots, James V, as Ireland's sovereign.[72] The destruction of the O'Mores and O'Connors was in part propelled by the need to expedite government control of the Midlands ahead of a long-anticipated French intervention;[73] likewise the devastation visited on the people of Antrim, for their overlords the MacDonalds were in the vanguard of growing Scottish interference in Ulster that was traceable to the Stuart royal court.[74] FitzMaurice's rebellion had been purposely framed as a religious challenge, literally a Catholic crusade, against Elizabeth as a heretic, and coincided with a new succession crisis in England sparked by the flight of Mary, Queen of Scots and rebellion in the north.[75] Baltinglass had followed a similar path to FitzMaurice and—a decade after Elizabeth's excommunication—dared to display papal banners at the head of his forces.[76] Desmond for his part had consorted with the papal legate Dr Nicholas Sander, the chief spokesman of English Catholics opposed to Elizabeth's rule, and in 1580 was joined by a small invasion force of Italian and Spanish troops sent into Kerry by Philip II.[77] O'Rourke had sought Spanish military assistance and offered aid to Armada survivors.[78] The Tyrone-O'Donnell confederacy had gone furthest, particularly from 1596, seeking to stir up religious resistance to Elizabeth in northern England as well as the Dublin Pale, and had drawn the Spanish to a renewed invasion effort, in Munster, in 1601.[79] Viewed collectively, the widespread slaughter and devastation that the English forces unleashed in response to these threats revealed the lengths to which the monarchy was prepared to go in order to deal with an Ireland-centred emergency, especially once English sovereignty was questioned or the ruling Protestant regime threatened. Genocidal campaigning was part of the menu, for as long as an emergency lasted. Once it had been contained, however, the level of extremity soon fell back. The viceroys who commanded the forces had another, bigger task to perform, to oversee the ongoing construction and development of a new state, the kingdom of Ireland. Without subjects to govern and tax, it would hardly amount to much. Effective subjection required an end to the killing.

Years later, even the Cromwellians would recognize this.

6

VIOLENCE IN SCOTLAND
THE BRITISH ARMY AND GOVERNMENT
AFTER CULLODEN

Murray Pittock

On 16 April 1746 (OS), Charles Edward Stuart's Jacobite army was defeated on Culloden Moor near Inverness by the British Army under the command of William Augustus, Duke of Cumberland (1721–65). On a dramatic level, the last Jacobite Rising was a deeply personal conflict between two dynasties; understood as politics not theatre, it was an ideological contest between supporters of the old Stuart three-kingdom composite monarchy with its strongly European-facing associations and the new centralised British imperial state. This was understood by contemporaries. Some Americans 'believed that the Jacobites…would have ceded large swathes of colonial territory to the Catholic French'. Thomas Prince's sermon in Boston on 14 August 1746 expressed the fear that Gibraltar, Minorca, and even Jamaica would have been returned to Spain and Cape Breton and Nova Scotia to France by a Jacobite victory, while the Stuart Crown would become a client of the Bourbons, as had been the case after 1670. Prince was far from alone. Throughout the American Colonies, Cumberland was seen as a deliverer, and his apologist Andrew Henderson was exaggerating, not inventing, when he remarked that 'the victory at Culloden gave birth to an inexpressible joy through the extensive dominions of the British empire'.[1]

The outcome of the Rising of 1745 thus had a global aspect. Culloden itself was not only ideologically, but also militarily, an international conflict. The French Crown had an envoy with the Jacobite Prince, and French regulars fought on the field, and indeed prevented the encirclement of the Jacobite army by British cavalry and dragoons. Several regiments on both sides had been engaged at Fontenoy only a year earlier on the British and French sides. Men from Dillon's, Bulkeley's, Clare's, Rooth's, Berwick's and Lally's battalions and Fitzjames's Horse stood with the Jacobites as they had with France at Fontenoy; British regiments present at both engagements included the Royal Scots in the front line at Culloden, as were the Scots Fusiliers and Handasyde's, with Sempill's, Howard's, Bligh's, Cholmondeley's, Pulteney's, men from Hawley's and Bland's dragoons and the Inniskillings behind or beside them. One of the Scottish or Irish officers in the French service produced a map shortly after the battle, showing the view they—and indeed the Jacobite command—took of the struggle: the two forces are labelled *L'Armée Ecossoise* and *L'Armée Angloise*.[2] And this was also substantively the view that Cumberland and other British general officers adopted in their own policy.

First and foremost, the British high command viewed the Jacobites from within Great Britain and Ireland as rebels, and not entitled to consideration as prisoners of war: an attitude which led to Friedrich (1720–85), later Landgrave of Hesse-Cassel, withdrawing his six battalions when Cumberland refused to negotiate a cartel for the exchange of prisoners; later Friedrich received Jacobite fugitives at Dunkeld.[3] But secondly, and equally critically, the Scottish Jacobites were viewed as foreigners ('Jacobitism...is a dependence on France', as one letter to Newcastle put it), threats not just to the current British government but to the British polity itself. No great distinction was made between Jacobites in particular and Scots in general: General Humphrey Bland (1686 –1763) complained of 'the connivance of the "Scottish" interests that pervaded every level of the administration' in the northern kingdom.[4] In addressing the challenge they posed, and in taking

94

vengeance on them in defeat, Cumberland and his senior officers were following a long tradition of military doctrine and practice in the English and British armies.

As in Ireland in the seventeenth century, non-combatants were viewed as potential rebels rather than civilians, or even as 'extraordinary Animals' as the Prime Minister, Henry Pelham (1694–1754), put it.[5] The policy carried out by Norfolk in France in the 1540s and by the English forces in southern Scotland at the same time and in Ireland in the 1520s, discussed by Neil Murphy and David Edwards, made a fresh appearance: artificial famine was created through desolation of arable land and the killing or removal of livestock, while depopulation—as practised in the Boulogne area of France in 1544–46—was widely advocated by the military, with what success we shall see. Just as Norfolk had recruited locals from the English side of the Border to identify and kill Scots in hiding, so Cumberland clearly advocated the same policy in England, once the Jacobite army was in retreat there. On 12 December 1745, he wrote from Macclesfield that 'as they have so many of our Prisoners in their hands, I did not care to put them to death, but I have incouraged the Country People to do it'.[6] By February, he was reflecting on the possibility of punishing a wide section of the population, far too many for the criminal justice system to deal with. Population transplantation, as pioneered in Ireland in Laois-Offaly in 1548–9 to expand the Pale, and then used by Cromwell's forces in 1652–3 (as in the 'Order for transplantation of native Irish to Connacht' of 2 July 1653), became the preferred option. In the hours, days and weeks after the end of the battle, the British Army revisited other Irish precedents, such as killing prisoners after quarter (following Drogheda in 1649) or the ascription of collective responsibility to the civilian population in disaffected districts (or those supposed to be disaffected), as in Tipperary in 1651. These historical exemplars were part and parcel of specific English military policy, used in both internal police actions and external war, where that war was—as in sixteenth-century France—seen as a reincorporation of prior English territorial rights. General John Huske (1692–1761) specifically spoke of 'reviving laws once used against the Irish, and offering a reward of £5 for every rebel head'.[7]

In the immediate aftermath of Culloden, the British Army tended to follow these inherited military policies, excusing them by claiming (falsely) that the Jacobites had seriously mistreated British prisoners. In the pursuit after the battle, when Kingston's Light Horse and some of Cobham's dragoons killed everyone on the road to Inverness, whether Jacobite or civilian, occasionally stopping to castrate the men and place their genitals in their hands, the approach was similar to that taken in Ireland a century before. Likewise, Colonel James Wolfe (1727–59) noted that as few prisoners were taken as possible. On the day of the battle itself, orders were given to 'bring off all *our* Wounded Men' [my italics] while 16 guineas was offered for each 'Colour & Standard' captured and 2s 6d for each broadsword and firelock, with a reward of a guinea for anyone captured by the Jacobites who had refused to join them. Measures such as these were intended as a 'replacement' offered the troops in compensation for the strict enforcement of military justice threatened to those found plundering. The Orders of the Day for 17 April sent a captain and company round all houses near Culloden with a 'licence to kill' on the pretext that 'The Officer and Men will take notice that the public orders of the Rebells Yesterday was to give us no Quarters', a reference to the almost certainly fake No Quarter order which had already been distributed. Some 500 under Colonel Cockayne went 'in Quest of them that should be found lurking': there is only a limited possibility that those they found survived. Only 154 prisoners were taken from the Scottish regiments, and General Bland 'made great slaughter & gave quarter to none' not in French or Spanish service: these soldiers, usually Irish or Scottish by origin or descent, were 'nation troops' (*gente de nacciones*) and not regarded as 'mercenaries' in the modern sense.[8] Some 70 summary executions by firing squad were carried out, with up to 32 burned alive in a barn (those trying to escape were forced back in), 36 deserters hanged and 19 officers shot or clubbed to death together at the 'Prisoners' Stone' (Ensign John Fraser survived to tell the tale), together with hundreds of nameless victims killed on the field. Officers stood by to watch the wounded being shot.[9] Later on, there was a show mass execution of British deserters at Hyde Park. News travelled swiftly: the Presbytery of Kilearnan recommended on 21 April (the day after the Army's compulsory 'Divine Service of Thanksgiving' for victory) that parish ministers should accept bare assurances of innocence to justify certifying the good conduct of their parishioners, while the Synod of Moray advised all its ministers 'to be very careful and cautious' in attesting to the guilt of anyone detained or suspected of complicity in the Rising.[10] These recommendations have important implications for the validity and comprehensiveness of primary documents based on reports from local parish ministers.

The thousand Jacobites who died in the battle were supplemented by another 2,000 in the days that followed. As in Ireland, the British Army probably manipulated its own casualty figures to make the most of the victory: army surgeon estimates were markedly higher than the figures finally released.[11] Two other elements of seventeenth-century Irish policy were immediately visible: women were 'specifically targeted' and a principle of 'collective responsibility' was applied to disaffected areas, the basis for the argument of mass transplantation of populations.[12] The day after the battle, 'Colonel' Anne Mackintosh was arrested by Colonel Cockayne, and the wounded and any others at Moy Hall were 'shot directly'.[13] While Major-General Bland's 1743 *Treatise on Military Discipline* called for 'a respectful attitude by occupying military forces towards the civilian population', on 22 May Bland wrote to Loudoun, ordering him to 'destroy all persons you can find who have been in the rebellion or their abettors'. Captain Moodie of the 57th termed all feudal dependants on the lands of the disaffected traitors 'in the Eye of the Law...and therefore their certain and unavoidable doom was to be hanged in England or at best to be sent to the plantations as Slaves for life', but this was in reality more Irish military than British civil policy. There was a debate about making an example of 'Advisers, Assister, Receptors and harborers Clerks and Servants', while livestock raiding and killing was commonplace: Sackville's Regiment alone gained 2400 live cattle from raiding by June, and even cattle under Loudoun's protection were driven off. It was very clear that had there been no Union and no Scottish jurisdiction, military doctrine would have carried transportation and constructive starvation far beyond what was actually practised. Cumberland certainly wanted to transport whole clans, preferably to the Indies.[14]

HARFLEUR TO HAMBURG

As it was, Gen. John Campbell and Captain Fergusson RN laid waste Sunart and Morven; Campbell militia were sent to burn Atholl, while Major Lockhart and a detachment from Cholmondeley's 34th carried out atrocities in Fort Augustus/Glenelg, where civilians—including at least one with a military safe conduct—were shot dead out of hand. At Fort William, Captain Scott hanged out of hand those who could not give information on the prince's whereabouts and also put to death three men who came in to surrender themselves, besides having Lochiel's gardener whipped to death. At Eigg, a captain in Clanranald's and his company surrendered and were all 'consigned to slavery in the plantations'. In Strathbogie, Elizabeth Small was flogged for seeking to support recruitment into the French service, and Episcopalian places of worship were routinely burnt. 'Spies' were hanged, and Albemarle was noted as hanging 'innocent men to obtain information'.[15] Even such moderates as Duncan Forbes of Culloden (1688–1747), thought 'more than half a Jacobite' by the British, favoured mass transportation and that 'No severity that is necessary, ought to be Dispensed with', while 'the Distruction of the Vermine' was called for in the correspondence of senior officers.[16] Personal vengeance was embedded in military and state policy: for example, Lt. Benjamin Moodie was deliberately given command of the naval expedition to Orkney, where the leading Jacobite, Sir James Stewart of Burray, had killed Moodie's father. On 17 May, Moodie (now a Captain) ordered his men to 'Destroy any lands, Cattle, houses, Boats or anything also belonging' to Jacobite landowners and to press their servants. Excess pressed men not needed by the Royal Marines or Navy would be sent away from Orkney elsewhere in the north.[17]

Unlike the case of Ireland under Parliamentary rule in the 1640s and '50s, the political administration in Westminster was not fully aligned with the proposed military solutions, not least because of the Union, which while it might permit suppression of rebellion, could not readily be reconciled with the removal of civil rights *en masse*. There was also an additional complicating factor: that Scotland remained a distinct jurisdiction within the Union, although treason legislation and trials had been removed from it following 1708. Scottish domestic legal governance—a critical part of the state apparatus in an early modern state—was in the ultimate hands of the Lord President, Forbes of Culloden, and the Lord Justice Clerk, Andrew Fletcher, Lord Milton and 5th Earl of Saltoun (1692–1766). Fletcher had been in effective command of Scotland's domestic administration from 1740 on, and in an additional complication, remained in charge of India patronage even after he stepped down as Lord Justice Clerk in 1748. His influence after the Rising has arguably been underestimated by contrast with Lord Forbes, who was unwell and whose direct interventions were often limited to saving individual Jacobites like Major John Rattray, who had laid down the laws of golf and been Forbes's golfing partner. The extension of East India Company patronage and placement to Scots had been a key part of Sir Robert Walpole's (1676–1745) strategy to wean the northern kingdom from Jacobitism, and true to this tradition, Fletcher 'knew the importance of reintegration and reconciliation'. The British Government under Henry Pelham followed this to some degree, and held in check more uncompromising views; Thomas Pelham-Holles (1693–1768), 1st Duke of Newcastle, Pelham's brother, was also reluctant to give Cumberland as free a hand as he would wish, and fell out with him altogether in 1748. After Pelham's death in 1754, Philip Yorke, Lord Chancellor Hardwicke (1690–1764), who was somewhat more hardline and remarked 'how desireable it was, that the laws of the two countries [Scotland and England] should not widely differ from each other', proceeded to push Jacobites out of official positions, which they had previously continued to be integrated into, to the infuriation of the military.[18]

Despite the increase in the 'publick stature and political power of the army' as a result of its victory over the Jacobites, and Cumberland's intervention in planned legislation (he recommended an additional session of Parliament), there was from the beginning political resistance to extreme measures: indeed, Hardwicke himself was proposing a general pardon while Habeas Corpus was still suspended.[19] Cumberland's view of 31 March that 'the whole Government & constitution in these parts of the Kingdom shall be changed' (he again wrote 'the whole of the laws of this ancient kingdom must be new modelled' a few days later) proved not nearly so simple as he imagined. On 23 April, he was still of the opinion that 'within a month or six weeks at the longest, we shall have done all that can be done by the military',[20] but this may already have been bravado, as on 30 April he wrote to Newcastle that 'the Jacobite rebellious principle is so rooted in this nation's mind that this generation must be pretty wore out, before this country will be quiet...nothing meddles with them except I send the Military force after them'.[21]

On 25 July, the Duke returned to England with his job of pacification still manifestly incomplete and with a telling instruction to his successor—the Earl of Albemarle—that he should be ready to take to the field immediately.[22] Despite the suspension of Habeas Corpus (initially until 20 November 1746, then 20 February 1747) and the immunity of British troops from being accountable for their actions up to 25 July, the military struggled in a territory where 'our geographers seem to be almost as much at a loss in the description of this north part of Scotland, as the Romans were to conquer it, and they are obliged to fill it up with hills and mountains, as they do the inner part of Africa with lions and elephants'.[23] In due course, the Roy-Sandby military survey—a key outcome of the occupation intended to 'lay open' the country—would address this problem, though it itself was hardly innocent of exaggerating the contours of the Scottish landscape. The Army also had difficulties because despite their belief in the ascendancy of 'military power', civil government kept breaking in and across it, despite the best wishes and intentions of the army.[24]

Action was nonetheless taken in short order with Jacobite prisoners put on trial or otherwise condemned in England. The justice system could not accommodate trials for all 3,500 or so prisoners: in the end only some 5% were tried, and others were sent *en masse* to Barbados, Jamaica and other destinations in the West Indies and the Chesapeake. We may never know the numbers entirely accurately, as—for example—the 70% mortality rate on the Tilbury hulks (prison ships) may have included false reporting by officials, but just under 1,000 in total were probably transported, and perhaps the same number died.[25] Prisoners on some ships such as the *Jane of Leith* and the *Thane of Fife* appear to have been drowned, in the former case in the process of drowning 'the vermine' at sea, in

100

the latter the binding together of sick and dead thrown overboard. Typically, transports were shipped for an agreed fee of £5–£6, and the merchant ships who carried them typically achieved another £5 a head for them at the quayside. Although mostly indentured for a period of only seven years (effectively a lifetime for many in the West Indies), transports were to stay in the plantations for life.[26] Women as well as men were transported: from a list of the transports on the *Veteran* liberated off Martinique by a French privateer, we can read names such as those of George Keith, a 35-year-old Aberdeen shoemaker who had served in Glengarry's, William Bell, a bookseller from Berwickshire (46), Anne Cameron (spinster, 28), Flora Cameron (40), Barbara Campbell (19) and Isabel Chalmers (25), who was recorded as having regimental affiliation to Glengarry's. There appears to have been some tendency to transport, e.g., Camerons and MacDonalds to Campbell-owned plantations in Jamaica, thus putting them in the power of their hereditary enemies. Some were also transported who might well have expected to be treated as prisoners of war, such as Peter McLean, a 27-year-old corporal in the French service.[27]

In Scotland itself, the conduct of some British officers during the Rising was examined (notably at Fort Augustus, accused of having surrendered too readily), but the major Scottish trial of Provost Stewart of Edinburgh for letting the Jacobites into the city ended in a not proven verdict, despite its being fairly clear from the evidence that Stewart's studied vagueness on issues of security and promise to 'order the Alarm bell to ring', which was not carried out, had materially advantaged the Jacobites and left the capital open.[28] Outcomes like this did not encourage the British high command to give much credence to the Scottish justice system. Even the Lord Justice Clerk himself—perhaps under pressure— favoured introducing army officers as justices of the peace in the localities, while there was fury that Jacobites were 'being appointed as sheriffs or sheriffs depute' and even on the Lord Advocate's staff, while disaffection was 'rife among the magistrates and justices of the peace'.[29] Forty-five customs, excise and salt duty officers were dismissed for disaffection, but this was seen as the tip of an iceberg.[30] Cumberland made no secret of his view that 'one half of the

Magistracy have been either aiders or abettors to this rebellion, and the others dare not act through fear of offending their chiefs or of hanging their own cousin', and—famously and more vehementlys—'The laws of the country! My lord, I'll make a brigade give laws!'[31]

The legal framework in which the army operated was that provided by Scots Law, combined with the major anti-Jacobite legislation at Westminster: the army provided a bridge between the two with the abolition of the Scottish Secretaryship.[32] Treason trials were not carried out in Scotland through concern that there would be no convictions, though there were some Scottish legal cases in connexion with the Rising under civil law, as for example James Grant's claim against Alexander Garioch for £44 12s 6d plus other costs, pursued by Grant as factor to the Earl of Kintore's estates, as Garioch was claimed to 'levy money unwarrantably...by an armed force & wrongous imprisoning the pursuer'. This kind of thing was all too mild for the British Army.[33]

The Westminster legislation in question included the Disarming/Proscription Act (19 Geo 2 c.39), which Cumberland had apparently insisted on, and which defined the 'Highlands' as including Aberdeen, Banff, Forfar, Kincardine, Perth, Stirling and (crucially) abolished wardholding for military service in favour of feu duty, a payment to the feudal superior which endured to the late twentieth century.[34] It was accompanied by the Act of Attainder (19 Geo. 2 c.46), the Vesting Act (20 Geo 2 c.41), the Heritable Jurisdictions (Scotland) Act (20 Geo 2. c.43), the Act of Indemnity (20 Geo. 2 c.52) which protected soldiers from any consequences of actions carried out before 25 July 1746, and the provision under the Treason Outlawries (Scotland) Act 1748 (22 Geo. 2 c.48) for automatic outlawry. The first proscribed arms, the Highland garb and the Episcopal Church—no peers were to vote who had been twice to an Episcopal Church since 1745 for example, and lesser mortals who had done the same might be 'forfeiting their employment'.[35] The Episcopalians were supposed to 'maintain many Popish Principles', and were seen by the Army—though less by an Anglican Parliament—as the home of Jacobite ideology and a priority for suppression. There were certainly signs of Episcopalians whose services had been suppressed moving into the Catholic fold as late as 1755.[36] The Heritable

VIOLENCE IN SCOTLAND

Jurisdictions Act strongly limited the feudal and judicial power of landlords: it was the most controversial, and was strongly resisted—including by the Court of Session, who regarded it as a breach of the Union and 'declined to comply' with an order of the House of Lords to work on the Bill—and was in the end watered down.[37] Among other measures, Lord Forbes and Lord Stair opposed the dress proscription, while James Erskine, Lord Grange, thought it should only apply to loose plaids.[38]

The Vesting Act placed confiscated estates under the control of the Crown through an arm's-length Commissioners system. This was later extended by the Annexing Act (25 Geo 2 c.41) to allow fourteen estates to be attached 'unalienably' to the Crown: in fact, this perpetual control largely ended in 1784.[39] The confiscated estates were administered by the Barons of Exchequer (the Chief Baron was in Hardwicke's pocket, and there were other direct lines of control from government). They largely proceeded on a 'care and maintenance' basis with the extraction of rents to Westminster. These confiscated estates were difficult to administer and there were suspicions of those responsible for collecting rents on the ground: on 2 April 1752, Newcastle wrote to the Barons of Exchequer that 'it were to be wished that no Highlander was ever employed'.[40] Factors refused to enforce the law, it became 'impossible to levy rents' without the Army, and Jacobite death threats were made to those who paid. Cameron of Fassifern (on whose land the white rose grew that was taken by Prince Charles as his badge) let his tenants know that they paid rents to the government agent Colin Campbell of Glenure (later murdered) 'at their peril'.[41] The valuation of many of the estates was modest, with annual rents in the hundreds, yet recovering even this could take considerable labour. For example, on 16 January 1750, two captains and forty men of Bury's at Perth, combined with some sixty-five to seventy from the Crieff and Dunkeld outposts were sent 'to join the party now at Tay Bridge...to assist Mr Ramsey appointed Factor for the Crown upon the Forfeited Estate of the late Strowan Robertson in Raising the Rents of the said Estate applicable to Law'. More than a hundred soldiers were needed simply to collect rents from the forfeited estate of a deceased landlord, who had himself in fact already acted as an adviser to the

British Army despite being a forfeited Jacobite Major-General who had been 'out' in four Risings from 1689 to 1745.[42]

Cumberland and his commanders acted deliberately to move troops every three months, 'to prevent Connections which may happen by their Staying too long in a place particularly Scotland'. In the early days of the occupation, there were signs of high anxiety reaching almost to paranoia. Five companies of Fleming's were sent to Montrose on the report of a 'great number of Ladies...with Bunches of White Roses' on 10 June, and a similar force of Fusiliers were ordered under arms to Leith on the report of a ball with tartan gowns and white ribbons for Charles Edward's birthday, to 'seize and secure...every Person in the said treasonable and Seditious Company'.[43] As Horace Walpole remarked, 'With all our victory... it was not thought safe to send' Lord Bury (who had received £1,000 for bringing the news of Culloden to London) 'through the heart of Scotland' by land, so he went by sea instead.[44] Tartan certainly continued to be used as a mute sign of defiance in the southern burghs not affected by proscription, in general remaining beyond the treason legislation of 1351 (25 Edward III). Lord Balmerino died on the scaffold in a tartan cap; James Baillie's shop in Edinburgh's Hie Gait (High Street) opposite the Tolbooth was archly promoting 'the newest patterns of TARTANS' just before St Andrews' Day 1748 in the *Caledonian Mercury*, which had published Charles's opposition to the Union in October 1745. Perhaps some of the tartan worn on these occasions came from the stock sold at 'our Highland Fair' (the reference was to a 1731 ballad opera) by British 'military Merchants at Inverness' after the battle of Culloden, for plaid was a subject of profiteering before it was banned.[45]

In 1746, there were some 13,000 British troops in Scotland, some 40% of the entire peacetime British Army.[46] But it was a national occupation, not an occupation of the 'Highlands' alone, as the order and letter books of the army make clear: the 'strong Jacobite sympathies of the whole country' were remarked on, while the 'Highlands' were taken as including land in Aberdeenshire, Angus, Banff, Dunbartonshire, Kincardineshire, Perthshire and Stirlingshire; potentially all eastern Scotland north of Dundee and much of the country south of it. 'Proposals for Civilizing the

Highlands' from 'their natural Barbarity', made by the Lord Justice Clerk to Newcastle at the end of 1747 might readily be interpreted as including locations such as Arbroath, Crieff or Forfar.[47] In 1746, there were six troops of Kerr's dragoons in the north-east, a similar number of Cobham's plus three of St George's in Aberdeen and Angus and six again of Hamilton's in Dundee. Burghs as far south as Kelso were placed under martial law. As late as the autumn of 1748, St George's Dragoon regiment had over 60 of their mounted infantry at such small settlements as Alloa and Culross in central Scotland.[48] The strength of the garrison reported on 1 September 1746 was 9,170 men, 778 sergeants and drummers, 376 officers, with a requirement for a further 2,200 troops—a major commitment set in the context of the continuing War of the Austrian Succession. There were repeated efforts to rotate troops to the Continent: in March 1747, five regiments (Howard's, North British Fusiliers, Dejean's, Conway's and Flemings) all sailed for the Netherlands, with a sailing by the Royal Artillery following on 30 April. It proved difficult however to reduce troop numbers, and although another battalion had left by February 1748, two battalions of the Royals returned from the Continent to central and eastern Scotland the following month. At Christmas 1747, there were ten regiments garrisoning Scotland from north to south (only one of which was Scottish), plus troops of dragoons and detached companies. In May 1748, thirty outposts were garrisoned with Independent Highland Companies, and by the close of the year there were still some eight regiments in Scotland, where on 23 November it was announced that 'the Several Regiments in North Britain' were to be 'Reduced to the Numbers...on the Establishment of Ireland'. As the War of the Austrian Succession ended that autumn, more and more of the troops that remained were deployed on roadbuilding and internal infrastructure, with between 1,350 and 1,750 troops seconded to extending Wade's road network in 1748 and 1749. As we shall see however, this was by no means the end of the story.[49]

Scots and Scotland in general were hated by the high command. Besides Cumberland's famous pronouncement that 'this vile spot may still be the ruin of this Island and of our Family' and Lord Chesterfield's typically blustery recommendation to Newcastle for 'mass starvation and the wholesale slaughter of Highlanders', Lt.-Col. Howard wrote on 23 August 1746 that 'a Scotch Soil can never suit an English Constitution' and Colonel Wolfe thought the 'Scotch excessively dirty and lazy'. Albemarle himself spoke of 'this cursed country' and of 'the ill intentions of the People' and wrote 'L'Ecosse est ma bete'. A week earlier, Colonel Naizon described the people of Ayrshire as 'Lazy, indolent, Proud, and of course miserable' even though he had been told that 'they have not had one man of the Country Joyn'd the Rebels'. Albemarle himself was uncompromising in his assessment to Newcastle on 6 September:

> notwithstanding the hopes entertained ... that this Kingdom was restored to Peace and quietness...nothing could Effect it but laying the whole Country waste and in ashes, and removing all the Inhabitants (excepting a few) out of the Kingdom.

Scotland was not in Albemarle's view the source of a local 'Highland' difficulty or a civil conflict with weak support for the Jacobites, but a nation in rebellion: 'Upon the whole I think this Kingdom can never be kept in awe but by a sufficient military force', Albemarle noted on leaving Scotland on 2 February 1747, adding 'My joy at leaving this country is inexpressible'. As Robert Cuningham put it to the Earl of Crawford in 1746 even among those 'obliged to put on the Appearance of being pleased' their 'good humour' at 'the Total Defeat of their Friends' was assumed; for Albemarle, 'very few now employed deserve the King's favour', and that included many senior law officers who were 'in their hearts Jacobites' or—as Robert Dundas of Arniston (1713–87), Solicitor General and later Lord Advocate was described—'violent patriots'. In these circumstances, it was clear to the British high command that more troops were needed.[50]

Scottish regiments were more likely to be seen as unsuitable for garrison duty, due no doubt to a tendency to go native: after all, as in 1715, no treason trials were held in Scotland itself. Neither British officers nor politicians trusted Scottish courts to convict, and likewise soldiers from outwith Scotland were those who might best preserve order. Thus on 6 August 1746, when Lt.-Col. Jackson noted that Fleming's Regiment stationed at Aberdeen was under strength by 141 men, he noted that recruits from England were needed, while

VIOLENCE IN SCOTLAND

the next day Brigadier Mordaunt was suggesting Berkshire as a good source of recruits.[51] In Aberdeen, over 200 families suffered material damage to their properties at the hands of the soldiery after there was no display of lights to mark George II's birthday on 1 August, and the magistrates complained to Albemarle. An embarrassed Andrew Fletcher of Milton (the Lord Justice Clerk) told them that 'I'm exceedingly sorry to hear so many Complaints from your Town of the Gentlemen in the Army'. Lord Sempill, who was sent to mediate, recommended that British officers should apologize. At Stirling on 29 July, the magistrates applied for a warrant against Lt.-Col. George Howard of Howard's Old Buff's and one of his subalterns when a wigmaker's apprentice was publicly whipped in the town on army orders. Provost Hossack was of the opinion that all the inhabitants of Inverness—some 9,000—were viewed as potential rebels.[52] It has been argued by recent scholars that 'the town [Inverness] was exploited and culturally suppressed for decades' after Culloden, and there were certainly acts of ritual humiliation, such as the Provost's having to personally supervise cleaning out regimental stables. The magistrates of Inverness thought 'the soldiers generally the greatest rogues in the British Army'. There was certainly a choice. For the Army's part, General Blakeney was unequivocal: 'if any inhabitants did meddle with Soldiers he woud give it in Orders that the Soldiers shoud Run them thorow'.[53]

Naturally, the presence of English troops led to many mistakes and insensitivities, as they were 'not over-considerate of Scottish susceptibilities, and by no means unready to confound friend and foe'.[54] In August 1746 alone, Viscount Arbuthnott complained to Albemarle that a sergeant had come ordering him to surrender his domestic arms or have his house burnt, while Sheriff Grant told the Lord Justice Clerk, Andrew Fletcher of Milton, that sixty men of Fleming's had forcibly searched his house 'for Rebels', requested billets for forty men and then robbed one of Grant's tenants, threatening to burn his house if he resisted.[55] In Arbuthnott's case, it was true that he had been involved in the 'Fifteen, but he had lived mainly peaceably since. On 26 August, Major Forrester reported that his men had burnt down the house of an octogenarian elder of the Presbyterian Kirk, John McLaren.[56]

107

HARFLEUR TO HAMBURG

In fairness to the British Army's anxiety however, the early stages of the occupation saw continued actual or threatened Jacobite activity. Jacobite troops returning home intact included the 1st and 2nd Ogilvy's and MacGregors, and some of Ogilvy's tenants who had been 'out' were later entrapped by a ruse involving the use of fake Jacobites.[57] Lochiel's and Clanranald's remained in the field, while Ardsheal's was paying its officers as late as June and 'Ardsheal and his Gang' were reported as 'still lurking' on 23 September. The 'Gang' was in fact a regularly organized and paid regiment, as its partially surviving Order Book makes clear. Lord Sackville had two battalions with him in Glenelg, but his force was still attacked by 'Glenmoriston Rascals'.[58] Jacobite expresses continued to be sent until August. Camerons were expected to be supplied from Ireland, while on 29 October Cluny Macpherson was reportedly paying £5 to every man in Appin who retained his arms (presumably the source of this largesse was the Loch Arkaig treasure) while 'fresh good Arms' were reportedly still in Jacobite hands in Badenoch, and arms landings were reported into 1748.[59]

On 20 August 1746, Major General John Campbell requested that the Independent Companies remain in active service to counter the continuing threat in Argyll, while General Blakeney wrote on 30 August from Inverness to request seven barrels of musket powder, flints and other *materiél*, 'not knowing how soon we may have occasion to make use of it against the Rebels'. The next day, Captain Munro was shot by a sniper and around a dozen armed Jacobites demanded £2,000 compensation on pain of death for British Army damage from Alexander Garden of Troup in Aberdeenshire, a government supporter in a Jacobite county. Between 500 and 1,000 militant Jacobites escaped to France to join the *Écossois Royales,* Lochiel's or Ogilvy's regiments in the French service.[60] These regiments were dissolved in 1763, somewhat earlier than the Franco-Irish regiments. The three Irish Jacobite regiments (Irlanda, Hibernia and Ultonia) in Spain survived until 1818, with Irlanda's officer corps still being Irish as of 1768, by which time the sole Scottish regiment, the Edinburgh Dragoons (Dragones de Edimburgo) in the service of the Spanish Crown had faded from view.[61]

As it became increasingly clear that the presence of the British Army at scale in Scotland was to be prolonged, adjustments were made more for reasons of practical policy than anything else. By December 1747, although General Bland remained frustrated that 'attainted Rebels' in Aberdeenshire were 'sensible that the Sheriffs & other Civil Officers, are very averse to putting the Laws in Execution', his continuing concern at the potential return of Jacobite exiles from France and his anxiety regarding increasing rates of desertion may have led him to order that English troops should not be sent 'to gather the cess' to avoid inflaming local populations.[62] In Elgin, compensation was paid for army damage and there was a sufficient concentration of soldiers to justify the opening of a hospital on 16 November 1747, which was situated in the basement of the lawyer James Wiseman's house and rented by the British Army at 1s 6d a week.[63]

The army's principal uses were first, 'to Enforce the Laws lately made relating to the Disarming and change of the Highland Dress', where enforcement could focus on trigger areas such as Glencoe, where 'John McPherson' was 'taken up for wearing the philibeg' even in the 1750s. Secondly, they were tasked with assisting 'the Officers of the Revenue' including the struggle 'against smugglers' and thirdly, to collect rents. Throughout, they were deployed against Jacobites who remained in the field or were conducting more covert acts of sabotage or violence against British forces: these incursions were almost always demilitarized and termed 'Depredations... Committed by the Highland Thieves'. There was an increasing stress on getting co-operation from the local inhabitants. The British Army might also be used to impose unwanted ministers, as were Rich's for example in May 1751, when over 200 of them were sent to Lanark, 'to Assist the Civil Power in Establishing a minister at that place who was opposed by a riotous mob'. Rich's (formerly Barrel's) was also regarded as among the most reliable for anti-Excise urban mobs: Rich had lost an arm at Culloden, while the officers of the regiment had been responsible for founding the 'Loyall and Friendly Society of the Blew and Orange' in the 1730s: thus Rich's was associated with Orangeism and ultra-Hanoverian loyalism.[64]

Although the Treaty of Aix-la-Chapelle and the end of the War of the Austrian Succession eased the pressure on the British Army, it proved very difficult to extricate much more of the substantial occupying force from Scotland. In the spring and summer of 1748, there were still fifty-six locations for the continuing surrender of Jacobite arms, including Dundee, Forfar, Perth, Stirling and Dumbarton.[65] As late as 8 December 1751 in the capital in a context of meal shortage and rising prices, Lord Provost Drummond could write to General Churchill, that 'if you withdraw the Dragoons, I dare not answer for the Town of Leiths continuing in quiet'. Leith was a centre of Jacobitism.[66] Struggles with the Scottish jurisdiction continued, and were to an extent addressed by giving 'Lieutenant Governors of the forts...a Warrant or Power...to act as Justices of the Peace', though whether that 'Warrant' would stand up in court was perhaps another matter. The military seem to have operated at least occasionally on the 'shot while resisting arrest' principle, as with 'A Soldier of Pulteneys ... [who] attempting to seize a man in the Highland Dress had the misfortune to shoot him Dead on the Spot', as General Churchill remarked on 1 October 1751. The same month, the Earl of Lauderdale—a Whig representative peer and former army officer—apologized to Churchill for assaulting one of his soldiers in an extraordinary exchange which reveals the power of the army.[67] Churchill appeared to sanction extra-legal action more broadly in his letter to Col. Crawford of 3 December that year. Four months later, reliable customs officers were being asked to inform on the 'not well Affected' (not even 'disaffected'), to report directly to the military and to be 'Secret'. There was thus a continuing separate parallel system of military 'justice'. As late as 7 April 1756 a senior customs officer was asked to ensure that in 'discovering, seizing & securing' of the disaffected, it was important to take 'due care not to appear...Yourself...Unless a Legal Warrant is produced... act with the greatest Secrecy...and with the Utmost Zeal'. Where legal warrants existed, senior officers were not above bullying the judiciary. On 3 October 1754, General Bland gave a more than broad hint to the Sheriff Substitute of Inverness in these terms: 'it is Incumbent upon, and indeed you cannot do a more important Service to the Government, than instantly to find Evidence...your hanging the Piper...is become the most important Service you can do for the State'. Eight years after Culloden, Inverness was still viewed as 'that Disaffected Shire'.[68] In 1746, Bland had reported that 'in the Inverness region, no JP was willing to assist the army'. More directly, in 1751 General Churchill released a soldier convicted of killing a Cameron and gave him a guinea. Men at large carrying 'pistols & Broad Swords' were still being reported. As late as 1754, General Bland was advising one of his senior officers that a 'Bishop cannot Legally be laid hold of without a Warrant', while there were persisting concerns regarding 'the Loyalty of some of the Revenue Officers'.[69] There was continuing anxiety which penetrated even into English politics that the will of the military to cut across political and judicial decision-making was a potential threat to the state: in 1751, a pamphlet was sent to every member of both Houses of Parliament which suggested that Cumberland's role as a military commander and his tendency towards 'usurping a Dominion over *Law*' might lead to a coup d'état. Cumberland was passed over as a potential Regent, a slight for which the Duke blamed Pelham and his brother Newcastle, who had certainly garnered enough experience between them of Cumberland's impatience with constitutional niceties. As Christopher Whatley notes, 'Scotland was not settled until the 1750s, and then only through the imposition of "systematic state terrorism"'.[70]

Even up to the brink of recruiting Scottish regiments for the war of 1756–63, stubborn problems of public order remained, despite the creation of infrastructure funds to seek to re-establish the northern Scottish economy on a sounder footing.[71] 'Deficient Cess' was widespread thanks to withheld taxes or inefficient collection, while as General Bland wrote to the Lord Advocate, 'Smuggling…is carried on to so great a height', 'exemplary Punishment' is necessary: once again the Army was struggling with the law, as Bland admitted that things might look otherwise in London. Smuggling was certainly a political crime: during the 'Forty-five itself, 'smugglers were carrying French agents…under the orders of the Conte de Lally-Tollendal, who commanded a regiment of the Irish Brigade', and the confluence between excise avoidance and Jacobitism remained a major anxiety.[72]

In January 1755 (in which month there was 'Riot and rescue' of a prisoner at Dornoch), Bland noted that 'the Jacobites will be a good deal elated upon the Reports' of French mobilization, and even at the end of that year was continuing to order revenue vessels to report on 'French Emissaries and other Enemies to the Government among the Disaffected'. On the brink of a global war that would claim a million lives it was still a Jacobite attempt that was feared by the substantial British forces north of the Tweed, and this continued to be the case into 1756, when Cluny was reported in Orkney disguised as a merchant 'who has gone wrong in his Business'. Arrests continued and Bland himself wrote directly to at least one subaltern requesting him to apprehend a 'disagreeable Neighbour of yours… very Obnoxious to the Government'. No other crime was specified. In February 1755, Captain Ferguson was sent 'to press Men in North Britain' for almost the first time for the Royal Navy; repeated orders to support him imply his lack of success. The Army still considered itself short of the troops needed to maintain order, and there was some scraping of the bottom of the manpower barrel. On 29 October, Bland ordered two new Independent Companies 'to be Formed from the Out-Pensioners of Chelsea Hospital in North Britain', some of whom had been accommodated at Loch Rannoch from 1748. The next month those Chelsea pensioners residing in Scotland were examined at Edinburgh, Glasgow, Aberdeen, Perth and Inverness to establish whether they were suitable for duty. The majority—which included men up to 102 years old—were assessed as unable to perform any duties, but a significant minority (71 from 190 at Perth for example) were passed for light, typically garrison, duty. They were apparently still needed: in June 1756, Bland ordered two companies to Ruthven in Badenoch and one to Corgarff in Strathdon to keep order, and at the end of that month there were still five companies stationed at Inverness. Continued strong efforts were made to secure Jacobites still at large such as Lord Forbes of Pitsligo and Gordon of Avochie to forestall any 'Rebellious Scheme in Agitation'. Officers on the ground were recommended to 'Cultivate a Personal Acquaintance' with those who might be sources of evidence as to the whereabouts of such dangerous individuals. Even while Scots recruits prepared to flood into North America, the last Jacobites remained in the sights of the high command. Pitsligo was 78 years old.[73]

VIOLENCE IN SCOTLAND

By this time, military doctrine had led to the imposition of planned solutions for Scotland in other theatres, to rid the country of its troublesome surplus of potential rebels. As early as 1746, recruitment to the Dutch service had been suggested: the Scots Brigade there marched under the saltire until their formal incorporation into the Dutch Army in 1782.[74] In 1748, it was proposed that Loudoun's troops themselves—used in garrisoning and 'defending' Moray against 'thieving Highlanders' as recently as the previous September—should be moved to Nova Scotia, a deportation in all but name, 'where their presence would counter... the French Acadians'. Under the influence of Cumberland's concepts and practices, the British forces in Canada would come to initiate *Le Grande Dérangement* of 1755, which led to the expulsion of over 80% of the 14,000 French settlers in Nova Scotia, New Brunswick and Prince Edward Island with major loss of life as 'food supply was marginal'. Six thousand 'peaceful farming people' were deported. Even further from the public eye, Cumberland's policies could be put into more thorough effect. As the Duke himself said, he looked forward to the French being 'drove out' as he had once hoped to do in Lochaber. By this time, on a recommendation of Wolfe's to William, Lord Barrington, passed to Pitt, Scottish troops were poised to flood into the North American theatre and the persisting enemy of the north was at length recruited to the public good of the British Empire.[75]

7

'ALAS POOR DANES!'
THE BOMBARDMENT OF COPENHAGEN, 1807

Brendan Simms[1]

At the height of the Napoleonic Wars, Britain launched an unprovoked assault on a small neutral state. It bombarded the Danish capital of Copenhagen and seized the fleet moored there. Nearly two hundred civilians were killed and tens of thousands were displaced. The attack was hugely controversial, even in Britain itself, and the government's claims that it was acting pre-emptively to forestall an imminent danger were widely rejected. Many condemned the horrors inflicted on innocent civilians, so that the operation became a byword for British brutality, and even entered the English language as a verb: to 'Copenhagen'. It was one of the more spectacular examples of the British state's use of calculated violence for geopolitical ends.[2]

* * *

Britain's bombardment of Copenhagen in 1807 was the culmination of a long engagement in the Baltic Sea region going back at least to Cromwell. The Royal Navy was very active there during the early eighteenth century to safeguard the security of the King's patrimony of Hanover and secure the supply of vital 'naval stores', such as masts, hemp, pitch and tar for ship-construction and maintenance, as well as to uphold the European balance of power more generally—in this case against Russia.[3] In the late eighteenth century, the Baltic loomed large again when Russia, Denmark, Sweden, and later Prussia set up the League of Armed Neutrality (1780), an association designed to curb British attempts to interrupt neutral commerce between France, Spain, the Dutch, and the rebel colonists during the American War of Independence.[4]

These concerns came to the fore once more after the outbreak of the Revolutionary and Napoleonic Wars, which Britain joined in 1793. The Royal Navy resumed its traditional strategy of attacking enemy commerce, boarding neutral shipping suspected of carrying enemy 'contraband' and often confiscating it. In international law, the position was clear enough. Any contact with a belligerent was a violation of neutrality. The only truly neutral trade in wartime was that conducted directly between two neutral states via neutral ports. In practice, though, there were many gradations in between, and much 'neutral' trade was tolerated for one reason or another. The potential profits were enormous. This meant that Britain's claim to police neutrality on the high seas was bitterly resented as an infringement of sovereign rights by the young United States and many European countries.

The Baltic Sea region was a particular area of contestation.[5] Britain took a close interest in the area for two reasons. First, because of the Royal Navy's enduring dependence on the region for its naval stores, manifest in the escalating 'hemp crisis' of the time.[6] Knowledge of the region was eagerly sought.[7] Secondly, because the states of the Baltic littoral were increasingly unwilling to accept what they saw as British high-handedness. This was true of the two great powers, Russia and—to a lesser extent—Prussia, but also of Denmark and Sweden. Their merchant navies and commerce were growing exponentially thanks to the opportunities opened up by neutrality in wartime, but threatened by British counter-measures.[8] In other words, the Baltic had become a key space in the Anglo-French confrontation long before the first Napoleonic soldier had arrived at its shores.

In late 1800, matters came to a head when Russia, Prussia, Sweden, and Denmark formed the Second Armed Neutrality, and excluded all British ships from trading with the Baltic. This was in retaliation for London's insistence on the 'right to search' on the high seas. Shortly after, in mid-January 1801, the British government responded by placing an embargo on all Danish, Russian, and Swedish ships in British ports. Three months later, the Prussians occupied Hanover, of which King George III was Elector, in order to put pressure on the British.[9] By then, though, the British had decided to force the issue by taking radical action against the League at its weakest point.

London picked on Denmark, a small power, to be sure, but far from an insignificant one. Territorially, it included Norway, Greenland, Iceland, the Faroe Islands, and the two German provinces of Schleswig and Holstein. Geopolitically, Denmark controlled access between the Baltic and the North Sea, either through the 'Sound', where it continued to levy lucrative tolls on commerce, or the Great and Little Belts to the west. Last but not least, the Danish fleet was the fifth largest in the world.

An amphibious operation was considered, but because there were not enough troops available, a purely naval expedition was launched instead. This was commanded by Sir Hyde Parker, with Horatio Nelson as second in command. The British fleet engaged the Danish reserve fleet, much of it not seaworthy, in Copenhagen Roads in April 1801 and defeated it. The Royal Navy prepared to bombard Copenhagen itself if Nelson's negotiations proved unsuccessful.[10] Then news arrived of the death of the Tsar; Denmark left the Armed Neutrality, which soon fell apart. One way or the other, Britain's political objective had been achieved. Militarily, though, the contest had been indecisive. The main Danish fleet was still intact.[11]

The attack on Denmark in 1801 provoked some controversy in the (British) political nation. Its defenders justified the mission as unfinished business from the American Revolutionary War and as a measure necessary to maintain the British maritime supremacy on which they believed the European balance of power rested. In the House of Lords, the Earl of Darnley condemned the principle of Armed Neutrality as 'directly contrary to the known law of nations' which threatened 'the most fatal consequences to our existence as a maritime power'.[12] Lord Hawkesbury went so far as to claim that it was this naval strength to which 'the continent of Europe owed what it retained of independence'.[13]

Not everybody was convinced. Some critics accused the ministry of wrapping themselves in the naval flag.[14] Others argued that British high-handedness had provoked the Armed Neutrality in the first place.[15] The main concern, though, was that the attack on neutral Denmark constituted a violation of international law. One senior opposition figure, the former Foreign Secretary, Earl Grey, did not believe that British naval dominance should be based 'on any claim inconsistent with the interest of other independent nations'. 'True policy', he argued, 'can never be incompatible with justice'.[16] Grey accepted 'the principle universally admitted by all publicists, that it is just to attack a power in the course of preparation with a hostile intention', but he denied that Denmark had had any such intent.[17] The Earl of Caernarvon argued that British policy had been 'precipitate' and 'doubt[ful] under the law of nations'.[18]

It is therefore not surprising that the government wheeled out the Solicitor-General, Sir William Grant, to defend its actions over Denmark. The situation, he argued, was one of 'difficulty and danger' which required 'vigour, exertion and promptitude', not 'doubt, hesitation and enquiry'. Those who set up the Armed Neutrality, Grant continued, did so 'in defiance of the long established law and usage of European nations, to deprive us of our indisputable and essential right [of search on the high seas]'.[19] This had been 'exercised ... for time almost immemorial', and without it Britain's 'maritime superiority would be reduced to complete insignificance'.[20]

Instead, Grant advanced an expansive view of the nature of warfare. He dismissed the idea that one made war only 'against a metaphysical being called the state, as if the state was anything but the aggregate of the people'. It was right, Grant went on, to 'attack their property in order to reduce the resources of the state which derives all its vigour from them'.[21] As for the intent of the supposedly neutral signatories, 'as soon as we understand that a convention is signed which we have every reason to think hostile to our rights and interests' it was right to 'put ourselves in a posture to be prepared against the consequences'. Having done so, the other side 'may not push their pretentions to the extent apprehended'.[22]

In other words, the British action against the Armed Neutrality in general, and Copenhagen in particular, had been pre-emptive.

When full-scale war broke out again between Britain and France in 1803, followed a year later by the establishment of a new European coalition against Napoleon, the Baltic was soon back in the eye of the storm. After defeating the Austrians, Russians, and Prussians in Central Europe, the emperor advanced to the Baltic and, with some difficulty, crushed the Prussian and Russian armies there by the middle of 1807. At the subsequent treaty of Tilsit, the Tsar not only made his peace with Napoleon, but undertook to enforce mediation on London. Britain was completely isolated in Europe. In mid-July 1807, the ambassador to Russia, Granville Leveson Gower, feared 'the probability of a coalition of the whole continent against us'.[23]

A large part of the challenge was economic. On 21 November 1806, Napoleon promulgated his Berlin Decree. The resulting Continental System forbade any part of the French Empire from trading with Britain. Because Denmark was not under French control, this measure in and of itself did not affect her directly. London responded with an Order in Council on 7 January 1807. This determined that all vessels which sailed from harbours which excluded British shipping could be seized. This was certainly a blow to neutrals, but again the direct impact on Denmark, which had given up on the idea of 'free ships, free goods' after her defeat in 1801, was not great.[24] Despite renewed tensions, therefore, the impending conflict was not a re-run of that of 1800–01 about maritime rights.

Likewise, the Baltic in general and Denmark in particular, remained vital to Britain's maritime predominance. Access to the region and its naval stores via the Sound or Belts was still critically important. For example, despite many attempts to source hemp elsewhere—in America, in India, the Mediterranean or the Black Sea—the Royal Navy of 1807 was still totally dependent on supplies from the Baltic.[25] All the same, neither the control of the Danish Sound nor the need to secure these naval supplies would play a decisive role in the confrontation to come. That would be driven by a different, though related, rationale.

* * *

The primary motivation behind British policy in the summer and autumn of 1807 was the question of whether Denmark could sustain its neutrality, and what the failure to do so might mean for the future of the Danish fleet. With the collapse of Prussia, the country was horribly exposed. In November 1806, the Danish observation corps in Holstein was withdrawn under French pressure, much to Britain's frustration. Napoleon could now march in at will and most likely overrun Jutland in short order. Not long after, Denmark was isolated still further, when the French surged into Pomerania, forcing the Swedes to fall back on the Baltic port city of Stralsund. A relief force of the King's German Legion found the city close to surrender and so landed on the nearby island of Ruegen instead.[26] To make matters worse, the Danes no longer allowed the British to run their packet boats carrying letters to and from the continent from Husum across the North Sea, cutting an important line of communication.

It was thus evident that Denmark's ability and willingness to resist French demands was extremely doubtful. To Britain, this rendered her neutrality ineffective. The most important issue now was the future of the Danish fleet. Despite the losses of 1801, with twenty ships of the line and eighteen frigates, this was still the fifth largest navy in Europe, behind only that of Britain, France, Spain, and Russia. If Napoleon could get his hands on these vessels, it would make a material difference to the naval balance of power. In early December 1806, the then-British Foreign Secretary Viscount Howick stressed that Britain could never 'acquiesce in any arrangement whereby the whole or any part of the Danish navy might be placed at the disposal of France...in order to secure the German Dominions [that is Schleswig and Holstein] of the Crown of Denmark'.[27] In the end, the question was whether Denmark, once unable to sustain her neutrality, would more fear a war with Britain or with France?

This made intelligence on Danish intentions, and those of Napoleon and Tsar Alexander, vital. Unfortunately, the information reaching London in July and August 1807 was alarming, contradictory, and sometimes false. Rumours of an anti-British alliance between Napoleon and Alexander at Tilsit swirled. 'The two emperors have shaken hands', one Russian general was reported as saying, 'Europe has cause to tremble'.[28] These accounts, much magnified

120

and distorted in communications to Foreign Secretary Canning by a French émigré agent, were in essence true.[29] By contrast, reports that the Danish fleet was being readied for action, presumably against Britain, were in fact false.[30] So were stories that Napoleon planned to use the Danish fleet to invade Ireland,[31] or to invade Holstein.[32] In the end, there was no single piece of intelligence which drove the decision to act—indeed some of the most reliable reports arrived after that decision was taken; rather, the cumulative weight of information received drove British strategic decision-making.[33]

On 6 August 1807, Napoleon told the Danish envoy in Paris that his country would have to either declare war on Britain and join the economic blockade against her or expect a French declaration of war herself.[34] He did not, however, demand the surrender of their fleet.

By then, though, the British government had come to a momentous decision. They would send an expedition to Copenhagen.[35] The instructions issued to the commanders of the expedition on 19 July 1807 showed that it was motivated by several concerns, but one over-riding anxiety. The Minister for War, Lord Castlereagh, wrote:

> His Majesty cannot but entertain the most anxious apprehensions that the maritime power, position and resources of Denmark may shortly be made the instrument in the hands of France not only of excluding our commerce from the Baltic and of depriving us of the means of naval equipment, but also of multiplying the points from which an invasion of His Majesty's dominions may be attempted under the protection of a formidable naval force.... The state of forward equipment in which the Danish navy has been of late kept was surely alone done in contemplation of being compelled by France at no distant period to adopt a course of conduct which must involve her in hostilities with Great Britain.

In other words, while the threat of Danish naval aggression was deemed real, the main driver of the operation was fear of French intentions.[36]

Because the fortifications of Copenhagen had been improved since 1801, Castlereagh decreed that it would have to be 'a conjoint operation'—what we would today call an amphibious operation.[37] Luckily for Britain, a substantial force was already nearby, deployed on the island of Ruegen. A senior diplomat, Francis James Jackson, who had previously served as envoy to Prussia, was sent to present the British demands to Denmark. 'You will carefully bear in mind', his instructions ran, 'that the possession of the Danish fleet is the one and indispensable object to which the whole of your negotiation is to be directed, and without which no other stipulation or concession can be considered as of any value or importance'.[38]

That said, there was a broader strategic aim behind the deployment. Foreign Secretary George Canning wanted to dispel the notion, as he put it in June 1807, that Britain was 'half-beaten already'.[39] This required radical, even brutal action. Canning came back to this argument after the attack had taken place, when he said that 'We must not disguise the fact from ourselves, we *are* [emphasis in original] hated throughout Europe, and that hate must be cured by fear'. He also stated that a major motivation had been 'to stun Russia into her senses again'.[40]

In short, the British government saw the expedition to Copenhagen as an exercise in prevention, pre-emption and deterrence. They genuinely, if mistakenly, believed that Denmark was close to surrendering its fleet to Napoleon, and that even if that were not the case, the danger of this happening at some future date warranted taking anticipatory action. They also hoped that firm measures against that state would deter others, in particular Tsarist Russia. What the government did not stipulate was the bombardment of civilians in pursuit of these aims.[41] The question of how to execute the mission was left to the commanders.

This latitude was widely understood at the time. For example, Castlereagh instructed the army commander, Cathcart, that in the event of the outbreak of hostilities, diplomacy would cease and that matters would then be left to the 'judgment' of himself and Admiral Gambier. He specifically denied wanting to 'fetter' their judgment, but offered only the 'informed general mode' of the government's thinking, in particular London's determination not to allow the Danes to play for time.[42] Cathcart, in turn, told Castlereagh that once he had occupied the approaches to Copenhagen, he would be 'better able to judge, what are the most expedient steps to be taken towards the accomplishment of the object set forth in my instructions'.[43]

Likewise, when Castlereagh was looking to the future deployment of the forces involved after the objective had been achieved, he specifically told the army commander, Lord Cathcart, that he should use his 'discretion' in the light of 'the state of circumstances as may exist on the spot'.[44]

Such preventive and pre-emptive action was not unprecedented, either in Europe more generally, or in Britain in particular. The most spectacular example, of course, was Frederick the Great's attack on Saxony in 1756, which was designed to forestall the Austrian, French, and Russian coalition assembling against him. By then, Britain had already engaged in radical preventive action herself, for example when she destroyed the Spanish fleet at Cape Passaro off Sicily in 1718. Later, shortly before the Seven Years' War formally broke out, Britain launched a pre-emptive attack on the French fishing fleet at the Great Bank of Newfoundland. During the conflict itself, the Elder Pitt even suggested that Britain attack Spain before it could join the coalition against her.[45] At that time, Pitt had referred to acting '*a la Prusse*'. Moreover, in European political and international legal thought, the concept of pre-emptive and even preventive action was well established. Nearly 200 years earlier, Francis Bacon had called for an attack on Spain on the grounds that 'Wars preventive upon just fears are true defensives'.[46]

Even so, the ruthlessness of what was being contemplated at Copenhagen is striking. In these earlier cases, French and Spanish hostility had been manifest. This time, Britain was proposing to force a neutral state to surrender its principal means of self-defence in order to safeguard its own maritime supremacy. The absolute security of the former was to be bought with the absolute insecurity of the latter. This was a step further than the action taken in 1801. There is no evidence, though, that ministers consulted either the Attorney-General or the Solicitor General about the legality of the planned operation, and in any case this was not customary at the time. There does not seem to have been dissent within the cabinet on the matter, but King George III was deeply unhappy. He called it 'a very immoral act'.[47]

That said, the objective was not the application of force, but the delivery of effect. The diplomat sent to deliver the British ultimatum, Francis Jackson, was advised that coercion would be used if necessary, but that 'if at any moment after the commencement of military operations a disposition shall be shewn on the part of the Danish government to recur to negotiation, all hostile measures should instantly cease and discussion begin'.[48] In other words, military force was to be used *strategically*, even if the term itself was not yet in use at the time, in order to assist diplomacy, not replace it.

* * *

In late July 1807, the British force assembled under the command of Admiral James Gambier. Once fully constituted, it was a formidable armada of 25 ships of the line, 71 smaller escort vessels, 377 transports, and 30,000 men.[49] The force clearly meant business, being armed with 8-inch howitzers and a plentiful supply of Congreve rockets.[50] By 2 August, Gambier was anchoring off Elsinore at the opening of the Sound; a squadron was detached to cut Zealand off from the rest of Denmark. A day later, he passed the Danish Sound unopposed. The ultimatum delivered by Francis Jackson, on 8 and 9 August, however, was rejected; Denmark refused to surrender her fleet for safe-keeping. Shortly thereafter, the Danish Chief Minister, Count Bernstorff, dismissed Jackson's threat of 'immediate operations of a vast military and naval force upon a populous and commercial city'.[51] By mid-August 1807, the British had landed on Zealand and surrounded Copenhagen.

It was now clear that the assumptions made before the dispatch of the expedition would have to be revised. The French had not occupied Holstein, and had made no demand for the surrender of the Danish fleet, not yet anyway; the Danes were showing no signs of joining any Franco-Russian maritime League; and their navy was in no fit state to do so anytime soon anyway. There was apparently no immediate threat; Napoleon's ultimatum in Paris was not yet known. In these circumstances, Jackson wondered, as he later wrote, whether 'it was advisable to proceed in my original intention and persist in the demand of the navy'.[52] His instructions, however, were clear; the fleet would have to be handed over, come what may. From now on, though, the operation was no longer a partly *pre-emptive* strike designed to ward off an imminent danger, but a purely *preventive* one intended to anticipate a possible challenge further down the line. As the subsequent debate showed, these terms were not in contemporary use, but the distinction was certainly made at the time.

Now, the military leadership would have to force the Danes to destroy or surrender their fleet. This was easier said than done. The seaward defences were so strong, the waters so shallow, and Danish gunboats so active, that the Royal Navy would not be able to get close enough to attack the Danish warships, nor was the fleet in range of the British artillery on land.[53] There was nothing for it: the city would have to be taken and physical possession of the fleet ensured.

The initiative now passed to the commander of the land force, General Cathcart. But while the garrison of Copenhagen was outnumbered and outgunned by the British, the sturdy city fortifications meant that it could not be taken by storm. 'The [defensive] works are stronger and more complete than has generally been imagined', Cathcart reported in late August 1807, warning that a '*coup de main*' was not possible.[54] 'It is far from certain', he elaborated a few days later, 'that the place will yield to bombardment and they [the Danes] may have provisions to hold out until the bad weather sets in'. Cathcart did not have the resources to dig trenches. Worse still, he had heard from intercepted Danish communications that the garrison had been ordered 'to defend the place to the last extremity'.[55] A lengthy siege would be unavoidable. This took time, and that was one commodity Cathcart did not have. The onset of winter meant that Gambier would be obliged to withdraw his ships by the beginning of November.

There was only one way of settling the matter quickly, and that was to terrify the Danes into compliance. 'If it is found by experience', the Deputy Quarter-Master General of the expedition George Murray argued, 'that the destruction of the fleet is actually not within the power of our mortar batteries, we must then on necessity resort to the harsh measure of forcing the town into our terms'. This, he continued, would be done 'by the suffering of the inhabitants themselves'. The action should be directed against 'all persons of whatever description', who should be forced to 'undergo the same hardships and dangers'.[56] In other words, the civilian population of Copenhagen was to be subjected to collective indiscriminate violence in support of a strategic objective.

Cathcart and Gambier were far from home. Even had they thought to consult them, there were no government lawyers to hand. Nor could they refer back to London for political guidance. The decision to attack the civilian population of Copenhagen was theirs, not the administration's, though not inconsistent with the directions the administration had supplied.[57] Neither man was happy about the morality of it. Jackson later sneered that Cathcart had a 'horror of knocking down the houses and of the chance of a shell falling on a girls' boarding school'.[58] Some of the officers also had qualms. The second-in-command of the land forces, Arthur Wellesley, later the Duke of Wellington, stated that 'it behooves us to do as little mischief to the town as possible, and to adopt any mode of reducing rather than bombardment'. His preferred method, though, was starvation, which was hardly more humane or less indiscriminate.[59] Jackson, for his part, ridiculed Cathcart's objections as 'considerations very unworthy of a General placed between the necessity of obtaining his object or of the danger of incurring irretrievable disgrace'.[60]

On 18 August 1807, the British commanders issued two warnings, one a public proclamation, the other a private summons to the Danish commander of the city.[61] The first, an 'Appeal', began by noting that the 'increased influence of France on the continent of Europe' made it 'impossible for Denmark, though it desires to be neutral, to preserve its neutrality'. This, the proclamation went on, made it 'absolutely necessary for those who continue to resist the French aggression to take measures to prevent the arms of neutral powers from being turned against them'. In the case of Denmark, this was her fleet, whose 'temporary deposit' was required. The British, it argued, came 'to your shores...not as enemies but in self-defence', and compliance would allow them to 'sheath [their] swords'. That was the velvet glove. Then followed the mailed fist. 'If', the 'appeal' threatened, 'the machinations of France render you deaf to the voice of reason, and the call of friendship, the innocent blood that will be spilt, and the horror of a besieged and bombarded capital, must fall on your heads and those of your evil advisors'.[62]

126

If this sounded menacing, the other document, a 'Summons' from Cathcart and Gambier was even more so. It warned that if the Danish capital—which was 'the seat of sciences and commerce and full of inhabitants of all ranks, of every age and sex', should be 'determined to abide the horrors of a siege', in other words to resist British demands, 'then the same shall be annoyed by every possible means of devastation'. Failure to comply would mean 'that most absolute orders are given by our government to attack this city by land and sea' would be put into effect. The authors ended by asking the Dane 'to think of the irreparable injury which may be caused by the operations of a few days; and that you are still in a situation to avert it'.[63] Charles Chalmers, then a surgeon aboard the Royal Navy fireship HMS *Prometheus* put it even more brutally. Cathcart, he wrote, had summoned the Danes and threatened to 'blow their town about their ears'.[64]

Francis Jackson was certainly in no doubt about what would happen. He wrote to his bother George in Berlin that the 'people [of Copenhagen] are said to be anxious to capitulate before a conflagration takes place, which must happen soon after a bombardment begins, when not improbably, the fleet as well as the city will become a prey to the flames'.[65] A day later, Jackson warned George that '[y]ou must expect to hear me not a little abused on the continent, and perhaps, even among our own countrymen'. But Jackson stressed that he had done what in his 'conscience even independent of [his] instructions' he thought 'to be right and just'. The Danes, Jackson believed, 'must be lashed a little before they will give in'.[66]

The purpose of the impending bombardment was thus clear. It was intended not to destroy the defences of the city, even at the cost of civilian casualties—what is today sometimes referred to as 'collateral damage'. The entire *objective* was to target civilians and thereby deliver political effect to the Danish leadership and induce them to hand over their fleet. The deliberations before the attack and the scarcely disguised rhetoric of these public and private 'appeals' and 'summons' leave no room for doubt.

Of course, the intentional harming of civilians during military operations was nothing new. Contrary to widespread belief, *ancien regime* commanders could be extremely ruthless—witness the 'ravaging' of the Palatinate and Bavaria by Louis XIV's armies—and their Revolutionary successors could be as brutal. Sieges were particularly vicious.[67] The era saw several brutal sackings with considerable civilian casualties.

That said, the planned attack went beyond contemporary practice in that it envisaged not the taking of a city by storm, nor its reduction through starvation, but its immediate surrender through the use of devastating fire-power against non-combatants. This was, if not unprecedented, then certainly unusual. Some of the weaponry to be used such as the Congreve rockets were so wildly inaccurate that one suspects that their main purpose was to frighten the population, especially at night when the visual effects were intensified.[68] The Danish commander, Peymann, later described them as 'weapons that are not usually used by refined [that is civilized] nations'.[69] It is therefore no exaggeration to speak of an attempt to 'terrorize' the civilian inhabitants as some later authors have done.[70]

* * *

The bombardment of Copenhagen began on 2 September at 7:30 in the evening. The first cannonade lasted until 7am the following day. It caught the citizenry completely unawares. Many were out promenading and killed or injured while trying to take cover. The second cannonade was longer, starting at 6pm on 3 September and ending at 8am on 4 September. After resting during the day, the gunners resumed firing at 7pm and continued to do so throughout the night.[71] That night, the spire of the Church of Our Lady, a prominent landmark, which the British gunners had been using as an aiming point, collapsed spectacularly. In all, about 6,000 projectiles were fired.[72] The damage to the city was relatively concentrated, encompassing about ten streets, but the risk that the fires would spread was high.[73] On 6 September, the Danes gave way and agreed to hand over their fleet.

Those who ordered and carried out the attack were in no doubt about what they were doing. In his report to the Admiralty the day after the Danish capitulation, Admiral Gambier described how 'the town was set on fire, and by the repeated discharges of our artillery, was kept in flames in different parts'. He continued, 'A considerable part of it [the city] being consumed [by fire], and the conflagration having arrived at a great height, threatening the speedy destruction of the whole city'.[74] That said, despite the obvious relish with which some Britons observed the spectacle, referring to it as a 'sport', the bombardment was carefully calibrated, or at least was intended to be. Cathcart reported that although 'the bombardment and cannonade have made considerable havock and destruction in the town not one shot [had] been fired into it', until the ultimatum had been refused and 'nor [was] a single shot [fired] after [the Danes had shown] a disposition to capitulate'. Indeed, the shelling had been 'considerably abated' during the second night in order to give the enemy a chance to reflect.[75]

It was still a traumatic experience for the Danes in two senses. First, the bombardment itself was horrific. Quite apart from the resulting deaths, injuries, and damage to property, the psychological impact of the shelling was immense, particularly that of the Congreve rockets. 'As they rushed through the air in the dark', one British observer wrote, 'they looked like so many fiery serpents, which must have dismayed the besieged terribly'.[76] Contemporary colour prints show the night sky above Copenhagen lit up with exploding shells and streaking rockets and much of the city in flames. One witness, Captain Thomas Browne, wrote that 'the fire from our batteries' and the Danish response 'resembled a constant succession of flashes of lightning and the very firmament shook with the unceasing explosions'. Another observer saw an 'awful yet magnificent spectacle' from the stern gallery of his ship. Even after going to bed, his cabin was 'illuminated by an intensely red glow, then suddenly wrapped in deep gloom as the flames rose and fell'. He concluded, 'Alas poor Danes! I could not but feel for them'.[77]

In the stricken city, rumour ran rife. It was said that the British shells penetrated all the way to cellars, where people instinctively sought shelter, increasing the panic. About 20,000 Copenhageners, a fifth of the population, streamed out of the city to nearby Christianhavn or Amager. The probable death toll was lower than often suggested, but at 195 civilian deaths was very substantial.[78]

The physical damage done to the city was considerable. One contemporary print shows a completely wrecked quarter of the city, in which women, children, and other civilians—including one man with two peg legs—walk about. 'I was astonished to see the havoc our bombardment had made', one British rifleman wrote. 'Whole streets lay in ruins; churches burnt down' and the roads were 'blocked up with bricks, stones, tiles and timber'. 'Many houses were still smouldering', recalls another British soldier, 'mothers were bewailing the fate of their slaughtered children'. Yet another observer saw a 'sight both 'dreadful' and 'truly magnificent', especially the destruction of the Church of Notre Dame of which 'nothing is standing but the bare foundation'. There was little heart-searching, however, about the action itself. Perhaps one Captain Leach came closest when he spoke of his 'bitter regret' that 'our government should have considered it necessary to adopt such rigorous measures'.[79]

Secondly, the outcome of the operation compounded the hurt. Because they had not submitted to the ultimatum, the Danes were forced to surrender not merely their ships of the line but their entire fleet, and that not just for the duration of the conflict but in perpetuity.[80] Over the next few weeks, the British were engaged in destroying or seizing all naval equipment. Then, on 16 and 21 October in two huge convoys, the British set sail with their captured ships, all bursting to the seams with confiscated—or stolen, as the Danes saw it—materials. To the watching Danes, the sight was a truly heartbreaking and humiliating one.[81] It marked the complete, and as it turned out, permanent, destruction of Denmark's naval status. She was relegated in one fell swoop from one of the major maritime actors to complete irrelevance.

* * *

The bombardment was much discussed at the time and widely regarded as damaging to Britain's reputation. During the shelling itself, one Dane, after seeing a child killed by a rocket before his eyes, exclaimed, 'O! Britain! Queen of Nations! Mother of such noble and manly sons! Is this thy work!'[82] Another Dane, writing in mid-September 1807 shortly after his country's capitulation, described how 'the Englishman had played a hellish role as a common pirate', by burning one third of Copenhagen and carrying off the

130

entire fleet.[83] Across the Atlantic, the young American midshipman William Henry Allen wrote of England's 'infamous attack on the Dane'.[84] US President Thomas Jefferson also condemned the attack, as did—more predictably—the Russian Tsar.[85]

Nowhere was the attack so intensively discussed, however, as in Britain itself. Here the government faced an immediate public relations problem. It was clear that the Danish fleet had been in no fit state to attack the home islands, as claimed. 'As few of the ships are in any considerable progress of equipment', Gambier's dispatch to the Admiralty of 7 September stated, 'it will require some time to complete them for sea, but not a moment will be lost in bringing the whole of them to England'.[86] This embarrassing sentence was simply excised from the version of Gambier's report presented to the public.[87]

The bombardment of Copenhagen was vigorously defended by the administration and its supporters, inside and outside of Parliament. Unlike the debates of 1801, the help of the Attorney-General's office was not sought, or at least not given. Instead, the advocates of the attack argued that Britain had acted from 'necessity' and thus within international law. It was only the 'maritime power of Great Britain', one pamphleteer wrote, which stood between Napoleon and the 'subjugation of the continent of Europe'. He would therefore have to be denied control of the Danish fleet and ports. In this context, Denmark's neutrality was void, because 'the want of power, and the absence of all defensive preparation' were effectively equivalent 'to the want of inclination' to resist Napoleon. Beyond this, the author justified the attack as an exercise in deterrence. 'The Danish marine', he wrote, 'has been the victim of a new experiment', adding that other powers 'will inevitably share the same fate' if they were 'forced' or 'seduced' to 'array themselves against us'.[88]

In Parliament, Foreign Secretary Canning justified the attack as a response to Napoleonic hegemony. It was the emperor's intention, he argued, to exclude British commerce from the continent and to bring all European powers into the lists against Britain. 'There was not now a community of states in Europe connected by the solemnity and sanction of public law', he argued, 'but one devouring state that swallowed up every one that it brings within its grasp'. In effect,

131

Canning said, international law was redundant and the action taken 'had saved us from imminent dangers that menaced us'.[89] Likewise, Castlereagh claimed that the expedition was 'no breach of the law of nations'. He continued, 'There was an engine of war [the Danish navy], which an enemy meant to turn against us, and we anticipated him by getting possession of it first'.[90]

All this was not enough to head off a ferocious parliamentary and pamphlet critique of the attack. According to its detractors, the government had supplied no satisfactory evidence of the 'necessity' of the operation. They were unpersuaded that Napoleon was about to demand the Danish Navy or that Denmark had pledged to join any attack on Britain. In the House of Lords, the Earl of Darnley said that 'the only ground on which [the operation] could be justified was actual necessity, which was not proved to exist by any documents before the house'.[91] And yet, as the veteran opposition MP Richard Brinsley Sheridan pointed out, 'the British government had bombarded Copenhagen, levelled its houses, churches and hospitals; sacked its arsenals and carried off its fleet, because it was given out that it was necessary to do so'.[92] They did not, in other words, accept that the attack was pre-emptive.

To many critics, the violence and illegality of the attack on Copenhagen was a blow to what we would today call Britain's 'soft power'. The government, Sheridan lamented, was trying to fight 'Bonaparte with his own weapons', rather than using the 'lenity and moderation' which was supposedly Britain's trademark. It was futile, his colleague William Windham argued, to 'attempt running a race of violence and injustice with the ruler of France because they were sure to be beat'.[93] The 'national character', Darnley argued, had been 'degraded and the national honour stained by this expedition', which had 'above all shaken our own persuasion of the justice of our cause a sentiment which had hitherto supported us through all our difficulties, commanding the respect of other powers, and encouraging us in an humble but confident reliance on the ultimate blessing and protection of providence'.[94]

Similar arguments were being made in the public sphere. The author of the pamphlet *The real state of the case respecting the late expedition* claimed that the government had failed to show that there

'ALAS POOR DANES!'

were any secret articles at the Treaty of Tilsit, and that in any case the expedition had been readied long before anything that did or did not happen at Tilsit could have been known. He also decried the 'massacre' that had taken place at Copenhagen. 'Greatly to the honour of this country', the author asserted, 'public opinion is rapidly turning against the flagitious proceedings which threatened the ruin of our national character'.[95] It would appear that the government's attempts to justify its actions largely failed. Already a fortnight after the bombardment, Francis Jackson was lamenting the public 'disposition to commiserate the Danes', which seems only to have grown with the passage of time.[96]

For the most part, though, it was the inherent violence of the operation's objective, rather than the actual violence of its execution, which was primarily at issue. Interestingly, government supporters made little attempt to justify the extreme use of force involved in the operation and the severe loss of civilian life. Even more interestingly, the expedition's detractors placed greater emphasis on the inherent illegality of the attack than its brutality, which was not out of the ordinary for its time.

The young American midshipman who deplored 'the infamous attack on the Dane', added an important rider. 'But I hope', he continued, 'their navy will ever possess a preponderating influence to that of Bonaparte as I conceive that bias in favor of the peace and safety of mankind generally'.[97] The ambivalence expressed here may well have been typical of those who were appalled by Britain's action in this particular case, but who were otherwise sympathetic to her role in containing Napoleonic France. There seemed to be no other way of maintaining the supremacy of the Royal Navy, on which the survival of international society rested, but by neutralizing the Danish fleet, one way or the other. The paradox here was that Britain needed to break international law in the specific case in order to uphold it more generally.

* * *

The controversy over Copenhagen in London eventually fizzled out, but the expedition was to enjoy a significant afterlife. From the 1830s, as Andrew Lambert's chapter in this volume shows, the Russians

133

feared that the Royal Navy would inflict another 'Copenhagen' on their capital, St. Petersburg, which was cruelly exposed to naval attack. The attack became a byword for British ruthlessness, praised by Anglo-American writers such as the naval historian Alfred Thayer Mahan and roundly condemned by continental European authorities.[98] Sometime in the early twentieth century, the word 'Copenhagen' entered the English language as a verb. As imperial Germany built up its navy, the First Sea Lord, Admiral Jackie Fisher suggested 'Copenhagening' the Kaiser's fleet through surprise attack on its bases. The German leadership feared exactly such a blow.[99]

During the Second World War, after the fall of France in the summer of 1940, the British actually did carry out a preventive strike.[100] The Vichy French fleet was destroyed in an unprovoked attack on its anchorage at Oran in North Africa in order to prevent it from falling into Hitler's hands. There was, though, another reason for the move. 'The elimination of the French navy as an important factor almost at a single stroke by violent action produced a profound impression in every country', Churchill later wrote.[101] 'Here was this Britain which so many had counted down and out, which strangers had supposed to be quivering on the brink of surrender to the mighty power arrayed against her, striking ruthlessly ... it was made plain that the British War cabinet feared nothing and would stop at nothing'.[102] The same thought, it will be recalled, had animated Canning and Castlereagh in 1807.

Looking back, Churchill called the attack at Oran 'a hateful decision, the most unnatural and painful in which I have ever been concerned'. The operation led to the deaths of nearly 1,300 French sailors. Of its necessity, though, he had no doubt, because the 'life of the state and the salvation of our cause were at stake.... It was Greek Tragedy', by which he seems to have meant a clash between two heroes in which both sides were confronted with morally impossible choices. The closest analogy Churchill could think of was 'the destruction of the Danish fleet at Copenhagen'.[103] Clearly, what had started in the Baltic did not stay in the Baltic.

134

8

BRITISH-ARMY VIOLENCE AGAINST CIVILIANS IN THE PENINSULAR WAR

Charles Esdaile

If the Peninsular War of 1808–14 is replete with some of the British army's proudest battle honours, it was also the scene of episodes that cannot but give rise to many qualms, if not outright condemnation. Most famously, 19 January 1812, 6 April 1812, and 31 August 1813 saw the troops of the Duke of Wellington take the fortresses of Ciudad Rodrigo, Badajoz, and San Sebastian by storm, the men concerned in each case running amok as soon as they had broken though the defences and engaging in behaviour that, at worst, descended into an orgy of rape, pillage, and even murder. In the context of a British state that was ever ready to push violence to its utmost bounds to achieve its political and strategic ends, this at first sight might appear to be the fruit of, say, a willingness to use terror tactics to discourage an entrenched enemy from resistance. In this case, however, it is clear that this simply is not the case. Far from being a deliberate strategy, such violence was frowned upon by Sir John Moore and the Duke of Wellington alike, and, as this essay will show, sprang not from above but from below. What this chapter shows is that when it suited commanders, they would try to ensure violence was not committed; and this would ameliorate the

135

actual incidence of violence. But what it also shows is that atrocity is difficult to avoid even when every effort is being made to wage war within the strictest of parameters.

Let us not delude ourselves: at the beginning of the nineteenth century as much as at the beginning of the eighteenth or the beginning of the twentieth, the British state was a ruthless war-machine that was wedded to the maintenance, if not extension, of its empire and had little compunction in pushing violence to its utmost bounds should it judge it necessary to do so. If proof is necessary that this was the case, one has only to turn to the so-called 'Battle of Cape Santa Maria' of 5 October 1804. Fought off the southern coast of Portugal, this witnessed a squadron of four British frigates under Sir Graham Moore challenge a Spanish squadron of equal composition and size that was making its way to Cádiz with a consignment of bullion from South America and demand its immediate surrender. The Spanish commander, José Bustamente, refused to be overawed, and Moore opened fire. Utterly unprepared, for Spain and Britain were not at war when the clash occurred, the Spaniards did their best to fight back, but within a short time they had been completely overcome, though not before the magazine of one of their four frigates had exploded, sending the ship to the bottom. In all, 349 Spaniards, many of them women and children who had been travelling back to Spain with husbands who had served out postings to Buenos Aires or Montevideo perished, compared with a mere nine British fatalities. That there was a strategic rationale for Moore's conduct is true enough—in brief, remain neutral though she had when the Peace of Amiens broke down in 1803, Spain was an ally of France, and it was generally—and, quite rightly—believed that the Spanish government was only waiting for the bullion carried by Bustamente's ships to get to Cadiz to resume its former belligerency: hence the orders that had been sent to Graham ordering him to detain the Spanish convoy come what may—but the affair had scarcely added renown to the annals of the Royal Navy and, in fact, remains little known to this day.[1]

Moving on a few years from this unfortunate affair, we come to the Peninsular War of 1808–14, and, with it, the acts of violence mentioned in the introduction to this chapter. In this conflict, of

BRITISH-ARMY VIOLENCE AGAINST CIVILIANS

course, having famously changed sides in 1808, alongside Portugal, Spain was an ally of the British. In this situation, it is self-evident that there were limits to the extent to which the British commanders sent to the Iberian peninsula could engage in behaviour that went beyond certain basic norms: as they recognized, they needed the assistance, co-operation, and support of the political and military authorities and the populace alike and could not behave as if they were in enemy country. This being the case, both Sir John Moore and the Duke of Wellington repeatedly urged their subordinates to exercise restraint with regard to the inhabitants and, in principle at least, paid for all the supplies that they extracted from the countryside, whilst Wellington made strenuous efforts to co-operate with the Patriot authorities, going out of his way, for example, to have the Constitution of 1812 proclaimed in every town and city that he liberated, and that despite the fact that he disapproved of many of its provisions. Only in one instance, in fact, can either commander be accused of stepping beyond the bounds of civilized convention, and this, of course, concerns Wellington's successful defence of Portugal in 1810 against the overwhelming forces sent against him by Napoleon under the command of Marshal Masséna. As is well known, the strategy adopted by the Duke consisted of a number of inter-connected elements ranging from the incorporation of the Portuguese army and militia into his forces through the devastation of the countryside in the face of the French advance to the construction of an impregnable line of redoubts and other fortifications blocking the only feasible approach to the Portuguese capital. Many British historians have written as if all this cloaked one intention and one intention only, namely to lure Masséna into a trap under the guns of the fortifications of Lisbon— the so-called Lines of Torres Vedras—and break the resistance of his army through the physical deprivation consequent upon Wellington's employment of a 'scorched-earth' policy involving, not just the destruction of every resource that might be of use to the French, but the flight of the entire populace to such coastal refuges as Lisbon and Peniche. In fairness, such pundits are not wrong—the invaders did, indeed, march all the way to the Lines of Torres Vedras, only to be forced to retreat by months of semi-starvation—but it should not be thought that Wellington was irrevocably wedded to this solution.

On the contrary, all the evidence suggests that his intention was to stop the French well before they reached Lisbon, either at the border fortress of Almeida, or, at the very worst, the towering Serra do Buçaco, but in this he was disappointed, the result being that a far wider area of the countryside had to be stripped of its resources than he had originally hoped. On top of this, meanwhile, it should also be pointed out the invaders withstood the utter misery to which they were subjected for far longer than the British commander ever anticipated—this, too, having the effect of intensifying the sufferings of the populace.[2]

That these sufferings were terrible indeed, no-one would deny. Amongst the many soldiers in Wellington's army who noted them, for example, was Rifles officer, John Leach. As he wrote of the winter of 1809–10:

> Thousands of the unfortunate inhabitants of the provinces through which our army had recently retreated ... were endeavouring to exist between Lisbon and the Lines. There was, therefore, an immense population hemmed up in a small space of country, hundreds of them without a house to cover them or food to eat ... It was not unusual to see hordes of these poor wretches, old and young, male and female, in rags, the very picture of death, round a miserable fire, on which was placed an earthen vessel full of such herbs as could be gathered in the fields and hedges. Thousands contrived to drag on a miserable existence on this vile sustenance. Their death-like, emaciated faces were sufficient to have touched the heart of the most callous and unfeeling.[3]

What we have here, then, is a human tragedy of immense proportions that is generally reckoned as having cost the Portuguese a minimum of 100,000 civilian lives—as many as one tenth of the population—and represented a greater disaster than even the Lisbon earthquake of 1755. However, that said, do we also have a war-crime? Both at the time and since, those favourable to the cause of Napoleon have entertained few doubts in this respect. To take just one example, here is André Delagrave, a French officer who experienced the campaign as an *aide de camp* of General Junot. Thus:

BRITISH-ARMY VIOLENCE AGAINST CIVILIANS

On reaching Viseu, the army was astounded to find hardly a single person. The town, a place of from 8,000 to 10,000 souls, was entirely deserted. The rich had fled to Oporto or Lisbon, while the common folk had hidden themselves in the woods and mountains at some distance from the town ... The sight of this pretty ... settlement filled the hardest hearts with pity and sadness when we thought of its unfortunate inhabitants wandering among the trees and rocks. There are few peoples among whom the resolve to flee at the approach of an enemy is so general. It is a custom that has characterised the Portuguese since the earliest centuries ... On this occasion, however, the disposition of the nation was somewhat changed. Having had the opportunity to become familiar with them on a number of occasions, many of the inhabitants did not feel any great alarm at the arrival of the French. They knew that, while there was some reason to fear the French soldier in the heat of the first moments of conquest, the latter resumed his naturally humane and sociable character so long as he was not exasperated by resistance or unnecessary privations. In consequence, there was no urge to flee the foreign yoke ... and so ... a great number of people, and certainly the most sensible elements of the populace, would have been quite happy tranquilly to await the result in their homes. But these sentiments did not suit the English, who had conceived of the idea of turning the whole country ... into a desert. The most rigorous orders laid down that the inhabitants should abandon anywhere that seemed likely to be occupied by the French after having first destroyed everything that they could not carry away. Secret emissaries of [the] Regency supervised their execution with a fury that recalled the conduct of the Inquisition in days gone by. Breaking into people's homes, at the slightest sign that these tyrannical measures were not being obeyed, they would immediately arrest the entire family and confiscate their goods; often enough, meanwhile, one person or another would be handed over to the daggers of the mob, which was always ready to look for scapegoats. Still worse, more than one of the barbarous tortures Lord Wellington had used on the soldiers of Tippu Tib during his campaigns in India were used on those Portuguese who wished to stay neutral and tried to remain in their homes by barricading themselves in. Fires were lit to smoke them out, and, when they came out, their noses or big toes were cut off. Inaccessible to all sentiments of pity, the English general excused his atrocities with the words 'the needs of war'.[4]

All this, however, is so much froth. In this particular instance, Wellington was driven by strategic necessity—and that denying Lisbon to the French was a strategic necessity of the first order no-one can possibly deny—to take measures that had a terrible impact on the civilian population, but he did not deliberately target the latter, and, when he could avoid it, refrained from doing so. In none of his three Peninsular-War sieges of fortress-cities, then, did he resort to the use of indiscriminate bombardment, while, offered the assistance of rockets in respect of that of San Sebastián, he famously refused to make use of them on the grounds that the only thing they were good for was burning down towns, this being something he had no desire whatsoever to do.[5] Unfortunately, however, this desire to expel the French from Spain and Portugal by strategies that did not transgress the limits of what was considered to be acceptable behaviour was not matched by the chief instrument by which the war was waged. We come here to the British redcoat.

Several times over, the Duke of Wellington famously damned the common soldiers of his army as 'the scum of the earth'.[6] Nuanced though this remark was on occasion by the admission that service with his army turned soldiers into 'fine fellows', it is one that has occasioned much protest in the more progressive age in which we live. According to the author of this chapter's good friend, Edward Coss, for example, if 'scum of the earth' was taken to refer to the criminal classes, and, more particularly, men who had been given the choice of enlistment or the gallows, this was simply not true. Whilst it was perfectly fair to say that the vast majority of British soldiers came from the humblest elements of British society—Irish peasants, Highland crofters, unskilled labourers and textile workers displaced from their traditional occupations by the march of industrialization—men with a criminal record were few in numbers, and cases of the object of court proceedings enlisting directly into the ranks few and far between, the most that he was prepared to accept being the presence of a minority of 'bad apples'—the so-called 'king's hard bargains'—who were a constant source of trouble. Happen though disorder did, then, it was in the vast majority the fruit either of hardship— in other words, desperately hungry men taking what they needed in order to survive—or the temporary madness induced by the profound psychological trauma involved in storming the walls of a defended fortress. Here, for example, is Coss's peroration:

> The British soldier was not, as has often been presumed, a brute forced to choose between the army and incarceration. The man who enlisted in the British army during the war against Napoleon most likely did so out of economic necessity. He was usually young ... an unemployed agricultural or manual labourer, textile worker, shoemaker or tradesman from any one of a hundred occupations. He chose the army because it offered the promise of regular food and pay. It was not his fault that the army failed miserably to fulfil its end of the bargain. Left without means to survive in Portugal, Spain, France and Belgium, the ranker did what anyone would do ... Commissariat failure and army neglect, not character flaws, caused the redcoat to steal in order to clothe and feed himself.[7]

This argument, however, has always struck this observer, at least, as being much too narrow in its definition of the term 'scum of the earth': in the eyes of the ruling classes of the day, to be poor was quite enough in itself to merit the term. At the same time, even granted that, as Coss argues, a substantial minority of the rank and file were artisans and, especially, such men as handloom weavers, it cannot but be felt that he protests too much: just because men were not criminals when they joined the army does not mean that they did not become criminalized by their experiences. As Thomas Browne, a captain in the Twenty-Third Foot who was serving on Wellington's staff, wrote in his diary in the wake of the retreat from Burgos in 1812:

> I think it was about this time that I began to remark the different effects of a continued warfare like that of the Peninsula on the character of the ... common soldiers. The latter appeared to me to become daily more ferocious and less fit for return to the

duties of citizens, and I sometimes apprehended that when they should be disbanded in England after the restoration of peace the country would be over-run with pilferers and marauders of every description.[8]

At the same time, much though Coss might deny that there is any concrete evidence of such a thing occurring, the army continued to be a refuge for men in trouble with the law, such as Thomas Norris, a butcher's boy from Watford who enlisted in the Fifty-Seventh Foot in December 1803 whilst on the run from a sentence of seven years' transportation, even if, in his case, his crime was no more than that of stealing two loaves of bread, while we learn from Phillip Haythornthwaite that, in 1803 alone, however small a proportion it represented of the punishments handed out to convicted malefactors (less than two per cent), fifty-three men were dispatched from the courts directly into the army or navy.[9] That said, however, even at the time, there were those who would have agreed with Coss. Here, for example, is Captain Joseph Sherer of the Thirty-Fourth Foot:

> My opinions of the moral excellence of soldiers is very superior to that generally entertained, and I think that we should find as much virtue, and as many amiable qualities, among 10,000 soldiers as among a similar number of individuals taken without selection from the bosom of civil society.[10]

This is not to say that Sherer was blind to the problem of discipline—on the contrary—but, like Coss, he was inclined to put it down to the situation in which the men found themselves in Spain and Portugal rather than to any innate criminality. Thus:

> Soldiers are often placed in situations which from their nature ... give birth to an elevation of spirits it is difficult to control. I have seen common men distributed through a suite of rooms in the empty palace of a nobleman ... surrounded by mirrors and marble, and I have observed in their countenances a jocular eagerness to smash and destroy them. But this does not arise out of cruelty. No: in such a case, a soldier feels himself lifted for a moment above his low and ordinary condition, while the owner of the proud mansion in which he lodges appears

BRITISH-ARMY VIOLENCE AGAINST CIVILIANS

humbled below him, and that mind must be superior to human infirmity which did not at such a thought carelessly exult. But I am persuaded that the sudden appearance of the sufferer and his weeping family in ninety-nine cases out of a hundred would reproduce ... generous feelings of pity ... Again, on the subject of plunder, setting aside assaults or battles, the soldier is often harassed with toil and hunger, impatient and penniless. It is the object and end of discipline to prevent and punish plunder under circumstances like these ... But when troops are neither fed, clothed or clothed with regularity, they are tempted beyond their strength, and the military man ... learns how and when to make allowances for those disorders which the world is ever too forward to characterise as barbarous and licentious.[11]

All this is true enough, but the fact remains that British soldiers misbehaved with extraordinary regularity in season and out. If what is wanted is example, the most obvious place to start is the terrible scenes that accompanied the successful assaults on Ciudad Rodrigo, Badajoz, and San Sebastián in 1812 and 1813, but these events have been discussed *ad inifinitum*, and so time will not be spent on them in this paper. What will be looked at is the constant low-level disorder, albeit some of it of a very unpleasant nature, that British officers found themselves dealing with on an almost daily basis.[12] Here, for example, is Sir John Moore (writing in the course not of the exhausting retreat through the mountains of Galicia to which he later committed his army, but the much easier advance from Lisbon to Salamanca):

> Some change must take place or matters cannot prosper. I saw the Sixth Regiment ... Their conduct has been bad, and their officers shamefully negligent. I spoke to them with great severity, and told them I should not take them into Spain: they were unworthy of it. One man had been sentenced to death by a general court-martial, and I ordered him to be executed.[13]

Here, Sir Arthur Wellesley:

> I cannot with propriety omit to draw your attention again to the state of discipline of the army, which is a subject of serious

143

concern to me, and well deserves the consideration of His Majesty's Ministers. It is impossible to describe to you the irregularities and outrages committed by the troops. They are never out of sight of their officers, I may almost say never out of the sight of the commanding officers of their regiments and the general officers of the army, that outrages are not committed, and, notwithstanding the pains which I take ... not a post or a courier comes in, nor an officer arrives from the rear of the army, that does not bring me accounts of the outrages committed by the soldiers who have been left behind on the march, having been sick or left behind by their regiments, or who have been left in the hospitals.[14]

And, finally, here Sir James Willoughby Gordon, who served as Wellington's Quartermaster-General in the latter half of 1812:

It is with the greatest concern that I feel it a duty I owe to Your Royal Highness and to the public service to report the extraordinary and, I hope, unprecedented state of indiscipline which prevails in the whole of this army, but, particularly amongst the British troops, in any matter whatever relative to plunder of private and public property. I do not exaggerate, Sir, when I assert that it is unexampled in any service, nor can it be equalled by the cossacks or guerrillas. Lord Wellington is extremely uneasy about it, nor can any order or regulation of his prevent it ... We owe our sickness to this kind of irregularity, which nothing but great severity can prevent. The provost is not equal to the thing: he must, if he did his duty, hang by dozens.[15]

Lest it be thought that all this is but the language of outraged property owners; common soldiers were just as likely to record the mayhem that all too often accompanied the Peninsular armies' movements. As Edward Costello of the Rifles remembered of one village through which he passed during the retreat to the Lines of Torres Vedras:

Arruda ... presented a picture of most wanton desolation. Furniture of a most splendid description in many instances was laid open to the spoliation of the soldiery. Elegant looking glasses wrenched from the mantelpieces were wantonly broken

BRITISH-ARMY VIOLENCE AGAINST CIVILIANS

to obtain bits to shave by, and their [frames] with chairs, tables, etc., etc., used as common firewood.[16]

Nor, despite Coss's protestations that there was no violence—or, for that matter, Sherer's that the soldiery's 'blameable disposition to waste and destroy' was 'the heedless and mischievous wantonness of the schoolboy, not the vindictive malice of the man'—was it just plundering, vandalism, or simple high-jinks. Outright murder was probably uncommon, but on occasion it did occur. In the admittedly desperate circumstances of the retreat to La Coruña in January 1809, then, a number of Spanish civilians, including several justices of the peace, fell to the muskets and bayonets of British stragglers.[17] If this was an isolated case, it might be put down to the fury many soldiers felt at the manner in which they had not only seemingly been betrayed by the Spaniards— 'The apathy with which the inhabitants of this mountain country ... have witnessed our misery is revolting', wrote German commissary, Auguste Schaumann. As he continued:

> They were to be seen in large armed hordes far away from us in the mountains ... when ... they might have been very useful to us and covered our retreat. But not only did these puffed-up patriots ... give us no assistance, but they also took good care to remove all cattle and all foodstuffs out of our way ... and in addition murdered and plundered our own men who fell out left and right along the road.[18]

But, unfortunately, in many instances there were no such mitigating circumstances, as witness a series of incidents in which stragglers shot dead civilians who refused them food and shelter or gangs of marauding red-coats broke into isolated dwellings in search of loot and murdered the inhabitants in conditions that were often marked by extreme brutality.[19] And, finally, there were even cases when soldiers engaged in the legitimate performance of their duties and, in particular, the requisition of draught animals and other livestock, responded to civilians' attempts to defend their property by shooting them down in cold blood.[20]

Second only to murder, of course, is the crime of rape. For a variety of reasons, of which the most important was probably a desire

145

both to shield the women concerned and to protect the reputation of the regiments to which their assailants belonged, sexual violence is almost completely absent from the court-martial records as such (of the many men sentenced to the lash in the course of the war by general courts martial, in only one case was the charge rape)—it was probably dealt with under the heading of common assault—but it would be naïve to think that it did not take place. That matters were at their worst in the special circumstances that pertained at Ciudad Rodrigo, Badajoz, and San Sebastián cannot be doubted. While it is probable that the French were far worse behaved in this respect, the memoir literature contains plenty of hints that there were other instances of rape, and, in addition, extensive sexual harassment, with the commissary Auguste Schaumann, in particular, appearing to be a positive menace to women.[21]

From where did all this come? The fact of the matter was that, whilst the social classes from which common soldiers were recruited were not inherently criminal, neither had they in any way been assimilated into polite society. If it were not enough to consider the general affinity for such activities as bare-knuckle boxing, shin-kicking contests, cock-fighting, dog-fighting, bull-baiting and football (still, of course, a sport played according to its rough and ready medieval origins), to suggest that this was so, we can once again look to voices from the ranks. These were by no means devoid of men of a little education who had fallen on hard times or sought to escape domestic troubles of one sort or another, and such men quickly found their situation difficult, if not intolerable. One man so affected was Private Joseph Donaldson of the Ninety-Fourth Foot:

> I was very far from being contented ... There were few of those with whom I could associate that had an idea beyond the situation they were in: those who had were afraid to show they possessed any more knowledge than their comrades for fear of being laughed at by their fellows, who, in other circumstances, they would have despised. If a man ventured to speak in a style more refined than the herd around him, he was told, 'Everyone [does] not read the dictionar' like [you]', or 'Dinna be gi'en us ony o' your grammar words, na.' If a man ... did not join with

146

BRITISH-ARMY VIOLENCE AGAINST CIVILIANS

his neighbours in their ribald obscenity and nonsense, he was a Methodist; if he did not curse and swear, he was a Quaker; and, if he did not drink the most of his pay, he was called a miser [or] a mean scrub, and the generality of his comrades would join in execrating him. In such society it was a hard matter for a man of any superior opinion or intellect to keep his ground, for he had few to converse with on those subjects which were most congenial to his mind, and to try to inform his colleagues was a vain and, by them considered, a presumptuous attempt. Thus, many men of ability and information were, I may say, forced from the intellectual height which they had attained down to the level of those with whom they were obliged to associate ... Blackguardism was fashionable, and even the youngest were led into scenes of low debauchery and drunkenness by men advanced in years.[22]

No better off, meanwhile, was another Scottish soldier, one Joseph Sinclair of the Seventy-First Foot:

I could not associate with the common soldiers: their habits made me shudder. I feared an oath; they never spoke without one. I could not drink; they loved liquor. They gamed; I knew nothing of play. Thus was I a solitary individual among hundreds. They lost no opportunity of teasing me: 'Saucy Tom' or 'the distressed Methodist' were the names they distinguished me by.[23]

If we are to believe such accounts, many of Wellington's soldiers were brutal and licentious because they came from a brutal and licentious society. Some places, true, were worse than others—Liverpool's dependence on aspects of maritime life such as privateering and the slave trade that were especially violent, for example, made it a social environment that was particularly grim.[24] Let us begin with the question of violence. Modern research has shown that the eighteenth century saw a marked decline in the murder rate. To quote Gregory Durston, for example, 'In England as a whole, it seems that there was an average of 2.3 homicides per 100,000 head of population during the first half of the eighteenth century. In the second half, however, it dropped to only 1.4.'[25] Too much should not be made of this, however. In Ireland, the place of origin for at least one third

147

of the rank and file, the murder rate was much higher, as much as four times so in the 1730s.[26] At the same time, too, many of the factors that have been argued as making society less murderous— among them, the rise of notions of 'polite society', the gradual disappearance of the sword as an item of habitual apparel, and the decline in the practice of duelling—had their greatest impact among the propertied classes and the 'middling sort', leaving the stews largely untouched. Meanwhile, murder was but one form of violence, with bare-knuckle fist fights being a feature of street life on which many foreign visitors were quick to comment: often conducted though these were within the parameters of certain informal rules that barred such actions as blows below the belt, the fact remains that among the lower classes it was very much the norm for disputes to be settled by force, and all the more so given the fact that men who died as a result of such clashes were rarely, if ever, treated as the victims of murder or even manslaughter.[27] What is more surprising, meanwhile, is that the same latitude extended to cases of common assault: a man could hit another, break his head with a club, and even stab him or attempt to cut his throat without fear of being tried for anything other than a misdemeanour, a class of crime that attracted penalties that could be seen as being extraordinarily lenient. By the beginning of the nineteenth century, true, attitudes were hardening, with a number of new Acts of Parliament subjecting cases of assault to much harsher penalties, but it would be a long time before the change had a significant impact in the streets.[28]

Assault and murder, of course, were not restricted to the street or the tavern, situations whose public nature ensured that there was at least a chance of them entering the historical record through the workings of judicial process. Out of sight, and by convention to a large extent beyond the purview of the courts, was a dark world of domestic violence in which wives, servants, children, and apprentices found themselves subjected to horrific abuse. As Gregory Smith has written, 'Hanoverian Britain was characterised by a high degree of ... private inter-personal violence, and, more importantly, a general toleration of such violence'.[29] Despite the many difficulties, wronged wives in particular were sometimes able at least to secure a hearing from justices of the peace, and the fact

BRITISH-ARMY VIOLENCE AGAINST CIVILIANS

that such individuals seem to have been hearing somewhere between two and three such cases each week suggests that the actual number of the sort of incident concerned must have been great indeed.[30] For all too many children of the lower classes, as well, life was an endless series of beatings and other acts of casual cruelty, with one young girl even being reported as having been thrown into a fire. To quote Smith again:

> The registers of the children admitted to the [Philanthropic] Society's care offer brief glimpses into the shocking circumstances of their young lives, and suggest that, for many desperately poor children on the margins of society, emotional and physical cruelty accompanied by neglect was not uncommon ... These children were able to escape the violence in their lives by the intervention of a charity. Other children were not so fortunate.[31]

To this dismal litany, there can, of course, be added the phenomenon of the riot. 'Certainly, when pushed too far, eighteenth-century English men and women, lacked neither courage nor initiative', wrote Dorothy Marshal in her pioneering *English People in the Eighteenth Century*. In her view, indeed, deference had definite limits. Thus

> And, if they took a modest idea of their rights, and demanded little beyond a roof for their heads, sufficient food to feed their bellies and clothes that would cover them, with a sauce of drink and idleness to give a relish to the monotony of life, when these things were jeopardised, their protests were vigorous enough.[32]

Throughout the eighteenth century and beyond, popular discontent therefore found expression in outbreaks of popular violence, or, at least, protest, whether the cause of these was the erection of turnpikes on important local roads (Kingswood in 1727); increases in the price of gin (London in 1736 and 1737); the spread of Methodism (Pendle in 1748); the formation of a new militia recruited by conscription (York, Beverley, Lincoln, Doncaster, Sheffield, Mansfield, Nottingham in 1757); the activities of the press-gang (Liverpool in 1759, 1762, and 1793); the introduction of new machinery that threatened the livelihood of textile workers (Shepton Mallet in 1776, Bolton in 1779, Bradford-on-Avon in

149

HARFLEUR TO HAMBURG

1791); the relaxation of discrimination against Catholics (London in 1780); hostility to sympathy for the French Revolution (Birmingham in 1791, Cambridge in 1792); the extension of the county militia system to Scotland (Tranent in 1797); and, over and over again, the soaring cost of bread (Falmouth in 1728, Penrhyn in 1737, Dewsbury and Newcastle-upon-Tyne in 1740, Sheffield and Taunton in 1756, Frome in 1757, Exeter, Birmingham, Nottingham, Norwich, and many other places in 1766).[33] Such outbursts were not always violent in the first instance, but opposition from the authorities, let alone attempts at repression, almost invariably led to serious trouble: the commonalty felt that they had both legitimate interests and a right to be heard. To quote John Stevenson:

> While there is no doubt that vicious and bitter violence could occur, it remains the case ... that many disturbances sought to inflict humiliation or exert pressure rather than indulge in indiscriminate bloodshed for its own sake. The attitude to property was similar ... What remains striking is less how often crowds turned to indiscriminate damage than how often they refrained from doing so.[34]

As, lamentably, in the twenty-first century, much public and private violence alike was linked to the excessive consumption of alcohol: in 1728, for example, one Joseph Barrett murdered his son in the course of a herculean drinking bout; in 1774, two Glasgow sisters named Margaret and Agnes Adam murdered a female neighbour named Janet MacIntyre while in drink; and in 1780, the initial aims of Lord George Gordon, the nobleman who summoned the anti-Catholic assembly from which sprang the riots that bear his name, were very soon at least partially submerged in a tidal wave of beer and gin.[35] By the time that the French Revolution broke out in 1789, the worst days of the appalling 'gin craze' were past, but things were still bad enough, not the least of the problems being that ale and liquor were often cheaper than beer. Amongst many concerned observers, drink was irrevocably associated with poverty and despair, and there were no doubt countless paupers who took whatever chance they could to drown their sorrows. Yet it was by no means as simple as that. Thus, since time immemorial,

150

excessive drinking had been one of the few ways that members of the lower classes had of demonstrating a measure of success within the parameters of their small world, whilst copious amounts of beer or gin were for many people a necessity if they were to get through day after day of labour as back-breaking as it was tedious in field, mill, or workshop. It was not, then, just the desperate who thronged the tavern and the gin-shop—the only venues, of course, where those excluded from respectable society were welcome— but also the employed and industrious, though, of course, too much indulgence on the part of the latter was all too likely to plunge them into the ranks of the former.[36] And, finally, drink was at the centre of many of the customs of lower-class life—one thinks here of wassailing, harvest suppers and the Irish 'wake'—an integral part of the political process as the chief means by which the crowd was treated at the hustings; and, finally, an expression of the cultures of both masculinity and British superiority over foppish 'frogs' and greasy 'dagos'; in the words of James Nicholls, 'Few people in Georgian England were sober in the sense that we would understand today, and the kind of freedom implicit in the act of getting drunk chimed with a certain model of individualistic liberty that underpinned [notions] of Englishness.'[37] Where society led, of course, the army followed: as Phillip Haythornthwaite has written, 'The consumption of alcohol was prodigious in the extreme.'[38]

Moving on, we come to robbery. In many of its aspects, this was clearly a normal part of the economy of the lower classes. While there were undoubtedly professional criminals in Georgian Britain, some of them very violent, the majority of crime against property was the work of men, women, and children facing destitution and even starvation who grabbed a cheese here, a chicken there, or a loaf somewhere else in order to get them through the next couple of days, or alternatively made off with items of limited value that they could either pawn or make use of themselves, generally clothing, tools, or domestic utensils. Such people were law-breakers, certainly, but they were in a different category altogether from such notorious underworld characters as Dick Turpin, almost invariably only turning to violence when they were cornered by constables or set upon by outraged householders. In the countryside, meanwhile, alongside the same sort of subsistence crime, there could be found other traditional practices that formed part of the same pattern, namely the poaching of rabbits and game-birds, the gleaning of mushrooms, berries, nuts, and firewood, and the sequestration of the odd farm animal. As to the argument that is being made here, it is devastatingly simple—namely that, in the eyes of the poor, necessity knew no law, a point driven home still further by the fact that indictments for petty crime invariably rose and fell in line with the cost of basic foodstuffs.[39]

Viewed in the context of all this, the issue of British-army violence in the Peninsular War appears in a new light. Thus, the campaigns in Spain and Portugal subjected the soldiers of Sir John Moore and the Duke of Wellington to strains that were all but unbearable: a war which must from the viewpoint of the rank and file have appeared as futile as it was endless; a theatre of operations characterized by harsh terrain, immense distances, and a climate that alternated between blazing heat and bitter cold; a supply system that could barely keep the men supplied even with the hopelessly inadequate rations to which they were entitled; a local populace who all too often came over as indifferent to their sufferings, if not downright hostile; a military hierarchy that could offer them little in the way of reward; a culture and society which were beyond their comprehension; a loss rate that led to the death of around one fifth of all the men who disembarked at Lisbon or, later, Santander; the list is endless. Faced by this situation, many redcoats responded in exactly the same way they would have done back home in the British Isles, seizing what they could to render their situation more bearable, revenging themselves on groups whom they regarded as being in some way responsible for their misery, and exploiting the temporary collapse of social control offered by such circumstances as the fall of Badajoz to engage in riot and revelry. There are complicating factors, true, including not least the fact that over half the British soldiers who fought in Spain and Portugal were not English, but rather Scottish, Irish, or even German, this last being something that cries out for further study. But it is nonetheless clear that it was not just muskets and bayonets that British aid transported to the Peninsula but an entire social *mentalité*. For all that, however, dreadful though the record of the Peninsular army frequently was away from the battlefields, the violence which it so often brought upon the heads of the unfortunate populace was anything but a weapon of war that was wielded by Wellington and his fellow commanders with deliberate attempt, but rather a phenomenon which they despised and sought to limit, if not wipe out altogether.[40]

9

'YOU HAVE NOT HAD A SUFFICIENT NUMBER KILLED AND WOUNDED'[1]
THE BALTIC CAMPAIGNS OF THE 'CRIMEAN' WAR, 1854–56

Andrew Lambert

After 1815, British policy towards Europe was shaped by anxieties about the national debt created in the Napoleonic conflict, the expansion of global trade, industrialisation, the challenge of radical politics, and the emerging impact of mass circulation media. Having endured 22 years of unlimited conflict, British decision-makers were anxious to avoid any resumption of such warfare in the near abroad. The so-called 'Crimean' War would be waged with restraint, diplomatic, economic, operational, and tactical, remaining a 'limited' conflict.[2] It would challenge long-held assumptions about the limited strategic value of British naval power on the continent, while reinforcing the consensus that Europe was a strategic risk, to be managed, rather than an opportunity. As a unique maritime-global hegemon, British interest in European conflicts was essentially negative. In 1814–15 Britain worked to 'order' Europe, which enabled it to balance critical areas of the continent from offshore. This ambition helps to explain why the Crimea was the only significant example of British violence

155

in Europe between Waterloo and the First World War.[3] Throughout the crisis and the war that followed, the Baltic remained the primary strategic theatre.

The Baltic campaigns of 1854 and 1855, and the public display of the fleet on St. George's Day 1856, emphasized the reality that this was the primary theatre of the 'Crimean' War. However, the campaigns were soon forgotten, because they witnessed little fighting, produced few casualties, and provided no examples of aristocratic incompetence, or mould-breaking roles for women. There was no great book about the Baltic, let alone memorable poetry... yet these campaigns, the culmination of a forty year 'cold war', dominated the next half century of Anglo-Russian relations.[4] Popular culture preferred sensation to strategy. Britain began preparing for conflict in the Baltic from 1702, when Russia acquired a coast on the Gulf of Finland.

The British approach to Europe might be described as a combination of 'Offshore Balancing' and 'Ordering', using diplomatic, naval and economic power to shape an international order that it could sustain with minimal intervention because it had the consent of a majority of the great powers. This consent was usually secured by negotiation at peace conferences. As a global maritime power, Britain used this approach to counter the aims of proto-hegemonic continental powers, notably Imperial Russia, Bourbon, and Bonapartist France. This approach sustained Britain's great power status by exploiting the unique building blocks of national power, insularity, sea-based national security, maritime economic power, and extra-European resources. From the early sixteenth century, English/British statesmen understood that they could not control continental Europe, even the strategically critical Scheldt Estuary.[5] This would require co-operation with major European powers to restrain potential hegemons, preserving the balanced state system Britain had worked for at Vienna in 1815, and avoid binding continental military commitments in peace time.[6] British strategic choices reduced the need for land operations in Europe, large-scale land battles, and the risk of brutalizing civilians.

The American concept of 'Offshore Balancing' emerged in the late 1990s, as an alternative to 'Preponderance', securing hegemony

THE BALTIC CAMPAIGNS OF THE 'CRIMEAN' WAR, 1854–56

through the large-scale overseas deployments of military force in Western Europe, Japan, South Korea, and elsewhere. By definition, 'offshore balancing' is only relevant for insular or quasi-insular powers, who can exploit the asymmetric advantages that accrue from command of the sea. As Christopher Layne argued:

> Insular great powers are substantially less likely to be affected by instability than are states that face geographically proximate rivals… In multi-polar systems, insular great powers have a much broader range of strategic choices than less fortunately placed powers. Because their strategic interdependence is low, they can avoid being entrapped by alliance commitments, and need worry little about being abandoned by actual or potential allies. Offshore great powers also have the choice of staying out of great power wars altogether or of limiting their involvement—a choice unavailable to states that live in dangerous neighbourhoods in which rivals lurk nearby.[7]

Layne assumed post-1815 Britain had been a hegemonic power.[8] However, the diminutive British Army of 1854–6 suggests this is incorrect. As Lord Acton stressed in 1894, 'A fleet with an army is an instrument of militarism. A fleet without an army is not'.[9] Britain had not maintained a continental army in peacetime. It struggled to find 25,000 troops to fight Russia in 1854, and a year later had hardly doubled that strength. Acquiring a proto-hegemonic army in 1916–18 made Britain a continental power, with serious economic and diplomatic consequences that emphasised the wisdom of nineteenth century decision-makers, their choices disciplined by the crippling financial legacy of an earlier 'Great War'.

While 'Offshore Balancing' might meet American needs in the twenty-first century, Britain had always been too close to Europe, and too weak, to impose balance; for that it would need a powerful military ally or allies. It was able to stay out of many European conflicts, the Franco-Prussian War of 1870–71 being a key example, because overt deterrence had secured the core aim, the integrity and independence of Belgium, before the war began.[10] It is significant that the American debate, like nineteenth-century British decision-making, has been driven by economic realities.[11]

157

American political scientists largely ignored the response of continental powers that do not wish to be 'balanced'. These responses would also be asymmetric, reflecting continental security concerns. Continental powers often counter maritime balancing by naval arms racing, challenging the legal basis of maritime strategy, attempting to close land-locked seas like the Baltic and Black Sea, and countering maritime economic power, building strategic land communications, notably Russia's Trans-Siberian Railway and the contemporary Chinese One Belt One Road. In war, they have seized critical naval bases and economic access points from the land. In 1807, Napoleon briefly occupied the strategic harbour at Lisbon, to exclude British trade from Iberia. Britain sent an amphibious army to recover the port, and pre-empted him at Copenhagen.

For Britain, 'Offshore Balancing' was never an alternative to continental 'preponderance'; it was the only option that might sustain Britain's great power status. Defeating the Spanish Armada in 1588 turned this approach into a quasi-religious element of national identity. Balancing multi-polar European systems helped ensure insular security, maritime dominion, and economic advantage. The policy was re-active.

When Napoleon abdicated in April 1814, the first thought of Prime Minister Lord Liverpool was to leave the continent as soon as the system could be balanced, leaving a small British army in France and Belgium until the strategic border had been secured, and France was ready to rejoin a multi-polar system. He balanced France out of Antwerp and the Scheldt Estuary, reducing the risk of invasion, and attacks on British shipping. At the same time, Britain worked with France and Austria to balance Russian attempts to dominate post-war continental politics. Napoleon's return in 1815 threatened Britain's hard-won balance. The Government acted decisively, providing subsidies to revive the Four Power alliance, and rushing troops to Belgium. Waterloo preserved the Congress of Vienna balance, and with that Britain's freedom from continental commitments.[12]

Proto-hegemonic powers have attempted to exclude offshore balancers from 'their' continent, to avoid being 'balanced'. Rome solved this problem by annihilating Carthage, the contemporary

THE BALTIC CAMPAIGNS OF THE 'CRIMEAN' WAR, 1854–56

'offshore balancing' power, in a conflict of unparalleled savagery. The British were well aware of this example, Napoleon thought it an insult to call them 'Carthaginians'.[13] At the height of their power and influence, the British demobilized their army, and paid off most of the fleet, ensuring no one would think they were seeking hegemony, other than at sea.

While Britain relied on command of the sea to protect the home islands, overseas possessions, and oceanic trade routes, British strategic culture was strikingly offensive. It focussed on the ability to command the sea in any conflict, destroy enemy naval bases and coastal cities, clear their commerce from the ocean, and impose economic blockades. The ability to defeat rival great powers through the asymmetric use of sea power made Britain a great power, and shaped the post-1815 development of technologically advanced maritime offensive strategies, based on those that had been effective against France and the United States between 1803 and 1814. These strategies were shaped by the reality that Britain might be obliged to act without allies, when it would have to rely on the offensive component of sea power to counter terrestrial threats. Command of the sea would enable Britain to fight prolonged limited wars at relatively low cost.

After 1815, the strategic impact of sea power was refined by industrial technologies, including steam propulsion, explosive shells, and rifled artillery that enhanced the offensive power of naval forces. The local threat posed by the French fortified naval base at Cherbourg prompted the development of a new concept, a 'Cherbourg Strategy' using steam gunboats to destroy hostile naval bases. This operational development reflected Britain's focus on deterrence over war fighting, preferring stability and peace in Europe while it pursued commercial expansion in the wider world, not least in response to rising European tariff barriers.

In the absence of a first-class army, British strategy would counter strategic threats by launching an asymmetric counter-stroke at an enemy's most vulnerable point. British statesmen recognized the best defence of Turkey against Russian aggression involved threatening Cronstadt and St. Petersburg. By contrast, the strategic culture of Imperial Russia drew strength from the geographic heart of the

159

state. Major western invasions of Russia were defeated deep inside Russian territory, where advantages of surprise or superior fighting power were negated by casualties, poor logistics, and an adverse climate. Threatening or attacking the Baltic coast enabled Britain to deal with Russia.

Britain was never a preponderant power in the international system, merely a relatively weak state exploiting asymmetric economic and strategic leverage. British 'Offshore Balancing' reflected weakness, not choice, and the concept should be used with care. Too close to Europe to stand aside, lacking the manpower to shape the near abroad, it worked the 1814–15 settlements, including the Peace of Ghent with the United States, to balance Europe, and preserve British interests and strategic advantages, critically the legal basis of maritime economic warfare.

Britain had long used the mobilization or movement of fleets to reinforce diplomatic communication. These deployments targeted the weak points of rival powers, rather than the location at issue. British fleets were mobilized for the Baltic when Russia attacked the Ottoman Empire, and Afghanistan, because St. Petersburg, the imperial capital, was critical to the regime's credibility. The naval threat obliged Russian rulers, from Peter the Great onward, to transform nearby Kotlin Island into Cronstadt, the world's largest naval fortress.

British policy in the peace process of 1814–15 has been described as 'Ordering' the system to support British interests. Recognizing Russia as a threat to the stability of the post-Napoleonic European system, Foreign Secretary Lord Castlereagh 'ordered' the post-war system to enable it to be sustained by 'offshore balancing', while seeking alternative supplies of critical naval stores that Russia had used as an economic weapon in the previous century. For Castlereagh, the greatest threat to British power would be an alliance between France and Russia, the second- and third-ranking naval powers, something he made explicit in the 'Two Power' naval standard. At the same time, Castlereagh refused to allow maritime belligerent rights, the basis of British strategy, to be discussed at Vienna, or Ghent. This repeated the British position in 1801, when Liverpool had been Foreign Secretary.

THE BALTIC CAMPAIGNS OF THE 'CRIMEAN' WAR, 1854–56

The key to diplomatic tension or conflict with Russia, which emerged as the dominant military power on the continent in 1814, was secure access to the Baltic. Since the early eighteenth century, British fleets had entered the Baltic to protect British economic interests, mostly the trade in shipbuilding stores, timber, flax, hemp, pitch, and tar, without which British ships, naval and mercantile, could not be built or operated. Russian rulers exploited this dependence to influence British policy. Catherine II and Czar Paul had created Leagues of Armed Neutrality in 1780 and 1801 to demand Britain abandon the hard-line economic warfare policies that formed the backbone of national strategy, and threatened to exclude British ships from the enclosed sea.[14] These plans, along with those of Napoleon and Czar Alexander in 1807, were thwarted by rapid naval or amphibious operations. These offensive operations enabled Britain to command the Baltic and block Russian exports, which devastated an economy kept liquid by foreign sales of forest products and pig iron. By 1811, the Anglo-French economic war had obliged Czar Alexander to break with Napoleon. Russian leaders understood the 'Continental System' would 'undermine the financial and economic bases of Russia's position as an independent power', enabling Napoleon to push Russia back into Asia, and control the Baltic coast, shutting down Russia's export trade.[15] When France demanded Russia live up to the terms of the Treaty of Tilsit, the Czar preferred a war with Napoleon to economic struggle with Britain.

British statesmen understood that access to the Baltic would be essential to restrain Russian aggression in Europe or Asia. Naval control enabled effective economic warfare, an asymmetric response. Castlereagh and his Cabinet colleagues changed the tariff system to privilege Canadian forest products; by 1854, Britain no longer depended on Russian exports.[16]

The Russian reaction to Scandinavian neutrality was hostile, rejecting all attempts to improve trade with Britain. In 1836 Alexei Orlov, the minister responsible for internal security, claimed the British were preparing a naval attack on Cronstadt, like the one that had destroyed Copenhagen in 1807.[17] This concern was echoed by the Czar's strategic advisor, Baron Jomini, who expected Britain would use sea power, an asymmetric advantage, to destabilize the

European system. Anxiety about naval power led Russia to claim that territorial waters extended 12 miles from the shore. Most other states, including Britain, were content with 3 miles, the extreme range of heavy cannon. Anglo-Russian relations were further complicated by clashes at the Bosphorus, in Persia and Central Asia.[18] Britain was well-informed about the Baltic before 1854; all it needed was a suitable fleet.

Wartime experience enhanced the Royal Navy's ability to operate in the Baltic, and challenge Russian assumptions of regional dominance. That expertise would be developed over the next four decades, as industrial technologies altered the balance of strategic and economic advantage between Britain and Russia; steam-powered warships enabling fleets to operate more effectively against forts.[19] Russia feared a British attack on St. Petersburg.[20] As the balance of geo-strategic advantage shifted the fortress at Cronstadt was reinforced, the mobile Royal Navy and a fixed Cronstadt represented strategic and cultural identities of Britain and Russia.

After 1815, Russian strategists concentrated on defending an extended European empire, notably the Polish and Finnish *glacis*, keeping Sweden quiet under the 'Policy of 1812', and encouraging Denmark, a client, to close the Straits against the British. However, the economic importance of British Baltic trade meant that any attempt to close the sea would have caused a war.

Britain responded by adjusting tariffs, to reduce the dependence on strategic Baltic products that had necessitated major campaigns between 1807 and 1812. Baltic timber and naval stores were replaced by Canadian produce. By 1820, the Baltic had become a major offensive opportunity rather than a strategic weakness. Britain's post-war Baltic policy was dominated by the requirement for unfettered commercial and naval access, enabling it to challenge Russian regional hegemony. The Royal Navy's Hydrographic Office improved British understanding of Baltic navigation, the key to any offensive operations in the shallow rock-studded sea. Information lay at the heart of British war-planning, the Hydrographer leading the Navy's planning section. Anglo-Russian relations reached a low point in 1833–4, with Russian troops occupying Istanbul, and Russian diplomacy attempting to undermine British policy in Belgium,

THE BALTIC CAMPAIGNS OF THE 'CRIMEAN' WAR, 1854–56

Portugal, and Spain. Lord Palmerston, the Foreign Secretary, seized the initiative, encouraging Swedish and Danish neutrality. Confident liberalism would triumph over reaction, Palmerston was delighted to report: 'Sweden and Denmark have formally declared that in the event of a rupture between us and Russia, they would be *neutral*; this is all we want'.[21] Neutrality ensured the Royal Navy could enter the Baltic, in peace and war. Palmerston saw Sweden as the key to ending Russian domination of the Baltic, a judgement that informed his policy during the Crimean War. Britain had recognized the projected fortress and naval base at Bomarsund in the Åland Islands would restrain Sweden, and support Russian attempts to seize the Danish Narrows.

In March 1853, at a critical stage in 'Holy Places' Crisis, Russia would demand a protectorate over the Sultan's Christian subjects. This posed an existential threat to the Ottoman Empire. Foreign Secretary Lord John Russell advised sending a fleet to the Baltic to emphasize the seriousness of the situation. Nothing was done.[22] Russell's colleagues assumed post-1815 political, economic, and strategic developments had transformed the balance of power in their favour, while hardly anyone expressed a desire for war with Russia. They thought France had created the problem, and were unwilling to align themselves with the new regime in Paris. Furthermore, French and Russian challenges to the 1815 settlement had been resolved without violence. Avoiding European wars enabled defence cuts, and promoted trade. In the spring of 1853, the 'Holy Places' appeared to be merely another flare-up of the long running 'Eastern Crisis', settling the future of the Ottoman Empire, something that would be resolved by diplomacy. However, the issues raised were unusually important to all involved. Britain wanted to preserve the Ottoman Empire as a trade partner; France looked to enhance the prestige of the new Bonapartist regime, and religious concerns prompted the Czar's aggressive slavophile nationalism, while the continued existence of the Sultanate focused Ottoman decision-making. The Ottomans declared war in October 1853.

The British elite's confidence in liberalism and progress shaped their response to the crisis. Despite a war on the Danube from October, ministers delayed mobilizing the armed forces, to avoid

163

unnecessary expense. Forty years of successful crisis management made them confident a great power conflict could be avoided. Nowhere was this confidence more obvious than in the appointment of a commander-in-chief for the Baltic fleet. The standing Mediterranean fleets of Britain and France had already taken control of the Black Sea, but there were no other fleets that could be sent to the Baltic. Although the Admiralty began assembling ships, and selected an admiral in the autumn of 1853, the Cabinet only approved the appointment of Vice Admiral Sir Charles Napier (1786–1860) on 9 February 1854, and delayed the official announcement for another two weeks, despite the Anglo-French ultimatum for Russia to evacuate the Principalities expiring on 27 March. Napier had a stellar record as a skilful fighting commander stretching back to the Napoleonic conflict. His timely application of violence had solved complex diplomatic problems in Portugal and Syria, earning the admiration of Lord Palmerston. As a radical Liberal and former MP, Napier was the obvious symbol of 'British' power and progress for the 'liberal' Whig/Peelite coalition Government. He was on good terms with John Delane, editor of the dominant *Times,* acting as his correspondent in the Baltic fleet.[23]

On 7 March, three days before he sailed, Napier was feted at the Reform Club, spiritual home of British Liberalism. Lord Palmerston and Sir James Graham, respectively Home Secretary and First Lord of the Admiralty, made highly politicized speeches praising the liberal hero, lacking the decorum many expected with war imminent. Graham emphasized the fact that both senior admirals afloat were members of the Reform. The occasion so unbalanced the judgement of the ministers that some in the audience assumed they were drunk. By contrast, Napier tried to limit the expectations of an audience that anticipated easy victory in a war between progress and reaction. His failure to offer suitably uplifting sentiments led the *Times* to craft their own: 'Sir C Napier is sent out to do all the harm he can to the Russians, and a dozen or two ships of the line and a few fortresses battered to pieces, and several thousand killed or wounded will be the probable—and indeed the wished for result', claiming Napier had promised to 'be in Cronstadt or in Hell' within the month. This was pure invention. Napier knew his small, newly mobilized fleet lacked vital equipment for coastal offensive operations, it could not strike early blows. He promised to do his best, but urged his audience not to expect miracles.[24]

A sense of what British liberals anticipated was captured in George Butler Earp's contemporary account of the campaign.[25] Dispatching a fleet would keep the Russian fleet locked up, although few expected the Russians would risk combat. It would also support diplomacy: extending the coalition, and encouraging rebellion all along Russia's Baltic coast. However, the Government's failure to provide steam gunboats, mortar vessels, war rockets, and troops left Napier's battleships unable to approach, let alone attack the Russian coast defences. Earp attributed this failure to unwarranted confidence that the appearance of a fleet would encourage Sweden, Prussia, and Austria to join a grand alliance against Russia.[26] Sending a fully equipped fleet, and securing an early success would, in Earp's (and Napier's) judgement, be essential to creating that coalition.

> It was in not adopting this course that we failed from the outset and throughout the whole war, and were, in the end compelled to patch up an inconclusive peace. Our national means were abundant, had they been rightly directed; but in place of so directing them as to attach the German powers to us, those means could not have been better diverted had our object been to detach them from us-and in this we succeeded...
>
> Had the Allies confined themselves to securing the integrity of Turkey, and directed their main strength to the Baltic, nothing could have saved Russia.

Earp found the proof of his case in the speed with which Russia accepted terms in January 1856, when a naval force capable of assaulting Cronstadt/St. Petersburg was ready. Until then, the German courts, led by Russian-dominated Prussia, believed Russia had little to fear from the Royal Navy, encouraging Austria to stand aside from the Anglo-French coalition.[27] Furthermore the essential Swedish alliance hinged on Austria joining the allies.[28] Ultimately Earp believed the war had been waged in the wrong place, attacking a secondary maritime flank when the enemy's capital was exposed.[29] This ignored the critical role of asymmetry in British strategy.

165

There were sound 'liberal' reasons for delaying mobilization—the influence of small-state economic radicals, followers of Richard Cobden and John Bright. They had secured the repeal of the Corn Laws and Navigation Acts, powerful instruments of national strategic power abandoned to provide cheap bread, in the belief that increased trade would end international conflict. Lord Aberdeen's Cabinet depended on radical votes. The radicals also urged changing the legal basis of economic warfare, the basis focus of naval strategy, to reduce the cost of the Royal Navy. When Cobden took his ideas to Russia, they were greeted with the wry amusement usually accorded to impractical monomaniacs. Czarist economics were protectionist, aware that Free Trade would promote liberalism in Russia.

The radicals urged the need to insulate private property from seizure in wartime, their own private property it should be noted, and espoused the pacifism of Dissenting Christianity, anticipating perpetual peace. They believed war was a moral stain on the nation, and feared it would enhance the power of the British aristocracy.[30] Such views reflected their confidence that Russian troops would not reach Manchester. The radicals turned against the Government in December 1854, joining a wartime critique of aristocratic incompetence, promoting the virtues of middle-class men and methods. In 1856, Cobden attacked the legal basis of maritime blockade, which he compared to the Corn Laws. His arguments achieved a brief popularity before cynical realists like Disraeli demolished the illusion of perpetual peace.[31]

This war remained limited because the allies agreed a set of war aims that emphasized restoring the 1815 European system and preserving the Ottoman Empire. Britain and France renounced territorial ambitions to stress the moral basis of their actions, in the 'just war' tradition, adjusting war aims to encourage wider participation, seeking the sanction of Europe. When the Cabinet discussed strategy, Chancellor of the Exchequer William Gladstone considered the intervention of Austria 'morally necessary' to their cause, conveying the 'judgement of Europe' against Russian aggression.[32] This approach, which had wider traction, may have influenced the decision to attack a purely military target, the naval base at Sevastopol, rather than a regional economic centre like Odessa.

166

THE BALTIC CAMPAIGNS OF THE 'CRIMEAN' WAR, 1854–56

After the horrors of total war in the Napoleonic era limiting war was attractive—although limitation was restricted to conflicts with other 'civilized' peoples. The restraints in place during this war were generic tropes of European Christianity, which it was widely assumed were not applicable to extra-European conflicts. All three major combatants had experience of colonial/imperial warfare, where different standards were accepted. Contemporary British culture, suffused with quasi-romantic concepts of honour, propriety, and gentlemanly behaviour, abhorred violence against non-combatants, the wounded, and prisoners, as morally repugnant. They expected gentlemanly officers to control the use of force, even as they exhorted their men to fight.

Russian behaviour on the Crimean battlefields was frequently held up as immoral, wounded soldiers shooting British stretcher parties after the Battle of the Alma, some dubious use of flags of truce including the *Cossack* incident in the Baltic, ending with the Russian decision to leave sick and wounded men in wrecked hospitals when Sevastopol was evacuated. While Russian soldiers were frequently described as 'barbarians', or 'Asiatic', their officers were considered honourable, unless they violated the code. It helped that many Russian officers spoke French or German.

As essentially naval campaigns, the only moral outrage generated by the war in the Baltic concerned the capture of Finnish merchant shipping, and the destruction of Finnish property, largely shipbuilding materials and vessels on the stocks that were thought to be gunboats.[33]

At the strategic level, the allies adopted a British approach, using naval and amphibious power to destroy Russian naval forces and impose an economic blockade, while supporting allies and potential allies, including Sweden-Norway; extending the coalition also had a moral dimension.

This was a war against the instruments of Russian aggression, not Russian civilians, very few of whom would be caught up in the restrained use of violence. There were no Finnish civilians at Sweaborg in August 1855, only Russian military personnel, who had ample time to evacuate their families. Russian casualty figures for that operation were implausibly low, reflecting a wider propaganda effort to downplay the defeat. The Finns did not believe them. Those of the allies were restricted to wounds; there were no fatalities, which greatly reduced the interest of the London media. Yet without a heavy 'butcher's bill' to linger over press and public alike assumed the action had not been 'serious', or interesting. The contrast with the 'Charge of the Light Brigade' is telling. William Howard Russell's original dispatch grossly inflated the casualties, because he assumed the initial muster of survivors was complete, when most of the men were still making their way back up the valley on foot, or with wounded horses, while others had been captured. The casualties were strikingly low, but by then Lord Tennyson had published a poetic response, which he knew to be incorrect, and it endured. Contemporary culture, fascinated by heroism and heroic sacrifice, had been shocked by the realities of war on land, and appalled to realize that most soldiers died of disease, as they had in every previous conflict. This war would generate an obsession with sanitation rather than violence.

The Baltic and the war

The primacy of the Baltic in the strategy of the 'Crimean' War should be obvious. It contained the capital city of the Russian Empire, the main fleet and major trading ports, including those in Finland, and part of Poland. Furthermore, Russian influence on other regional powers, Sweden, Denmark, and Prussia had turned the enclosed sea into a Russian lake. At the operational level, the allied ultimatum to Russia was timed to expire when the Baltic ice broke up, enabling the British to enter the sea before Russian naval bases in the Gulf of Finland were free of ice.

As the Holy Places crisis deepened in 1853, the Assistant Hydrographer, Captain John Washington, travelled to St. Petersburg, by way of Sweden and Finland, ostensibly to discuss lifeboat stations. In reality he would report on the Russian fleet, naval bases and coastal fortresses, including Bomarsund. Washington wrote the war plan for the Baltic early the following year. He emphasized an early attack on the Russian battle squadron that normally over-wintered at Reval (Tallinn) and capturing Bomarsund. Reval, one of three Russian Naval bases in the Gulf of Finland, would be ice-free before Cronstadt and Sweaborg. Nelson had planned the operation during his 1801 Baltic campaign: the Russians may have known that, moving the Reval squadron the previous autumn. The hydrographer appointed Captain Bartholomew Sulivan as Baltic Fleet Surveying Officer, effectively Chief of Staff (Plans), working closely with the commander-in-chief in both campaigns. Charting key areas of the Russian and Finnish coasts and planning offensive operations, Sulivan found ways to outflank the fixed defences of Bomarsund, Sweaborg, and Cronstadt, demonstrating the central role of the coastal offensive in British strategy.

The Reval plan explains why the Baltic fleet sailed earlier than expected in 1854. Reports reached London that the sea ice was breaking up. Sir Charles Napier cancelled the operation on 25 March, just as his fleet entered the Baltic, when HMS *Miranda* reported Reval harbour was empty.[34]

Without the Reval option, Napier was left to visit Stockholm, plan for an economic blockade, and investigate Åland. The Government hoped that offering the islands to Sweden would secure an alliance, Sweden providing the gunboats and troops needed to support the British fleet in further offensives. The Swedish King, Oscar I rejected the offer, to avoid earning the undying enmity of Russia. After his second set-back Napier sailed east to inspect the Russian and Finnish coasts. Over-zealous British raids in the Gulf of Bothnia caused complaints in Finland and Britain, destroying large quantities of shipbuilding materials, much of it already purchased by British merchants. This campaign came to a dramatic conclusion on 19 June when the steam warships *Vulture* and *Odin* sent over 200 Royal Marines and sailors into the harbour of a small Finnish town in the north of the Gulf of Bothnia, then known by the Swedish name Gamla Carleby, today Finnish Kokkola, with orders to destroy 'gunboats' and timber stores. Ambushed and driven off by Russian and Finnish troops, backed by local militia, the British lost fifty men killed, wounded, or captured, along with a boat, a flag, and gun. The gun, a military trophy, was sent to St. Petersburg, to show how the Empire was being defended. Nine British sailors were buried in the local cemetery. Their bullet-holed boat is the centrepiece of the 'English Park'.[35] Finnish casualties were minimal.

The battle at Kokkola was the exception in a series of otherwise unopposed coastal raids. Not only were Finnish casualties in these Bothnian raids generally negligible, but the consideration shown for private property, and the interests of the local people, demonstrate that British sailors understood the rules, formal or otherwise, of war, together with the distinction to be drawn between the local populace and the Russian government. One contemporary estimate of the value of the materials destroyed reached £365,000.[36] British merchants were still trying to recover their losses from the Government in 1858.

After Kokkola the British shifted their attention to Bomarsund. In late May Napier sent Sulivan to examine Åland, where he earned the gratitude of local people by supplying Bibles in their language.[37] He also secured the essential intelligence about the fort, and found a viable passage for steamships into the central anchorage of Lumpar Bay through the Angosound, a channel the Russians had failed to guard, and spent a few hours sketching Bomarsund from a distance of 2,500 yards. Sulivan rejoined Napier on 10 June with a thorough report that emphasized the need to demolish new structures that had just been started. It would require a regular siege using 10,000 men.

Napier had inspected the Baltic coast, reporting the Russian fleet was securely blockaded in the Gulf of Finland. He could not attack Cronstadt without gunboats, mortars and rockets, and the Russian fleet would not come out to fight. Similarly, Sweaborg (outside modern Helsinki) would require heavy guns and troops, close range attacks by battleships were impossible from the intricacy of the navigation, and overwhelming defensive firepower. Well-aware that merely maintaining a blockade would be unpopular at home, Napier urged the newly arrived French Admiral to land 10,000 allied sailors and marines on Åland. Admiral Parseval Deschenes refused, being anxious to appear off St. Petersburg. The allies found the Russians had anchored their ships to reinforce the fixed defences of Cronstadt. They had no intention of offering battle to the smaller, but more capable allied force.

On 18 June the British Cabinet belatedly agreed to carry a French army of 10,000 men to take Bomarsund. On 23 July Sulivan piloted four coast assault battleships and a frigate through the Angosound,

THE BALTIC CAMPAIGNS OF THE 'CRIMEAN' WAR, 1854–56

isolating Bomarsund from the rest of the island, and securing an excellent beach to land troops and heavy artillery. What followed was little more than a clearing operation. Bomarsund, like most sea forts, was relatively weak on the land side, while sending so many troops made success inevitable. After a bombardment by ships and naval guns mounted in shore batteries the fortress surrendered on 16 August. Isolated by naval power, it was easily taken by a superior amphibious force. When Sweden rejected the allied offer to transfer the islands, the fortress had to be demolished. One section was used as a target by a British coast assault battleship, which smashed the walls with concentrated broadsides at 500 yards. The symbolism of a British battleship giving the *coup de grace* to the Russian fort should not be missed.

Throughout the siege Napier left a screen of cruisers off Cronstadt, while the allied battlefleet waited over the horizon, just in case the Russians tried to relieve Bomarsund. This was a faint hope, Russia let the fortress fall.

News of Napier's success received a decidedly mixed response. While naval professionals were impressed, the press took a very different line. First Sea Lord Admiral Sir Maurice Berkeley observed:

> Your work, and the work of your fellow-labourers, has been done admirably. Some of the newspapers are not satisfied because you have not had a sufficient number killed and wounded, while the whole government are pleased beyond measure at your trifling loss, and may well praise your skill and DISCRETION in having succeeded in striking the first blow at so small a sacrifice.[38]

The Russian response to Bomarsund was to abandon every small, isolated fortress that was exposed to allied amphibious power. Russian troops hurriedly destroyed the forts at Hango Head when allied ships steamed past, removed cannon from other small coastal positions, and redoubled their efforts to improve the three major fortresses, Reval, Sweaborg, and above all Cronstadt.

At this point the development of British Baltic strategy was interrupted by problems elsewhere, and a breakdown of civil military relations. As the Bomarsund operation began, Sir James Graham, the First Lord of the Admiralty, hoped for more dramatic successes.

171

He wanted Napier to attack the much stronger works at Sweaborg. Lacking the political courage to issue public orders, he insinuated his ideas into his private correspondence, hoping the veteran Admiral would act without official instructions. In the event of failure Napier, not Graham, would be blamed. Graham had violated the time-honoured method of directing strategy from London. Official orders were issued by the Cabinet to attack Sevastopol, despite the known opposition of the British army and Navy commanders on the spot. A week later Graham suggested attacks on Abö (Turku) or Reval, while sharing the concerns of his senior naval advisor to bring the fleet home before the weather deteriorated. These private letters were in stark contrast to Admiralty orders urging caution that arrived in the same mail. Graham's attempt to manipulate Napier into actions the Admiralty Board had expressly opposed shattered relations between Napier, Graham and the Board. The resulting public dispute would overshadow the achievements of the campaign. The sudden change in Graham's private letters reflected growing demand for action.

The newspapers judged Bomarsund a trifling event, because the casualties were so low. Bomarsund had not satisfied the blood-lust of a public starved of major wars for a generation. The Crimean campaign produced far more human suffering. As the press complained some of Napier's Captains were equally disappointed—they expected to conduct a major war against a great power in the same fast paced, aggressive manner that Britain had dealt with pirates, slavers and extra-European states. Sulivan, who understood the realties of the campaign, was entirely satisfied with Napier's methods. Relations between Napier and the Admiralty reached a crisis in late September, when erroneous reports that Sevastopol had fallen to a *coup de main* reached London. Graham imagined something similar could be done at Sweaborg, despite the sickly French troops returning home from Åland, and his own failure to provide any of the coastal attack vessels Napier had repeatedly requested. He urged a close-range attack by battleships, mentioned in the private letters of two hot-headed young Captains. Napier, who had attacked many coastal forts across his long career, knew Sweaborg was far too strong for the fleet under his command. His views were unpalatable in London, especially as reports of the fall

THE BALTIC CAMPAIGNS OF THE 'CRIMEAN' WAR, 1854–56

of Sevastopol proved false. Mounting disappointment at home only increased pressure on Graham: his political instinct was to shift the blame to Napier, who he had appointed only six months earlier. Napier was rewarded for a successful, largely bloodless campaign with an order to strike his flag. This disgraceful act overshadowed the Baltic campaigns, prompting generations of historians to ignore or underestimate their significance.

Graham finally ordered twenty of the steam gunboats and mortar vessels Napier had requested in October, along with five iron armoured floating batteries designed to engage coastal forts. The initial plan for the Baltic campaign of 1855 included a significant force of British troops, but the disastrous winter in the Crimea shifted priorities. Neither Britain nor France sent any troops in 1855. Instead, an entirely steam powered British fleet, supported by a small French squadron that arrived later in the season, re-imposed the blockade, and maintained it throughout the campaign, undermining the Russian economy by blocking the export of bulky products like timber and grain and the import of advanced weapons and technologies.

Russia did not protest the blockade because it was imposed under long-standing internationally agreed legal rules, which the British had refused to discuss at Ghent and Vienna in 1814–15. The intent was to deny the Russian state the revenues generated by export trades. It impacted civilian traders to deny Russia the funds it needed to wage war. The Baltic was the main source of Russian exports. The impact of the Baltic blockade was primarily a question of blocking Russian exports—like oil and gas since 2022—to weaken the state revenue stream. Perceived as a relatively benign measure designed to impact the Russian treasury, not the populace generally, it did reduce employment, contributing to a spate of bread riots and conscription protests in 1855 that challenged Russia's ability to sustain the conflict. State censorship deprived public opinion of an outlet, but the Czarist police state was well aware of popular unrest, which was discussed by at the Czar's Crown Council meeting that agreed to accept the allied peace terms. As Richard Connolly observed, Russia's political economy has been defined by 'an excessive focus on security, a dominant state, and a weak market'.[39]

173

The blockade made neutrality profitable for Prussia, which smuggled goods into and out of Russia, until the British threatened to include Prussian ports in the blockade in early 1856. This prompted Berlin to advise St. Petersburg to make peace. Austria was pleased by Allied action that re-opened the Danube for trade, and intervened to remove Russia from the Danubian Principalities. Vienna was keen to limit the war, and Britain was happy to oblige, because Austrian actions could be seen as a moral judgement on Russian aggression. Limited war avoided forcing the German Powers to choose a side. While their threat to join the coalition in 1856 shifted the balance and put pressure on Russia to concede, both were anxious to avoid being caught up in a wider war.

Hardly a life was lost on the blockade until a controversial violent incident on 5 June 1855. Boats from the steam corvette HMS *Cossack* landed near Hango Head on the south coast of Finland, to return Finnish seamen whose ships had been captured. As they walked along the jetty, they were fired on by Russian soldiers; five men were killed, two of them Finns. Most of the British sailors surrendered, and one escaped to warn the ship. The incident caused outrage in London, but on closer inspection it proved more complicated. *Cossack*'s signal requesting to land under a flag of truce had not been acknowledged, so the British should not have landed, nor should they have stowed rifles in the boat, loaded or not. The Russians were entitled to reject a request, but not to ignore it and then shoot men landing under such a flag. They could have warned off the boat. Unbeknownst to the British, the Russian Minister of War had restricted the use of flags of truce to Cronstadt, Reval, and Sweaborg, alleging, with some foundation, that the British were abusing the system to spy on Russian defences.[40]

The blockade worked well in 1855: attempts to carry Belgian and American rifles and machinery through Prussia were thwarted by diplomatic intelligence. The new commander-in-chief, Admiral Sir Richard Dundas, a cautious officer with limited experience, was expected to follow orders. He relied on Sulivan, who guided him to Sweaborg, and then Cronstadt, where Sulivan's ship ran into a Russian minefield. The mines, too small to cause serious damage, were easily swept. When part of the coast assault force arrived, without the

THE BALTIC CAMPAIGNS OF THE 'CRIMEAN' WAR, 1854–56

armoured batteries, in mid-summer Sulivan persuaded Dundas to attempt a long-range bombardment of Sweaborg dockyard, which housed an important Russian gunboat flotilla. The attack would combine rifled artillery, mortars, and rockets with steam-powered flotilla craft, using hydrographic expertise to solve the classic strategic problem of destroying an enemy fleet that hid behind shore defences. These developments had focussed on the French naval base at Cherbourg, occupying a threatening strategic position on the English Channel, but the concept was equally applicable to Russian and American bases. Sulivan placed the bombarding vessels at extreme range. Just after midnight on 9 August the attack began, sixteen British and five French mortar vessels firing, supported by a small French mortar battery on an offshore islet. At a range of over 3,000 yards (3,500 metres) from the forts, the mortar vessels were beyond the effective range of Russian artillery. They were screened by the steam gunboats, which laid down a heavy covering fire on the Russian defences, avoiding damage by remaining underway. Two British gunboats armed with Lancaster rifled cannon drove a Russian battleship from its moorings in the main channel leading up to Helsingfors (Helsinki). During the short northern nights mortars and guns were replaced by rocket fire. The attack continued until the 11 August, by which time the dockyard and gunboat flotilla had been destroyed, and a major powder magazine had exploded. The defences remained largely untouched because the allies had no need to engage them. The allies fired 6,000 mortar shells. No allied servicemen were killed, and remarkably few wounded. The only problem was rapid degradation of the mortars, which became unserviceable. There were no spare barrels. After the war, Russia admitted that six battleships, two frigates, and a corvette had been destroyed, and 250 men killed and wounded. They were less forthcoming about the damage to the base. The Finns thought the Russian casualty figures absurdly low. The attack on Sweaborg made the best use of the limited coast attack force, destroying dockyard buildings and ships, without engaging the fortifications. The correspondent of the *Times* was ecstatic, 'the blow … will be severely felt by Russia. It shakes her confidence in her stone walls, and makes her tremble for every town along her coasts'.[41] Graham's replacement as First Lord

175

of the Admiralty was delighted by the success, and the low cost in human life.

Sulivan left the Baltic in late October, encouraged by the successful attack on Kinburn by the allied Black Sea Fleets on October 17, when armoured batteries, mortar vessels, gunboats, and battleships had destroyed a Russian fortress, and captured the garrison. Sweaborg and Kinburn demonstrated that British coast assault flotillas could bombard any sea fort, and had opened the way to Cronstadt. Sulivan and his Royal Marine Artillery colleagues understood the destruction of Cronstadt, a more powerful defensive system, would require sustained mortar bombardment over several days, followed by concentrated close range fire. Sulivan was confident the enlarged flotilla and armoured batteries prepared for 1856 could force the barrier to the north of Cronstadt Island, using underwater demolition techniques pioneered by the Royal Engineers in the1830s, bombard the arsenal from angles not covered by major forts, and then engage the individual fortresses in detail. The fall of Cronstadt would open the Russian capital to attack, inflicting a tremendous blow on the prestige of the Russian state.

In a sign of desperation, the Czar ordered General Totleben, the engineer who had defended Sevastopol so skilfully, to improve the defences of Cronstadt, despite being wounded and in poor health. While some historians have dismissed the possibility of a British success, largely on the basis of Russian statements, Sulivan's track record, and the high esteem in which the Admiralty held his work over the next two decades indicate it was entirely possible. After the war Sulivan and Totleben discussed the operation, leaving Sulivan satisfied with his plan. The 1856 plan required 100 mortar vessels, 250 steam gunboats, more armoured batteries, a floating industrial base and stores depots.

It is hard to judge the impact of British operations on the Russian people, as the state actively prevented any manifestations of public opinion in the reign of Nicholas I, and after his death in January 1855 little changed. Alexander II replaced state censorship with a state-controlled media that upheld autocratic imperial rule.[42] Russian wartime propaganda, including published material passed by the censor, focused on religion, loyalty, and Russian success. It was simple, positive, and largely unconnected with reality. Peasants and serfs expressed little enthusiasm for the war, and few volunteered to fight. The only wartime event to generate real interest was the defence of Sevastopol.[43] Furthermore, the civilians impacted by the Baltic campaigns were Finns, Estonians, Lithuanians, Latvians, and Poles, who did not share language, faith or identity with their imperial masters.

A warfare state?

After 1815, Britain had demobilized both the armed forces and large elements of the warfare state that had mobilised money, ships, and munitions to fight Napoleon. While the extraordinary National Debt made these cuts imperative, ordering and balancing allowed them to be sustained for 40 years, despite occasional alarms. Predictably both Navy and Army had problems mobilizing for war in 1854. The Navy could not attract experienced sailors—the global shipping market was booming and wages were high, while the existing naval reserves only provided limited numbers. The Army managed to recruit significant numbers of men from the 1852 Militia, but was reduced to hiring mercenaries in Italy, Switzerland, and Germany.

By contrast, Britain had the industrial capacity to mass produce weapons; the 1855 pattern Enfield rifle and Colt Navy pistol were produced with machine tool made interchangeable parts. Heavy artillery production increased quickly, while the leading marine steam engine manufacturers in London mass produced 300 sets of gunboat machinery, and local shipyards built the hulls. At the same time the Royal Dockyards were engaged in a naval arms race with France, in large wooden steam-powered battleships. Both programmes were successful. Although the British military-industrial complex had revived with surprising speed, this was not thought worthy of comment at the time.

In financial terms, the costs of the war were covered by increased taxes, which Gladstone as Chancellor of the Exchequer in 1853–4 felt were a moral judgement on a belligerent nation. His successor in 1855, George Cornewall Lewis, increased borrowing, raising the National Debt to levels not seen since the 1820s, without any difficulty in the capital market.[44] Britain could afford European wars, but Victorian governments displayed no enthusiasm for waging them. They preferred deterrence and stability to war and risk. After 1830, debt reduction had become an imperative, one which Gladstone turned into a political morality test.

The 'Great Armament'

The revived 'warfare state' produced the British 'Great Armament' of 1856 to threaten St. Petersburg, and the Government used print media to ensure the Russians were kept fully informed of its progress. They used the threat of overwhelming firepower to persuade the Czar to accept the allied peace terms. The scale of British naval offensive operations in the Baltic in 1855 created strategic problems for the Russians. Although the fleet had no troops, using Royal Marines and sailors for minor amphibious operations, Russia deployed 250–300,000 high grade troops along the coast. Frequent coastal operations, cutting out ships, blowing up isolated positions and anchoring the fleet within a few miles of Cronstadt provided a demoralising reminder of the Royal Navy's moral ascendancy. In the last months of the 1855 campaign, the British scoured the eastern end of the Gulf of Finland, identifying an anchorage it could use for the armada that would support the attack on Cronstadt, tested local shore defences and updated the surveys. The bombardments of Sweaborg and Kinburn on 17 October 1855 refined the tactics of coast attack, and exposed minor technical failings. Industrial sea power could target military assets without the need to fire on civilian populations: Bomarsund, Sweaborg, and Cronstadt were fortresses, not cities.

The improved understanding of littoral power projection dovetailed with the diplomatic and strategic developments of late 1855.After the fall of Sevastopol on 9 September 1855, France, having recovered the military reputation lost at Waterloo, began to disengage, encouraging Austria to join the effort for a compromise peace without consulting Britain. When Austria threatened to join the allies unless Russia accepted the 'Four Points', the 'Great Armament' provided a strategic threat that focussed Russian thinking, ensuring Britain would secure its' war aims. This threat was directed at the seat of Russian power and the location of the capital city, the Royal Navy having already destroyed two sea fortresses with impunity. Everything pointed to the Baltic becoming the decisive theatre if the war continued into 1856. Baltic plans were discussed by the allies at the Paris Council of War in early 1856. Ultimately, the new Baltic strategy provided the military threat that, along with Russian bankruptcy, persuaded the Czar to accept the allied terms. With British naval power fully mobilized, Sweden joined the allies, reinforcing the threat to the Czar's northern flank. Sweden acted after receiving an Anglo-French guarantee of Swedish-Norwegian territory in November 1855. Facing further defeats, and those far closer to the centre of Russian power than Sevastopol, the Czar accepted the allied terms.

The Russian decision for peace was shaped by two key issues: the accession of Sweden, and potentially Austria, to the allied coalition, and the economic impact of the blockade. Russia lacked the money to continue the war. The additional humiliation of having the imperial capital destroyed would have called into question the legitimacy of Russian rule over subject peoples.[45] Economic warfare, including fiscal measures, broke a Russian economy that relied on advance sales of bulky materials, and the cheap transport provided by British merchant shipping. In 1853, Russian exports to Britain stood at 68 million roubles, by 1855 they had fallen to zero, while total exports collapsed from 143 million to 40, with grain exports falling by 90%.[46] With state expenditure doubling, the collapse of revenue streams, and the inability to access foreign capital, due to British pressure on the Dutch, Russia could not wage war.

Palmerston, now the Prime Minister, insisted on an additional clause, that Åland be demilitarized. This weakened Russia's strategic posture in the Baltic, increasing the possibility of more effective British naval action in future. Introducing the peace treaty to the House of Commons Palmerston singled out the capture of Bomarsund as the great naval success of the war, the first allied victory, a permanent shift in the regional balance of power, and praised Napier, the only Admiral named in the speech.

179

HARFLEUR TO HAMBURG

The peace signed in Paris in March 1856 broke Russia's control of the Baltic, preserved the Ottoman Empire, and temporarily patched up the 1815 system. The demilitarization of Åland, the one wholly British clause in the Peace of Paris, rounded off 20 years of mounting concern over Russian expansion in the Baltic, at the Bosphorus and in Asia. While it might seem a trifling point, the Åland terms have held, unlike the demilitarization of the Black Sea, which Russia renounced in 1870: it ended the forward policy of Nicholas I in the Baltic. Defeat forced the Russian navy back inside the Gulf of Finland, restricted to defending Cronstadt/St. Petersburg. Bomarsund had been a vulnerable over-extension of Russian strength, inconsistent with the continental assumptions of Russian strategic culture. With Bomarsund left in ruins, Sweden could move into the western camp.

Although peace had been made, the 'Crimean' War witnessed one last act of violence, albeit simulated. On 23 April 1856, St. George's Day, the British staged a victory parade, the Queen reviewed the Baltic fleet and the 'Great Armament' created to attack Cronstadt and St. Petersburg. There were 240 warships, very different to the fifteen ships reviewed by the Queen on 10 March 1854. After the fleet had been reviewed at anchor and underway 120 gunboats conducted a mock bombardment of Southsea Castle, standing in for Cronstadt, Cherbourg, or Charleston. The scale and sophistication of the event, the carefully projected image of overwhelming naval power annihilating land-based defences, had been designed to impress. It reminded the audience that not only did Britannia rule the waves, but she could annihilate hostile fleets skulking in fortified bases. The primary audience was the assembled diplomatic corps, and their military attaches. The American Minister refused to attend. The potency of steam age sea power was obvious, as the *Times* observed:

> A new system of naval warfare had been created.... We have now the means of waging really offensive war, not only against fleets, but harbours, fortresses and rivers, not merely of blockading, but of invading, and carrying the warfare of the sea to the very heart of the land.[47]

After the review, gunboats were sent to China, for another war about economic interests and market access, but most were hauled ashore at

Haslar, on a gigantic railway designed by Isambard Kingdom Brunel, and stored for the next great power crisis. In December 1861, the *Times* announced that the gunboats were being mobilized, the American Minister in London immediately advised his Government to back down in the crisis caused by the illegal seizure of passengers from the British mail steamer *Trent* by a Union warship.[48] The threat of British violence from the sea was a global phenomenon: targeting the naval bases of hostile powers.

After 1856, the role of the Baltic in British strategy was enhanced by improved access, and Russian weakness. Russian battleships no longer anchored at Copenhagen for months on end. With Russia a crippled and defeated shadow of its' former self, the British had only to mobilize a powerful fleet designed for coastal power projection at Spithead to coerce St. Petersburg. Alexander II could not forget that a British fleet had anchored off Cronstadt throughout the summer of 1855, a few miles from his capital. Only dynastic pride kept him from moving the centre of power back to Moscow, the true capital of Russia, where the Royal Navy could not act. This strategic retreat would be made by the Bolshevik regime, well-aware of the danger posed by an attack from the sea.

In conclusion

The Baltic campaigns emphasized the reality that although mid-nineteenth century Britain had become a unique global maritime power, it was far too close to Europe to ignore continental politics, and the possibility that a European Great Power could threaten British security. The obvious threats were a French occupation of the Scheldt Estuary and northern Flanders, or a Russian seizure of the Danish Narrows, and/or Istanbul and the Bosphorus. Further afield, Russian expansion in the Caucasus, Persia, and Central Asia posed strategic/economic threats to British interests. Countering French aggression relied on long-standing ties with the German powers: countering Russia depended on taking control of the Baltic and using economic pressure to restrain Russia. These campaigns consciously built on the experience of 1807–12, their effectiveness enhanced by the post-1833 neutrality of Denmark and Sweden, improved charts acquired from Russia, steam-powered warships, long-range artillery, and a portfolio of economic warfare methods dominated by the central role of the City of London in international finance and shipping services to exploit Russia's dependence on low value bulky exports for revenue.[49]

These campaigns were asymmetric: they were intended to secure the independence and integrity of the Ottoman Empire, and if Lord Palmerston had plans to liberate Poland and Finland, his Cabinet colleagues were less ambitious, and in the end, Palmerston was content to compromise. After 1856, Russia no longer dominated the Baltic, and newly guaranteed Sweden moved into the western orbit. Russian leaders recognized the vulnerability of St. Petersburg to sea-based threats, and looked for their own asymmetric counter in Central Asia, as far from the ocean as possible.

These were remarkably peaceful campaigns, with very little fighting, and strikingly limited impact on civilians. The British were well aware that the Finns, while subjects of the Czar, were not Russian, and aside from the loss of some merchant ships, which sailed under the Russian flag, and some shipbuilding timber, they were allowed to live in peace. Captain Sulivan was especially proud of distributing Finnish language Bibles on both sides of the Gulf of Finland. The population of the Baltic states was largely non-Russian. In both areas, small Russian military posts were abandoned before the British had the chance to attack. Casualties at the taking of Bomarsund were light, as befits a skilful operation where an isolated island garrison faced an overwhelming force. Most of the garrison were not Russian, but mainly Finnish volunteers and Polish-Jewish conscripts. The Russian garrison of Sweaborg suffered heavier losses, although there are no reliable figures. British deaths, less than 100 over two years, were dominated by a brief outbreak of cholera in 1854.

These calm, clear-headed professional naval campaigns lacked the high drama and pageantry of the Crimea, where courage and resolve compensated for incompetence in so many aspects of war. They were quickly forgotten by a public that preferred sensation to sense.

Russia lost the ability to dominate the Baltic during the 'Crimean' War; the demilitarization of the Åland Islands, the Anglo-French

THE BALTIC CAMPAIGNS OF THE 'CRIMEAN' WAR, 1854–56

guarantee of Sweden-Norway in November 1855 and the inability of Russian fleets and fortresses to resist advanced warships secured a key British war aim, the maintenance of asymmetric strategic leverage in the Baltic. Russia rebuilt its coast defences, turned its Navy into a coast defence force, and radically rebuilt the imperial system to generate modern industries and weapons.

After 1856 'Offshore Balancing' became more overt as a generation that could recall the unlimited Napoleonic conflict passed. Palmerston was the last of them, a man who knew how to use talk of war to secure important interests. In 1878 and 1885 Britain and Russia came close to war, over Turkey and Afghanistan. On both occasions British resolve was signalled by assembling Baltic fleets at Spithead, with Captain, later Admiral Lord 'Jacky' Fisher as the chief of staff, and Russia backed down before the fleets sailed. In 1905 Fisher sent the Channel Fleet into the Baltic to deter German aggression against France, in the First Moroccan Crisis. The diplomatic endgame of the crisis took place at Algeçiras, under the guns of Britain's Mediterranean and Atlantic Fleets, anchored in full view of the delegates. The violence had been implicit, as it usually was when Palmerston or Fisher were involved. In 1907 Russia and Germany signed the Treaty of Björko, to ban non-riparian warships from the Baltic, but Denmark refused to join them, and the idea was abandoned.

Britain used the threat of violence in Europe for almost a century after 1815, but the strikingly limited use of violence in the Baltic campaigns of 1854–5, and the threatened 1856 campaign, secured key strategic and diplomatic objectives, and sustained a reputation for strikingly effective power projection from the sea, supporting a policy of deterrence that helped avoid increasing the burden of the National Debt.

All that changed in 1914. Britain made no attempt to deter the looming conflict by sending a fleet towards, or into, the Baltic. This failure surprised the German High Command, which had expected a repetition of the 1905 demonstration. The Cabinet of 1914 included Gladstone's biographer John Morley, and others who had served in Gladstone's administrations. Despite his moral stance in 1854 Gladstone had used the threat of naval and military force to secure

183

British interests on more than one occasion, notably over Belgium in 1870, and Afghanistan in 1885, issues that Morley's massive biography had explained in detail. It appears British liberalism had forgotten that it was occasionally necessary to threaten or use violence to secure national and international interests.

10

THE BLOCKADE IN THE FIRST WORLD WAR

Mary Elisabeth Cox

The British Blockade, as it is commonly known, was the interdiction of goods into and out of Germany by the Allied Powers during the First World War. While the amount and type of goods that were interdicted changed over time, the blockade itself lasted from the outbreak of the War until July 1919, after the Treaty of Versailles had been signed by the Associated Governments.[1] As others have pointed out, the name 'British Blockade' is not entirely accurate.[2] While it was initially designed and directed by the British government, the blockade was operated under close cooperation with British Allies and Associated Powers, most notably the French, and later the United States.[3] Furthermore, it was largely tolerated, though not without criticism, by neutral countries. A more accurate name for this military action might be the 'Anglo-French Blockade', or the 'Allied Blockade'. While the use of the term 'Allied Blockade' has increased recently, the 'British Blockade' or 'English Blockade' are still common monikers, as they were during the time of blockade itself.

In addition to a name that lacks full descriptive power of the nations that operated it, the Allied Blockade impacted more countries than just Germany: Austria-Hungary, Bulgaria, and Turkey were also subjected to the blockade.[4] And of course, since the First World War ended over a hundred years ago, the United Kingdom has led or participated in other blockades, both alone[5] and in conjunction with others.[6] Yet despite these discrepancies, for a variety of historical and political reasons, when 'the British Blockade' is mentioned, this usually refers to the United Kingdom's blockade against Germany during the First World War.

The historical nature of the blockade's nomenclature likely has to do with the status of the Royal Navy as the most powerful naval power on earth at the outbreak of the First World War, as well as the deference that other countries gave to the British Government's edicts on naval policy.[7] Indeed, the United Kingdom issued eight Maritime Orders in Council throughout the War that confirmed, adjusted, changed, and finally negated the most recent previous international agreement on blockades, the 1909 Declaration of London.[8] Other countries followed suit.[9] It also issued fifteen Contraband Proclamations during the conflict explaining what His Majesty's government would or would not consider contraband for trade.[10] Finally, the German government and people focused primarily on what they termed the *Englische Hungerblockade* during and following the First World War in their bitter complaints about the blockade, rather than on the Anglo-French or Allied blockade.

And why were their complaints so bitter? In large part because many Germans believed that some 763,000 of their fellow non-combatant citizens perished as a direct result of the blockade.[11] The estimates of excess German civilian deaths have since been reduced to 478,500,[12] with the total deaths from the blockade alone estimated by the German government at 424,00.[13] Neither figure includes the number of German civilians who suffered nutritional deprivation as part of the blockade who did not perish at that time, but who had diminished energy and stature and increased vulnerability to a variety of diseases. With a German population of approximately 70,000,000 people, and assuming the range of estimated civilian deaths from hunger to be 424,00–763,000, then about 0.5–1% of the German civilian population died because of the blockade.

Germany was extraordinarily vulnerable to a blockade because it depended on international trade to feed its citizens: it imported roughly 20%–30% of its entire food supply.[14] Furthermore, Germany's farms were dependent on access to foreign fertilizers, with some 40% of all fertilizer imported.[15] Yet dependency on foreign food was not unique to Germany.[16] Other European countries were also heavily reliant on food imports, some to a far greater extent than Germany. The United Kingdom imported some 60%[17]–75%[18] of all dietary calories in 1913. Perhaps it was this inherent vulnerability in its own food systems that allowed the UK to imagine how blocking food might negatively impact an enemy's morale and ability to fight.

The British government invited nine other countries to the London Naval Conference (4 December 1908–26 February 1909) 'in order to arrive at an agreement as to what are the generally recognised rules of international law' concerning maritime rights for belligerents and neutrals during wartime.[19] These meetings led to the famous 1909 London Declaration of the Laws of Naval War, better known as the Declaration of London. Many of the same British delegates, principally liberals who had attended the Second Hague Convention of 1907, believed that a way to create international peace was through international law which would lead to 'a stable world free from large-scale conflict where Britain could thrive unmolested.'[20] In a large sense, the British liberals got their way at the London Naval Conference, achieving what they could not at the Second Hague Convention in 1907, as the trading rights of neutral countries were given precedence over the rights of belligerents to run blockades during a future war.

The Declaration of London confirmed many existing norms on how blockades would operate in times of war, and settled more recent questions such as what constituted contraband by including itemised lists of goods considered to be absolute contraband, conditional contraband, and items that were not to be considered contraband. Free goods, or items that were not contraband, were 'articles which are not susceptible of use in war' and therefore 'may not be declared contraband of war'. Included in the list of items that could not be declared contraband of war were 'natural and artificial manures, including nitrates and phosphates for agricultural purposes',[21] and 'articles serving exclusively to aid the sick and wounded'[22] as well as many other medical supplies. Under the Declaration of London, non-contraband items could not be declared contraband.[23] Types of goods listed as 'absolute contraband' were goods considered to serve a military purpose, particularly 'articles exclusively used for war'.[24] These included goods with an obvious military use, such as 'arms of all kinds' and other materiel.[25] Items termed 'Absolute Contraband' were 'liable to capture if it is shown to be destined to territory belonging to or occupied by the enemy, or to the armed forces of the enemy.' Items listed as 'conditional contraband' were 'articles susceptive of use in war as well as for purposes of peace'[26] and could only be captured if the items were known to have a military purpose and were 'destined for the armed forces or of a government department of the enemy State'[27] with proof for their destination resting on the accuser. Otherwise, 'the destination is presumed to be innocent.'[28]

In theory, international agreement on these lists of contraband could protect maritime commerce of neutral countries in future conflicts, thus protecting their right to trade specific kinds of goods and be safeguarded from attack so long as neutrals followed the requisite trading guidelines, and adhered to the designated lists of absolute contraband, conditional contraband, and non-contraband.

With its support of the Declaration of London, Britain gave up the right to continuous voyage, a legal term that means that if ships are destined to a belligerent at any point in their journey— even if that journey begins and ends in neutral ports—then the entire voyage is considered to be one single, continuous voyage. By giving up the right to continuous voyage, 'continental powers could continue to receive food through neutral ports.'[29] While such actions would have protected British commerce in a war in which they declared neutrality—by allowing British merchants to trade largely uninhibited—surrendering rights to continuous voyage could hamper Britain as a belligerent in future conflicts, particularly if they sought to enforce a continental blockade.

The Declaration of London confirmed many previously held international norms on the use of blockades during war, including that a belligerent operating a blockade against an enemy must operate a 'close blockade', as agreed to in the 1852 Treaty of Paris,

188

THE BLOCKADE IN THE FIRST WORLD WAR

rather than a distant blockade. A 'close blockade' meant that any blockade should 'not extend beyond the ports and coasts belonging to or occupied by the enemy'.[30] The hope was that such an agreed proscription would limit naval and military conflict close to the coasts of the warring parties, thus leaving the larger oceans free for commerce. Interference with neutral countries that wished to maintain trade during hostilities would be minimised. It has been suggested that because of the Declaration of London, German leaders may not have been as troubled as they might have otherwise been in going to war: they believed that the Declaration of London would to an extent protect them from the impact of a blockade, and therefore reduced the deterrence value of the formidable Royal Navy. As Avner Offer concluded 'The Declaration of London must be considered as one of the causes of the war.'[31]

Plenipotentiaries for all ten countries present at the London Naval Conference unanimously confirmed the Declaration of London: Germany, the United States of America, Austria-Hungary, Spain, France, the United Kingdom of Great Britain and Ireland, Italy, Japan, the Netherlands, and Russia.[32] While the vote from all countries was unanimous, the Declaration of London was not ratified by all of those who signed, including the United Kingdom itself. While it passed the House of Commons in 1911, full ratification was later defeated in the House of Lords.

Just over five years after the 1909 Declaration of London, as the Great War raged, food was prevented from entering Germany, as was fertilizer and other goods. As foodstuffs were included in the list of 'conditional contraband', it had to be shown that they were 'destined for the armed forces or of a government department of the enemy State' if they were to be captured.[33] Britain reasoned that if the German government rationed food, then as the German government was leading a war this rationing could be considered military action.[34] In any case, food stopped from entering Germany would mean less food for both soldiers and civilians alike. Fertilizers such as 'natural and artificial manures, including nitrates and phosphates for agricultural purposes' were on the non-contraband list, and therefore formed a more difficult problem for the British if they wished their blockade to adhere to the dictates of the Declaration of

London. Given military exigencies, the British decided not to follow the Declaration of London. The tonnage of foreign fertilizers making their way into Germany during the War was therefore significantly reduced.[35] In the late nineteenth and early twentieth centuries, German agriculture relied heavily on foreign fertilizer to boost yields. The issue is complicated, however, as the Germans invented a process to synthesise artificial fertilizers. In the years preceding the First World War, German research scientists Fritz Haber, Carl Bosch, Alwin Mittasch and others created the Haber-Bosch-Mittasch synthesis method, which synthesised ammonia at an industrial scale and in an economic way. The first ammonia synthesis plant was opened in 1913, a year before the First World War broke out.[36] This ammonia could be used in the creation of artificial fertilizer, but also in the creation of deadly weapons such as chlorine gas and explosives. Given the vicious invasion of Belgium by Germany, how could the British believe that the manure, nitrates, and phosphates Germany imported would be used to continue its agricultural tradition of heavy fertilizer use to maintain agricultural yields, and not for the creation of weapons to kill?

The British government violated the original agreements made in the Declaration of London by operating a distant blockade, maintaining the right to continuous voyage, and changing and eventually negating the original contraband lists. The ambiguity of the unanimous confirmation of the Declaration of London by the plenipotentiaries, yet later failure of ratification by individual governments, led to debates about its legality. Because the Declaration of London had not been ratified at home, the United Kingdom was almost certainly within its legal rights not to follow it.

Nevertheless, these violations did not go unnoticed by neutral countries. The elaborate system created by England to limit goods from neutral countries from entering Germany, including food, was generally not met with enthusiasm by neutral countries. For the most part, they complained against the constraint of their rights as neutrals, reaffirmed by the Declaration of London, to trade goods with belligerents that were not absolute contraband or destined for the military. Complaints about the blockade because it could starve

THE BLOCKADE IN THE FIRST WORLD WAR

Germany were less common. The focus of neutral countries on their trading rights perhaps related to self-interest in their economies, as well as to the state of international law itself.

Still, some scholars from neutral countries confirmed the legal right of England to issue a blockade. Writing in 1915, famed American political scientist James W. Garner wrote that:

> Blockade as a war measure may or may not be a proper means of overcoming the enemy; whatever may be the opinion on this point, however, there can be no doubt as to its legitimacy; its existence is contemporaneous with the birth of international law itself. The German denunciation of the British measure as a cruel and inhuman attempt to starve the civil population of Germany by cutting off its food supply cannot be sustained either upon grounds of international law or practice. The legitimacy of blockade as a means of compelling a belligerent to surrender, by cutting off the supplies of the civil population, has been recognized by nearly all publicists from Gentilis to the present.[37]

Garner continued:

> ... On the other hand, there are not lacking authors who, while not contesting the legitimacy of blockade as a war measure, believe it should be abandoned.

Garner cited a number of scholars who argued against the use of commercial blockades previously. Cambridge professor of international law, John Westlake, wrote of 'the fearful evils which the country is now suffering' from the blockade of the Confederate States by the Union during the US Civil War.

> I have been obliged to come to the conclusion that commercial blockades ought to be abolished, from motives both of justice and policy: not, indeed, that we can suddenly repudiate our ancient doctrines at the moment when we begin to feel ourselves the evils which we have long inflicted on others; but our duty is to turn the present lesson to account, and use it at the first legitimate opportunity.[38]

Garner also cited Azuni's argument that a blockade against a country 'with a view to reducing the enemy by starvation was "barbarous and immoral"'.[39]

Still, some members of governments in other neutral countries failed to see both sides. Ernst Liljedahl, a member of the Swedish Parliament, argued against the English blockade on February 19, 1917:

> International Law established before 1914 is now largely shot to pieces. This has occurred mainly on the initiative of England ... The London Naval Conference of 1909, convened at England's invitation, laid a sound theoretical foundation for the right of the civilian population to food in a belligerent country. This was accomplished by the provision in the Declaration of London (Article 34) that conditional contraband, as opposed to absolute contraband (like arms, ammunition), should only be seized when they were destined for a fortified place or a place used by the enemy. In this way the [food] supply to other locations not directly serving the war effort would be secured.
>
> ... On August 20, 1914, England announced that it would, as far as possible, follow the London Declaration, but with some "additions and modifications" which concealed England's real intentions. A proclamation of September 21, 1914, also included a number of previously free articles as war contraband, and a new "Order in Council No. 2" of October 29, 1914, expanded the contraband list so considerably that the London Declaration became useless. Thus... the hunger blockade against Germany came into operation.[40]

Liljedahl complained in the same article that 'England, the "protector" of us and other small nations ... has violated the rights of the neutrals.'

Beyond questions of legality and the concerns of neutral countries, there were also questions about the letter of the law versus the overall meaning of the law. Technological improvements in weaponry were dramatic in the early twentieth century. The new German ability to fix atmospheric nitrogen was dangerous. Furthermore, 'the development of mines, submarines, torpedoes, and long-range coastal artillery made the traditional close blockade of the enemy coast impractical, if not suicidal'.[41] Hence, 'the basic conflict was between a focus on the adherence to specific rules and a focus on the adherence to the deeper principles that arguably underlay the surface rules'.[42] So, to the chagrin of Germany and many neutral countries who had hoped to trade freely, the Declaration of London was referred to repeatedly yet carefully negated by the Government in London.

Implementation of the blockade was relatively straight-forward, though with an endeavour so complex, the blockade required constant maintenance, adjustments, negotiations, and political oversight. The British operated a distant blockade safely away from the German coastline and long-range coastal artillery. They patrolled the entrance to the North Sea between Scapa Flow, the Shetlands, and Norway. This made it impossible for German ships to leave or enter the Atlantic—which would have opened them up to trade— without the German navy leaving their coasts and coming out to battle the Royal Navy.[43] The British Channel Fleet defended entrance or exit from the Channel, preventing German ships from exiting the North Sea via this route.[44]

For many contemporaries, the blockade was controversial, and for some a diplomatic embarrassment, especially given the recent Naval Conference and Declaration of London, which the British Government itself had instigated.[45] As such, arguments were made as to why the blockade was necessary. One theme in support of the blockade related to retribution. It was claimed that the blockade was a valid response to previous actions of the enemy.

It is important to separate the events leading to war from acts committed during a war, yet Germany's brutal and illegal attack on neutral Belgium starting on 4 August 1914, and the prolonged and painful occupation the followed, could not be ignored by the British. The terrible violence that occurred there was a point that galvanised much of the world against Germany, and indeed led to the entry of the United Kingdom into the War. In effect, the response of the United Kingdom, including the blockade and the negative consequences it entailed, was a response to German aggression. There were other more mundane retribution arguments to support

193

the blockade. For example, early accusations that the Germans illegally placed 20 to 30 mines off of the Aldeburgh Napes were made. However, under the rules of war, doing so was not illegal. Rather 'the Admiralty would have been well advised to accuse the enemy only of disregarding a custom of war, which every other nation would have considered binding'.[46] Claims were also exaggerated: Germany 'only laid one single minefield' yet they were accused of having scattered 'contact mines indiscriminately about the North Sea'.[47] The aim of these statements was to warn neutral countries about German danger while proffering British protection, and thereby engendering cooperation.

Another theme in arguments in support of the blockade against Germany related to German cruelty. In essence, Germany would have done the same to England and others if given the chance. There is some evidence for this, particularly if one looks at how Germans treated their enemies and people under their occupation. German soldiers frequently and routinely requisitioned food from the lands they occupied, and not only to feed their own army. Food was also shipped back to Germany. While food requisition seems to have often been used to relieve the hunger of their own people rather than as an instrument to inflict hunger on others, very often little care or consideration was shown for civilians. The German military's requisition of food in Belgium was 'official policy'; soldiers there were instructed at least initially to take more than was needed for the military.[48] German actions in East Central Europe also drew particular ire. For example, German soldiers requisitioned foodstuffs in Tsarist Poland and shipped the goods back to the German home front, to the detriment and often total disregard of the local population, though this varied depending somewhat on timing and which German leaders were in charge.[49] Such actions caused intense suffering. The Treaty of Brest-Litovsk in 1917 between Russia and the Central Powers further showed how mercilessly self-interested Germany could be.

But what about an actual blockade of the United Kingdom? Would Germany have tried to starve England out with a blockade if given the chance? Some have argued that the German U-boat campaign was an attempt to do just that, an equivalent action to the British blockade.[50] German Admiral Alfred von Tirpitz stated on November 21, 1914, 'England wants to starve us into submission; we can play the same game, blockade England and destroy each and every ship that tries to run the blockade'.[51] When on February 1, 1917, Germany announced an unrestricted submarine campaign, they contended that this was in response to the English hunger blockade, using arguments of retribution of their own. It was argued that the '"disorder" caused by raw material and food shortages would bring the British economy to a grinding halt within five months of unrestricted submarine warfare'.[52] The U-boat attacks did destroy food meant for British consumption, especially after Germany announced its unrestricted submarine campaign. An average of some 642,833 tons of Entente shipping were lost per month between February and July 1917. When only British shipping is included, the amount is approximately three-fifths of that, or 385,700 tonnes per month.[53] It is estimated that German and Austrian-Hungarian submarines combined killed some 15,000 Allied military personnel.[54]

Food prices in both countries increased. In Germany, the magnitude of cost increases in food caused the state to begin to lose its legitimacy as people turned to black markets and illegal activities to provide for their families.[55] Many women of lesser means felt that they were shouldering the food burden unevenly, and participated in collective action to demand lower prices and more food in cities like Berlin.[56]

A key difference in the German U-boat campaign and the British blockade is that the German U-boat campaign was instantaneously violent. Innocent civilians aboard vessels were attacked and killed, seemingly indiscriminately, and people died quickly through the initial explosion or by drowning. In comparison with the Allied Blockade, civilians in Germany did not die speedily. Rather, people who were negatively impacted by the blockade suffered slowly and often incrementally, with less and less energy to complete basic functions of life such as fighting disease and regulating their body temperature. Many who did not have outside sources of foodstuffs or money and connections to pay those who did, died. Whether the lower estimate of excess civilian deaths in Germany given earlier of 424,000 is used, or the initial higher estimate of 763,000, the total deaths from the Allied blockade are many times greater than the approximately 15,000 or so souls who died from the U-boat campaign. This difference goes a way towards showing the kinds of violence that, while not accepted, are more easily discounted. Death inflicted slowly through nutritional deprivation from a blockade seems to be easier to countenance than death that is inflicted instantaneously through explosions.

In addition to the main themes concerning the blockade's legality and an act of retribution against a ferocious enemy, there are arguments that question the physical impact of the blockade itself on German civilians. During the armistice period, as the blockade continued, some believed that the German people had eaten way too much before the hostilities anyway. As an American charged with reporting actual German need during the armistice period wrote internally:

> 75% of the adult population was overweight. Every one recalls the fat Germans with triple chins, ponderous and pendulous abdomens, and pudgy legs. After three years of war they were reduced so they looked like other people. Perfect 42s became perfect 36s. Now they are somewhat thinner than most people like to be.'[57]

The message was clear: if the German diet had been reduced because of the blockade, they could afford to lose the weight. Starling's report is more diplomatic. He presented large tables that showed the total calorie consumption per head of the average German, and argued that compared to France or England, 'Germany before the war was extremely well fed both as to quantity and quality'.[58] In effect, even if caloric consumption did go down during the War, the Germans could afford a reduction in calories. Yet a problem with large assessments of total calories available in a country divided by that country's total population, even accounting for different ages as most surveys did, is the underlying assumption that calories were divided equitably. They were not.[59] In my own research on the nutritional status of German civilians, I found that the greatest predictor of children's height and weight before the war was their socio-economic background.

196

These inequalities were made worse during the War, which served to deepen existing inequalities.[60] In addition to differences between families, calories were also not dividedly evenly *within* families, with women of child-bearing age taking the greatest hit. In Leipzig in 1917, for example, 30%–48% of women in the sample between the ages of 20 and 40 suffered from chronic energy deficiency.[61]

Another argument that has been made over the past century about the efficacy of the blockade relates to its overall impact on the outcome of the war. While early on it was 'the unanimous opinion of Allied leaders in 1918–19'[62] that a large part of the Entente's victory was due to the blockade, military historians have argued that Germany lost the war because the United States joined the Allies,[63] and because it lost on the battlefield.[64]

Another argument along the lines of German hunger being due to German culpability looks at German domestic policy decisions. While well-meaning, these decisions rarely had the impact German authorities sought. In the beginning, they included a piece-meal approach by the different municipalities to the crisis, creating national competition for foodstuffs. In May 1916, the Bundesrat organised the Kriegsernährungsamt to assist in food distribution. This new organisation had the unfortunate position of being able to make suggestions and even rules, yet did not have the support of the military to enforce them. Price controls on basic foodstuffs were created in an attempt to ensure that the most basic foods remained affordable. Instead, the price controls incentivised farmers to produce less needed staples, and more luxury goods that could be sold for higher profits.[65] Naturally, this had negative impacts on an already weakened food supply.

To ignore the blockade, which by its design and function reduced food and fertilizer imports into Germany, does not make sense. Of course a reduction of foodstuffs across society impacted food supplies in the country. It is also true that the German response to these actions often made the impact worse.[66] Yet given an absolute shortage of food and the restraints and capacity of the German government, there were not many other options available to the leaders of Wilhelmine Germany. 'There were no unplayed cards up Imperial Germany's sleeve'.[67]

HARFLEUR TO HAMBURG

Finally, another argument goes that if the Germans did go hungry during the war, they had themselves to blame. 'Germany chose to go to war with its principal trading partners' thus naturally limiting their resources.[68] This argument may help explain part of the reason why at least some in the German command were loath to induce the United States to join the war. In addition to fresh manpower and a large economy, the blockade against Germany tightened after the United States joined on the side of the Entente in 1917. By 1918, the blockade had 'contributed greatly to the reduction of the supplies of food from all sources of the Central Powers by over 50 per cent'.[69]

The blockade of Germany reached its greatest geographic spread during the winter months of the armistice, between the winter of 1918–1919, when physical fighting on the Western Front had stopped. In addition to the persistence of the blockade during the armistice period, which some argued was a safety measure against renewed violence and others viewed as a bludgeon to ensure Germans signed the peace treaty, the blockade was expanded into the Baltic Sea, and fishing of all kinds was banned along the Germany coasts.[70]

During the second half of the armistice—at the end of March— the blockade was partially lifted after Germany negotiated with the Allies to purchase precise amounts of food from them in gold. There was fear on both sides of exploitation—the Allies feared that the Germans might not pay, and the Germans feared that the British might sell them rancid goods. This does not appear to have happened. Indeed, purchased food made its way into Germany from late March through August 1919 after the blockade was fully lifted.[71]

That the blockade existed for the duration of the armistice was particularly galling to many Germans, as was the fact that they had to endure an entire winter with the blockade still in force after their representatives had signed armistices. It was also upsetting to many civilians in the UK. One famous example comes from Eglantyne Jebb, whose moral horror led her to protesting the continued blockade against Germany and Austria and to her founding of the charity Save the Children, which quickly spread to helping needy children beyond German and Austrian borders.[72] Jebb was not alone in her criticisms that the blockade was continuing during the

198

THE BLOCKADE IN THE FIRST WORLD WAR

armistice. On February 15, 1919, as the blockade was still in force, *The Nation* published Henry W. Nevinson's opinion:

> We must allow distress alone to become sufficient call for human sympathy; nor do I wish to believe that a large majority of English people desire a massacre of the innocents, or even of the guilty...The World's peace will not be ensured either by the destruction of a great and laborious people, or by implanting among them the poisonous seed of revenge.[73]

What responsibility then, if any, did the United Kingdom have in its blockade against Germany in reducing the living standards of civilians? This is a difficult question to answer. The blame, so to speak, has often been side-stepped or outright rejected by scholars who emphasise the legality the blockade, the poor economic and policy decisions by the Germans which negatively impacted food production and food distribution, or outright German viciousness in other parts of the war. In the complex and changing calculus of the First World War, who can say outright that anything was due to a single cause? On the other hand, who could fairly argue that a major reduction of foreign fertilizer for an agricultural economy dependent on it, in addition to 20–30% of total food outright because of blockade, would not impact a state's ability to feed its citizens?

While the Allied blockade of Germany is the most studied of the First World War, other countries were also impacted by blockades, even those that were not fighting. Sweden, which was formally neutral during the War, though with obvious German sympathies at the highest levels of government, experienced hunger riots and the resignation of their prime minister in part because of their refusal to give in to British blockade demands and their infrangible belief in their rights to free trade as a neutral country as espoused in the Declaration of London.

Research on blockades in parts of the Ottoman Empire suggests that impacts on civilians there were far worse than they had been in Germany. In the area around Mount Lebanon, one third of the total population—150,000 people—died of hunger and hunger-related diseases between 1915–17. Despite less rain and locusts, 'in no sense was the famine a "natural disaster"'. Rather, the novel disease environment brought by the war, and the blockade operated by the Triple Entente Fleet, were responsible for many of those deaths.[74]

There is ample evidence that the blockade against Germany was a deliberate and 'central weapon of the war'.[75] There is also evidence that not everyone agreed with the blockade during or after the War, and that not all sides of government had thought through the implications of the Declaration of London or what a blockade of Germany might look like before Britain entered the war. Perhaps more interesting, more than a century after it occurred, and despite the spicy title of this book, is to ask other questions of the blockade. Rather than use it to attach blame and culpability, a more useful discussion would be to examine the impacts, both intended and unexpected, of the blockade on Germany and beyond. By doing so, policy makers and the public will be better informed when considering the use of similar blockades today.

11

LEGITIMISING VIOLENCE IN THE BRITISH ATTACK ON THE FRENCH FLEET AT MERS-EL-KÉBIR

Karine Varley

At 5:53pm on 3 July 1940, British air and naval forces opened fire on French ships stationed at the French naval base of Mers-el-Kébir, near Oran in Algeria. The operation, codenamed Catapult, resulted in the sinking of one French battleship, damage to five other ships, and the loss of 1,297 French servicemen, with a further 351 wounded. Coming less than a fortnight after the French had defied London's wishes and signed armistices with the German and Italian governments, the attack sprang from British fears that the French fleet might fall into enemy hands. The British therefore issued an ultimatum to the French navy. The ultimatum gave four options: first, to sail French ships to British ports and continue to fight; second, to sail to British ports from where the crews would be repatriated; third, to sail to a French port in the West Indies where the ships would be demilitarised; or fourth, to sink the ships within six hours.[1] As commander of the Force de Rade at Mers-el-Kébir, Admiral Gensoul deemed all the options unacceptable.[2] The French government insisted that as a matter of national honour, it would never surrender its fleet. When the British made good on their threat, the French government was therefore outraged.

The episode gave rise to a controversy that has remained alive to this day.[3] For French sailors to have been killed by men with whom they had served as allies just a few days earlier in ships that were unable to retaliate seemed not merely an act of treachery, but an act of callous brutality. Indeed, if he maintained that no undertaking had ever been 'more necessary for the life of Britain', Winston Churchill nevertheless conceded that it was a 'hateful decision, the most unnatural and painful in which I have ever been concerned'.[4] While the British had neutralised a significant potential threat, the operation resulted in an immediate diplomatic rupture with France and pushed the new government in Vichy towards active collaboration with the Nazis and Italian Fascists.[5] It played directly into Axis propaganda as well. The German government claimed that 'all crimes in history pale before this new act of piracy', while the Italian press alleged that the British had 'danced' around the French sailors' corpses.[6] In France, the episode inaugurated a propaganda narrative of ruthless global ambition in which Mers-el-Kébir had unmasked the British as the true enemies of the French people.[7]

This chapter explores the motivations and justifications behind the British use of force at Mers-el-Kébir on 3 July 1940. As an attack conducted against the forces of a friendly nation that had ceased to fight, the operation contravened the accepted use of military violence in war. It displayed an apparent ruthlessness that seemed at odds not only with Britain's status as a liberal democratic pillar of the international community but with the supposed British values of decency and fairness as well. Nevertheless, the action gained wide domestic and international support as being both necessary and legitimate. Churchill justified the use of violence with a wider argument that the exceptional moral exigencies of defeating the Nazis warranted breaching the very codes, laws, and values his government was fighting to uphold.

In some respects, however, the British action was neither exceptional nor without precedent. The 1807 bombardment of Copenhagen saw the Royal Navy mount a similar pre-emptive strike to prevent neutral Danish ships from falling into Napoleon's hands. As in 1940, the British justified the attack, and the civilian and military deaths that resulted from it, by claiming it was conducted in the interests of European peace. For some international observers, however, it revealed the harsh realities of British imperial and capitalist power, exposing an 'utter ruthlessness behind a humanitarian mask'.[8] The ready recourse to violence and the reasoning that lay behind it indicate that the British attack at Mers-el-Kébir was more than merely a pre-emptive military strike for self-defence. Bolstered by the precedent of 1807, the British government was not simply engaged in an exercise of power without reference to morality. Rather, it conceived its own national interests as being so inextricably bound with those of the wider international community as to justify violence in the cause of peace and civilisation.

The chapter begins by exploring how British action in Norway earlier in 1940 helped establish a rationale for Mers-el-Kébir that centred on notions of supreme emergency. The second section outlines how Franco-British tensions over strategy and political and military obligations shaped London's decision to mount the attack. The third section deals with how the strategic use of violence was central to the planning and execution of Operation Catapult. The fourth section analyses how the British government justified its actions politically on the domestic and international stages. The chapter finishes with an examination of how military codes of honour militated against the use of violence in the circumstances presented at Mers-el-Kébir, highlighting the political impulsions behind the operation.

Supreme Emergency

British intervention in Norway played a significant role in shaping the government's approach towards the Mers-el-Kébir operation. It established a moral reasoning for violating international law and exposed tensions between military and political thinking about the conduct of the war. Following the Soviet invasion of Finland on 30 November 1939, as First Lord of the Admiralty, Churchill proposed mining Norwegian territorial waters to prevent iron ore exports from reaching Germany and to hinder a German invasion of Norway.[9] Even after the Winter War had ended in March 1940, Churchill continued to press his plans, against resistance from British army and naval officers who opposed the violation of Norwegian neutrality and the likely bloodshed that would ensue.[10] In so doing, he revealed a determination not to be hindered by Britain's values and international commitments but rather to turn them into a justification for action. In a memorandum dated 16 December 1939, Churchill argued that Britain had entered the war to uphold the values of the League of Nations Covenant and to 're-establish the reign of law'.[11] The country had a powerful moral duty not merely to fight but to be victorious, because 'defeat would mean an age of barbaric violence' for Britain and the rest of Europe.[12] In such circumstances, Churchill maintained, 'we have a right, and indeed are bound in duty, to abrogate for a space some of the conventions of the very laws we seek to consolidate and reaffirm'.[13] Indeed, in the face of a 'supreme emergency', Churchill argued, 'the letter of the law' must not prevent Britain from taking action, because 'humanity, rather than legality', must be its guide.[14]

The episode was significant for two main reasons. It showed that Churchill was prepared not merely to inflict harm on a neutral state but to embed the moral justification for action within an abrogation of international law. The problem was, however, that the circumstances of war did not mean that decisions and their consequences occurred in a 'moral vacuum'.[15] Even if international law could be temporarily abrogated, that did not justify a free-for-all. As Michael Walzer observes, Churchill adopted a 'sliding scale' rationale, in which the graver the injustice that would ensue from defeat, the more the rules could be broken to avoid that defeat. According to such reasoning, the rights of those whose cause is just become greater, while those of their enemy are diminished.[16] With much of Europe under Nazi control and fears of an imminent German invasion of Britain, the case for declaring a 'supreme emergency' was much stronger at the time of the Mers-el-Kébir operation than during the Norwegian intervention. However, the moral imperatives for defeating Nazism did not correspondingly give the British the right to kill sailors from another state, especially one which was no longer an active belligerent.

The British government was in no doubt that if the French fleet were to fall into enemy hands, it would create a significant threat to British security and prospects in the war more broadly. London therefore legitimately cited supreme national emergency as its main justification for action, arguing that Britain faced an existential danger. But while dealing with such a threat might have been a military necessity, the use of violence was less clear-cut. Operation Catapult fulfilled international law requirements that pre-emptive strikes must be in response to an imminent threat and that force must be proportionate to that threat.[17] However, the manner with which force was deployed and the loss of life that resulted from it was a political as much as military choice.

Franco-British Tensions

The fact that the victims of British violence at Mers-el-Kébir were not German but French was a significant complicating factor in justifying the violence of Operation Catapult. For the British government to have taken such action against a hitherto friendly state with which it had a history of close political and military cooperation implied a ruthless determination to prioritise national interests that stood in marked contrast with principled assertions of Britain's moral duties to the international community. It also went against the direction of British policy up to that point. If London had tended to be suspicious of European entanglements and to limit military commitments on the continent in the 1930s, it had come to realise its reliance upon the strength and willingness of the French army to fight.[18] Moreover, by 1938 there had been a marked strategic convergence with Paris as London increasingly accepted that it could not remain detached from developments on the continent.[19] The Foreign Office even went so far as to propose an Act of Union with France that would have seen the two states combine their armed forces, foreign, and economic policies as well as their political institutions.[20]

However, the military disasters of May and June 1940 revived old Franco-British tensions, culminating in a breakdown of trust between the two governments. For all their shared interests and values, the alliance between London and Paris had always been built on uneven foundations. While the two countries had fought alongside one another during the First World War, the alliance was in many respects a 'marriage of convenience'.[21] The ease with which it dissolved into fractiousness after 1918 was a measure of how differently the two parties viewed it.[22] A pragmatic British mindset conflicted with the deeper significance that French policy-makers attached to the alliance. Under the strain of the German invasion, past French suspicions mixed with new fears that London was putting its own interests first in failing to commit the necessary resources to the battle for France. Such concerns were intensified by the Dunkirk evacuation, when the proportionately lower numbers of French soldiers evacuated led to accusations that the British had abandoned the French to their sorry fate.[23] For the British, meanwhile, the rapid collapse of the French army was not merely the result of poor planning but was a consequence of defeatism.[24]

The weeks leading up to the French surrender fuelled a mutual misunderstanding that drove the decision to mount Operation Catapult. Repeated British attempts to gain the French government's assurance that it would not seek armistice terms without prior consultation were met with refusal and incomprehension. Repeated British demands for action to prevent the French fleet from falling into enemy hands were taken as an affront by French ministers and admirals.[25] On 16 June, Churchill informed his counterpart Paul Reynaud that London would only consent to a French request for armistice terms on condition the French fleet sailed to British ports first.[26] Reynaud rejected the demand. His resignation and replacement by Marshal Philippe Pétain only exacerbated the tensions. A last-ditch British offer of union as an inducement to continue fighting was dismissed by French ministers as a ploy to exploit France's fall and seize its empire.[27] By 17 June, the British and French governments had adopted fundamentally opposing approaches to the war. Whereas Pétain's experiences in the First World War led him to believe that his government's duty was to protect the French people from further suffering by seeking armistice terms, Churchill insisted that the British people would fight to the bitter end and would 'never surrender'.[28] The fallout over the French armistice terms and the subsequent British decision to take action at Mers-el-Kébir was a consequence of these irreconcilable positions.

LEGITIMISING VIOLENCE IN THE BRITISH ATTACK

Whereas Pétain's government was satisfied with Axis assurances on the security of the French fleet, London maintained that the armistice terms provided no guarantee that it would not fall into German or Italian hands.[29] In the agreements signed on 22–24 June 1940, the German and Italian governments declared that they did not 'intend' to use French ships under their control for the purposes of war.[30] The French government accepted the terms as being consistent with national honour and providing significant scope for the exercise of sovereignty.[31] The British, by contrast, maintained that neither Berlin nor Rome could be trusted to uphold their pledges and that the French would be unable to resist any attempts to seize their ships.[32] The experiences of occupied France and the impotence of Petain's Vichy government in the face of Axis interventions would go on to vindicate the British assessment.[33] However, as the British Ambassador to France Sir Ronald Campbell noted, the armistice terms were 'diabolically clever' for bolstering French delusions and driving a wedge between the two allies.[34] Any further demand for assurance on the fleet would imply a mistrust of the French that distracted from the severity of the threat with which the British were confronted. On the evening of 22 June, Campbell told French officials that the failure to safeguard the fleet could make the difference between victory and a defeat that risked jeopardising the entire future of France.[35]

Operation Catapult

Having decided to take military action to deal with the threat posed by the French fleet, on 2 July the War Cabinet agreed the wording of a telegram to be sent to Admiral Gensoul before it issued an ultimatum. The telegram reiterated the British government's position on the armistice terms and expressed a determination to fight to the end and restore the 'greatness and territory of France'.[36] However, it also restated the demand for French ships to sail to French ports in the West Indies or Martinique where they could be demilitarised or entrusted to American safekeeping. If the French refused these 'fair' offers, the telegram warned, the British must 'with regret' demand that the French sink their own ships.[37] The tone and language of

207

the message conveyed a reason and courtesy that deflected from its violent intentions. The carefully-worded expression of support for France sought to express the notion that military action would be taken in the French, rather than the British, interest. Reminding the French of the close relationship between their armed forces, it sought to forestall any accusations of treachery by insisting that the Germans were the real enemy.[38]

Up until the last moment on 3 July, Admiral Somerville, commanding the Royal Navy's Force H at Gibraltar, remained convinced that he could persuade Gensoul to accept the terms and that violence could be averted.[39] Somerville portrayed the ultimatum not as a sign of mistrust in the French but rather as a lack of faith in the Germans and Italians. Seeking to take the onus away from Gensoul and to allow the French to honour their armistice undertakings, he argued that if the French admiral accepted the British terms, he would be acting under *force majeure* and would therefore be absolved from blame.[40] In response, however, Gensoul maintained that he would only break the armistice terms if the Germans or Italians breached them first. If the British fired on French ships, he would treat such action as tantamount to a declaration of war.[41] Gensoul even showed Somerville the secret orders to prevent French ships from falling into enemy hands that Admiral Darlan had issued as commander of the French navy on 24 June.[42] By 5pm, Gensoul had failed to agree to any of the British terms, conceding only his willingness to demobilise reservists the following morning.[43] With the ultimatum deadline having expired, at 5:53pm, Somerville gave the order to open fire on the French fleet.

Despite the repeated British demands in relation to the French ships, and despite the ultimatum of 3 July, French ministers and admirals refused to believe that London would carry out its threat to attack. On receiving the news, French Foreign Minister Paul Baudouin therefore responded with 'stupor'.[44] Darlan took it as a particularly personal afront. According to one observer, his whole mentality changed overnight, going from clarity and reason to 'internal frenzy' and rage.[45] The French Ministry for Naval Affairs issued a statement accusing the British of callously exploiting France's misfortunes to advance their own global ambitions.[46] Refuting British claims that the fleet had been in danger of falling into German or Italian hands, the statement insisted that French sailors had not wanted to be placed under Churchill's command. By positioning magnetic mines in the harbour before the ultimatum deadline had expired, the Ministry claimed, the British had engaged in a 'deliberately hostile' act.[47] Using highly emotive language, it claimed that the dead sailors had been stabbed in the back by the British, despite having selflessly given their all to help the Royal Navy.[48]

The use of violence in the operation was, however, neither unconsidered nor unconstrained. On 2 July, the Cabinet agreed that if the French rejected the ultimatum, air and naval forces should use all means at their disposal to destroy the French ships, especially the battleships *Dunquerque* and *Strasbourg*. In considering the options for carrying out the operation, the Admiralty and Cabinet had to balance achieving their strategic objectives with the likely military and political repercussions. Such were the risks that on 24 June, First Sea Lord Sir Dudley Pound had warned that the military gains would not be worth the potential British losses and advised against the whole operation. The naval staff took the view that capturing French ships or sinking them would drive French crews into active hostility and would prompt the Germans to seize the rest of the fleet.[49] The decision not to allow the evacuation of French sailors was to prove particularly contentious, not merely for the many deaths that resulted but for its apparent callousness. Nevertheless, in considering the options, the British government took steps to minimise military and civilian casualties. It ordered that bloodshed should be avoided in the capture of the battleship *Richelieu*, which had set sail from Dakar on 25 June.[50] Minimal force was deployed in the seizure of French ships at British ports as well.[51] Moreover, while the Cabinet opposed offering the French fleet the option to demobilise itself, to avoid unnecessary bloodshed it conceded that it would accept such a proposal if it came from the French themselves.[52] The Cabinet also agreed that a similar operation at nearby Oran would only go ahead if it did not involve 'considerable loss of civilian life'.[53] It rejected a separate operation in Algiers on the grounds that it would cause significant damage to the town and its civilian population.[54]

Despite the limitations on the use of violence, British admirals maintained their opposition to Operation Catapult on grounds of its judiciousness and morality. Indeed, Churchill later conceded that only the most direct orders had compelled naval officers to open fire on their former comrades-in-arms.[55] Whereas ministers and civilian officials in London took a detached view of French sailors, British admirals and their crews had developed a camaraderie with their French counterparts. On 30 June, as commander of the North Atlantic fleet at Gibraltar, Admiral North convened a meeting of captains and flag officers to express opposition to any use of force at Mers-el-Kébir.[56] The following day, Somerville sent the Admiralty a telegram stating that he and the other naval commanders in the Mediterranean also opposed the use of force.[57] Even after having fulfilled his orders, Somerville expressed his disapproval in his report to the Admiralty.[58] Cunningham did not hold back either, describing the operation in his memoirs as 'utterly repugnant' and nothing less than an 'act of sheer treachery'.[59]

In marked contrast with the violence at Mers-el-Kébir, an analogous operation at Alexandria was averted by Cunningham negotiating an agreement with his French counterpart, Admiral Godfroy. On being presented with a similar ultimatum, Godfroy opted to place the French ships in a non-seagoing condition. Unable to communicate with his government, however, he told Cunningham that he would have to sink the ships and requested forty-eight hours to make the necessary arrangements.[60] The Admiralty was unwilling to agree any extension to the ultimatum deadline. Cunningham therefore took the initiative, sending a private letter to Godfroy to seek a way out of the impasse. By 5.30pm on 3 July, the two men had agreed a compromise. Godfroy was to remove oil from the French ships and remove the torpedo warheads, but would only reduce the crews if his government approved.[61] Once again, however, the Admiralty rejected the proposal. In a tersely-worded signal sent at 8:15pm, it ordered the immediate reduction of French crews, insisting 'do not, repeat, not fail'.[62] Filled with 'indignation', Cunningham ignored the signal and continued the negotiations.[63] Having learned of the developments at Mers-el-Kébir overnight, however, the following morning Godfroy repudiated his previous undertakings, declaring that he would sail his ships out of the harbour and would fight the British to do so. As a final resort, Cunningham appealed directly to the French sailors. Under pressure from his crews, Godfroy agreed to discharge the oil from his ships and to place his ships in a non-combat condition. Cunningham's compromise therefore averted the use of force, earning fulsome praise from the Admiralty and even from Churchill.[64]

Political Justifications

Ultimately for Churchill, however, it was the desire to show that the British government would stop at nothing in the pursuit of victory that lay behind Operation Catapult. In his statement to the House of Commons on 4 July, the Prime Minister declared that the operation would end the 'lies and rumours' circulating in the United States and in German propaganda that the British were on the verge of surrender.[65] Churchill later argued that 'ruthlessly' taking 'violent action' against his country's 'dearest friends of yesterday' at a time when many observers had written Britain off proved that London was fearless.[66] Operation Catapult was therefore designed to be decisive and to appear so. Indeed, Martin Thomas and Richard Toye have gone so far as to suggest that it was 'intended as a symbolic or even rhetorical act'.[67]

If British action sailed close to the wind in its morality and legitimacy, it did so deliberately. Churchill wanted to show British resolve to friendly governments, while showing British ruthlessness to unfriendly governments. Above all, he sought to demonstrate that his country's defiance was more than a match for Nazi aggression and that being a liberal democracy was no hindrance to the pursuit of victory. His strategy had the desired effect. The *New York Herald Tribune* observed that 'Britain has at last the one thing which the democratic Powers have lacked through all these fantastic years— the will to fight regardless of consequences, the will to victory.'[68] The *Chicago Daily News*, meanwhile, noted that the decisiveness of the operation signalled that the British government would not be hampered by its liberal democratic values: 'There was a widespread fear that the rot of indecision—that disease of Democracy—had eaten as deeply into the British, as it was proven to have spread into the French'.[69] In France, there was widespread shock at how the action seemed the very opposite of the values the British claimed to represent. Far from behaving like 'gentlemen' according to notions of 'fair play', Darlan claimed, British sailors had been 'accomplices to premeditated murder'.[70] In the press, the 'civilised' conduct of the French was contrasted with the 'gangster' behaviour of the British.[71] German propaganda, meanwhile, berated the British for betraying their supposed values of 'honesty, decency and chivalry', expressing outrage at the 'triumph of pirate morals'.[72]

In making such a show of defiance, the British government consciously drew upon the precedent of Copenhagen in the Napoleonic Wars. Despite the public uproar at the time, in British memory Copenhagen had become a shorthand for decisive pre-emptive action that helped secure ultimate victory against Napoleon. Indeed, Cabinet minutes dated 27 June 1940 claimed that public opinion was 'strongly insistent' that the government take similar action to that against the Danish fleet in 1807.[73] A *Times* editorial on 6 July explicitly drew parallels between the two episodes, arguing that if the 1807 attack had been justified to prevent Danish ships from potentially falling into enemy hands, the 1940 attack was even more justified because French ships were already under enemy control.[74] Several regional papers followed suit, drawing positive comparisons between the two operations.[75] In Germany, by contrast, Copenhagen had become a byword not merely for pre-emptive action but for British violence and disregard for international law as well. Four months earlier, officials had claimed that British sailors boarding the German supply ship *Altmark* while in Norwegian territorial waters was part of a pattern of British violations of international law that stretched back to 1807.[76] The German minister in Oslo compared the killing of four members of the Altmark's crew with the violence witnessed in 1807.[77] It was perhaps because Nazi propaganda had been so quick to draw parallels between the two episodes that Churchill avoided any direct comparisons at the time and in the period thereafter.[78] In his memoirs, he likened the Mers-el-Kébir operation to the less contentious British action against the Danish fleet at Copenhagen in 1801. Striking a more remorseful tone than

LEGITIMISING VIOLENCE IN THE BRITISH ATTACK

in July 1940, he claimed that Mers-el-Kébir had been even more painful than the Copenhagen attack of 1801 because the French 'had been only yesterday our dear Allies'.[79]

In the days immediately following the operation, however, Churchill mounted a more bullish defence of British actions. Addressing Parliament, he focused on justifying the action in military and political terms. Beginning by expressing his regret at the losses, he quickly moved on to rebuff French claims of treachery with accusations of his own. Charging the French government with 'abandoning the conflict and leaving its whole weight to fall upon Great Britain and the British Empire', he went on to condemn its 'callous and perhaps even malevolent treatment' of the British.[80] He ended with what Rachel Chin describes as a 'classic rhetorical device' that encouraged the audience to draw its own conclusions on the legitimacy of the operation.[81] Throwing down the gauntlet, Churchill challenged the United States, the world and 'history' to make their judgement.[82] In a similar vein, Foreign Secretary Lord Halifax told the House of Lords of his 'distress and sorrow', but insisted that the operation had been justified, accusing the French government of prioritising its promises to the enemy over the 'fulfilment of a solemn pledge to its ally'.[83]

Managing media reporting on the operation was critical to the British government's efforts to legitimise it politically. The Ministry of Information advised that the story's release must be carefully timed so that the government could control the narrative. On 2 July, in conjunction with the Admiralty, it proposed a statement for release to the press once the operation had been completed. The statement began by outlining how the German and Italian armistices included terms that affected the 'vital interests' of the British empire and claimed that the French government had placed itself in a position where it would be unable to prevent the enemy from seizing its ships.[84] Under such circumstances, the statement explained, the British government 'felt constrained' to take action.[85] In anticipation of the potential losses resulting from the action, it concluded on a conciliatory note that emphasised the British government's hopes that French sailors would join their 'British comrades' in continuing the fight for the 'freedom of France'.[86]

213

The British press faithfully followed the government line in conveying the necessity of the operation while highlighting the painful nature of the decision.[87] Many reports focused on Churchill's emotion as he delivered the news to Parliament, seeking to quash any suggestions of triumphalism or that the British government revelled in the misfortunes of its former ally.[88] Several newspaper editors and columnists welcomed the change in the tone of the British engagement, praising not merely the decisive nature of the intervention but its ruthlessness as well. *The Scotsman* noted the Prime Minister's promise to handle the situation with 'patience and resolution', commenting that hitherto, patience had 'been shown perhaps to excess', but resolution had 'now been brought into play with heartening and decisive success'.[89] A columnist for *The People*, meanwhile, was 'thrilled' to see 'John Bull drive into battle again, resolute, full of fight', noting that the British government had abandoned its earlier 'hesitations and over-nice scruples'.[90]

Careful management of how domestic public opinion responded to the news was also vital in helping to legitimise the operation. Ministry of Information monitoring suggested that such efforts were largely successful. The British people generally welcomed the decisive nature of the action as a turning-point for the nation's war effort. Having been on the back foot in May and June 1940, many believed that they were finally showing Hitler what they were capable of.[91] The public were said to have hailed the 'strong action' as evidence of government 'vigour and decisiveness'.[92] For many, the violent character of the attack was central to its appeal, with one report noting the public's 'cheerful aggressiveness'.[93] Antipathy towards the French was exacerbated rather than generated by the episode, with some claiming that Britain had never been 'real friends with the French'.[94] Overall, the Ministry of Information deemed Operation Catapult to have had a positive effect on British morale, with members of the public showing little concern about the French casualties.[95]

The decisiveness of the operation gave it a powerful simplicity that was designed to resonate in the wider international community.[96] In the weeks that followed, Britain's network of ambassadors reported favourable responses from across the globe.[97] Above all, however,

Churchill was determined that the operation should send a signal to the United States. Desperate for greater support from Washington, he wanted to demonstrate his government's resolve.[98] The response was overwhelmingly favourable. Reuters reported that Washington saw the operation as evidence that 'the iron will has not yet rusted out of the British character'.[99] There was widespread relief at the development on Capitol Hill as well.[100] Churchill's radio broadcast a few days later did much to consolidate this view, especially within American public opinion.[101] Coverage in the American press was also positive, with newspapers praising the 'boldness' and 'efficiency' of the operation.[102] The *New York Post* said that any lesser action would have been 'criminal madness'.[103] The *New York Times* agreed that without the operation, the French fleet would 'inevitably' have fallen into enemy hands.[104]

The British handling of the French government was, perhaps inevitably, rather less successful. The gulf between British confidence in the legitimacy of the operation and French outrage at the apparent treachery was most starkly exposed in the diplomatic fallout between the two countries. After protesting in the 'strongest terms' against the 'unacceptable' nature of the British ultimatum, on 4 July the French government formally broke off relations with London.[105] In a note delivered to Halifax a few days later, the French government emotively invoked memories of their countries' alliance to highlight the apparent callousness of the attack, arguing that such a close relationship should have deterred the British from their 'repeated acts of aggression'.[106] Nevertheless, the Foreign Office remained sanguine about the prospects of reconciliation, believing that simply by repeating its defence of the operation along with a perfunctory 'expression of regret', the French would come to accept the just nature of the action.[107] In reality, however, the French government had already decided to pivot its foreign policy to an alignment with the Axis, having seriously considered declaring war on Britain.[108]

Honour

If British policy-makers were confident in the legitimacy of Operation Catapult, they nonetheless had to square it with notions of honour. Despite modern warfare having become more total and more deadly, professional officers and servicemen continued to uphold a set of restraints rooted in respect for enemy combatants.[109] Many of these restraints had their origins in ancient aristocratic chivalric codes and served to distinguish professional combatants from mere killing machines. They have therefore often led to clashes with civilian political leaders' pursuit of victory.[110] Such was the case in July 1940.

Whereas Churchill assessed the necessity for action in strategic and political terms, French and British naval commanders clung onto the inviolability of military codes of honour. In the days prior to Operation Catapult, Darlan's repeated rejection of British demands to hand over or sail French ships from the Mediterranean was accompanied by an incomprehension as to why such action was necessary. Having given his word that he would never surrender the fleet and that he had ordered its scuttling if the Germans or Italians tried to seize it, Darlan saw no need for further measures.[111] The Admiralty took a similar view. Many naval officers trusted that the French would not allow their ships to fall into enemy hands.[112] Dudley Pound retained his faith in Darlan's honour as a fellow admiral.[113] Cunningham, meanwhile, insisted that Godfroy was a 'man of honour' and considered the prospect of Darlan willingly handing over the fleet 'unthinkable'.[114] By contrast, Churchill, the Cabinet, and the Foreign Office were unwilling to risk the nation's defences on the private word of men they believed had already betrayed Britain.[115] As well as seeking a decisive resolution to the crisis, they took a more pragmatic view of France's military and political leaders than the Admiralty, with one Foreign Office official noting that Pound had 'too much confidence in old friends and sailors of other races'.[116] Despite their differing approaches, however, the Admiralty and the Cabinet agreed on the importance of avoiding any unnecessary affront to French honour. The Admiralty therefore informed the French navy that it did not doubt the 'good faith' of Darlan's assurances on the French fleet but feared he would not be in a position to oppose German or Italian attempts to seize it.[117] The Cabinet showed a similar sensitivity. Rather than telling Gensoul that it would be 'dishonourable' to allow the French fleet to fall into

LEGITIMISING VIOLENCE IN THE BRITISH ATTACK

enemy hands, it suggested that communications should stress how the British proposals were consistent with French honour.[118]

The British government's contention that it had acted on behalf of a French nation whose political and military leaders had betrayed it was supported by General de Gaulle.[119] The Free French leader maintained that Pétain's government did not represent the 'true' France and that the honour of the nation could only be served by continuing the war.[120] Despite not having been consulted by the British before the operation, de Gaulle publicly gave it his endorsement in a BBC radio broadcast on 8 July. Speaking directly to the French people, he asked them not to think about the 'deplorable and detestable' events at Mers-el-Kébir but about the wider goals of victory and liberation.[121] Seeking to refute accusations that he was a puppet of the British government, he described his 'grief and anger' at the losses and condemned attempts to glorify the operation as a military victory. Nevertheless, de Gaulle accepted that the ships had to be destroyed to prevent them from being used by the enemy, insisting that the defeat of Britain would seal the 'enslavement' of France.[122] For all the many resentments he was to hold against the British over his long political career, de Gaulle's endorsement of the Mers-el-Kébir operation was truly remarkable. It stood as a powerful testimony to the legitimacy of the action and the British government's justification of it.

Conclusion

Much of the bitterness of the French response to Operation Catapult derived from a sense that the British government seemed to treat the loss of French sailors, ships, and diplomatic relations as mere collateral damage. The apparent callousness of the attack was taken as evidence that it was merely a cover for Britain to pursue its global ambitions at France's expense.[123] Moreover, when the French fleet at Toulon scuttled itself in November 1942, Darlan claimed moral vindication for the position he had adopted in July 1940. The arrival of German and Italian forces to the unoccupied zone saw the French navy take action to prevent its ships falling into Axis hands, defying even the instructions of the Vichy government. Writing to Churchill in early December 1942, Darlan claimed that the French navy's action showed that he had been right all along.[124] In the circumstances of early July 1940, however, the British government faced a supreme emergency that meant it could not risk the nation's security on mere verbal promises. Pétain's government may have insisted that the armistice terms preserved French sovereignty, but it was a delusion that the British government saw through from the outset. Quite simply, there was no guarantee that France's navy would remain in French hands. The issue was therefore not so much the reason for Operation Catapult as the nature with which it was conducted.

A *Times* editorial of 6 July 1940 summed up the difficulties facing the British government. While the British maintained that they had higher moral values than other nations, the article claimed, they needed to avoid those moral values seeming a hindrance to their ability to undertake difficult and contentious military action.[125] In pursuit of domestic and international support for its continuing war effort, the British government used violence to send a signal of its determination to pursue victory at any cost. At the same time, however, it had to ensure that such violence did not undermine its claims to be acting legitimately and in the moral interest. While Operation Catapult was not the first such use of military force, the British government centred its justification on claims of the wider exigencies of defeating the extraordinary threat posed by Nazism. The violence at Mers-el-Kébir was not a deviation from Britain's moral undertakings, nor was it a sign that the 'mask' had slipped. It was rather that the British government's belief in the moral superiority of its cause became at once a driving factor and a justification for its use of violence.

12

OPERATION GOMORRAH
RUTHLESSNESS AND THE BRITISH AIR WAR, 1943

Richard Overy

Shortly after the end of the Casablanca Conference in January 1943, Air Chief Marshal Arthur Harris, commander-in-chief of RAF Bomber Command, wrote that the German city of Hamburg had so far enjoyed a 'lucky escape' from being 'devastated' by British bombing. He planned to carry out six so-called devastations in the course of the year: Bremen, Kiel, Duisburg, Wilhelmshaven, and Hamburg (whose great size qualified it for devastation twice over).[1] Much has been written about the subsequent bombing of Hamburg, which until the bombing of Dresden recorded the highest number of dead in one night of raiding.[2] The purpose of this chapter is not to revisit the story of Operation Gomorrah and its consequences for the urban population but to explore the broader context, both political, strategic, and technical, that allowed Bomber Command to pursue the deliberate obliteration of city areas and the ruthless mass killing of their civilian inhabitants.

It is necessary, nevertheless, to begin by briefly outlining the nature of the attack. The plan for the raids on Hamburg was finalized on 27 May 1943 under the operational title Gomorrah. The operation was to take place over a ten-day period to ensure that 'devastation' was indeed the result, and between the nights of 24/25 July and 2/3 August Bomber Command carried out five large-scale raids, the last of which had to be aborted through bad weather. The aiming point, detailed to the squadron commanders, was the working-class residential districts clustered along the Elbe River. The first raid killed 10,289 people, by far the largest number in any raid so far on a German target. The raid that is best known came on 27/28 July when British bombers laid waste a large area of working-class Hamburg, created an unstoppable firestorm and killed an estimated 18,474 people. The United States Eighth Air Force carried out two small raids by day, but the pilots could see little because of the smoke from the night raids and the impact was slight by comparison, though American reports did observe that 'the amount of residential damage is very great'.[3] Over the ten-day period, between 34,000 and 37,000 people lost their lives; other estimates suggest even higher figures, but the lower one is the result of careful reconstruction by local historians and the city council.[4] Some 61% of the houses and apartments in the city were destroyed or damaged, and one million people fled from the city. Gomorrah was by far the worst set of raids throughout the war, but it has always excited less publicity than the bombing of Dresden in February 1945, which has become emblematic of the callous strategy of 'area' bombing.

The first question raised by Gomorrah is to ask why Bomber Command was permitted by the political and military leadership in London to conduct operations the principal purpose of which was to attack and destroy the civilian milieu of German cities and kill, injure, or displace the inhabitants who lived there. The initial policy of the government and the military chiefs-of-staff was to insist on restraint in the bombing war. Bomber Command was told by the Air Ministry in 1939 that night bombing or bombing through cloud was not permitted, to protect civilians from harm; only military targets could be attacked, but not if they were sited in residential areas where 'negligent' bombing would produce civilian casualties. An inter-departmental committee reported in August 1939 that 'it is clearly illegal to bombard a populated area in the hope of hitting a legitimate target'.[5] The prevailing view was that the deliberate targeting of civilians was entirely contrary to the rules of war, a view reiterated by Neville Chamberlain's government at the outbreak of war, which wanted no risk of justified German retaliation. The laws of war nevertheless allowed a relaxation of these restrictions if, or when, the enemy ignored them. When Winston Churchill's cabinet, successor to Chamberlain's in May 1940, debated whether German cities could be attacked to ease pressure on Allied forces in France, it was generally agreed that the moral issue could be side-stepped because of the atrocious behaviour of German armed forces in Poland. From 12 May onwards, Bomber Command flew regular bombing missions against German cities at night, in violation of the initial constraints, long before the German Air Force initiated the Blitz. Over the course of the summer of 1940, Bomber Command was given greater opportunity to bomb targets where civilians might be victims, though not deliberate victims, until by October the restraints imposed in late 1939 were virtually abandoned. [6]

The German bombing campaign against British cities did not prompt the RAF bombing offensive, which had already begun four months before, but it did provoke a more radical departure for Bomber Command from the initial campaign against military and economic targets. Assessment of the damage done by German bombing suggested that it made greater strategic sense to bomb civilians and civilian areas intentionally and to abandon the hitherto unsuccessful attempt to hit small, individual objectives. The new strategy was candidly laid out in an Air Ministry memorandum in April 1941:

> carefully planned and continuous BLITZ attacks delivered on the centre of the working-class area of the German cities and towns ... is undoubtedly the most effective weapon available to our bomber force within the limitation of night operations. It is felt [sic!] the aiming point of the first aircraft over the target should if conceivably possible, be the centre of the working-class area and not the centre of the industrial zone. [7]

The change was not regarded as a shift to terror bombing, which was still regarded as something only the Germans did, but as a means to multiply the strategic impact bombing operations would have. Research on Britain's blitzed cities showed that far more damage was inflicted by incendiary bombs than high explosive. City fire

HARFLEUR TO HAMBURG

chiefs reported to the Ministry of Home Security that between 80% and 90% of urban destruction had been caused by fire.[8] It was also realised that destruction of residential areas and amenities, and killing workers, would affect many more factories than bombing just one of them. The Ministry of Economic Warfare, which drew up a survey of all German cities and their economic significance, encouraged the Air Ministry to adopt bombing of whole working-class areas for just this reason.[9] The weapon of choice for the campaign was now the incendiary bomb, dropped in tens of thousands on the target city.

If Bomber Command needed persuading, the evidence that emerged on how inaccurate British bombing was made the attack on large area targets seem a sensible operational choice. In the discussions surrounding the change it was clear that Bomber Command could not be directed to kill civilians indiscriminately, which is what the new strategy amounted to, so the euphemism of attack on working-class 'morale' was substituted.[10] The first directive to attack civilian morale came in July 1941, but the development of operations with this objective evolved slowly over the rest of the year. By late autumn 1941, the Air Ministry Bombing Directorate had outlined how to develop operations that would destroy homes and civilian amenities by fire, kill or injure workers, and undermine key services and the general morale of the population.[11] In January 1942, a draft directive for Bomber Command explained that now 'The attacks against industrial areas should be concentrated primarily on the civilian population'.[12] The final directive, published on 14 February 1942, stated more equivocally that the sole principal aim of the Command from now on was 'the morale of the enemy civil population and in particular of the industrial workers', but the surrounding discussion at the Air Ministry made it clear that killing workers and burning down their homes was the real purpose.[13] Morale nevertheless remained the code word used in all discussions of Bomber Command targeting with other Ministries, political leaders, and the American allies.

It was against this background that the eventual obliteration of Hamburg was to be based. The city had already featured in the planning for the new strategy. In November 1941, the Bombing Directorate in the Air Ministry concluded that among the cities within range, Hamburg presented the best conditions for a large-scale area raid. To achieve saturation-point with incendiaries, it was argued that the target area should be 'the congested city and housing areas north of the Elbe'.[14] A further study in February 1942 on choosing a city to destroy had Hamburg at the top of the list, its vulnerability described as 'outstanding'. Harris, now commander-in-chief, wanted the city obliterated in one or at most two nights through an 'inextinguishable conflagration'.[15] The first 'Thousand Bomber Raid' in May 1942 was supposed to be directed at Hamburg, but had to be changed at the last moment to Cologne because of poor weather. Instead, Hamburg was regularly subjected to minor raids, a total of 137 recorded between 1940 and summer 1943. The ten raids in 1943 prior to Gomorrah killed 142 people and destroyed 200 buildings.[16] Finally, in April 1943, the Air Ministry Target Committee defined Hamburg as the 'No 1 priority' and three months later the special status accorded to the city as a target was redeemed with the devastation Harris wanted.[17] Only by this stage was Bomber Command in a position to inflict serious damage. If Hamburg had been the object of the first 'Thousand bomber raid' in 1942, the city would not have experienced the 1943 firestorm.

The critical factor in the change to bombing city areas was the incendiary bomb. It was this that made possible a firestorm on the scale of Hamburg. But for the RAF, the incendiary had always been a minor weapon; real damage was expected to come from the impact of high explosive bombs. Incendiaries had been used for colonial policing against tribal villages in Africa, the Middle East, and South Asia, used in order to burn down huts and crops and to scatter livestock. Many of those in command in the war had had experience of these operations against what the RAF War Manual called 'semi-civilized peoples', including Portal and Harris. Indeed, at one point in 1941, in response to Churchill's declining enthusiasm for the bombing campaign, Portal argued that raiding Germany was just a larger version of the 'outstandingly successful' colonial air policing, which Churchill had helped to initiate in the 1920s.[18] In combat against colonial peoples there was little sense of ethical restraint, since air policing was seen as both cheap and effective.

Nevertheless, incendiary use against 'civilized' Europeans was regarded by British airmen and politicians as sheer terror, symbolised

HARFLEUR TO HAMBURG

by the bombing of the Basque town of Gernika in 1937. In 1936 the ICI company was invited to develop a small magnesium incendiary bomb, but the subsequent 4-pound bomb was initially produced in small numbers as at most a subsidiary weapon in any future air war—although in the end, over 76 million of them were produced during the war.[19] In the first British raids on Germany, a few incendiaries were mixed into the bombload, but it was the discovery that up to two-thirds of German bombloads were made up of incendiaries that gave the small bomb a sudden importance. By January 1942, the Bombing Directorate in the Air Ministry no longer regarded the incendiary as subsidiary. Instead, the high explosive bomb was now 'secondary and supplementary', assisting the incendiary effect by blasting windows and terrorising the enemy civil defence service.[20] The sudden shift in priorities produced a crisis in the manufacture of the incendiaries with severe shortages of the necessary magnesium. Efforts to get more production from the United States failed to provide what Bomber Command now needed in 1942. Churchill was alerted and threw his weight behind production to avoid reducing 'the scale of fire-raising attacks', whose purpose he clearly understood.[21] Production in the end expanded at an exponential rate so that by early 1943 magnesium production and imports amounted to seven million tons a quarter, adequate to meet the demands of Harris's devastating operations during the spring and summer.[22]

The advent of the incendiary as the principal weapon was the only means to achieve the level of fire destruction envisaged by the Air Ministry for the change in strategy. The new operations required significant alterations in tactics, which were developed by Harris over the course of 1942. These alterations have not usually been attributed to the introduction of mass incendiary bombing, but they were designed to ensure that the city centre burnt down effectively. They included the introduction of a 'pathfinder force' to lead the operation and to drop target markers to illuminate the city area; the employment of a bomber stream to ensure that the area was hit every few seconds by an incendiary load; navigation aids to ensure that the right city was bombed (a problem earlier in the war); and around ten per cent of the incendiary bomb load composed of incendiaries with a high explosive charge that killed or maimed civil defenders who

224

tried to tackle them. High explosive bombs were included to hinder fire-fighting and to encourage the spread of fire.

The new tactics also depended on being able to identify readily the right area of a city to attack, like the instruction to hit working-class residential housing in Hamburg. The advantage of starting an 'unmistakeable conflagration' by the lead aircraft, wrote deputy chief of staff Norman Bottomley to Harris, was for all the crews following to have something obvious to bomb.[23] The Bombing Directorate, beginning in October 1941, drew up a zoning scheme based on a study of the geography of German cities and towns. The key targets were Zone 1 ('central city area, fully built up'), Zone 2(a) ('compact residential area, fully built up' and Zone 2(b) ('compact residential area, 40% to 70% built up'). The priority was to hit these central zones where a large proportion of the working class lived; Zone 4 ('industrial areas') was no longer regarded as a priority since the industrial area was generally more difficult to burn down.[24] One final innovation was introduced for Gomorrah: the use of 'Window', small metallic strips dropped from lead aircraft to confuse enemy radar with a mass of information on the screen. Based on the new operational tactics, Portal with remarkable candour informed the chiefs-of-staff committee in November 1942 that over the following eighteen months Bomber Command could kill 900,000 Germans and seriously injure a further million, destroy six million homes, and leave 25 million homeless.[25] In any other context, these claims might be regarded as genocidal.

The key problem was to work out exactly how to burn a city down. This had scarcely been a problem when towns were scorched in medieval and early modern warfare, but cities were now large and spread out, built of materials not easy to ignite, with roads and parks that separated off one residential block from another. The answer was to employ civilian scientists and engineering experts to work out the ideal pattern and intensity of incendiary bombing to achieve a major conflagration. There were many sources used to study the technical nature of incendiary bombing. The Ministry of Home Security established a research department, RE8, to assess the effects of the German Blitz, but it soon became involved in applying these lessons to the bombing of German cities. To work out how best to damage German buildings by fire, the Building Research Station and the Road Research Laboratory helped to evaluate the efficacy of different types of incendiary device. Model German buildings and houses were constructed for the purpose, using advice from émigré German architects, including the founder of the modernist Bauhaus, Walter Gropius. By October 1941, it was already possible to conclude that 'a German house will burn well once the fire has caught on'.[26] It was realised early on that wind speed and direction were very important multipliers in spreading an uncontrollable fire and at the government experimental centre at Porton Down the scientist (and former pacifist) J. D. Bernal recommended wind trials on models of urban areas to calculate the typical spread of fire. In many German cities, the centre consisted of tightly packed residential areas easier to incinerate. The Bombing Directorate concluded that igniting 'the terraces of box-like buildings dating from the Middle Ages' would almost certainly 'yield good dividend'. [27]

To further the research, the Air Ministry invited fire-fighting engineers from the United States to study their conclusions and to provide advice on the basis of the major conflagrations that had occasionally engulfed American cities. In late 1942, Horatio Bond, chief engineer of the National Fire Protection Association stayed for four months to help the RE8 scientists with their calculation of vulnerability to fire. A few months later, another senior American engineer from the Association, James McElroy, arrived and stayed for the rest of the war producing fire vulnerability maps of German cities. 'It is clear,' McElroy later wrote, 'that the application of peacetime fire engineering experience to the offensive use of fire is profitable and valuable...'.[28] The advice was complemented by inviting British scientists and technologists to join an informal committee to consider 'Tactics of Incendiary Attacks'. The first meeting convened in the Senior Common Room at Imperial College, London in November 1942 and continued through to the end of the war, by which time it had been constituted in April 1944 more formally as the 'Incendiary Panel'.[29] The members included J. D. Bernal and, later in the war, Jacob Bronowski, both pacifists who nevertheless found it possible to work on the technical issue of how to burn down a typical German (and later Japanese) home. The group at Imperial

College spent, according to the minutes, much time discussing, and occasionally arguing over, the necessary density of incendiary bombs per acre, the optimum bomb for penetrating the roof and floors of a typical German home, and how to smother the enemy's fire-fighting force. The aim was to achieve a 'fire storm' on every major raid (a term first used on 12 August 1942), but that depended, as the meeting in May 1943 concluded, on the wind velocity and air flow characteristics. If there were turbulent air, sucked into the fire zone from the sides, then a major conflagration would result.[30] Hamburg three months later was to prove the experts right.

* * *

How is it possible to explain not only the willingness of the air force to pursue the deliberate destruction of the civilian milieu and the civilians who inhabited it, but to win the endorsement and co-operation of a cohort of politicians, civilian experts, scientists, and engineers to ensure that the strategy would have optimum effect? For RAF commanders this did not seem to be an issue of military ethics, but of military efficiency. This was also Churchill's priority when he endorsed the shift to city bombing after disappointment with the results achieved by 1942, and he too expressed no scruples about the change in strategy until after the bombing of Dresden in February 1945. Area bombing of industrial cities was regarded as the best that night bombing under current technical conditions could achieve. As the government scientist Solly Zuckerman put it in late 1942, 'a ton of IB kills more Germans' than a ton of high explosive.[31] There was also a positive desire to demonstrate ruthlessness, rather than be accused of weakness in the face of any moral qualms. In a private speech to the Thirty Club (a group of senior businessmen) in November 1941, the then-commander-in-chief of Bomber Command, Air Chief Marshal Richard Peirse, told his audience that the campaign was now against 'the people themselves', but even if the government liked to pretend 'that we still held some scruples', continued Peirse, 'I can assure you, Gentlemen, that we tolerate no scruples.' There was, he concluded, 'no false sentiment in Bomber Command'.[32] Harris was notorious for his hostility to 'humanitarian sentiment', and dismissive of the idea that bomber crews might be affected by the strategy they were now being asked to carry out. Any 'weaker sisters', he told the publicity department in the Air Ministry, would be weeded out.[33] Harris himself took an evident pride in conducting a campaign in which any ethical considerations were reserved for his crews, not for those whom they incinerated.

Acceptance of the strategy was made easier for those conducting it and for the wider public because the results of city bombing were always presented in a morally neutral format by measuring success in terms of the area destroyed rather than the numbers killed, injured, or displaced. For Harris, the bombing of Hamburg was a great success. A week after the end of the Gomorrah campaign, he wrote to Portal, who was in Quebec for the QUADRANT Conference, that Hamburg opened the way to 'the final show-down' in the bombing war: 'I am certain,' he continued, '...that we can push Germany over by bombing this year'.[34] For the Air Ministry, Hamburg overnight transformed the statistics on damage to German cities and strengthened their hand in defending the achievements of the bombing campaign. The abstract nature of the statistics masked the human cost in the areas designated as devastated. The following table shows the impact that the bombing of Hamburg had on the statistical model used by Bomber Command to measure impact:

Destruction by fire of the inner-city areas of German cities, 1941–43[35]

Date	Acres in Inner Zones 1 and 2	Acres devastated	Percentage devastated
End 1941	70,300	86	0.12
31 Mar 1942	71,000	276	0.38
30 June 1942	71,000	1,705	2.40
30 Sept 1942	72,900	2,350	3.22
31 Dec 1942	74,600	2,350	3.15
31 Mar 1943	75,200	4,280	5.68
30 June 1943	78,000	9,583	12.27
31 Oct 1943	84,200	20,990	24.94

[The increase in Inner Zone acreage is due to adding additional towns to the list]

OPERATION GOMORRAH

This proved to be the only effective way to measure what the force was doing, since details on German deaths, housing destroyed, and production hours lost only became available once the war was over, although this did not prevent wartime speculation on the probable statistics. Air Intelligence also used Hamburg as the starting point for using acres destroyed as a means to define statistically three operational outcomes, 'effort', 'efficiency', and 'success', again a way of masking the consequences of bombing for those under the bombs.[36]

There was evidently some sensitivity in the Air Ministry over advertising exactly what Bomber Command was doing. Every effort was made to mask the reality of the area attacks by insisting that they were legitimate military-economic targets. When the term 'industrial populations' slipped into a document, it was changed to 'industrial centres' to ensure that the deliberate targeting of civilians was erased from the record through the use of abstract language.[37] In a famous exchange between Harris and the Air Ministry in October 1943, the commander-in-chief of Bomber Command requested that the purpose of the campaign be properly advertised as 'the obliteration of German cities and their inhabitants as such'. The bomber crews, Harris insisted, could not understand why the Ministry was not honest about 'the killing of German workers and the disruption of civilised community life'.[38] The Air Ministry refused on the ground that the directive to Bomber Command only talked about attacking the morale of the German working-class, not bombing civilians directly, a piece of sophistry that the Ministry sustained down to the end of the war and beyond.[39] The reason given to Harris was caution over the existence of 'religious and humanitarian opinion'.

There was less reticence in telling the German people what to expect. In a leaflet bearing Harris's signature with the title 'Why We Bomb You', dropped over Germany in summer 1942, the population was told that in bombing industrial cities 'we hit your houses—and you—when we bomb them. We regret the necessity for this. But this regret will never stop us...'[40] The leaflet was part of a broader campaign to break enemy morale organised by the Political Warfare Executive in collaboration with Bomber Command, to instil fear in the German urban population of the consequences of being bombed, and to encourage them to sabotage the war effort. In November and December 1943 leaflets were dropped with pictures of the destruction of Hamburg's residential areas under the heading 'Wann soll es enden?' [When will it end] or 'Volk im Abgrund' [A people in the abyss]. 'More industrial cities', ran one leaflet, 'will be made into heaps of ruins', unless the Germans capitulated.[41] The language used by PWE was always abstract. 'Morale' rather than real people was the euphemism employed in what the PWE Director of Operations called the 'indivisibility of Total War', but undermining morale meant destroying houses, amenities, and services and killing or displacing workers, which perhaps explains why little effort was devoted to defining it.[42] By the last months of war, PWE encouraged ever greater levels of bombing on the assumption that more destruction and death must break morale and bring the war to an end.[43]

It was certainly true that some opposition to the bombing campaign against cities existed among the wider British public. The Bombing Restriction Committee, established in 1942 by Christian pacifists, ran a propaganda campaign against bombing which, though limited in its impact, was sufficiently vocal to worry the Air Ministry. Hamburg became the focus of the Committee's activity in the second half of 1943. In the pamphlet *What Happened in Hamburg*, detail from Swiss newspapers described the physical facts of the firestorm in the city. A number of senior scientists contested the claim as an 'intrinsic absurdity', but a firestorm was exactly what the Incendiary Panel at Imperial College were hoping to create.[44] There was even opposition from within the government establishment. A few days before Gomorrah, the government senior scientific adviser, Henry Tizard, voiced strong objections over the operation to Churchill and Portal on the grounds that the population was 'anti-Nazi and anti-Prussian' and might soon be 'anti-war'. Portal rejected the plea because Hamburg was too important a target. 'It is a moot point,' he wrote for the prime minister, 'whether bombing produces a more desirable effect when directed upon anti-Nazis than upon the faithful', and Churchill took this as a reason to ignore Tizard's intervention.[45]

Tizard was an exception among the cohort of scientists and engineers recruited to support Bomber Command's lethal campaign, and remained sceptical throughout the war about the wisdom of the bombing strategy. More puzzling is the involvement of prominent pacifists and anti-war activists from the 1930s who not only shed their pacifism, but in some cases actively collaborated with an air strategy that could only have the effect of deliberately killing enemy civilians and destroying their urban milieu. A good example is the physicist J. D. Bernal, one of the founding members of the RE8 research department and a regular contributor to the Incendiary Panel. His personal papers, deposited in the Royal Society's archive, contain almost nothing on his wartime activities; the most recent biography notes only Bernal's work together with Zuckerman in compiling a survey of the German bombing of Hull and Birmingham, which provided little evidence that bombing really undermined either production or popular morale.[46] What is missing is Bernal's substantial contribution to the technical study of the impact of incendiary bombing and assessment of the vulnerability of German urban targets to fire. Once his work in assessing the effect of German bombing was over, he continued as one of the scientific advisers attached to the RE8 department to provide advice on how best to bomb German targets, particularly the effect of fire. In a meeting on incendiary bomb development in June 1942, Bernal contributed to the discussion of bombing domestic properties with the advice that incendiaries should be designed to penetrate to lower parts of a German house to ensure a greater level of destruction.[47] He was a regular member of the Incendiary group, where he could have been in no doubt that the purpose was to find ways of burning down German homes in urban residential districts, particularly the meetings in the months before Gomorrah where the subject was 'Fire-Raising'. In July 1942 he became a member of an Operational Research Committee to advise on bombing tactics, where he provided advice on the effect of wind currents on spreading fire. In a September 1942 meeting of the advisory group, Bernal wanted to survey bomb loads necessary 'to render a city incapable of dealing with the immediate problems raised by an air raid', a key objective later in the Gomorrah operation.[48]

In understanding how Bernal and his fellow scientists could accept a strategy that defied the moral concerns of the 1930s in its level of ruthlessness, the analyses of Zygmunt Bauman and Eric Markusen on the possibility of extreme violence contained within the context of 'modernity' can help.[49] They emphasise the importance of the fragmentation of responsibility in modern institutions, and the psychological significance of distance from the violent consequences of research and experiment carried out in the domestic context of scientific or technical enquiry. That distancing renders the victims, in this case of a bombing war aimed at civilians, as invisible to those making the plans or providing the necessary expertise. In the minutes of the Incendiary Panel there is not a single mention of any moral concern about the purpose of the meetings and the advice they generated. 'None of us ever saw the people we killed,' wrote Freeman Dyson, a young scientist recruited to work in Operational Research for Bomber Command. 'None of us particularly cared.'[50] Indeed, the archive evidence shows that the scientists involved were most concerned about the technical issues they were asked to analyse. Any arguments were over the technical evidence—for example the quantity of incendiary bombs needed per square mile of area attacked—rather than the value of the strategy or its ethical implications. Scientific *amour propre* also played a part since those involved wanted to be taken seriously by their air force patrons and resented the points when the research was distorted or ignored, but not what the research was for.

The capacity to accept working for a strategy that in the cold light of day might have evoked resistance was captured well by Freeman Dyson in his memoir of work for Bomber Command:

> Since the beginning of the war I had been retreating step-by-step from one moral position to another, until at the end I had no moral position at all. At the beginning of the war I believed fiercely in the brotherhood of man … and was morally opposed to all violence. After a year of war I retreated and said, Unfortunately nonviolent resistance against Hitler is impracticable, but I am still morally opposed to bombing. A few years later I said, Unfortunately it seems that bombing is necessary in order to win the war, and so I am willing to go to work for Bomber Command, but I am still morally opposed to bombing cities indiscriminately. After I arrived at Bomber Command I said, Unfortunately it turns out

that we are after all bombing cities indiscriminately, but this is morally justified as it is helping to win the war.[51]

The scientist Patrick Blackett, like Tizard a sceptic during the war of the way the bombing campaign was carried out, but not of its ethical ambiguity, later claimed to find it extraordinary, after listening to a lecture by C. P. Snow at Harvard in 1961, that for the first time a 'modern nation had deliberately planned a major military campaign against the enemy's civilian population rather than against his Armed Forces'.[52] But for all Blackett's scepticism during the war about the claims made for bombing, he could still argue in 1941 that 'the bombing of the civilian population is a very important accessory and ought to be continued'. A few months before Gomorrah, he still believed bombing should be continued, but thought it should be conducted after proper scientific assessment of its effects by a committee of the Royal Society.[53] Here too, scientific interest was what counted rather than ethics.

One final factor in explaining the willingness to conduct a strategic air campaign that made possible the deliberate destruction of Hamburg's working-class residential areas and the killing of more than 34,000 people in three nights is the punitive element directed against a totalitarian system and the people who sustained it. When Harris was asked in April 1945 why he was still bombing almost ruined cities with high explosive bombs, he scribbled in the margin 'To kill Boche!'[54] Although never admitted publicly, that was the heart of the incendiary campaign against an enemy regarded on the Allied side as the epitome of evil, to be exorcised by any means available. There was in this ambition an almost Biblical character, expressed in the name chosen for the raids on Hamburg. The city of Gomorrah together with Sodom were the victims of God's wrath for their wickedness and destroyed (Genesis, 19), even though Abraham pleads unsuccessfully for the righteous in the cities to be spared. Other major operations used a similar idiom: Operation Millennium against Cologne, Operation Chastise against the Ruhr dams. The apocalyptic trope was continued in the codenames given to bomb loads with a different mix of bombs: ARSON, FIREBRAND, BAKE, SEAR.[55] Bombing was not intended to be mere vengeance, but

HARFLEUR TO HAMBURG

the exercise of justice against the wicked. In what will now seem an unfortunate Biblical metaphor, the head of Bomber Command Operational Research regretted in September 1943 that the force had, except for Hamburg, failed on most raids 'to create a conflagration in the sense of an all-consuming holocaust'.[56]

* * *

At almost every point in the British wartime establishment, there was support for a bomber offensive directed at enemy cities, and muted concern about any ethical implications for a campaign always presented by the air force authorities as one of military necessity against targets defined in abstract ways. Only a week before Operation Gomorrah, the Archbishop of Canterbury, William Temple, wrote to the Air Ministry to express his concern about the many letters he received from Christians anxious that the RAF had not changed its policy to one of bombing civilians and the city environment. A response was drafted by the Publicity Directorate to reassure the archbishop that no cities were being bombed that did not contain legitimate military-economic targets whose products would otherwise kill British 'husbands, brothers, and sons'. Temple replied four days before the first raid on Hamburg, content that his mind and those of his correspondents had been set at rest that civilians were not a deliberate target.[57] The private brief prepared for the Air Minister, Archibald Sinclair, was more candid than the published statement, confirming that the RAF was indeed bombing and killing civilians. 'We have, of course,' continued the report, 'a far stronger right for we are fighting for the freedom of mankind'. This moral relativism was used throughout the air campaign to justify a ruthless destruction of enemy civilian life, in the belief that this would contribute to the victory of the Allied powers, shorten the war, and display to the German people the error of their ways.

The bombing of Hamburg was to serve one further purpose for the post-war government when the Air Ministry was asked in 1960 by the JIGSAW committee (Joint Intelligence Group on the Study of All-Out Warfare) to provide analytical material on how to 'kill a city', using nuclear weapons. The ministry used Operation Gomorrah as the reference point in how to render a city incapable of survival.

234

OPERATION GOMORRAH

Hamburg was bombed, so it was calculated, with the equivalent of five kilotons, but even small nuclear weapons would achieve greater destruction and so destroy a city more comprehensively than had been possible in 1943. Unlike acres destroyed, however, the JIGSAW committee considered that 'people were the scale to be used in assessing the effects of damage', and looked for Soviet targets by considering 'only effects on the population'.[58] Here once again was ruthless scientific calculation elbowing out any concern about massive loss of life. Rather than the awkward example Hamburg should have been in post-war reflection on the ethics of bombing civilians, it was the best result Bomber Command achieved to compare with nuclear war.

pp. [1–4]

NOTES

1. INTRODUCTION

1. See, e.g., Holger Janusch, 'Normative Power and the Logic of Arguing: Rationalization of Weakness or Relinquishment of Strength?', *Cooperation and Conflict*, 51 (2016), 504–21.

2. See Boyd Hilton's volume in the New Oxford History of England, *A Mad, Bad, and Dangerous People? England 1783–1846* (Oxford: Clarendon Press, 2006).

3. David Edgerton, *Warfare State: Britain, 1920–1970* (Cambridge: Cambridge University Press, 2008). For an application of the concept to the US, see James T. Sparrow, *Warfare State: World War II Americans and the Age of Big Government* (New York: Oxford University Press, 2013). Andrew Lambert, in Chapter 9 in this volume, engages briefly but explicitly with the idea of a 'warfare state' but transferred to the nineteenth century.

4. The pioneering work in this connection is John Brewer, *The Sinews of Power: War, Money, and the English State, 1688–1783* (Cambridge, Mass.: Harvard University Press, 1990); for a survey of the literature relating to the concept see Mark Knights, 'Fiscal-Military State', *Oxford Bibliographies*, https://www.oxfordbibliographies.com/display/document/obo-9780199730414/obo-9780199730414-0073.xml, reviewed Nov. 18, 2022. On the earlier period and the place of war in Anglo-British state development, see James Scott Wheeler, *The Making of a World Power: War and the Military Revolution in Seventeenth-Century Britain* (Stroud: Sutton, 1999); Mark Charles Fissel (ed.), *War and Government in Britain, 1598–1650* (Manchester: Manchester University Press, 1991); Mark Charles Fissel, *English Warfare 1511–1642* (London: Routledge, 2001).

237

NOTES

pp. [4–16]

5. Cf. Alan Cromartie (ed.), 'Introduction' to *Liberal Wars: Anglo-American Strategy, Ideology, and Practice* (New York & Abingdon: Routledge, 2015), 18; Mark Mazower, *Hitler's Empire: How the Nazis Ruled Europe* (New York: Penguin Press, 2008), 586. See also, in this volume, Chapters 9 and 12, by Andrew Lambert and Richard Overy.

6. That said, the fact that British air commanders had experience of colonial 'policing' and of using extreme violence in extra-European conflicts probably made ruthlessness against Germany easier in the twentieth century, as Overy shows in Chapter 12.

7. British action against Copenhagen had meanwhile affected Russian strategic decision-making in 1836, as Andrew Lambert shows in Chapter 9; thus, strategic ruthlessness had a legacy beyond British shores.

8. Paul Langford, *A Polite and Commercial People: England 1727–1783* (Oxford: Clarendon Press, 1989).

9. D. J. B. Trim, '"Put all to the sword": The Effects of Reformation on the Ethics of War in Sixteenth–Century Germany and England', in Dorothea Wendebourg and Alec Ryrie (eds.), *Sister Reformations II / Schwesterreformationen II: Reformation and Ethics in Germany and England / Reformation und Ethik in Deutschland und in England* (Tübingen: Mohr Siebeck, 2014), 275, 276, 292.

10. As Murphy shows in Chapter 3, the Habsburg allies of Henry VIII's general Thomas Howard were 'shocked by the severity of his scorched earth strategy', while contemporaries thought that, of all contemporary combatants, the English were the most skilled at burning.

2. STRATEGY, PIETY, AND CHIVALRY

1. Etienne Marcel letter in Jean Froissart, *Œuvres*, ed. Kervyn de Lettenhove (repr., Osnabrück: Biblio Verlag, 1967), VI, 469.

2. Guy Bois, *Crise du féodalisme: économie rurale et démographie en Normandie orientale du début du 14ᵉ siècle au millieu du 16ᵉ siècle* (Paris: Presses de la fondation nationale des sciences politiques, 1981), 299–308.

3. Jean Juvénal des Ursins, 'Loquar in tribulacione,' in *Écrits politiques*, ed. P. S. Lewis (Paris: SHF, 1978), I, 311.

4. Thomas Basin, *Histoire de Charles VII*, ed. and tr. Charles Samaran, vol. 1 (Paris: Les belles lettres, 1933), 86.

5. Clifford J. Rogers, 'By Fire and Sword: *Bellum Hostile* and 'Civilians' in the Hundred Years War,' in *Civilians in the Path of War*, ed. Mark Grimsley and Clifford J. Rogers (Lincoln: University of Nebraska

238

pp. [16–22]   NOTES

Press, 2002), 45–6 and n. 62; *Chronique de Jean le Bel*, ed. J. Viard and E. Déprez (Paris; SHF 1904), II, 84–85

6. Clifford J. Rogers, 'The Battle of Agincourt,' *The Hundred Years War (Part II): Different Vistas*, ed. L. J. Andrew Villalon and Donald J. Kagay (Leiden: Brill, 2008): 37–132, at 104, 104–05n; Clifford J. Rogers, 'The Anglo-Burgundian Alliance and Grand Strategy in the Hundred Years War,' *Grand Strategy and Military Alliances*, ed. Peter R. Mansoor and Williamson Murray (Cambridge: Cambridge University Press, 2016), 222 n. 10.

7. Bordeaux's population of around 20,000 indicates an adult male population around 4,000–5,000. The army was mostly made up of townsmen, and the lowest figure for the number of slain given by any chronicler is 1,200. 15–20% is thus a conservative estimate; it could well have been 25%. Vincent Haure, 'Bordeaux à la fin du Moyen Age, une puissance militaire. Composition et organisation de ses forces armées,' *Annales du Midi* 126 (2014), 139–59.

8. See the introduction to this volume, 1–2.

9. Unless, that is, he could gain what he considered his rights (sovereign rule over a large part of France) without having to fight—but that was not at all likely.

10. Clifford J. Rogers, *War Cruel and Sharp. English Strategy under Edward III, 1327–1360* (Woodbridge: Boydell, 2000), chs. 5 and 8; Clifford J. Rogers, 'The Anglo-French Peace Negotiations of 1354–1360 Reconsidered,' in *The Age of Edward III*, ed. James Bothwell (York: York Medieval Press, 2001): 193–213.

11. Rogers, *War Cruel and Sharp*, 322–4.

12. Rogers, *War Cruel and Sharp*, chs. 13–16; idem, 'The Anglo-French Peace Negotiations.'

13. For this period see J. J. N. Palmer, *England, France and Christendom, 1377–99* (Chapel Hill: UNC Press, 1972).

14. Though not universal: the Burgundian-Armagnac war in France, for example, was quite brutal, as noted below. But we see little mention of ravaging following Isabella's invasion of 1326 (leading to the deposition of Edward II), and comparatively little during the Wars of the Roses. For example, in J. R. Lander's collection of texts on the latter conflict, the words *burn, devastate, devastation, ravage,* and *ravaging* never appear with reference to England. J. R. Lander, *The Wars of the Roses* (New York: G.P. Putnam's Sons, 1966).

15. 'Wrangit': William Fraser, *The Red Book of Menteith*, 2 vols. (Privately printed: Edinburgh, 1880), I, 170. Rest of paragraph: Stephen I Boardman, *The Early Stewart Kings* (East Linton: Tuckwell, 1996),

NOTES pp. [22–23]

226–38; Chris Given-Wilson, *Henry IV* (New Haven: Yale U.P., 2016), 167–71, 224–25; Anne Curry et al., 'Henry IV's Scottish Expedition of 1400,' *EHR* 125 (2020), 1382–1413; Rory Cox, 'A Law of War? English Protection and Destruction of Ecclesiastical Property during the Fourteenth Century,' *EHR* 128 (2013), for 1385. On the level of devastation, see ibid., n. 65, and consider that the Scottish chroniclers were in a better position to know the truth, and had no motive to depict Henry showing more restraint than he actually did. Similarly, according to the report of several senior French clergymen, when the duke of Clarence chose to restrain his troops after a sort of armistice in 1412, they 'comported themselves better than French troops would have done' while making their way out of French territory. [Michel Pintoin], *Chronique du religieux de Saint-Denys,* ed. L. Bellaguet, 6 vols. (Paris: SHF, 1839–52), IV, 721. Hereafter *Saint-Denys.*

16. *Chronicon Adae de Usk, 1379–1421*, ed. and tr. E. Maunde Thompson, 2nd ed. (London: Royal Society of Literature, 1876), p. 208. Likewise the rebels in 1402 'cruelly harried…the country-side with fire and sword…carrying off the spoil of the land and especially the cattle' (p. 239); in 1404, Owain 'marched through Wales with a great power as far as the sea of the Severn, and brought into subjection with fire and sword all who made resistance and also those beyond the same sea wherever the Welsh had, as such, been pillaged by the country people, sparing not even churches…' (p. 254); in response the men of Bristol 'pillaged the church of Llandaff' (p. 255); the French arrived to support the rebellion, and 'wasting all the march with fire and sword they did no small hurt to the English' (p. 255).

17. Ibid., 237.

18. Ibid., 247; Thomas Walsingham, *The St Albans Chronicle. The Chronica maiora of Thomas Walsingham,* ed. and tr. John R. Taylor et al., vol. 2 (Oxford: Clarendon, 2011), 314, 323. Some historians would dismiss such claims as propaganda, but students of the whole history of human violence will know that the assertion is not inherently unlikely.

19. Rhidian Griffiths, 'Prince Henry's War: Armies, Garrisons and Supply during the Glyndŵr Rising,' *Bulletin of the Board of Celtic Studies* 34 (1987); Christopher Allmand, *Henry V* (Berkeley: University of California Press, 1992), ch. 2; R. R. Davies, *The Revolt of Owain Glyn Dŵr* (Oxford: O.U.P., 1995). On the development of bombards, see Clifford J. Rogers, 'Gunpowder Artillery in Europe, 1326–1500: Innovation and Impact,' in Robert S. Ehlers, Jr.; Sarah K. Douglas;

240

pp. [24–25] NOTES

and Daniel P. M. Curzon, eds., *Technology, Violence and War. Essays in Honor of John F. Guilmartin, Jr.* (Leiden: Brill, 2019), 39–71.

20. Clifford J. Rogers, 'Henry V's Military Strategy in 1415,' *The Hundred Years War: A Wider Focus*, ed. L. J. Andrew Villalon and Donald J. Kagay (Leiden: Brill, 2005): 399–427. It was understood in the French court that Henry sought to capture Harfleur as a first step towards the recovery of Normandy. *Saint-Denys*, 5:532.

21. Anne Curry, 'The Military Ordinances of Henry V: Texts and Contexts,' *War, Government and Aristocracy in the British Isles, c. 1150–1500. Essays in Honour of Michael Prestwich,* ed. Chris Given-Wilson et al. (Woodbridge: Boydell and Brewer, 2008), 214–49, at 231–2, suggests the Latin version of the ordinances in Upton's *Studio militari* may be a translation of the 1415 Middle English ordinances, probably with some retrospective alterations or elaborations; I concur. Proclamation: in different places in different versions, e.g., *Black Book of the Admiralty,* ed. Travers Twiss, vol. 1 (London: Rolls Series, 1871), 295, 471; Nicholas Upton, *De studio militari libri quator* (London: Roger Norton, 1654), 133–4.

22. Anne Curry, 'Disciplinary Ordinances for English and Franco-Scottish Armies in 1385: An International Code?' *Journal of Medieval History* 37 (2011), 269–94; Maurice Keen *The Laws of War in the Late Middle Ages* (London: Routledge & Kegan Paul, 1965). See also Andrew Martinez, 'Disciplinary Ordinances for English Armies and Military Change, 1385–1513,' *History* 102 (2017), 361–85. Cf. Cox, 'Law of War?' esp. p. 1417.

23. Enguerrand de Monstrelet, *The Chronicles*, tr. Thomas Johnes, 2 vols. (London: Bohn, 1840–53), II, 225.

24. Perceval de Cagny, *Chroniques,* ed. H. Moranvillé (Paris: SHF, 1902), 77 (1412). Standard practice: Nicholas Wright, 'Ransoms of Non-combatants during the Hundred Years War,' *Journal of Medieval History* 17 (1991): 326–27; idem, *Knights and Peasants. The Hundred Years War in the French Countryside* (Woodbridge: Boydell, 1998), 64–76; Honoré Bonet [Honorat Bouvet], *The Tree of Battles,* tr. G. W. Coopland (Liverpool: Liverpool U.P., 1949), 153.

25. Monstrelet, *Chronicles*, I, 223; idem, *Chronique,* ed. L. Douët d'Arcq, 6 vols. (Paris: Société de l'histoire de France, 1857–62), II, 285.

26. At least, that is how I read clause 3: as forbidding the robbing or pillaging of a church, or killing [*destruir*] or capturing [*prendre prisoner*] of any man of the church, or any woman, unless bearing arms— which would imply by omission that robbing a churchman outside of a church, or killing or capturing an unarmed lay man, is permissible.

NOTES   pp. [25–25]

Anne Curry, however, reads this clause as protecting from capture all unarmed people. ('Ordinances,' 289.) It seems illogical, though, to protect all unarmed persons from *capture*, but only some of them from *killing*. Moreover, my reading matches the (more clearly expressed) version of the same clause in Henry V's ordinances. *Black Book*, 283, 460; St Johns College, Oxford, MS 57, fo. 236v (my thanks to St Johns and Ms. Rosslyn Johnston for a digital copy); Upton, *Studio militari,* 134–5.

27. Those things would certainly have been frowned upon, and *might* even have been judged illegal by the general law of arms, but that was up for debate. The semi-official French *Chronique du religieux de St.-Denys* makes no bones about the brutality of the Franco-Scottish attack on England: 'they slaughtered without pity all the peasants and other inhabitants they encountered, without sparing anyone based on rank, age, or sex, so that one could say of them [quoting Psalm 93 and Deut. 32] *they killed the widow and the resident alien and slaughtered the orphan, the stripling along with the maiden, the nursing infant with the venerable elder*.' *Saint-Denys*, I, 366. According to the same source, the French also slaughtered the garrisons in fortresses they captured. The chronicler pitched such conduct—'killing, pillaging and burning'— as 'that which enemies are accustomed to do to enemies,' not meriting complaint or reproach (other than being acknowledged as 'cruelties'). (Ibid., 370, 368, 366.) The Scottish ordinances of the March in time of war, drawn up in 1448 but based on practices 'kepit in blak Archibald of Douglas [d. 1400] days' has nothing to say about protection of enemy non-combatants. *Acta parliamentorum domini Roberti Tertii, regis Scotorum,* vol. 1 part 2 (Edinburgh: Queen Victoria, 1844), Appendix IV, pp. 350–52; likewise the 1430 version (Records of the Parliaments of Scotland to 1707, https://www.rps.ac.uk/, 1430/32–53). On the Continent, similarly, the *Livre des trahisons* has the duke of Berry order his men-at-arms to enter Burgundian territory and 'kill men, women, and children, and set fires all around': but in this case, at least according to the perspective of the other side, that *did* merit reproach, as the chronicler reports that their actions made a mockery of God and religion. *Livre des trahisons de France envers la maison de Bourgogne,* in Kervyn de Lettenhove, ed., *Chroniques relatives à l'histoire de la Belgique sous la domination des ducs de Bourgogne,* vol. 2 (Brussels: Hayez, 1873), 78, 80; cf. also 229.

28. In addition to the copies of the ordinances cited above (notes 21, 26), see *Gesta Henrici Quinti: The Deeds of Henry V,* ed. and tr. F. Taylor and J.S. Roskell (Oxford: O.U.P., 1975) [Hereafter *Gesta*], 27.

pp. [25–29] NOTES

29. Upton, *Studio militari,* 139; *Black Book,* 293, 470; St. Johns MS 57, fo. 240r.
30. Jean Juvénal des Ursins, *Histoire de Charles VI,* ed. Theodore Godefroy (Paris: Abraham Pacard, 1614), 486.
31. *Gesta,* 61.
32. See note 24.
33. Juvénal des Ursins, *Histoire,* 369.
34. Philippe Contamine, 'Rançons et butins dans la Normandie anglaise (1424–1444),' *Actes du 101e Congrès national des Sociétés savants, Lille 1976* (Paris: Bibliothèque Nationale, 1978); Upton, *Studio militari,* 90.
35. The army was provided with wages for the first quarter (which expired shortly after the siege of Harfleur ended), and royal jewels had been pawned to the captains to cover the costs of a second quarter.
36. Rogers, 'Henry V's Military Strategy.'
37. *Gesta,* 61; Rogers, 'Henry V's Military Strategy.'
38. *Gesta,* 63, 69; Le Févre, *Chronique,* I, 234.
39. Juvénal des Ursins, *Histoire,* 373.
40. Antoine-Henri Jomini, *Précis de l'art de la guerre,* new ed., vol. 1 (Paris: Anselin, 1837), 69: 'to calm the popular passions by all possible means; to wear them out over time; to employ a powerful mix of politics, mildness and severity, and above all great justice: these are the first elements of success.' Cf. R. A. Newhall's 'recognized principle of soldiering': 'Henry VI's Policy of Conciliation in Normandy, 1417–22,' *Anniversary Essays in Mediaeval History by Students of Charles Homer Haskins* (1929; repr. Freeport, NY: Books for Libraries Press, 1967), 205.
41. *Gesta,* 69 (pyx). Diplomatic context: Allmand, *Henry V,* 237–56. Doubts: John Barnie, *War in Medieval English Society: Social Values in the Hundred Years War 1337–99* (Ithaca: Cornell University Press, 1974), 128–138.
42. Bouvet, *Tree of Battles,* 153 (emphasis added).
43. Philippe de Mézières likewise considered it a rule of the discipline of chivalry that even in hostile territory churches should be protected, clergy and women should remain untouched, and small children should not be killed. *Le songe du vieil pélerin,* ed. G.W. Coopland (Cambridge: C.U.P., 1969), I, 517. Eustache Deschamps, the greatest French poet of the age, held that the way war was commonly waged in his day, with much plundering, murdering, and ransoming, 'turned honor into dishonor': 'he who conducts war in such a way

243

NOTES pp. [29–30]

damns himself.' *Oeuvres complètes de Eustache Deschamps,* ed. le marquis de Queux de Saint-Hilaire (Paris: Firmin Dido, 1878), 159–62.

44. How successful Henry was in enforcing his disciplinary code is beyond the scope of this chapter and would be difficult to determine. The story of Raoul le Gay suggests, as one might have guessed *a priori*, that the ordinances were taken seriously but complied with imperfectly. Le Gay was a priest robbed and taken prisoner by English soldiers, but was eventually brought before the king himself, who asked if he had been taken in arms (which he apparently had been, since he notes having lost a *jupe*, a form of padded armor), then released without a cash ransom, in exchange for a promise to carry a letter to another churchman in Paris. James Hamilton Wylie, *The Reign of Henry the Fifth,* vol. 2 (Cambridge: C.U.P., 1919), 25–29.

45. *Chronique de Ruisseauville,* 142, though the French is difficult to interpret. It literally says 'or robbed anyone or any church,' but it is quite possible the chronicler was confused, or the manuscript was incorrectly transcribed, with 'hommes ne eglises' given for what should have been 'hommes de eglise,' so that the meaning would be 'men of the church' (as in the ordinances) rather than 'men or churches.' In any case, the caveats, which presumably would not be included if this was simply a rhetorical ploy to criticize the French by contrast, suggest this is otherwise an accurate account of the king's words, provided by an eyewitness, not simple hearsay or invention. Note also the independent testimony of Thomas Elmham that before the battle Henry called upon God, St. George and the Virgin Mary (as well as Edward the Confessor) to support the English, seemingly echoed in the *Chronique's* words. *Liber metricus,* in *Memorials of Henry the Fifth,* 121. See also *The First English Life of King Henry the Fifth,* ed. Charles Lethbridge Kingsford (Oxford: Clarendon, 1911), 28–30, 34, 40–41, and *Chronique de Jean le Févre, seigneur de Saint-Rémy,* ed. François Morand, vol. 1 (Paris: SHF, 1876), 261, for the mindset.

46. To make a dangerously sweeping generalization, there seems to be a tendency for historians to be willing to accept that medieval society as a whole was profoundly shaped by religion, yet to be very skeptical of any professed religious motivations given by individual rulers. Certainly, there were wolves in sheep's clothing who ruthlessly pursued self-interest while proclaiming themselves champions of Christian values—but equally surely, not all kings who proclaimed Christian motives were simple hypocrites.

47. *Foedera, conventiones, litterae etc.,* ed. Thomas Rymer, v. 10 (London: J. Tonson, 1727), 106–8.

pp. [30–33]   NOTES

48. Ian Mortimer, *Henry V: The Warrior King of 1415* (London: Rosetta Books, 2013), 533. Anne Curry, *Agincourt: A New History* (Stroud: Tempus, 2005), 250–51, concurs that Henry's attribution of the victory to God's favor 'is not to be dismissed as medieval "spin."' For another example of piety trumping military expediency, see Titus Livius, *Vita*, 7–8.

49. The threat was made by referring to Deuteronomy 20 and 'penis legis Deutronomii' rather than spelling the penalties out. The Bible commands enslavement of the women and children, but among Christians the medieval laws of war substituted ransoming for enslavement. The Chaplain repeatedly emphasizes Henry's attention to the law of Deuteronomy, which he 'wrote out for himself…in the volume of his breast,' and this is not mere priestly imagination, as it is confirmed by Henry's explicit reference to the same passage in a letter to Charles VI. See *Gesta*, 34, 48, 154; *Saint-Denys*, 5:528; note also Juvénal des Ursins, *Histoire*, 366–7.

50. *Gesta*, 39, 48.

51. Walsingham, *St. Albans*, 667; see also *Gesta*, 39.

52. *Gesta*, 41.

53. Nonetheless, had the attackers fought their way past walls and therefore found it possible again to inflict lethal violence on lay men while sparing the lives of women, children, and clergy, English soldiers would have generally done so here, just as they did two years later when Caen was taken by storm, Elmham, *Liber metricus*, 113; Titus Livius Frulovisi, *Vita Henrici Quinti*, ed. T. Hearne (Oxford: Sheldonian Theater, 1716), p. 39; cf. Morosini, *Chronique*, 146–149 ('tuty…da XII any in suxo' presumably meaning all *males*). See also, Monstrelet, *Chronique*, III, 242; Puisieux, *Siège*, 81.

54. Cf. Rémy Ambühl, 'Punir la résistance: Henri V et la reddition du Marché de Meaux, mai 1422,' in *Eroberung und Inbesitznahme. Die Eroberung des Aargaus 1415 im europäischen Vergleich*, ed. Christian Hesse et al. (Ostfildern: Jan Thorbecke Verlag, 2017), 109–25.

55. Letter of Henry V in Jules Delpit, *Collection générale des documents français qui se trouvent en Angleterre* (Paris: Dumoulin, 1847), 217 ('nostre dite ville et leurs personnnes et biens soubzmettre a nostre grace sans nulle condition'); Walsingham, *St. Albans*, 668–71; *Gesta*, 52; see also Monstrelet, *Chronique*, III, 85; cf. Le Févre, *Chronique*, I, 227 ('la vie saulve') and Elmham, *Liber metricus*, 47, for an arrangement that only thirty leading defenders would be at risk of death. These were probably the same thirty men-at-arms and bourgeois who were kept as prisoners, some under harsh conditions, for a long period.

245

NOTES   pp. [33–34]

Rémy Ambühl, *Prisoners of War in the Hundred Years War: Ransom Culture in the Late Middle Ages* (Cambridge: Cambridge U.P., 2013), 72–5. Quotation: Juvénal des Ursins, *Histoire*, 373. Maurice: Ian Mortimer, *1415: Henry V's Year of Glory* (London: The Bodley Head, 2009), 369.

56. *Saint-Denys*, 544–5.

57. *Gesta*, 53.

58. The defenders (presumably meaning the group who made the formal submission) surrendered with nooses around their necks to symbolize that their lives were at the king's mercy—a doubtless intentional reprise of the surrender of Calais in 1347. Adam of Usk, *Chronicon*, 125. Thomas of Elmham states that thirty of the leading defenders were to be at the king's will, to do with as he wished, specifically 'whether death or ransom.' *Liber metricus,* 47; similarly, Titus Livius, *Vita*, 10. There are many instances of unconditional surrender followed by the execution of at least some of the defenders.

59. Juvénal des Ursins, *Histoire*, 374; *Gesta,* 54, 55n4, 57; Monstrelet, *Chronique*, III, 94; Le Févre, *Chronique*, I, 229; *Saint-Denys*, 544. Although it was common for surrender terms to allow the defenders to leave with some agreed quantity of goods or wealth, it was very rare to provide anything more than was agreed. The Chaplain (*Gesta,* 54) says that the escort was needed to protect the refugees from 'those of our men, who were more interested in plunder than piety'; note the implication that Henry was the reverse.

60. This was the overall strategy for the campaign, and typical for English strategy in the period; Edward III, likewise, had used the siege of Berwick to force the battle of Halidon Hill, and tried to use the siege of Calais to provoke a reprise of Crécy. Rogers, 'Henry V's Military Strategy'; idem, *War*, chs. 4, 12. Nonetheless, I should admit my assertion is a deduction on those grounds, not something stated in the sources.

61. Which accorded with his father's deathbed advice; see *First English Life*, 14–16.

62. *Gesta,* 51. It is unclear to what extent the king distributed the booty among the soldiers.

63. Juvénal des Ursins, *Histoire*, 373.

64. Ibid., 373–4.

65. Orderic Vitalis, *Ecclesiastical History,* ed. and tr. Marjorie Chibnall, vol. 6 (Oxford: Clarendon, 1969), 241; Clifford J. Rogers, 'The Military Revolutions of the Hundred Years War,' in idem, ed., *The Military Revolution Debate* (Boulder: Westview, 1995), 62–3.

246

pp. [35–37]   NOTES

66. Rogers, 'Agincourt,' 58–9; 104 n. 234.
67. John Keegan, *The Face of Battle* (London: Penguin, 1976), 78.
68. The whole subject is brilliantly examined by Keen in *The Laws of War in the Middle Ages*.
69. The Chaplain described the deaths as 'quite contrary to any wish of ours'; the *Chron. St. Denys* has Henry pronouncing himself 'horrified' and feeling 'heartfelt compassion' at the effusion of so much human blood. *Gesta*, 93, 99; *Saint-Denys*, 5:568.
70. Keen, *Laws of War*, 104–6; Andy King, '"Then a Great Misfortune Befell Them": The Laws of War on Surrender and the Killing of Prisoners on the Battlefield in the Hundred Years War,' *Journal of Medieval History* 43 (2017), 108–11.
71. Rogers, 'Agincourt,' and idem, *Soldiers' Lives through History:The Middle Ages* (Westport, CT: Greenwood, 2007), 171–73, 179–81, 214–16.
72. *Gesta*, 91–93, 100–101; see also *Saint-Denys*, 5:568.
73. Le Févre, *Chronique*, 258. Despite Le Févre's omission of other reasons, it is not justified to generalize, as an expert on the subject recently did, that the reaction 'had nothing to do with compassion for their prisoners,' any more than it would be to discount the importance of ransom in explaining why some English soldiers avoided the order to kill Scottish prisoners after Halidon Hill, though Andrew of Wyntoun attributes their action only to 'pity.' The motivations are by no means mutually exclusive. Rémy Ambühl, 'The French Prisoners,' in *The Battle of Agincourt*, ed. Anne Curry and Malcom Mercer (New Haven: Yale U.P., 2015), 207; King, 'Great Misfortune,' 114.
74. Le Bel, *Chronique*, 337–8.
75. Pizan, *Book,* 169 (*Livre*, 419), following Bouvet, *Tree*, 152; followed by Caxton, *Fayttes*, 222. Hence, when King Pedro killed without trial a Castilian knight who had surrendered to a Gascon knight, the latter 'felt greatly dishonored that a knight who had surrendered to him and whom he held in his power should thus be murdered,' even by a sovereign. Pedro López de Ayala, *Crónica de Pedro I*, tr. in L. J. Andrew Villalon and Donald Kagay, *To Win and Lose a Medieval Battle* (Leiden: Brill, 2017), 385. But cf. note 79 below.
76. Bouvet, *Tree*, 152; *Arbre* 138 ('hors de la bataille'; 'en la prison'); Pizan, *Book,* 169.
77. The main concern was certainly the large French force still on the field in front of the English—the original French third line plus defeated men who had rallied to it, and possibly also the late-arriving contingent of the duke of Brabant (though more likely that force had already made its attack when the death order was given). The attack

NOTES pp. [37–38]

on the English baggage train may also have contributed to the order, or may have happened after the order was given.

78. *Tree,* 152; *Arbre,* 138 ('senon que l'on doubtast qu'il n'eschappast don't plus grant guerre, dommaige ou mischief en peut advenir'); Giovanni da Legnano, *Tractatus de Bello,* tr. James Leslie Brierly (Oxford: O.U.P., 1917), 274, 254: 'quarter should be granted to one who humbles himself and does not try to resist, *unless* the grant of quarter gives reason for fearing a disturbance of the peace.' (Emphasis added.)

79. If a prisoner was killed *on the battlefield,* even after one side was clearly defeated, the killer might be held liable for the property loss to the original captor, but not for the homicide itself (implying that a man who killed his own prisoner, on the battlefield, would not be culpable). Henry V's ordinances in Upton, *Studio militari,* 141; Ambühl, *Prisoners of War,* 26; Stephen Muhlberger, *Charny's Men-at-Arms. Questions Concerning the Joust, Tournament and War* (Wheaton, IL: Freelance Academy Press, 2014), p. 102, question 80 (for the original French see Brussels, KBR, Ms. 1124-1126, ff. 78r-v). It was even open to question (*Questions,* p. 100, no. 71) whether a captor could legitimately, in cold blood, execute a prisoner who failed to produce his ransom within an agreed term. Certainly that was done in practice. Ambühl, *Prisoners,* 48–50. However, Joan of Arc and her interrogators seem to have agreed that it would be a mortal sin to take a man for ransom then kill the prisoner ... unless it was done after a trial for a crime. *Procès de condamnation,* ed. and tr. Pierre Champion, 2 vols. (Paris: Champion, 1921), I, 218. Christine di Pizan, *Book,* 169 and *Livre,* 418, agrees that would be inhumane and contrary to law (*droit*) and chivalry (*gentillesce*).

80. Bouvet, *Arbre,* 138. Quotation from Pizan, *Book,* 169 and *Livre,* 418, though she adds that the victim must have well deserved execution for this to be licit.

81. *Gesta,* 92. Meron's view that the prisoners were 'hardly a menace' and that therefore 'the justification of the killings on grounds of necessity is unpersuasive' is itself entirely unpersuasive, and not shared by any military historian that I am aware of. Theodore Meron, *Henry's Wars and Shakespeare's Laws* (Oxford: Clarendon, 1993), 165–6.

82. Jean Froissart, *Chroniques,* ed. Léon Mirot, vol. 12 (Paris: SHF, 1931), 161–3.

83. Cuvelier, *La Chanson de Bertrand du Guesclin de Cuvelier,* ed. Jean-Claude Faucon, vol. 1 (Toulouse: Editions universitaires du Sud, 1990), DCCLXXVI, p. 470. This event is not well substantiated, but the

pp. [38–42]   NOTES

point here is mainly about Cuvelier's attitude (in 1387) to what he *believed* happened.

84. With the possible exception of Titus Livius Frulovisi, whose elaboration of his source material may be 'a sign that the author thought an excuse was needed.' Curry, *New History*, 217.

85. Craig Taylor, 'Henry V, Flower of Chivalry,' in *Henry V: New Interpretations*, ed. Gwilym Dodd (Woodbridge: Boydell, 2013), 235. Cf. Curry's opinion that the order resulted from panic and amounted to failure to 'follow chivalric customs'; Juliet Barker's that 'in chivalric terms, it was reprehensible,' and 'violated every principle of decency and Christian morality' (despite being militarily justified); and Ian Mortimer's that 'by all the standards of the time, the killing was an ungodly act, and no way to win the love or respect of the people whom he sought to rule as king.' Curry, *New History*, 250; Juliet Barker, *Agincourt: Henry V and the Battle that Made England* (New York: Little, Brown and Co., 2005), 289, 292; Mortimer, *1415*, 453, and see also 447. Yet it is undoubted that in the end Henry was widely respected, as a ruler and a model of chivalry, even by some French writers hostile to his cause. E.g., see *Mémoires de Pierre de Fenin*, ed. Dupont (Paris: SHF, 1837), 186–7.

86. Letters translated in Mortimer, *1415*, 378–9, 372.

87. Taylor, 'Flower of Chivalry.'

88. An ordinance of Henry VII for 1486 is even more protective than Henry V's, as might be expected since it is for an army operating within England. Francis Grose, *Military Antiquities Respecting a History of the English Army*, vol. II (London: S. Hooper, 1788), 83–5. But Henry VIII's, for operations in France, also protected boys under 14 (unless the son of an important man), women, and churchmen from ransoming, as well as forbidding rape, and forbade burning any house or town without command of an appropriate officer, though with an exception if 'the king's enemies be within it, and it cannot bee noe otherwise taken.' It was also forbidden to rob or murder any man 'except he bee the king's enemy': I am not sure if that category is meant to be limited to combatants. Ibid., 92, 97, 105.

3. THOMAS HOWARD AND THE CHARACTER OF ENGLISH VIOLENCE DURING THE REIGN OF HENRY VIII

1. Edward Hall, *The Triumphant Reigne of Kyng Henry the VIII*, 2 vols. (Edinburgh, 1904), 2: 49; British Library [hereafter BL], Cotton MS Vespasian C I, f. 80 (*Letters and Papers, Foreign and Domestic, of the Reign*

249

NOTES   pp. [42–45]

of Henry VIII, ed. J. S. Brewer J. Gairdner and R. H. Brodie, 21 vols. (London, 1862–1932) [hereafter *LP*], I, pt. 1, no. 1327).

2. *I diarii di Marino Sanuto*, ed. F. Stefani, 58 vols. (Venice, 1879–1902), XIV, 580; XV, 9 (*LP*, I, pt. 1, no. 1291); *Calendar of State Papers and Manuscripts Relating to English Affairs, Existing in the Archives and Collections of Venice and Northern Italy*, ed. R. Brown et al, 38 vols. (London, 1864–1934), II, 183; *Letters and Papers Relating to the War with France, 1512-1513*, ed. A. Spont (London, 1897), XVII, 26–7, 37–8; *Grafton's Chronicle*, 2 vols. (London, 1809), I, 248.

3. *Holinshed's Chronicles of England, Scotland and Ireland*, 6 vols. (London, 1807–8), III, 571.

4. B L Cotton MS Caligula D/VIII, ff. 225r-225v, 259r-259v, 263r-264v, 266r-266v, 268r, 269r-270r, 271r-272v, 273r-273v, E/II, ff. 18r-18v (*LP*, III, nos. 2549, 2499, 2511, 2517, 2526, 2530, 2540, 2541, 2551); *Grafton's Chronicle*, II, 331.

5. 'Enquête faite en 1578 par le maître particulier des Eaux et Forêts de Boulonnais', ed. A. de Rosny, *Mémoires de la Société académique de l'arrondissement de Boulogne-sur-Mer*, 27 (1912), 364; D. Potter, *War and Government in the French Provinces: Picardy 1470–1560* (Cambridge, 1993), p. 202; *Grafton's Chronicle*, II, 325.

6. R. Robson, *The Rise and Fall of the English Highland Clans: Tudor Responses to a Medieval Problem* (Edinburgh, 1989), p. 149.

7. *LP*, III, pt. 2, no. 2958.

8. BL, Cotton MS Caligula D/VIII, ff. 269v-270r (*LP* III, pt. 2, no. 2530); The National Archives, Kew [hereafter TNA], SP 1/26, f. 96r (*LP* III, pt. 2, no. 2592).

9. BL, Cotton MS Caligula B/VI, ff. 374r-374v (*LP* III, pt. 2, no. 3321).

10. BL, Cotton MS Caligula D/VIII, f. 266v (*LP* III, pt. 2, no. 2517).

11. Hall, *Henry VIII*, I, 68. See also: BL, Cotton MS Caligula D/VIII, ff. 269r-269v (*LP* III, pt. 2, no. 2530).

12. BL, Cotton MS Caligula E/II, ff. 20r-20v (*LP* III, pt. 2, no. 2560), D/VIII, f. 278r (*LP* III, pt. 2, no. 2579).

13. *State Papers Published under the Authority of His Majesty's Commission: Henry VIII*, 11 vols. (London, 1830–52) [hereafter *StP*], IV, 10. See also: *LP* III, pt. 2, no. 3222.

14. BL, Cotton MS Caligula D/VIII, ff. 266r-266v (*LP* III, pt. 2, no. 2517).

15. BL, Cotton MS Caligula B/II, f. 162r (*LP* III, pt. 2, no. 3241); *LP* III, pt. 2, nos. 3104, 3110.

16. TNA, SP 1/189, f. 97v (*LP*, xix, pt. 1, no. 795).

17. TNA, SP 1/191, f. 234r (*LP*, xix, pt. 2, no. 176). See also: *Holinshed's Chronicle*, III, 843; *LP*, XX, pt. 2, no. 494.

pp. [45–47]   NOTES

18. A. Morin, 'Chroniques du siege de Boulogne, en 1544', in *Revue des sociétés savants de la France et de l'étranger*, 4th series, 2 (1875), 260.

19. *Chronqiues de Flandre et d'Artois par Louis Brésin. Analyse et extraits pour servir à l'histoire de ces provinces de 1482 à 1560*, ed. Mannier (Paris, 1880), p. 293; D. Potter, *Henry VIII and Francis I : The Final Conflict, 1540–1547* (Leiden, 2011), p. 270.

20. TNA, SP 1/202, f. 84r (*LP*, XX, pt. 1, no. 962).

21. *Elis Gruffydd and the 1544 'Enterprises' of Paris and Boulogne*, ed. J. Davies and trans. M. B. Davies (Farnham, 2003), p. 28.

22. Ibid., p. 38.

23. See: *Acts of the Privy Council of England: New Series*, ed. J. R. Dasent et al, 46 vols. (London, 1890–1964), I, 246, 289, 301, 335, 347, 356, 387, 426, 498, 508, 515, 538, 557–8, 559.

24. C. S. L. Davies, 'Henry VIII and Henry V: The Wars in France', in J. L. Watts (ed.), *The End of the Middle Ages? England in the Fifteenth and Sixteenth Centuries* (Stroud, 1998), p. 255; M. H. Keen, *The Laws of War in the Middle Ages* (London, 1965), p. 123; T. Meron, *Henry's Wars and Shakespeare's Laws: Perspectives on the Law of War in the Later Middle Ages* (Oxford, 1993), pp. 22–23.

25. *LP*, III, pt. 2, no. 2958; *Grafton's Chronicle*, II, 325.

26. BL, Cotton MS Galba B/VII, f. 362r (*LP* III, pt. 2, no. 2595); M. E. Delgove, *Histoire de la ville de Doullens* (Doullens, 1865), 99; *Mémoires de Martin et Guillaume du Bellay*, ed. V.-L. Bourilly and F. Vindry, 4 vols. (Paris, 1908–19), I, 294; BL, Cotton MS Galba B/VII, f. 359v (*LP* III, pt. 2, no. 2593).

27. Hall, *Henry VIII*, I, 269.

28. *LP* III, pt. 2, no. 3360.

29. BL, Cotton MS Caligula B/VI, f. 352r (*LP* III, pt. 2, no. 3364).

30. *Grafton's Chronicle*, II, 490–91; *Holinshed's Chronicle*, III, 835.

31. Francis Godwin, *Annales of England Containing the reignes of Henry the Eighth. Edward the Sixt. Queene Mary* (London, 1630), p. 190; *Holinshed's Chronicle*, III, 835; 'The Late Expedition into Scotland, made by the King's Highness' army, under the conduct of the Right Honourable the Earl of Hertford, the year of our Lord God 1544', in A. F. Pollard (ed.), *Tudor Tracts, 1532–1588* (London, 1903), p. 41.

32. Thomas Lanquet, *An epitome of chronicles* (London, 1559), no pagination.

33. G. Le Jean, *Histoire politique et municipale de la ville et de la communauté de Morlaix* (Morlaix, 1846), pp. 70–1.

34. *Gruffydd*, p. 67.

35. Morin, 'Chroniques', p. 260; *Chroniques de Flandre*, p. 185

251

NOTES

pp. [47–48]

36. *Gruffydd*, pp. 30–1; *Chroniques de Flandre*, p. 185.

37. S. Bowd, 'Mass Murder in Sacks during the Italian Wars, 1494–1559', in T. Dean and K. Lowe (eds.), *Murder in Renaissance Italy* (Cambridge, 2017), pp. 249–68.

38. *Double d'un letter missive, envoyee par le seigneur Nicholas Nicholai, geographe du Roy, á Monseigneur du Buys, vicebaillif de Vienne. Contenant le discours de la guerre faicte par le Roy nostre Sire, Henry, deuxieme de ce nom pour le recourvrement du païs de Boulongnoys, en l'an mil cinq cens quarante neuf* (Lyon, 1550).

39. R. Clifton, '"An Indiscriminate Blackness"? Massacre, Counter-Massacre, and Ethnic Cleansing in Ireland, 1640–1660', in M. Levene and P. Roberts (eds.), *The Massacre in History* (New York, 1999), p. 109.

40. R. G. Asch, '"Wo der soldat hinkömbt, da ist alles sein": Military Violence and Atrocities in the Thirty Years War Re-Examined', *German History*, 18 (2000), 296–7; D. Hall and E. Malcolm, '"The Rebels Turkish Tyranny": Understanding Sexual Violence in Ireland during the 1640s', *Gender and History*, 22 (2010), 66; Christina Lamb, *Our Bodies, Their Battlefield: What War Does to Women* (London, 2020); D. Wolfthal, *Images of Rape: The 'Heroic' Tradition and its Alternatives* (Cambridge, 1999).

41. P. J. B. Bertrand, *Précis de l'histoire physique, civile et politique, de la ville de Boulogne-sur-Mer et des ses environs*, 2 vols. (Boulogne, 1828), pp. 101–2 ; 'Récit du siège et de la prinse de Boulogne par les anglais en 1544, et de la reprise de cette ville par les anglais en 1544, par Guillaume Paradin', ed. D. de Haignerè, *Mémoires de la Société académique de l'arrondissement de Boulogne-sur-Mer*, 15 (1889–90), 285–304; 290.

42. *Chroniques de Flandre*, p. 279; S. J. Gunn, D. Grummitt and H. Cools, *War, State and Society in England and the Netherlands, 1477–1559* (Oxford, 2007), p. 273; Potter, *War and Government*, p. 217; J. Thieulaine, 'Un livre de raison en Artois (XVIe siècle): extraits historiques', ed. X. de Gorguette d'Argoeuves, *Mémoires de la Société des antiquaires de La Morinie*, 21 (1881), 160–1 ; Jean de Beaugé, *Histoire de la guerre d'Escosse: pendant les campagnes 1548 et 1549*, ed. W. Smith (Edinburgh, 1830), p. 104.

43. Hall, *Henry VIII*, II, 349; *A Chronicle of England during the Reigns of the Tudors, from A. D. 1485 to 1559 by Charles Wriothesely, Windsor Herald*, ed. W. D. Hamilton, 2 vols. (London, 1875–7), I, 149.

44. G. Walker, 'Rereading Rape and Sexual Violence in Early Modern England', *Gender & History*, 10 (1998), 1; *Statutes and ordynances for the warre* (London, 1544), p. 15.

pp. [48–53]   NOTES

45. J. Bradbury, *The Medieval Siege* (Woodbridge, 1992), pp. 317–19, 322; Keen, *Laws of War*, pp. 65, 121; T. Meron, *Henry's Wars and Shakespeare's Laws*, pp. 40–1; R. C. Stacey, 'The Age of Chivalry', in Howard, Andreopolous and Shulman, *Laws of War*, p. 38.

46. *Chroniques de Flandre*, p. 185; E. Deseille, 'Introduction à l'histoire du pays Boulonnais: notes et documents', *Mémoires de la Société académique de l'arrondissement de Boulogne-sur-Mer*, 9 (1878–9), 46–7; Récit du siège et de la prinse de Boulogne, 290; Morin, *Chroniques*, p. 259; A. Marmin, *Le siège de Boulogne en 1544* (Boulogne, 1825), p. 87.

47. *Chroniques de Flandre*, p. 185.

48. TNA, SP 1/192, f. 137v (*LP*, xix, pt. 2, 270).

49. TNA, SP 1/190, f. 78r (*LP*, xix, pt. 1, no. 933).

50. *Grafton's Chronicle*, II, 326; 'Enquête faite en 1578', p. 405.

51. 'Enquête faite en 1578', pp. 404–5; *Chroniques de Flandre*, p. 179; L. F. J. Deschamps de Pas (ed.), 'Pièces d'extraites d'un manuscript de la bibliothèque communale de Lille', *Bulletin historique trimestriel. Société académique des antiquaries de la Morinie*, 1 (1852–6), 123.

52. *Chroniques de Flandre*, p. 293.

53. *StP*, X, 10, 15–16.

54. *Gruffydd*, p. 29; J. H Leslie (ed.), 'The Siege and Capture of Boulogne – 1544', *Journal of the Society for Army Historical Research*, 1 (1922), 189.

55. C. T. Allmand, *Lancastrian Normandy, 1415–50: The History of a Medieval Occupation* (Cambridge, 1983), pp. 229–40; N. Wright, *Knights and Peasants: The Hundred Years War in the French Countryside* (Woodbridge, 1998), p. 87; Alberico Gentili, *De jure belli libri tres*, trans. J. C. Rolfe, 2 vols. (Oxford, 1933), II, 22.

56. C. J. Rogers, 'Edward III and the Dialectics of Strategy, 1327–1360', *Transactions of the Royal Historical Society*, 6th series, 4 (1994), 83–102.

57. BL, Cotton MS Caligula D/VIII, f. 273r (*LP* III, pt. 2, no. 2540).

58. BL, Cotton MS Caligula D/VIII, ff. 266r-266v (*LP* III, pt. 2, no. 2517).

59. BL, Cotton MS Caligula B/II, f. 162r (*LP* III, pt. 2, no. 3241).

60. BL, Cotton MS Caligula B/VI, ff. 374r-374v (*LP* III, pt. 2, no. 3321). See also: *LP* III, pt. 2, no. 3096.

61. *StP*, III, 75–6.

62. TNA, SP 49/2, ff. 63-63v (*LP* III, pt. 2, no. 3570).

63. *StP*, IV, 54.

64. BL, Cotton MS Caligula B/VI, ff. 374r-374v (*LP* III, pt. 2, no. 3321).

65. *StP*, VI, 173.

66. James Morton, *The Monastic Annals of Teviotdale* (Edinburgh, 1832), p. 31.

NOTES pp. [53–57]

67. TNA, SP 1/193, f. 69v.
68. *StP*, X, 118
69. *StP*, X, 175
70. *Gruffydd*, p. 35.
71. *StP*, X, 386–7.
72. T. Rymer, *Foedera, conventiones, literae, et cujuscunque generis acta publica*, 20 vols. (London, 1704–35), XV, 57.
73. Rosny, 'Documents inédits', p. 404.
74. Elis Gruffydd, 'Boulogne and Calais. From 1545 to 1550', ed. M. B. Davies, *Bulletin of the Faculty of Arts of Fouad I University, Cairo*, 12 (1950), 2.
75. Rosny, 'Documents inédits', p. 404.
76. J. Bain (ed.), *Hamilton Papers*, 2 vols. (Edinburgh, 1890–2), II, 326.
77. BL, Cotton MS Caligula D/VIII, ff. 271v-272r (*LP* III, pt. 2, no. 2541).
78. BL, Cotton MS Caligula D/VIII, ff. 266r-266v (*LP* III, pt. 2, no. 2517).
79. BL, Cotton MS Caligula D/VIII, ff. 263r-264v (*LP* III, pt. 2, no. 2511).
80. A. Henne, *Histoire du règne de Charles-Quint en Belgique,* 10 vols. (Brussels and Leipzig, 1812–96), X, 30n.; Steven Gunn, *The English People at War in the Age of Henry VIII* (Oxford, 2019), p. 105.
81. *Hamilton Papers*, I, xciv; Gunn, *English People at War*, p. 110.
82. For violence against civilians during the Italian Wars, see: Stephen D. Bowd, *Renaissance Murder: Civilians and Soldiers During the Italian Wars* (Oxford, 2018).
83. Michelle Gordon, *Extreme Violence and the 'British Way': Colonial Warfare in Perak, Sierra Leone and Sudan* (London, 2020), p. 8.
84. H. E. Selesky, 'Colonial America', in M. Howard, G. J. Andreopoulos and M. R. Shulman (eds.), *The Laws of War: Constraints of Warfare in the Western World* (New Haven and London, 1994), p. 61. See also: N. P. Canny, 'The Ideology of English Colonization: From Ireland to America', *William and Mary Quarterly*, 30 (1973), 581; Ben Kiernan, 'Settler Colonies, Ethno-Religious Violence and Historical Documentation: Comparative Reflections on Southeast Asia and Ireland', in J. Ohlmeyer and M. O. Siochrù (eds.), *Ireland 1641: Contexts and Reactions* (Manchester, 2013), p. 255.

4. ENGLISH ATROCITIES IN THE REIGN OF ELIZABETH I AND THEIR CONTEXT
1. D. J. B. Trim, 'Fighting "Jacob's Wars". The Employment of English and Welsh Mercenaries in the European Wars of Religion: France and

pp. [58–62]   NOTES

the Netherlands, 1562–1610' (unpublished PhD thesis, University of London, 2002), pp. 123, 163, 185, 195.

2. [Anon.] to Elizabeth, n.d. [but clearly 1572], Hatfield House, Cecil Papers, MS 7, f. 78r (quoted by kind permission of the Marquess of Salisbury).

3. Arthur Champernowne to Elizabeth, 8 October 1572, British Library (London), Lansdowne MS 15, f. 200v.

4. This is in contrast to the near-contemporaneous case studies of Neil Murphy and David Edwards (Chapters 3 and 5 in this volume).

5. D. J. B. Trim, 'The "foundation-stone of the British army"? The Normandy Campaign of 1562', *Journal of the Society for Army Historical Research*, 77 (1999), 71–87.

6. See ibid., pp. 81–84.

7. Thomas Smith to Nicholas Throckmorton, 17 October 1562, The National Archives (Kew) [hereafter TNA], SP 70/43, f. 53r: 'pour avoir vennes contre la volunte de la Royne Dangleterre au service des Huguenots'.

8. See Bibliothèque Nationale de France (Paris), Fonds français, MS 3243, ff. 12–15, and MS 3881, ff. 117–18.

9. Smith's 'News', 29 October 1562, Patrick Forbes (ed.), *A Full View of the Public Transactions in the Reign of Elizabeth* (2 vols, London, 1740–41), II, 168.

10. Throckmorton to Elizabeth, 30 October 1562, *Calendar of State Papers, Foreign Series, of the Reign of Elizabeth I* [hereafter *CSPFor.*] *1562*, no. 407, p. 932.

11. Smith to Cecil, 7 November 1562, *CSPFor., 1562*, no. 996, p. 434.

12. For the servitude of English prisoners in the galleys, going beyond the end of the first war of religion, see Henry Killigrew to Sir Thomas Challoner, 12 June 1563, *CSPFor., 1563*, no. 871, p. 397; Paul de Foix (French ambassador to London) to Catherine de Medici, 23 January 1565, in *The Letters of Paul de Foix, French Ambassador at the Court of Elizabeth I 1562–1566*, ed. David Potter, Camden 5th series, 58 (Cambridge: Cambridge University Press, 2019), no. 93, p. 194.

13. See *CSPFor., 1566–68*, nos. 909–10, pp. 1568–69, for their petitions; see also Elizabeth to Charles IX, 6 August 1568, Archives du Ministère des Affaires Étrangères (Paris), Memoirs et Documents Angleterre 98, ff. 9r-10r; and Sir Henry Norris to Elizabeth, 10 February 1569, *CSPFor., 1569–71*, no. 105, p. 29.

14. D. J. B. Trim, '"Put all to the sword": The Effects of Reformation on the Ethics of War in Sixteenth-century Germany and England', in

255

NOTES pp. [62–64]

Dorothea Wendebourg and Alec Ryrie (eds.), *Sister Reformations II/ Schwesterreformationen II: Reformation and Ethics in Germany and England/ Reformation und Ethik in Deutschland und in England* (Tübingen: Mohr Siebeck, 2014), p. 275.

15. William Killigrew to William Cecil, 2 November 1562, TNA, SP 70/44, f. 84v; Edward Horsey to Cecil, 14 January 1563, TNA, SP 70/48, f. 207v.

16. Luke MacMahon, 'Killigrew, Sir Henry (1525x8–1603), diplomat', *Oxford Dictionary of National Biography*. 23 September 2004; Accessed 16 September 2022: https://www.oxforddnb.com/view/10.1093/ref:odnb/9780198614128.001.0001/odnb-9780198614128-e-15533.

17. Amias Paulet to Francis Walsingham, 12 August 1577, *Copy-book of Sir Amias Poulet's Letters, Written during his Embassy to France (A.D. 1577)*, ed. Octavius Ogle (London: J. B. Nichols & Sons, for the Roxburghe Club, 1866), p. 94 (emphasis added).

18. Trim, 'Fighting "Jacob's Wars"', p. 110.

19. D. J. B. Trim, 'The Huguenots and the European Wars of Religion, c.1560–1693: Soldiering in National and Transnational Context', in idem (ed.), *The Huguenots: History and Memory in Transnational Context* (Leiden: Brill, 2011), pp. 161–62.

20. Guillaume Baudart, *Les Guerres de Nassau: Portraits en taille douce, Et Descriptions des Sieges, Battailes, rencontres & autres choses advenues durant les Guerres des Pays bas, sous le Commandement des hauts & Puissants Seigneurs les Estats Generaux des Provincis Unies, & la Conduite des Tresillustres Princes Guillaume Prince d'Orange & Maurice de Nassau son fils*, 2 vols. (Amsterdam: 1616), I, 102.

21. Trim, 'Fighting "Jacob's Wars"', pp. 110, 114–16, 383.

22. Geoffrey Parker, *The Army of Flanders and the Spanish Road, 1567–1659*, 2nd edn (Cambridge: Cambridge University Press, 2004), p. 143.

23. Fernando González de León, *The Road to Rocroi: Class, Culture and Command in the Spanish Army of Flanders, 1567–1659*, History of Warfare 52 (Leiden: Brill, 2009), p. 211.

24. Roger Williams, *The Actions of the Lowe Countries*, ed. John Haywarde (London: 1618), p. 27 (in John X. Evans (ed.), *The Works of Sir Roger Williams* (Oxford: Clarendon Press, 1972), p. 79).

25. Edward Grimeston, *A generall historie of the Netherlands: continued unto 1608, out of the best authors* (London, 1609), 474–75; Jean-François Le Petit, *La grande chronique ancienne et moderne, de Hollande, Zelande, West-Frise, Vtrecht, Frise, Overyssel & Groeningen*, 2 vols. (Dordrecht; 1601), II, 225; Williams, *Actions* (1618), p. 54 (*Works*, p. 100); Gilbert to

256

pp. [64–67]   NOTES

Burghley, 29 August 1572, [Baron J. M. B. C.] Kervyn de Lettenhove and L. Gilliodts-van Severen (eds.), *Relations politiques des Pays-Bas et de l'Angleterre sous le règne de Philippe II*, 11 vols. (Brussels: Académie Royale des Sciences, des Lettres et des Beaux-Arts de Belgique, 1882–1900) [hereafter *RPPA*], no. 2455, VI, 500.

26. González de León, *The Road to Rocroi*, p. 211 n. 107.

27. Williams, *Actions* (1618 edn), p. 71 (*Works*, p. 110).

28. Williams, *Actions* (1618 edn), p. 78 (*Works*, p. 115).

29. Williams, *Actions* (1618 edn), p. 79 (*Works*, p. 116).

30. D. J. B. Trim, 'Williams, Sir Roger (1539/40–1595), Soldier and Author', *Oxford Dictionary of National Biography*. 23 September 2004; Accessed 16 September 2022: https://www.oxforddnb.com/view/10.1093/ref:odnb/9780198614128.001.0001/odnb-9780198614128-e-29543.

31. 'Theophile', *A Tragicall Historie of the Troubles and Civile Warres of the Lowe Countries*, trans. T[homas] S[tocker] (London: 1583), book iii, f. 99v.

32. All Souls College Oxford, Codrington Library, MS 129, ff. 27r-28r; repr. in David Caldecott-Baird (ed.), *The Expedition in Holland 1572–1574* (London: Seely Service & Co., 1976), pp. 134–35 (illustration), 137 (description of massacre). Baudart, *Guerres de Nassau*, I, 117–19; Geoffrey and Angela Parker, *European Soldiers 1550–1650* (Cambridge: Cambridge University Press, 1977), pp. 60–61 including reproduction of Baudart's illustration of executions at Haarlem.

33. Parker, *Dutch Revolt*, pp. 159–60; Stephen Turnbull, *The Art of Renaissance Warfare: From the Fall of Constantinople to the Thirty Years War* (Barnsley & Havertown, PA: Frontline Books, 2018), p. 195.

34. Baudart, *Guerres de Nassau*, I, 117: 'dix-huit Capitaines & Porte-enseignes, & cinq cens soldats, tant Walons, que François, Anglois & Escossois'.

35. Theophile, *Tragicall Historie*, f. 100v.

36. Baudart, *Guerres de Nassau*, I, 117: 'Aucuns qui par maladie ou bleçeure avoient esté gisans en l'Hospital, y furent executez à mort le dixneufiésme d'Aoust'.

37. Williams, *Actions*, (1618) p. 59 (*Works*, p. 130).

38. Anon. [Walter Morgan?] to [Burghley?], 23 Aug. 1574, *RPPA*, no. 2815, VII, 317.

39. See J. S. E. Smith, '"The Sword and the Law": Elizabethan Soldiers' Perception and Practice of the Laws of Armed Conflict, 1569–1587', PhD thesis (University of Glasgow, 2017), chaps. 3–4 for an overview

257

NOTES   pp. [67–70]

of how Spanish and English practice in the Netherlands conformed or diverged from contemporary laws of war.

40. González de León, *Road to Rocroi*, p. 211, quotation in fn. 107.

41. John Lothrop Motley, *The Rise of the Dutch Republic*, Chandos Classics edn, 3 vols. (London: Frederick Warne, n.d.), III, 311.

42. Rossel to Walsingham, 5 July 1579, *CSPFor.*, *1579–80*, p. 6, no. 5.

43. E.g., Le Petit, *Grande chronique*, II, 414.

44. Thomas Churchyard, *A plaine or moste true report of a daungerous service, by Englishmen, & other worthy soldiours, for the takyng of Macklin sette forthe* (London: 1580), sigs. B3v, C2r.

45. William Blandy, *The castle, or picture of pollicy* (London, 1581), f. 22r.

46. Smith, '"The Sword and the Law"', pp. 122–23.

47. English ransoming a Spanish prisoner: Martin Couche to Walsingham, Cobham to Burghley, and Norreys to Walsingham, 3, 4 and 5 August 1582, *CSPFor.*, *1582*, pp. 218, 220, 222, nos. 217, 219, 221. Spanish ransoming an English prisoner: *CSPFor.*, *1583–84*, p. 556, nos. 681–82.

48. William Camden, *Annales* (London, 1625), Book iii (second pagination), p. 5; Grimeston, *Generall historie*, p. 759.

49. Smith, '"The Sword and the Law"', pp. 121–22; D. J. B. Trim, 'Strategy and the Art of War in the Low Countries during the Eighty Years' War', at the conference 'Strategy and its Making in Early Modern Europe', University of St Andrews, 29–30 April 2016.

50. Cf. Smith, '"The Sword and the Law"', pp. 81–83.

51. D. Alan Orr, '"Communis Hostis Omnium": The Smerwick Massacre (1580) and the Law of Nations', *Journal of British Studies*, 58 (2019), 473–93 at 493.

52. Trim, 'Fighting "Jacob's Wars"', pp. 376-77; Cyril Falls, *Elizabeth's Irish Wars* (London: Methuen, 1950), p. 166.

53. *The Annals of Lough Cé*, ed. and trans. William M. Hennessy, 2 vols. (London: Longman, 1871), II, 493.

54. Angus Konstam, *The Spanish Armada: The Great Enterprise against England 1588* (Botley & New York: Osprey, 2009), pp. 185–86.

55. *Annals of Lough Cé*, II, 499; *Calendar of the Manuscripts of the Most Honourable the Marquess of Bath, Preserved at Longleat, Wiltshire*, vol. V, *Talbot, Dudley and Devereux Papers*, ed. G. Dyfnallt Owen (London: H. M. Stationery Office, 1980), p. 257.

56. See Beatrice Heuser: *Strategy before Clausewitz: Linking Warfare and Statecraft 1400-1830* (Abingdon: Routledge, 2018), chapter 4; and, on Essex, see Paul E. J. Hammer, *The Polarisation of Elizabethan Politics: The Political Career of Robert Devereux, 2nd Earl of Essex, 1585–1597* (Cambridge: Cambridge University Press, 1999).

pp. [71–74]   NOTES

57. *List and Analysis of State Papers, Foreign Series, Elizabeth I, Preserved in the Public Record Office*, ed. Richard Bruce Wernham, 9 vols. (London: HMSO, 1964-2000), VI, p. 72, nos. 22-23, p. 75, no. 28 (quotation). Cf. John Lothrop Motley, *History of the United Netherlands: From the Death of William the Silent to the Twelve Years Truce 1609*, 4 vols. (New York: Harper, 1879-80), III, 338, 340.
58. Motley, *United Netherlands*, III, 343.
59. William Shute, *The Triumphs of Nassau* (London: 1613), pp. 320, 321 (cf. Jean Janszoon Orlers and Henry de Haestens, *Les lauriers de Nassau* (Leiden: 1612), p. 232).

5.   STATE OF EMERGENCY

1. There is insufficient space to list all the many publications to have referenced Drogheda as part of these wider public debates in Ireland, let alone the political uses they have served. For a balanced assessment—and invaluable warning—see Jason McElligott, 'Cromwell, Drogheda, and the abuse of Irish history', *Bullán*, 6:1 (2001), pp. 109–32. For the evolution of Cromwell's monstrous reputation, see Sarah Covington, *The Devil from Over the Sea: Remembering and Forgetting Oliver Cromwell in Ireland* (Oxford: Oxford University Press, 2022).
2. John Morrill, 'The Drogheda Massacre in Cromwellian context', in D. Edwards, P. Lenihan and C. Tait (eds.), *Age of Atrocity: Violence and Political Conflict in Early Modern Ireland* (Dublin: Four Courts Press, 2007), pp. 242–65.
3. Ibid., pp 253–4. See also Micheál Ó Siochrú, *God's Executioner: Oliver Cromwell and the Conquest of Ireland* (London: Faber, 2008), p. 82.
4. McElligott, 'Cromwell', pp. 123–5; Barbara Donagan, 'Codes and conduct in the English Civil War', *Past and Present* 118 (1988), pp. 65–95. More generally, see Geoffrey Parker, 'The Etiquette of Atrocity: The Laws of War in Early Modern Europe', in idem., *Empire, War and Faith* (London: Allen Lane, 2003), pp. 143–68.
5. J.T. Gilbert, *A Contemporary History of Affairs in Ireland* (6 vols., Dublin, 1880), ii, pp. 271–2.
6. Anon, *Letters from Ireland, Relating the several great Successes it hath pleased God to give unto the Parliaments Forces there, in the Taking of Drogheda, Trym, Dundalk, Carlingford, and the Nury* (London, 1649).
7. Micheál Ó Siochrú, 'Propaganda, Rumour and Myth: Oliver Cromwell and the Massacre at Drogheda', in Edwards, Lenihan and Tait (eds.), *Age of Atrocity*, p. 280.

259

NOTES pp. [75–77]

8. Alan MacFarlane (ed.), *The Diary of Ralph Josselin, 1616-83* (London, 1976), p.183

9. The most recent discussion is Pádraig Lenihan, *Consolidating Conquest: Ireland 1603-1707* (Harlow: Longman, 2008), pp. 128–9; see also Anthony Wood, *The Life of Anthony à Wood from the year 1632 to 1672* (Oxford, 1772), pp. 68–9.

10. Author's estimate: accurate population figures are not possible for Ireland before the nineteenth century. For the general upward trend in urban settlement levels before 1641 see Anthony J. Sheehan, 'Irish Towns in a period of change, 1558–1625', in C. Brady and R. Gillespie (eds), *Natives and Newcomers:The Making of Irish Colonial Society, 1534–1641* (Dublin: Irish Academic Press, 1986), pp. 93–119.

11. The best guide to the subject is Aidan Clarke, 'The '1641 massacres'', in M. Ó Siochrú and J. Ohlmeyer (eds.), *Ireland 1641: Contexts and reactions* (Manchester: Manchester University Press, 2013), pp. 37–49; for an exemplary local investigation, see Hilary Simms, 'Violence in County Armagh, 1641', in B. Mac Cuarta (ed.), *Ulster 1641: Aspects of the Rising* (Belfast, 1993), pp. 122–38.

12. Vengeance for the Irish rebellion had long motivated him: Ronald Hutton, *The Making of Oliver Cromwell* (London and New Haven, CT: Yale University Press, 2021), pp. 73–4.

13. Ó Siochrú, *God's Executioner*, ch. 4–5; J. Scott Wheeler, *Cromwell in Ireland* (Dublin: Gill and Macmillan, 1999), ch. 3–6; Patrick J. Corish, 'The Cromwellian Conquest, 1649–53', in T.W. Moody et al (eds.), *New History of Ireland, III: Early Modern Ireland, 1534–1691* (Oxford: Oxford University Press, 1976), pp. 336–52.

14. Morrill, 'The Drogheda Massacre', pp. 259–61.

15. James Heath, *Flagellum, or the Life and Death, Birth and Burial of Oliver Cromwell, the late Usurper* (London, 2nd ed., 1663), p. 83. Corish, 'The Cromwellian Conquest', p. 341 offers a balanced discussion of this source.

16. The level of pillaging was extensive enough to dissuade Cromwell from his original plan of using Wexford as a winter base for the army; there was little or nothing of any value left (Ó Siochrú, *God's Executioner*, p. 97).

17. Elaine Murphy, *Ireland and the War at Sea, 1641–1653* (Woodbridge: Boydell Press, 2012), p. 72.

18. Morrill, 'The Drogheda Massacre', p. 256.

19. Ibid., pp. 242–5.

20. W.J. Smyth, *Map-Making, Landscapes and Memory: A Geography of Colonial and Early Modern Ireland, 1530–1750* (Cork: Cork University

260

pp. [78–79] NOTES

Press, 2006); John Cunningham, *Conquest and Land in Ireland: The Transplantation to Connacht, 1649–1680* (Woodbridge: Boydell Press, 2011); Micheál Ó Siochrú and David Brown, 'The Down Survey and the Cromwellian Land Settlement', in J. Ohlmeyer (ed.), *The Cambridge History of Ireland, II, 1550–1730* (Cambridge: Cambridge University Press, 2018), pp. 584–607; Micheál Ó Siochrú, Heather MacLean, and Ian Gentles (eds.), 'Minutes of the Courts Martial held in Dublin in the years 1651–3', *Archivium Hibernicum* 64 (2011), pp. 56–164.

21. D.B. Quinn and K.W. Nicholls, 'Ireland in 1534', in Moody et al (eds.), *New History of Ireland*, III, pp. 1–38; David Edwards and Brendan Kane, 'Contiguous Court Societies: The Renaissance Irish Lordships and the Tudor and Early Stuart Monarchy', in D. Edwards and B. Kane (eds.), *Ireland and the Renaissance Court, 1450–1640: Cultural Change from the Cúirteanna to Whitehall* (Manchester: Manchester University Press, forthcoming).

22. Jane Ohlmeyer, *Making Ireland English: The Irish Aristocracy in the Seventeenth Century* (London and New Haven, CT: Yale University Press, 2012); Patrick J. Corish, *The Catholic Community in the Seventeenth and Eighteenth Centuries* (Dublin: Helicon, 1981); Robert Armstrong, 'Establishing a Confessional Ireland, 1641–1691', in Ohlmeyer (ed.), *Cambridge History*, II, pp. 220–45.

23. Derek Hirst, *Dominion: England and its Island Neighbours, 1500–1707* (Oxford: Oxford University Press, 2012); William Palmer, *The Problem of Ireland in Tudor Foreign Policy, 1485–1603* (Woodbridge: Boydell Press, 1994); Hiram Morgan, 'British policies before the British state', in B. Bradshaw and J. Morrill (eds.), *The British Problem, c.1534–1707: State Formation in the Atlantic Archipelago* (Basingstoke: Macmillan Press, 1996), pp. 66–88.

24. There is no satisfactory general narrative of the Tudor and early Stuart conquest; however, for the larger wars James O'Neill, *The Nine Years War in Ireland, 1593–1603* (Dublin: Four Courts Press, 2017) is outstanding. See also Anthony McCormack, *The Earldom of Desmond, 1463–1583: The Decline and Crisis of a Feudal Lordship* (Dublin: Four Courts Press, 2005), ch. 8; idem, 'The Social and Economic Consequences of the Desmond Rebellion of 1579–1583', *Irish Historical Studies* 34/133 (May 2004), pp. 1–15.

25. In fact, regarding 'little wars' in early modern Europe, one authority has stated, 'What was known universally as 'small war' was waged on a scale that was anything but small': Simon Pepper, 'Aspects of Operational Art: Communication, Cannon and Small War',

261

NOTES pp. [79–80]

in F. Tallett and D.J.B. Trim (eds.), *European Warfare, 1350–1750* (Cambridge: Cambridge University Press, 2010), p. 182.

26. For the debate accompanying this change, see Clodagh Tait, David Edwards and Pádraig Lenihan, 'Early Modern Ireland: A History of Violence', in Edwards, Lenihan and Tait (eds.), *Age of Atrocity*, pp. 9–33, and Brendan Kane (ed.), 'Human Rights and the History of Violence in the Early British Empire', special issue of *History: The Journal of the Historical Association*, 99/3 (July 2014), esp. the essays by Kane, Andy Wood, Vincent Carey, Sarah Covington, and Malcolm Smuts.

27. David Edwards, 'The Escalation of Violence in Sixteenth-Century Ireland', and John McGurk, 'The pacification of Ulster, 1600–3', both in Edwards, Lenihan and Tait (eds.), *Age of Atrocity*, pp. 34–78, 119–29; Vincent Carey, 'The end of the Gaelic political order: The O'More Lordship of Laois, 1536–1603', in P.G. Lane and W. Nolan (eds.), *Laois: History and Society* (Dublin: Geography Publications, 1999), pp. 213–48; Brian Donovan, 'Tudor Rule in Gaelic Leinster and the rise of Feagh McHugh O'Byrne', in C. O'Brien (ed.), *Feagh McHugh O'Byrne: The Wicklow Firebrand* (Rathdrum: Rathdrum Historical Society, 1998), pp. 118–49; Patricia Palmer, *The Severed Head and the Grafted Tongue: Literature, Translation and Violence in Early Modern Ireland* (Cambridge: Cambridge University Press, 2013), ch. 1; David Heffernan, *Walter Devereux, first Earl of Essex, and the Colonization of North-East Ulster, c.1573–6* (Dublin: Four Courts Press, 2018).

28. David Edwards, 'Out of the blue? Provincial unrest in Ireland before 1641', in M. Ó Siochrú and J. Ohlmeyer (ed.), *Ireland 1641: Contexts and Reactions* (Manchester: Manchester University Press, 2013), pp. 95–114.

29. Malcolm Smuts, 'Ireland's Militarized Itinerate Court and the Tudor and Early Stuart State', in Edwards and Kane (eds.), *Ireland and the Renaissance Court* (forthcoming).

30. David Edwards (ed.), *Campaign Journals of the Elizabethan Irish Wars* (Dublin: Irish Manuscripts Commission, 2014), pp. x-xi and *passim*.

31. This has finally been challenged: see David Heffernan, 'The Reduction of Leinster and the origins of the Tudor Conquest of Ireland, c.1534–46', *Irish Historical Studies*, 40/157 (May, 2016), pp. 14–16.

32. St Leger to Henry VIII, 12 Sept. 1540 (*State Papers, Henry VIII*, iii, pp. 235–40); Lord Justice Brereton and the Irish Council to same, 22 Sept. 1540 (ibid., iii, pp. 241–5).

pp. [80–83]   NOTES

33. His absence lasted from 18 January–6 September 1580: Edwards (ed.), *Campaign Journals*, pp. 58, 110.

34. Ibid., p. 70.

35. Ibid., p. 72.

36. Ibid., p.74.

37. Ibid., p.83.

38. For a different view, contending that rape committed by the Crown forces was not a 'major issue', see James O'Neill, 'Spouses, Spies and Subterfuge: The role and experience of Women during the Nine Years' War (1593–1603)', *Proceedings of the Royal Irish Academy* 121 C (2021), pp. 17–19, quotation p.18. Just because Crown officers did not report it is hardly evidence of it not occurring. For a notorious case from 1606, involving the rape of an eleven-year-old girl in County Donegal by an English captain who, despite prosecution in a local court, escaped punishment and was subsequently promoted, see David Edwards, 'The Plight of the Earls: Tyrone and Tyrconnell's 'Grievances' and Crown Coercion in Ulster, 1603-7', in T. O'Connor and M.A. Lyons (eds.), *The Ulster Earls in Baroque Europe* (Dublin: Four Courts Press, 2010), pp 53–76. See also William Palmer, 'Gender, Violence and Rebellion in Tudor and Early Stuart Ireland', *Sixteenth Century Journal*, 23/4 (1992), pp. 699–712. Valerie McGowan-Doyle is currently researching this difficult and troubling subject; her findings are eagerly awaited.

39. Katherine Eggert, 'Spenser's Ravishment: Rape and Rapture in *The Faerie Queene*', *Representations* 70 (2000), pp 1–26.

40. Pelham to Elizabeth I, 1 April 1580 (TNA, SP 63/72/28).

41. J. O'Donovan (ed.), *Annals of the Kingdom of Ireland by the Four Masters* (6 vols., Dublin, 1854), v, p.1731.

42. Edwards (ed.), *Campaign Journals*, p. 82.

43. In the continued absence of a major study of English military rule in Early Modern Ireland, I have attempted to broach aspects of the subject in a series of essays, viz. David Edwards, 'Questioning the Viceroys: Towards a new model of English government in Ireland, 1536-94', in S. Covington, V. Carey and V. McGowan-Doyle (eds.), *Early Modern Ireland: New Sources, Methods and Perspectives* (Abingdon and New York: Routledge, 2019), pp. 147–65; idem, 'Ireland: Security and Conquest', in S. Doran and N. Jones (eds.), *The Elizabethan World* (Abingdon and New York: Routledge, 2011), pp. 182–200; idem, 'Legacy of Defeat: The Reduction of Gaelic Ireland after Kinsale', in H. Morgan (ed.), *The Battle of Kinsale* (Bray: Wordwell Books, 2004), pp. 279–99; idem, 'Political Change and

NOTES pp. [83–85]

Social Transformation, 1603–1641', in Ohlmeyer (ed.), *Cambridge History*, II, pp. 48–71. See also Joseph McLaughlin, 'The Making of the Irish Leviathan, 1603–25: Statebuilding in Ireland in the reign of James VI and I', unpublished PhD thesis (2 vols., NUI Galway, 1999), ch. 10–11.

44. For the distribution of the garrisons see Chart 1 in Edwards, 'Legacy of Defeat', pp. 286–7.

45. Edwards, 'Political Change', pp. 54–6; idem, 'Two Fools and a Martial Law Commissioner: Cultural Conflict at the Limerick Assize of 1606', in D. Edwards (ed.), *Regions and Ruler in Ireland, 1100–1650: Essays for Kenneth Nicholls* (Dublin: Four Courts Press, 2004), pp. 237–65; John M. Collins, *Martial Law and English Laws, c.1500–c.1700* (Cambridge: Cambridge University Press, 2016).

46. Dean G. White, 'The Tudor Plantations in Ireland before 1571', unpublished PhD thesis (2 vols., Trinity College Dublin, 1967); Michael MacCarthy-Morrogh, *The Munster Plantation: English Migration to Southern Ireland, 1583–1641* (Oxford: Oxford University Press, 1986); Nicholas Canny, *Making Ireland British, 1580–1650* (Oxford: Oxford University Press, 2001), ch. 4; Jonathan Bardon, *The Plantation of Ulster* (Dublin: Gill and Macmillan, 2011); Éamonn Ó Ciardha and Micheal Ó Siochrú (eds.), *The Plantation of Ulster: Ideology and Practice* (Manchester: Manchester University Press, 2012).

47. Chichester's note of services, May 1614 (*Calendar of State Papers, Ireland, 1611–14*, pp. 479–80). For one of the more unusual violent episodes associated with this see John McCavitt, 'Chichester, Ceannairc agus Cairlinn, 1609', *Cuisle na Gael: The Journal of the Newry Branch of the Gaelic League* (1986), pp. 19–23.

48. McCormack, *The Earldom*, pp. 193–4.

49. Hiram Morgan, ''Never any Realm Worse Governed': Queen Elizabeth and Ireland', *Transactions of the Royal Historical Society*, 14 (2004), p. 308.

50. David Edwards, 'Tudor Ireland: Anglicization, Mass Killing, and Security', in C. Carmichael and R. Maguire (eds.), *The Routledge History of Genocide* (Abingdon and New York: Routledge, 2015), pp. 23–4.

51. For civilian casualties in continental European conflicts see Frank Tallett, *War and Society in Early Modern Europe, 1495–1715* (London, 1992), pp. 105–12, 148–68.

52. Surrey to Henry VIII, June 1521 (*State Papers, Henry VIII*, ii, pp. 73–5); extraordinarily, this crucial item has been omitted from the recent revised edition of the Henrician state papers, *Calendar of State Papers,*

264

pp. [85–87]   NOTES

Ireland, Tudor Period, 1509–1547, ed. S.G. Ellis and J. Murray (Dublin: Irish Manuscripts Commission, 2017). For King Henry's change of attitude see D.B. Quinn, 'The Reemergence of English Policy as a major factor in Irish affairs, 1520–34', in A. Cosgrove (ed.), *New History of Ireland, ii, Medieval Ireland, 1169–1534* (Oxford: Oxford University Press, 1987), pp. 662–8.

53. J.J. Scarrisbrick, *Henry VIII* (London: Penguin Books, 1968), pp. 414–18 remains the best guide to the excommunication.

54. Palmer, *The Problem of Ireland*, ch. 3. The prospect of foreign aid for the Fitzgeralds who rose in rebellion in summer 1534 is discussed in Micheál Ó Siochrú, 'Foreign involvement in the revolt of Silken Thomas, 1534–5', *Proceedings of the Royal Irish Academy*, 96 C (1996), pp. 49–62.

55. David Potter, 'French intrigue in Ireland during the reign of Henri II, 1547–1559', *International History Review*, 5 (1983).

56. David Edwards, 'The first sacking of Rathlin, 1557: English Sovereignty in Ireland, the MacDonalds, and the Anglo-Scottish Wars', in S. Egan (ed.), *Beyond the Pale and Highland Line: New Narratives in Archipelagic History* (Manchester: Manchester University Press, forthcoming).

57. Gregory renewed the bull in 1583, as plans for an invasion of England were under discussion: John Bossy, 'The heart of Robert Persons', in T.M. McCoog (ed.), *The Reckoned Expense: Edmund Campion and the Early English Jesuits* (second revised ed., Rome: Institutum Historicum Societatis Jesu, 2007), p. 192.

58. Stephen Alford, *The Watchers: A Secret History of the Reign of Elizabeth I* (London: Allen Lane, 2012); Adrian Morey, *The Catholic Subjects of Elizabeth I* (London: George Allen and Unwin, 1978), ch. 4; Paul E.J. Hammer, 'The Catholic Threat and the Military Response', in Doran and Jones (eds.), *The Elizabethan World*, pp. 629–45.

59. Nicholas Canny, *The Elizabethan Conquest of Ireland: A Pattern Established, 1565–1576* (Hassocks: Harvester Press, 1976), pp. 123–8; Brendan Bradshaw, 'Sword, Word, and Strategy in the Reformation in Ireland', *Historical Journal*, 21 (1978), pp. 475–502; David Heffernan, *Debating Tudor Policy in Sixteenth Century Ireland: 'Reform' Treatises and Political Discourse* (Manchester: Manchester University Press, 2018), pp. 158–60.

60. B. Bailyn and N. Canny, 'Introduction', in B. Bailyn and N. Canny (eds.), *Strangers Within the Realm: Cultural Margins of the First British Empire* (Chapel Hill, NC, and London: University of North Carolina Press, 1991), pp. 25–6; G. Parker, *The Military Revolution: Military*

NOTES pp. [87–90]

Innovation and the Rise of the West, 1500–1800 (Cambridge: Cambridge University Press, 1988), p.118.

61. See Murphy, Chapter 3, above; see also his monograph, *The Tudor Occupation of Boulogne: Conquest, Colonisation and Imperial Monarchy, 1544–1550* (Cambridge: Cambridge University Press, 2019).

62. Surrey to Henry VIII, June 1521 (*State Papers, Henry VIII*, ii, pp. 73–5).

63. Writing to 'Little John' Heron, the keeper of Redesdale in 1540, the king insisted that in confronting rebels from neighbouring Tynedale Heron refrain from 'incontinent fire ... like as in extreme war between strange realms': Ralph Robson, *The Rise and Fall of the English Highland Clans: Tudor Responses to a Medieval Problem* (Edinburgh: John Donald, 1989), p.149.

64. His chief campaigns are charted in Edwards, 'The escalation of violence', pp. 64–5.

65. Edwards (ed.), *Campaign Journals*, pp. 8–9.

66. *Cal. Carew MSS, 1515–74*, no.212.

67. HMC, *Haliday MSS: Acts of the Privy Council in Ireland, 1556–1571* (London, 1895), p.42

68. Ben Kiernan, *Blood and Soil: A World History of Genocide and Extermination from Sparta to Darfur* (London and New Haven, CT: Yale University Press, 2007), ch. 5.

69. D.B. Quinn, *The Elizabethans and the Irish* (Ithaca, NY: Cornell University Press, 1966).

70. Canny, *Making Ireland British*, ch. 1; Ciaran Brady, 'The Road to the View: On the Decline of Reform Thought in Tudor Ireland', in P. Coughlan (ed.), *Spenser and Ireland: Interdisciplinary Essays* (Cork: Cork University Press, 1989), pp. 25–45; Richard A. McCabe, *Spenser's Monstrous Regiment: Elizabethan Ireland and the Poetics of Difference* (Oxford: Oxford University Press, 2002). See also Pauline Henley, *Spenser in Ireland* (Cork: Cork University Press, 1928); though dated it retains much of value.

71. Cowley to Cromwell, 1536 (*State Papers, Henry VIII*, ii, p. 329); Ackworth to Burghley, 20 May 1574, in *Calendar of State Papers, Ireland, Tudor Period, 1571–1575*, ed. M. O'Dowd (Dublin: Irish Manuscripts Commission, 2000), no. 982.

72. Alison Cathcart, 'James V, King of Scotland—and Ireland?', in S. Duffy (ed.), *The World of the Galloglass: Kings, Warlords and Warriors in Ireland and Scotland, 1200–1600* (Dublin: Four Courts Press, 2007), pp. 124–43.

73. Potter, 'French intrigue'.

74. Edwards, 'The first sacking of Rathlin'.

266

pp. [90–95] NOTES

75. McCormack, *The Earldom of Desmond*, pp 110–17; Connolly, *Contested Island*, pp. 159–61.

76. Christopher Maginn, 'The Baltinglass Rebellion 1580: English Dissent or Gaelic Uprising?', *Historical Journal* 47 (2004), pp. 205–32; Judy Barry, 'Eustace, James, (1530–1585), of Harristown, 3rd Viscount Baltinglass', Dictionary of Irish Biography (2009), http://dib.cambridge.org

77. McCormack, *The Earldom of Desmond*, pp. 180–3.

78. Hiram Morgan, 'Extradition and Treason of a Gaelic Lord: the case of Brian O'Rourke', *The Irish Jurist*, 22 n.s. (1987), pp. 285–301.

79. Hiram Morgan, 'Faith and Fatherland in sixteenth-century Ireland', *History Ireland* 3, no. 2 (1995), pp. 13–20; Thomas O'Connor, 'Hugh O'Neill: free spirit, religious chameleon or ardent Catholic?', in Morgan (ed.), *The Battle of Kinsale*, pp. 59–72; Ruth Canning, *The Old English in Early Modern Ireland: The Palesmen and the Nine Years' War, 1594–1603* (Woodbridge: Boydell Press, 2019), ch.2.

6.   VIOLENCE IN SCOTLAND

1. Thomas Prince, *A Sermon Deliver'd at the SOUTH-CHURCH in Boston* (Boston, 1746; Edinburgh, 1747), pp. 14–15; Geoffrey Plank, *Rebellion and Savagery: The Jacobite Rising of 1745 and the British Empire*, (Philadelphia: University of Pennsylvania Press, 2006), p.4; Andrew Henderson, *The Life of William Augustus, Duke of Cumberland*, ed. Roderick Macpherson (London: Pickering and Chatto, 2010), pp. xxv, 195–96.

2. See Murray Pittock, *Culloden* (Oxford: Oxford University Press, 2016), p. 70; discussed further by Carolyn Anderson and Chris Fleet, *Scotland: Defending the Nation* (Edinburgh: Birlinn/National Library of Scotland, 2018), p. 107.

3. See Christopher Duffy, *Fight for a Throne: The Jacobite '45 Reconsidered* (Solihull: Helion, 2015), p. 488.

4. Ibid., 500.

5. Jacqueline Riding, *Jacobites* (London: Bloomsbury, 2016), pp. 318, 365, 368.

6. Royal Archives [hereafter RA], CP/Main/8/25.

7. Mícheál Ó Siochrú, *God's Executioner: Oliver Cromwell and the Conquest of Ireland* (London: Faber, 2008), pp. xx, 84, 210–11; National Library of Scotland [hereafter NLS], Blaikie MS 35431; Evan Charteris, *William Augustus, Duke of Cumberland: His Early Life and Times* (London: Edward Arnold, 1913), p. 183.

267

NOTES   pp. [96–100]

8. RA, CP/Main/14/57; NLS, MS 303; Paul O'Keeffe, *Culloden: Battle and Aftermath* (London: Bodley Head, 2021), pp. 114–16, 155; Óscar Reico Morales, *Ireland and the Spanish Empire, 1600–1825* (Dublin: Four Courts, 2010), p. 128; Riding, *Jacobites*, p.427; Michael Hughes, *A Plain Narrative and Authentic Journal of the Late Rebellion*, 2nd edn. (London: Henry Whitridge, 1747), p.48; Victoria Henshaw, *Scotland and the British Army, 1700–1750: Defending the Union* (London: Bloomsbury, 2015 [2014]), pp. 68, 71.

9. O'Keeffe, *Culloden*, pp.156–57.

10. National Records of Scotland [hereafter NRS], CH 2/918/1; Henshaw, *Scotland and the British Army*, p. 70; Duffy, *Fight for a Throne*, p. 490.

11. O'Keeffe, *Culloden*, p. 152.

12. Ó Síochru, *God's Executioner*, pp.31, 92, 210–11.

13. Hughes, *A Plain Narrative*, p.48.

14. O'Keeffe, *Culloden*, pp. 170, 281–82; Riding, *Jacobites*, p. 460; Hughes, *A Plain Narrative*, p. 51.

15. Charteris, *Cumberland*, p. 184; Duffy, *Fight for a Throne*, p. 486; O'Keeffe, *Culloden*, pp. 170–73; Riding, *Jacobites*, pp. 379–80, 389.

16. RA, CP/Main/15/101; NLS, Advocates MS 23.3.28, ff. 120–21; Riding, *Jacobites*, p.459; Duffy, *Fight for a Throne*, p. 28.

17. R.P. Fereday, *Orkney Feuds and the '45* (Stromness: Kirkwall Grammar School, 1980), pp. 84–86, 91, 96.

18. George G. McGilvary, 'John Drummond of Quarrel: East India Patronage and Jacobite Assimilation, 1720–80', in Allan Macinnes and Douglas Hamilton (eds), *Jacobitism, Enlightenment and Empire, 1680–1820* (London: Pickering and Chatto, 2014), pp.141–57 (149–50, 156); Plank, *Rebellion and Savagery*, pp. 23, 120; Duncan Warrand (ed.), *More Culloden Papers*, Volume V (Inverness: Robert Carruthers & Sons, 1930), p.155.

19. *More Culloden Papers*, ed. Warrand, pp. 71, 137; Plank, *Rebellion and Savagery*, pp. 5, 106.

20. RA, CP/MAIN/14/99.

21. *More Culloden Papers*, ed. Warrand, p. 71.

22. Cumberland to Newcastle, RA, CP/MAIN/14/99; NA SP 36/85/2 f.51 and Riding, *Jacobites*, pp.379, 481.

23. *More Culloden Papers*, ed. Warrand, 102; *The Albemarle Papers,* ed Charles Sanford Terry, 2 vols. (Aberdeen: New Spalding Club, 1902), II, 325.

24. O'Keeffe, *Culloden*, pp. 303, 306; Riding, *Jacobites*, p.445; Anderson and Fleet, *Scotland*, pp. 118–19.

pp. [100–105]   NOTES

25. O'Keeffe, *Culloden*, p. 155.
26. Ibid., pp. 256–58, 261, 263–64, 283–85.
27. David Dobson, *Directory of Scots Banished to the American Plantations 1650–1775* (Baltimore: Genealogical Publishing Co., 1984), pp. 10, 19–20, 28, 85, 109, 121, 140.
28. NLS, MS 1081 (Stewart trial), MS 3142 ('Inventory of Papers relative to the Rebellion') ff. 148, 168.
29. *Albemarle Papers*, ed. Terry, II, 462.
30. Duffy, *Fight for a Throne*, pp. 500–01.
31. *More Culloden Papers*, ed. Warrand, p. 71.
32. Riding, *Jacobites*, p. 368.
33. NLS, MS 280.
34. Duffy, *Fight for a Throne*, p. 492.
35. *More Culloden Papers*, ed. Warrand, pp. 112–13.
36. Annette M. Smith, *Jacobite Estates of the Forty-Five* (Edinburgh: John Donald, 1982), p. 2; *Albemarle Papers*, ed. Terry, II, 463, 482; NRS, GD 95/11/11 (2) (returns of the Presbytery of Fordyce to the SSPCK).
37. Smith, *Jacobite Estates*, p. 2; *More Culloden Papers*, ed. Warrand, p. 177.
38. *More Culloden Papers*, ed. Warrand, pp. 113–15, 152–53; Henshaw, *Scotland and the British Army*, p. 74.
39. Smith, *Jacobite Estates*, pp. 23, 224.
40. Duffy, *Fight for a Throne*, p. 501.
41. Smith, *Jacobite Estates*, p. 11.
42. Ibid., pp. 3–4; Darren S. Layne, 'A Game of Dress Up', *History Scotland* (January/February 2022), pp. 50–51 (p. 51); *The Records of Invercauld 1547–1828*, ed. Revd John Grant Michie (Aberdeen: New Spalding Club, 1901), p. 429; Cantonments of the British Army, 16 January 1750, NMS collection, Edinburgh Castle.
43. *Albemarle Papers*, ed. Terry, II, 350–51.
44. O'Keeffe, *Culloden*, pp. 223, 232, 234.
45. *Caledonian Mercury*, 14 October 1745; 4 September 1746; 24 November 1748; British Library [hereafter BL], Add MSS 32707; Charteris, *Cumberland*, pp. 181, 185; Hughes, *A Plain Narrative*, p. 49.
46. O'Keeffe, *Culloden*, p. 318.
47. *More Culloden Papers*, ed. Warrand, p. 71; *Albemarle Papers*, ed. Terry, II, 448, 479.
48. National War Museum Library, Edinburgh [hereafter NWM], M. 1975.5.2: Cantonment Register of the British Army in Scotland 1746-52; NLS, MS 3142; Duffy, *Fight for a Throne*, p. 487.
49. NWM, M.1975.5.2: Cantonment Register Summer 1749; Henshaw, *Scotland and the British Army,* pp. 22, 169; Nigel Leask, *Stepping*

269

NOTES

pp. [106–111]

Westward: Writing the Highland Tour, c.1720–1830, (Oxford: Oxford University Press, 2020), p. 54. See also William Taylor, *The Military Roads in Scotland* (Exeter: SRP, 1996 [1976]).

50. BL, Add MSS 32706 f. 324; NLS, MS Adv MS 23.3.38 f.277; *Albemarle Papers,* ed. Terry, I, 4, 9, 10, 115, 163–64, 204, 214–15, II, 357.

51. *Albemarle Papers*, ed. Terry, I, 59.

52. Ibid., I, 59, 65, 116-17, 193, 210; *More Culloden Papers*, ed. Warrand, p. 123.

53. Amy Peteranna and Lindsey Stirling, 'Digging Beneath the Streets of Inverness', *History Scotland* 18:5 (2018), pp. 10–14 (12); O'Keefe (2021), p. 163; *More Culloden Papers*, ed. Warrand, pp. 129–30.

54. *Albemarle Papers*, ed. Terry, I, 79, 82.

55. Terry (ed.), in *Albemarle Papers*, II, xxxvii.

56. Ibid., I, 78–82, 175.

57. Layne, 'A Game of Dress Up', p.51.

58. *More Culloden Papers*, ed. Warrand, pp. 103–4.

59. NLS, MS 3787 (Appin Order Book); *Albemarle Papers*, ed. Terry, I, 239; II, 300, 339, 370, 550.

60. *Albemarle Papers*, ed. Terry, I, 195–96, 201, 216–17, 222–23

61. Morales, *Ireland and the Spanish Empire*, pp. 185, 190–91, 195.

62. NLS, MS 304, General Bland's Letter Book for 1st, 8th and 17th December 1747.

63. William Crawford, *The Records of Elgin 1234–1860*, 2 vols. (Aberdeen: New Spalding Club, 1903–8), I, 457–58.

64. NWM, M.1975.5.1 (Courts Martial Scotland, 1751-53); Cantonments of the British Army, 6 June, 25 November 1749, 15 May 1751 (National Museum of Scotland).

65. NLS, MS 304, 26 April-3 June 1748.

66. Courts Martial of the British Army in Scotland 1751-53 (National Museum of Scotland).

67. NLS, MS 308 (Churchill's Letter Book); NWM, M. 1975.5.1, Summer 1749, 9 October 1751.

68. NLS, MS 305 (Bland's Letter Book), 3 October, 7 November 1754, 7 April 1756.

69. NLS, MS 304.

70. NWM, M.1975.5.1 (Courts Martial); O'Keeffe, *Culloden*, pp. 327, 331; Christopher A. Whatley, 'Order and Disorder', in Elizabeth Foyster and Christopher Whatley (eds,), *A History of Everyday Life in Scotland 1600–1800* (Edinburgh: Edinburgh University Press, 2010), pp. 191–216 (191).

NOTES

71. Alistair J. Durie (ed.), *The British Linen Company 1745–1775* (Edinburgh: Scottish History Society, 1996).

72. NLS, MS 305 (Bland's Letter Book), 7 January 1755; Stéphane Robin, 'Jacobitism and Banditry', unpublished M.Res. thesis, (Bretagne Sud, 2014), p. 32.

73. NLS, MS 305 (Bland's Letter Book): 15, 30 January, 6 February, 18 February, 12 March, May, 13 June, 29 October, 13, 15 December 1755; 17, 31 January, 19 April, 3 June and 29 June 1756; Medical Reports on the Chelsea Pensioners, 1755 (National Museum of Scotland).

74. *Albemarle Papers*, ed. Terry, II, 325.

75. Andrew Hill Clark, *Acadia* (Madison, Milwaukee and London: University of Wisconsin Press, 1968), pp. 350, 363; Plank, *Rebellion and Savagery*, p. 164.

7. 'ALAS POOR DANES!'

1. I would like to thank the following for their comments on this chapter in draft form: Tom Bartlett, Ilya Berkovich, John Freeman, Joshua Meeks, Rose-Ann Melikan, Alexander Mikaberidze, Thomas Peak. Some of the content of this chapter was originally published in Brendan Simms and Thomas Peak, 'From Commerce to Violence. The Second Bombardment of Copenhagen (1807)', *Studia Historica Gedanensia*, 13 (2022), pp. 110–120.

2. I look at the international legal dimensions in greater detail with Thomas Peak in Simms and Peak, 'From Commerce to Violence. The Second Bombardment of Copenhagen (1807)'.

3. Brendan Simms, *Three Victories and a Defeat. The Rise and Fall of the First British Empire, 1714–1783* (Allen Lane: London, 2007); Robert G. Albion, *Forests and Sea Power. The Timber Problem of the Royal Navy, 1652–1862* (Harvard University Press: Cambridge, Mass., 1926); John J. Murray, *George I, the Baltic and the Whig Split of 1717. A Study in Diplomacy and Propaganda* (University of Chicago Press: Chicago and London, 1969).

4. Isabel de Madariaga, *Britain, Prussia and the Armed Neutrality of 1780: Sir James Harris's Mission to St. Petersburg During the American Revolution* (Yale University Press: New Haven, 1962).

5. National Archives [hereafter NA], FO 22/44

6. Thus James Davey, 'Serving the State: Empire, Expertise and the British Hemp Crisis of 1800–1801', *Journal of Imperial and Commonwealth History*, 46 (2018), 651–675.

271

NOTES

pp. [116–119]

7. See James Davey, 'The Advancement of Nautical Knowledge: The Hydrographical Office, the Royal Navy and the Charting of the Baltic Sea, 1795–1815', *Journal for Maritime Research*, 13 (2011), 81–103.

8. Silvia Marzagalli and Leos Mueller, '"In apparent disagreement with all law of nations in the world". Negotiating neutrality for shipping and trade during the French Revolutionary and Napoleonic Wars', *International Journal of Maritime History*, 28 (2016), 108–117, especially 111–113. See also Katherine B. Aaslestad, 'Lost Neutrality and Economic Warfare. Napoleonic Warfare in Northern Europe, 1795–1815', in Roger Chickering and Stig Förster (eds). *War in an Age of Revolution, 1775–1815* (Cambridge University Press: Cambridge, 2010), pp. 373–394.

9. Brendan Simms, *The Impact of Napoleon. Prussian High Politics, Foreign Policy and the Crisis of the Executive, 1797–1806* (Cambridge University Press: Cambridge, 1997), pp. 83–85. See also Philip Dwyer, 'Prussia and the Armed Neutrality: The Invasion of Hanover in 1801', *International History Review*, 15 (1993), 661–87.

10. Gareth Glover, *The Two Battles of Copenhagen, 1801 and 1807. Britain and Denmark in the Napoleonic Wars* (Pen and Sword Military: Barnsley, 2018), pp. 25–33, 77–88.

11. Ibid., p. 93 *et passim*.

12. *Parliamentary History of England from the earliest Period to the year 1803* [hereafter *PH*], Volume XXXVI, 1820, p. 198.

13. Ibid., p. 270.

14. *PH*, Volume XXXV, p. 1139.

15. Ibid., p. 1174, p. 1183.

16. Ibid., p. 896.

17. Ibid., p. 901.

18. Ibid., p. 1195.

19. Ibid., p. 921.

20. Ibid., pp. 923–924.

21. Ibid., p. 925.

22. Ibid., p. 926.

23. Quoted in Thomas Munch-Peterson, *Defying Napoleon. How Britain Bombarded Copenhagen and Seized the Danish Fleet in 1807* (The History Press: Stroud, 2007), p. 37. For the Swedish dimension see Christer Jorgensen, 'The beginning of the end. Tilsit, the battle of Copenhagen, the Franco-Russian "continental" coalition against Britain and invasion plans against Sweden, March 1807-March 1808', in Christer Jorgenson (ed.), *The Anglo-Swedish Alliance Against Napoleonic France* (Palgrave Macmillan: London, 2004), pp. 90–125.

272

pp. [119–122] NOTES

24. Henning Soby Andersen, 'Denmark between the wars with Britain, 1801–7', *Scandinavian Journal of History*, 14 (1989), 231–238 (especially, 231–32); Munch-Peterson, *Defying Napoleon*, p. 55.

25. James Davey, 'Securing the sinews of sea power. British intervention in the Baltic, 1780–1815', *International History Review*, 33 (June 2011), 161–184 (especially, pp. 174–175).

26. Glover, *Two Battles of Copenhagen*, pp. 88–100.

27. Munch-Petersen, *Defying Napoleon*, p. 51.

28. Quoted in J. Holland Rose, 'Canning and the Secret Intelligence from Tilsit (July 16–23 1807)', *Transactions of the Royal Historical Society*, 20 (1906), 63. This is now superseded by Thomas Munch-Petersen, 'The secret intelligence from Tilsit. New light on the events surrounding the British bombardment of Copenhagen in 1807', *Historisk Tidsskrift*, 102 (2002), 54–96.

29. See Munch-Peterson, *Defying Napoleon*, pp. 126–127.

30. A.N. Ryan, 'The causes of the British attack upon Copenhagen', *English Historical Review*, 68, (1953), 43–45.

31. Munch-Petersen, *Defying Napoleon*, p. 95.

32. See Barry O'Connell, 'Underground alliances and preventive strikes: British intelligence and secret diplomacy during the Napoleonic Wars, 1807–1810', *Intelligence and National Security*, 35 (2020), 179–196, especially 181–182.

33. Thus Rose, 'Canning and the secret intelligence', 77.

34. Glover, *Two Battles of Copenhagen*, p. 97.

35. A.N. Ryan (ed.), 'Documents relating to the Copenhagen Operation, 1807', *The Naval Miscellany* (London: Navy Records Society, 1984), V, pp. 297–329. I have only cited archival material directly where it was not available in this or other printed editions.

36. Castlereagh to the Commander in Chief of His Majesty's [sic] in the Baltic, Downing Street, 19 July 1807, in Ryan, 'Documents relating', pp. 304–305.

37. Quoted in Munch-Petersen, *Defying Napoleon*, p. 106. See also Christopher T. Golding, 'Amphibians at heart. The battle of Copenhagen (1807), the Walcheren Expedition, and the war against Napoleon', *Journal for the Society of Army Historical Research*, 90 (2012), pp. 167–188.

38. Quoted in Munch-Petersen, *Defying Napoleon*, p. 139.

39. Canning to Gower, 9 June 1807, in Ryan, 'Documents Relating', p. 302.

40. Quoted in Munch-Petersen, *Defying Napoleon*, pp. 245 and 116.

NOTES

pp. [122–125]

41. The only suggestion that they did is in Francis Jackson's account in NA FO 353/56 (entry for 18 August 1807), but it is not supported by any other evidence I have found. Jackson writes that when the commanders discussed whether one should 'proceed by bombardment or regular siege. I knew from the Lord Castlereagh that the former [i.e., bombardment] was to be tried first'.

42. Castlereagh to Cathcart, Downing Street, 3 August 1807, NA WO6/14, f. 35.

43. Cathcart to Castlereagh, Off Elsinore, 13 August 1807, [P.S. of 15.8.1807], NA, WO 188, f. 95.

44. Castlereagh to Cathcart, Downing Street, 27 August 1807, in Ryan, 'Documents relating', p. 319.

45. See Brendan Simms, *Three Victories and a Defeat. The Rise and Fall of the First British Empire, 1714–1783* (London: Allen Lane, 2007), p. 481.

46. Quoted in Mark Totten, *First Strike. America, Terrorism and Moral Tradition* (New Haven and London: 2010), p. 111.

47. Quoted in Munch-Petersen, *Defying Napoleon*, p. 111.

48. Dispatch to Francis Jackson and Taylor, Foreign Office, 30 July 1807, NA FO 22/54, f. 48.

49. Glover, *Two Battles of Copenhagen*, p. 130.

50. The Admiralty Minute of 19 July 1807 (NA ADM 3/161) notes that the Board of Ordnance was to be asked 'to issue such rockets as Mr Congreve may demand'.

51. Francis Jackson to Canning, Landscrona, 15 August 1807, NA FO 22/54, f. 97.

52. Quoted in Munch-Petersen, *Defying Napoleon*, p. 157.

53. The location of the Danish fleet in harbour and the difficulty of a seaward approach due to forts and floating batteries is clear from 'A plan of the City of Copenhagen with the adjacent ground', NA MPH 1/617. For the Danish preparation see also Rasmus Glenthoj and Morten Nordhagen Ottosen, 'The bombardment of Copenhagen in 1807', in idem *Experiences of War and Nationality in Denmark and Norway, 1807–1815* (London: 2014), pp. 36, 41 *et passim*.

54. Cathcart to Castlereagh, HQ before Copenhagen, 22 August 1807, ff. 98–99.

55. Cathcart to Castlereagh, before Copenhagen, 31 August 1807, f. 127. See also the account of Francis Jackson: 'Lord Cathcart declared [on 21 August 1807] to Admiral Gambier that the town could not be taken without a regular siege and that he had not the means of carrying one on'. NA 353/56, entry for 21 August 1807.

56. Quoted in Munch-Petersen, *Defying Napoleon*, p. 195.

274

pp. [126–129]   NOTES

57. Munch-Peterson, *Defying Napoleon*, p. 193.
58. NA FO 353/56, entry for 30 August 1807.
59. Quoted in Glover, *Two Battles of Copenhagen*, p. 140
60. NA FO 353/56, entry for 30 August 1807.
61. Both are printed in Glover, *Two Battles of Copenhagen*, pp. 232–34.
62. Ibid., pp. 232–233.
63. Ibid., p. 234
64. W.G. Perrin (ed.), 'The bombardment of Copenhagen, 1807. The Journal of surgeon Charles Chambers of H.M Fireship *Prometheus*', entry for 2 September 1807, *The Naval Miscellany*, *III*, Navy Records Society, Vl. 63 (1928), p. 405.
65. Mr F.J. Jackson to George Jackson, Landscrona, 15 August 1807, in Lady Jackson (ed.), *The Diaries and Letters of Sir George Jackson K.C.H.*, Volume II (London: Richard Bentley, 1872), pp. 197–198.
66. Mr F.J. Jackson to George Jackson, HMS *Prince of Wales* off Copenhagen, 16 August 1807, in Lady Jackson, *The Diaries and Letters of Sir George Jackson*, p. 199.
67. Gavin Daly, *Storm and Sack. British Sieges, Violence and the Laws of War in the Napoleonic Era, 1799–1815* (Cambridge: Cambridge University Press, 2022); this book is mainly about the Peninsula War, with only brief discussion of Copenhagen, pp. 186–187. For the brutality of sieges see also Gunther Rothenberg, 'The Age of Napoleon', in Michael Howard (ed.), *The Laws of War. Constraints on Warfare in the Western World* (New Haven: Yale University Press, 1994), pp. 86–97, especially pp. 86, 88, and 93.
68. Robert Wilkinson-Latham, *British Artillery on Land and Sea, 1790–1820* (Newton Abbot, 1973), p. 35 describes their performance as 'erratic'.
69. Quoted in Glenthoj and Ottosen, 'The bombardment of Copenhagen, 1807', p. 42.
70. E.g. John D. Grainger, *The British Navy in the Baltic* (Woodbridge: Boydell and Brewer, 2014), pp. 171–172; Mats Fridlund, 'Buckets, bollards and bombs: towards subject histories of technologies and terrors', *History and Technology*, 27 (2011), 391–416, especially 392; and Aaslestad, 'Lost neutrality and economic warfare', 382.
71. Glover, *Two Battles of Copenhagen*, pp. 151–154.
72. Thus Glover, *Two Battles of Copenhagen* p. 160.
73. See the map in NA MPH 1/617, in which the destroyed areas are marked in yellow.
74. Gambier to Hon William Wellesley-Pole, Secretary of the Admiralty, 7 September 1807, in Glover, *Two Battles of Copenhagen*, p. 261.

275

NOTES

pp. [129–134]

75. Cathcart to Castlereagh, Citadel of Copenhagen, 7 September 1807, NA WO1/188, f. 223.

76. Quoted in Munch-Petersen, *Defying Napoleon*, p. 202.

77. Mr George Jackson to Mrs Jackson, H.M. cutter *Surly*, 14 September 1807, Lady Jackson, *The Diaries and Letters of Sir George Jackson*, p. 210.

78. See Glover, *Two Battles of Copenhagen* p. 195.

79. Quoted in ibid., pp. 158–159.

80. 'A list of the Danish ships and vessels delivered up by the capitulation of Copenhagen to his Majesty's forces, 7.9.1807', in NA ADM 1/5.

81. See the description in Hans Christian Berg, '"To Copenhagen a fleet". The British pre-emptive seizure of the Danish-Norwegian navy, 1807', *International Journal of Naval History*, 7 (2008), pp. 10–12.

82. Quoted in the printed Account, p. 23, consulted in NA MPH 1/617.

83. The original letter is depicted in https://www.schwanke-philatelie.de/2021/12/aspekte-zur-hamburger-postgeschichte-16-zeitzeugen-die-bombardierung-von-kopenhagen/ [accessed 20 December 2021].

84. William Henry Allen, Edward H. Tatu and Marion Tining, 'Letters of William Henry Allen, 1800–1813. Part Two, 1807–1813', *Huntington Library Quarterly*, 1 (1938), p. 219.

85. Thus Glenthoj and Ottosen, 'The bombardment of Copenhagen, 1807', p. 50.

86. Quoted in Glover, *Two Battles of Copenhagen*, pp. 261–262.

87. A.N. Ryan, 'The Copenhagen Operation, 1807', *The Naval Miscellany*, V, p. 323.

88. *An examination of the causes which led to the late expedition against Copenhagen* by an Observer (London, 1808), pp. 1, 36, 41.

89. Hansard, X, 3 Februrary 1808.

90. Hansard, X, 21 March 1808.

91. Hansard, X, 3 March 1808.

92. Hansard, X, 25 February 1808.

93. Hansard, X, 25 February 1808.

94. Hansard, X, 3 March 1808.

95. *The real state of the case respecting the late expedition* (London: J. Ridgeway, 1808), pp. i, 1–3, and 13.

96. Diary entry, 26 September 1807, in Lady Jackson, *The Diaries and Letters of Sir George Jackson*, p. 218.

97. Allen, Tatu and Tining, 'Letters of William Henry Allen', p. 219.

98. For a dated overview see Carl J. Kulsrud, 'The seizure of the Danish fleet, 1807. The background', *American Journal of International Law*, 32 (1938), 280–311, especially 280–282.

pp. [134–142]   NOTES

99. Jonathan Steinberg, 'The Copenhagen Complex', *Journal of Contemporary History*, 1:3 (1966), 38, 24 *et passim*.
100. See Chapter 11, by Karine Varley.
101. Winston S. Churchill, *The Second World. Volume II. Their Finest Hour* (London: Cassell and Co, 1949), p. 211.
102. Ibid.
103. Ibid., p. 206. Oddly, he specified the first attack by Nelson in 1801, rather than the later one of 1807, perhaps because of its resemblances to British terror-bombing of German cities in World War II.

8. BRITISH-ARMY VIOLENCE AGAINST CIVILIANS IN THE PENINSULAR WAR

1. For details of the battle of Cape Santa Maria, see S. Millar, 'Seizing the Gold of Spain, the Action of Cape Santa María', https://www. napoleon-series.org/military-info/battles/1804/c_santamaria. html, accessed 6 October 2022.
2. For the author's views on Wellington's intentions with respect to the defence of Portugal, see C.J. Esdaile, *The Peninsular War* (London: Allen Lane, 2002), pp. 311–12. For alternative discussions of the same subject, see J. Grehan, *The Lines of Torres Vedras: the Cornerstone of Wellington's Strategy in the Peninsular War* (Barnsley: Pen and Sword, 2015), and D. Buttery, *Wellington against Masséna: the Third Invasion of Portugal, 1810* (Barnsley: Pen and Sword, 2007).
3. J. Leach, *Rough Sketches in the Life of an Old Soldier* (London: Longman, Hurst, Rees, Orme, Brown and Green, 1831), pp, 175–6.
4. E. Gachot (ed.), *Mémoires du Colonel Delagrave sur la campagne de Portugal* (Paris: Librairie Charles Delagrave, 1902), pp. 55–7.
5. See Esdaile, *Peninsular War*, p. 470.
6. E.g., Earl of Stanhope (ed.), *Note of Conversations with the Duke of Wellington, 1831–1851* (London: John Murray, 1888), pp. 14, 18.
7. E. Coss, *All for the King's Shilling* (Norman, Oklahoma: University of Oklahoma Press, 2010), p. 236.
8. R. Buckley (ed.), *The Napoleonic-War Journal of Captain Thomas Henry Browne, 1807–1816* (London: Bodley Head, 1987), p. 198. For an interesting discussion, see A. Parker, 'Incorrigible Rogues: The Brutalization of British Soldiers in the Peninsular War', *British Journal of Military History*, 1, No. 3 (June, 2015), pp. 42–59.
9. D.W. Norris, *Over the Hills and Far Away: The Life and Times of Thomas Norris, 1778–1858* (Enstone: privately published, 2005), pp. 58–61.

277

NOTES pp. [142–145]

P. Haythornthwaite, *The Armies of Wellington* (London: Brockhampton Press, 1994), p. 67.

10. J.M. Sherer, *Recollections of the Peninsula* (London: Longman, Hurst, Rees, Orme, Brown and Green 1824), p. 132.

11. Ibid., pp. 131–2.

12. For the most recent and, indeed, fullest treatment of Ciudad Rodrigo, Badajoz, and San Sebastián, see G. Daly, *Storm and Sack: British Sieges, Violence and the Laws of War in the Napoleonic Era, 1792–1815* (Cambridge: Cambridge University Press, 2022). On Badajoz, in particular, meanwhile, see Fletcher, I., *In Hell before Daylight: The Siege and Storming of Badajoz, 16 March–6 April 1812* (Tunbridge Wells: Spellmount, 1984).

13. J.F. Maurice (ed.), *The Diary of Sir John Moore* (London: Edward Arnold, 1904), II, pp. 278–9. Moore's complaints that much of the disorder was due to negligence on the part of the officers of the army was frequently echoed by Wellington, as witness, for example, the similar allegation that he made in the wake of the retreat from Burgos. However, whilst there certainly were officers who were, at best, lax in their approach to discipline, a great part of the trouble took place in situations in which officers were either absent altogether or hopelessly isolated. Herewith, for example, the senior commissary, Richard Henegan, on the small parties of men who were constantly making their way from Lisbon to the encampments of the army or vice versa. Thus: 'Relieved from the responsibility and discipline attached to each individual in an organised force, their route is marked, with few exceptions, by violence and rapine. The arms they bear for the service of their country are turned Against the peaceful inhabitants of the districts they pass through, and bloodshed but too often follows the commission of plunder.' R. Henegan, *Seven Years' Campaigning in the Peninsula and the Netherlands from 1808 to 1815* (London: Henry Colburn, 1846), pp. 70–3.

14. Sir Arthur Wellesley to Lord Castlereagh, 17 June 1809, cited in J. Gurwood (ed.), *The Dispatches of Field Marshal the Duke of Wellington during his Various Campaigns in India, Denmark, Portugal, Spain, the Low Countries and France* (London: Parker, Furnivall and Parker, 1852), III, pp. 302–3.

15. J.W. Gordon to Duke of York, 16 August 1812, British Library, Additional Manuscripts, 49473, ff. 56–8.

16. E. Costello, *Adventures of a Soldier, or Memoirs of Edward Costello, K.S.F., formerly a Non-Commissioned Officer in the Rifle Brigade and Late Captain in the British Legion comprising Narratives of the Campaigns in the*

278

pp. [145–150]   NOTES

Peninsular War under the Duke of Wellington and the recent Civil Wars in Spain (London: Henry Colburn, 1841), p. 73.

17. Marqués de la Romana to A. Cornel, 18 January 1809, Archivo Histórico Nacional, Sección de Estado, 18-8, ff. 32-4.

18. A. Ludovici (ed.), *On the Road with Wellington: The Diary of a War Commissary in the Peninsular Campaigns* (New York: Alfred A. Knopf, 1925), pp. 127–8.

19. G. Daly, *The British Soldier in the Peninsular War: Encounters with Spain and Portugal, 1808–1814* (Basingstoke: Palgrave Macmillan, 2013), p. 115.

20. E.g., P. Haythornthwaite, *Redcoats: The British Soldier of the Napoleonic Wars* (Barnsley: Pen and Sword, 2012), p. 89.

21. For the situation with respect to general courts martial, see C. Oman, *Wellington's Army* (London: Edward Arnold, 1913), p. 245, while the issue of sexual violence is discussed at some length in C.J. Esdaile, *Women in the Peninsular War* (Norman, Oklahoma: University of Oklahoma Press, 2013), pp. 189–216.

22. J. Donaldson, *Recollections of the Eventful Life of a Soldier* (Edinburgh: Robert Martin, 1852), pp. 44–5.

23. Anon., *Journal of a Soldier of the Seventy-First, or Glasgow Regiment, Highland Light Infantry from 1806 to 1815* (Edinburgh: William and Charles Tait, 1819), p. 15.

24. M. Mcilwee, *The Liverpool Underworld: Crime in the City, 1750–1900* (Oxford: Oxford University Press, 2011), pp. 1–26.

25. G. Durston, *Whores and Highwaymen: Crime and Justice in the Eighteenth-Century Metropolis* (Hook: Waterside Press, 2012), p. 80.

26. Ibid., p. 81.

27. Ibid., pp. 85–6.

28. Ibid., pp. 86–9.

29. G.T. Smith, 'Expanding the compass of domestic violence in the Hanoverian metropolis', *Journal of Social History*, 41, No.1 (Fall, 2007), p. 33.

30. Ibid., p. 34.

31. Ibid., pp. 40–1.

32. D. Marshall, *English People in the Eighteenth Century* (London, 1956), pp. 196–7.

33. For a wide-ranging discussion of the eighteenth-century riot, see A. Randall, *Riotous Assemblies: Popular Protest in Hanoverian England* (Oxford: Oxford University Press, 2006). Perhaps most relevant to the discussion here are the major bouts of disorder that broke out in response to the poor harvests of 1793, 1794, 1799 and 1800–1801.

279

NOTES pp. [150–153]

34. J. Stevenson, *Popular Disturbances in England, 1700–1870* (London: Longman, 1979), p. 313.

35. D. Reamer, "'Damn the bitches: they want gin!" The Eighteenth-Century English Gin Craze', *New England Journal of History,* 73, No. 1 (September, 2016), p. 94; A.M. Kilday, *Women and Violent Crime in Enlightenment Scotland* (Woodbridge: Royal Historical Society, 2007), pp. 49–50; N. Rogers, *Crowds, Culture and Politics in Georgian Britain* (Clarendon Press: Oxford, 1998), pp. 163–4. It was not, of course, just violence that was linked to drink, but also child abuse: one freezing day in January 1734 a certain Judith Dufour stripped her two-year-old daughter of all her clothes for the purpose of pawning them for drink, and left the little girl bound and gagged in a ditch, wherein she promptly died of exposure. See N. Allred, 'Mother Gin and the Bad Examples: Figuring a Drugs Crisis, 1736–1751' *Eighteenth-Century Fiction* 33, No. 3 (Spring, 2021), p. 376.

36. For all this, see G. Hirschfelder, 'The Myth of "Misery Alcoholism" in Early-industrial England: The Example of Manchester', in S. Schmid and B. Schmidt-Haberkamp (eds.), *Drink in the Eighteenth and Nineteenth Centuries* (London: Routledge, 2016), pp. 91–101.

37. J. Nicholls, *The Politics of Alcohol: A History of the Drink Question in England* (Manchester: Manchester University Press, 2009), p. 42; see also C. Luddington, *The Politics of Wine in Britain: A New Cultural History* (Basingstoke: Palgrave-Macmillan, 2013), pp. 183–220.

38. Haythornthwaite, *Armies of Wellington*, p. 67.

39. For all this, see A.M. Kilday, 'Criminally poor? Investigating the link between poverty and criminality in eighteenth-century England', *Cultural and Social History,* 11, No. 4 (December, 2014), pp. 507–26.

40. Critics of this essay will at this point doubtless revert to the sack of Ciudad Rodrigo, Badajoz, and San Sebastián, and, in particular, first, the fact that no measures were taken against any of the men involved in the disorder, something from which it is inferred that Wellington was not opposed to what took place, and, second, the suggestion that he had let it be known in the army that success at the breaches would carry with it the reward of at least a period of unlimited violence, plunder, and rapine. In so far as the latter claim is concerned, it has to be said that it is at the very least impossible to disprove, but, at the same time, from all that we know of Wellington, inherently implausible. As for the former, the simple fact is that, in practice, no action was possible, for summary punishment—the dispatch of squads of reliable soldiers into the three towns with orders to snatch particularly prominent malefactors and string them up forthwith—was a policy

pp. [155–156]   NOTES

that, in the circumstances, was unlikely to bear much fruit, and legal process—trial by court martial and execution thereafter—required the willing testimony of witnesses whose every word could not but amount to an admission of participation in the self-same disorders. That this situation was highly unsatisfactory cannot be denied, but, for all that, it can hardly be advanced as evidence that Wellington was prepared to go beyond the laws of war.

9. 'YOU HAVE NOT HAD A SUFFICIENT NUMBER KILLED AND WOUNDED'

1. George Butler Earp, *A History of the Baltic Campaign of 1854: from documents and other materials furnished by Vice Admiral Sir Charles Napier* (London: Richard Bentley, 1857), p. 382.
2. For the distinction between limited and unlimited wars see: Julian Corbett, *Some Principles of Maritime Strategy* (London: Longman, 1911), pp. 38–48, which develops the ideas of Carl von Clausewitz for a maritime power.
3. The obvious exception, the naval Battle of Navarino 20 October 1827, was criticized by Prime Minister Wellington as 'untoward'. Fought by British, French, and Russian forces against Ottoman and Egyptian fleets, it secured the independence of Greece.
4. The most important standard texts on these campaigns are: Henry Sulivan, *Life and Letters of Admiral Sir B. J. Sulivan* (London: John Murray, 1896), a first-hand account by the officer who planned all the major offensive operations, including the attack on Cronstadt/ St. Petersburg; David Bonner-Smith ed. *The Russian War, 1854* and *The Russian War, 1855: Baltic* (London: Navy Records Society, 1943 and 1944), reproduces the contemporary Confidential Cabinet Print, with significant scholarly analysis. Basil Greenhill and Anne Giffard, *The British Assault on Finland: A Forgotten Naval War* (London: Conway Press, 1988) addressed the impact on Finland and the Åland Islands, then a Grand Duchy ruled by the Czar, focussing on seafarers and coastal towns. Andrew Lambert, *The Crimean War: British Grand Strategy against Russia, 1853-56*, 2nd edn. (Ashgate: Farnham, 2011), focuses on strategic decision-making, economic warfare, and the role of the Baltic in the wider conflict, including the threat to St. Petersburg. Andrew C. Rath, *The Crimean War in Imperial Context, 1854-1856* (London: Palgrave Macmillan, 2015) examined all four theatres of the war, and stressed the significance of East Asia, including the 'opening' of Japan, along with the Russian seizure of the Amur River

281

NOTES pp. [156–161]

basin from China, the last act of the conflict. Trudie Tate, *A Short History of the Crimean War* (London: I.B. Tauris, 2019) a fine assessment of the conflict, recognizes the importance of the Baltic.

5. The Scheldt Estuary was the only secure base for an invasion of England in the sailing ship era (1350–1850). To avoid a Spanish invasion, England occupied key towns on the estuary in 1585, which prompted Philip II to declare war.

6. The first English language 'Offshore Balancing' text was a 1430s poem, the 'Libylle of Englysshe Policy', a humanist reaction to the collapse of the English Empire in France. Thomas More's *Utopia* identified and Henry VIII's Navy responded to the rising threat of Habsburg dominion. Kyle M. Lascurettes, *Orders of Exclusion: Great Powers and the Strategic Sources of Foundational Rules in International Relations* (Oxford University Press, 2020).

7. Christopher Layne 'From Preponderance to Offshore Balancing, American's Future Grand Strategy', *International Security* vol. 22, no.1 Summer 1997, pp. 85–124, at p.116 citing Daniel Baugh 'British Strategy during the First World War in the context of Four Centuries: Blue-Water versus Continental Commitment' in Daniel M. Masterson ed. *Naval History: The Sixth Symposium of the U.S. Naval Academy* (Wilmington, 1987).

8. Layne 1997, p. 118 fn.87.

9. Memorandum of 3.1.1894 sent to Gladstone via his daughter Mary Drew: John Neville Figgis & Reginald Vere Laurence eds. *Selections for the Correspondence of the First Lord Acton. Vol. 1* (London: Longman, 1917), pp. 246–50.

10. Richard Shannon, *Gladstone: Heroic Minister; 1865–1898.* (London: Allen Lane, 1999), p.88.

11. Layne 1997, p. 109.

12. John Bew, *Castlereagh: A Life* (London: Quercus, 2012); Gash, William Anthony Hay, *Lord Liverpool: A Political Life* (Woodbridge, Boydell & Brewer, 2018).

13. Napoleon's first abdication inspired J M W Turner to create 'The Dawn of the Carthaginian Empire' in 1814.

14. Isabel de Madariage, *Britain, Russia and the Armed Neutrality of 1780* (London: Hollis & Carter, 1962).

15. Dominic Lieven, *Russia Against Napoleon* (New York: Viking, 2009), pp. 100, 358–9.

16. For British Baltic policy see: Andrew Lambert, '"This Is All We Want": Great Britain and the Baltic Approaches, 1815-1914,' in Sevaldsen, J.

pp. [161–165]   NOTES

ed. *Britain and Denmark: Political, Economic and Cultural Relations in the 19th and 20th Centuries* (Copenhagen: 2003), pp.147–169.

17. Nicholas Riasonovsky, *Nicholas I and Official Nationality in Russia, 1825–1855* (Berkeley: University of California Press, 1959), p.47.

18. Harold N. Ingle, *Nesselrode and Russian Rapprochement with Britain, 1836–1844* (Berkeley: University of California Press, 1976), pp. 61, 69–73.

19. For British Baltic policy in the long nineteenth century: Andrew Lambert '"This Is All We Want": Great Britain and the Baltic Approaches 1815-1914.' In Sevaldsen, J. ed. *Britain and Denmark: Political, Economic and Cultural Relations in the 19th and 20th Centuries* (Copenhagen: 2003), pp. 147–169.

20. Ingle, *Nesselrode*, pp. 60–1.

21. Palmerston to George Villiers, Ambassador in Madrid 11.2.1834: in Bullen, R. & Strong, F. eds. *Palmerston: Private Correspondence with Sir George Villiers as Minister to Spain 1833–1837* (London: 1985), pp. 105–6.

22. Lambert, *Crimean War*, p. 53

23. *Times* editorial, April 24th, 1856: in Andrew Lambert & Stephen Badsey, eds. *The War Correspondents: The Crimean War* (Gloucester: Alan Sutton, 1994).

24. Lambert, *Crimean War*, p. 109. Napier would be used as a scapegoat by Sir James Graham to distract attention from the abject failure of the naval mobilization he had presided over, and the refusal to provide any of the coastal warfare equipment Napier requested before and during the campaign.

25. Earp, *Baltic Campaign*.

26. Earp, pp. 55–74. Although the title page claims the text was 'edited by' Earp, his role would now be described as ghost writer or as a book written by Napier 'with' Earp. Earp had an expertise in bringing the arguments of liberal naval heroes to the press, ghost writing Lord Cochrane's multi-volume memoirs, also published by Bentley, then the leading British naval publisher. Cochrane provided cogent support for Napier, in a stinging indictment of political failure, including his customary element of self-promotion in December 1856: Earp, pp. xiii–v. Earp's work with Cochrane ended in a court case, see: Brian Vale, *The Audacious Admiral: Cochrane. The True Life of a Naval Legend.* (London: Conway, 2004), pp. 207–8, 214.

27. Earp, pp. 63–5.

28. Earp, pp. 69–71.

29. Earp, p. 73.

NOTES

pp. [166–182]

30. Bernard Semmel, *Liberalism and Naval Strategy: Ideology, Interest and Sea Power during Pax Britannica* (London: Allen & Unwin, 1986), pp. 68–70.

31. Semmel, pp. 71–8.

32. Conacher, pp. 426–7.

33. Andrew Lambert, 'Looking for gunboats: British Naval operations in the Gulf of Bothnia, 1854–55', *Journal For Maritime Research*, 2005.

34. Lambert, *Crimean War*, p. 178.

35. Greenhill & Giffard, p. 116 and Lambert, 'Looking for gunboats'.

36. Plumridge to Napier 10 Jun. 1854: Napier Papers, British Library Additional Manuscripts (henceforth Add.) Add. 40,024 f237.

37. Lambert, *Crimean War,* p.191.

38. Berkeley to Napier 22.8.1854: Earp p. 382. Berkeley capitalized the word discretion to reflect the fact that Napier had been called 'indiscrete' by then Prime Minister Lord John Russell in 1849, and published the letter— earning himself the soubriquet the 'Indiscreet Admiral'.

39. Richard Connolly: *The Russian Economy: A Very Short Introduction* (Oxford: OUP, 2020), p.11. This penetrating study should be required reading for anyone attempting to comprehend the current crisis.

40. Lambert, *Crimean War*, p.288. Bartholomew Sulivan was not impressed by *Cossack's* proceedings.

41. Report of 11.8.1855 in Lambert & Badsey pp. 300–02.

42. W Bruce Lincoln, *Nicholas I: Emperor and Autocrat of all the Russias*, (London: Allen Lane, 1978 p. 316–24, 354).

43. Kezban Acar 'War Propaganda and Public Opinion in Russian Popular Culture' in Candan Badem ed. *The Routledge Handbook of the Crimean War* (Routledge: Abingdon, 2022), pp. 287–302.

44. Mitchell, B.R & Phyllis Deane, *Abstract of British Historical Statistics* (Cambridge University Press, 1962), pp.402–3.

45. Lambert, *Crimean War*, pp. 307–08 with fn

46. Mitchell, B. R. *European Historical Statistics.* 2nd edn. (London: 1980), pp. 360, 511, 580, 610, 750, 735.

47. *The Times* Editorial, April 24th 1856: Lambert & Badsey, pp. 304–5.

48. Andrew Lambert 'Winning without Fighting: British Grand Strategy and its application to the United States, 1815–1865' in Lee, B. & Walling. K. eds. *Strategic Logic and Political Rationality: Essays in honour of Michael J. Handel.* United States Naval War College, 2003.

49. Olive Anderson. *A Liberal State at War: English Politics and Economics during the Crimean War.* (London: St. Martin's Press, 1967) examined the development of economic war policy in an era of free trade, when

pp. [185–186]   NOTES

British liberal internationalists thought mutual economic interests would prevent future conflict.

10. THE BLOCKADE IN THE FIRST WORLD WAR

1. *Papers Relating to the Foreign Relations of the United States, The Paris Peace Conference, 1919*, Volume X, ed. Joseph V. Fuller, 'Twenty-sixth Meeting, July 10, 4.30 p.m. Document 25: 251, Removal of the Blockade on Germany' (Washington, DC: United States Printing Office, 1947), pp. 447–48.
2. Alan Kramer, 'Blockade and economic warfare' in *The Cambridge History of the First World War, Volume II: The State* (Cambridge: Cambridge University Press, 2014).
3. Marjorie Milbank Farrar, *Conflict and Compromise: The Strategy, Politics and Diplomacy of the French Blockade, 1914 – 1918* (The Hague: Martinus Nijhoff, 1974), pp. 2–3.
4. A. C. Bell, *A History of the Blockade of Germany and of the Countries Associated with Her in the Great War: Austria-Hungary, Bulgaria, and Turkey 1914–1919* (London: His Majesty's Stationery Office, 1937).
5. Perhaps the most famous twentieth-century example of the United Kingdom operating a blockade alone is the Beira Patrol. See Richard Moberly, 'The Beira Patrol: Britain's Broken Blockade against Rhodesia' *Naval War College Review*, 55, no. 1 (Winter 2002), pp. 63–84.
6. The United Kingdom was part of the 1990–2003 sanctions against Iraq, which blocked much trade in and out of the country.
7. Department of State, *Diplomatic Correspondence with Belligerent Governments Relating to Neutral Rights And Commerce* (Washington, DC: Government Printing Office, 1915).
8. Maritime Order in Council: 20 August 1914, Maritime Order in Council: 29 October 1914, Maritime Order in Council: 11 March, 1915, Maritime Order in Council: 20 October 1915, Maritime Order in Council: 30 March 1916, Maritime Order in Council: 7 July 1916, Maritime Order in Council: 10 January 1917, Maritime Order in Council: 15 February 1917. Bell, *A History of the Blockade of Germany*, pp. 711–719.
9. Marion C. Siney, *The Allied Blockade of Germany 1914–1916* (Ann Arbor, MI: University of Michigan Press, 1957), p. 14; Bell, *A History of the Blockade of Germany*, p. 40.
10. Bell, 'Appendix II' in *A History of the Blockade of Germany*, p. 721–740. Declarations of additions to the list of contraband were described

285

NOTES   pp. [186–188]

in Articles 23 and 25 in the Declaration of London. At the same time, however, Article 65 of the Declaration of London states that 'the provisions of the present Declaration must be treated as a whole, and cannot be separated.' For commentary published before WWI on why the Declaration of London was to be taken as a whole, see N. Bentwich, *The Declaration of London With An Introduction and Notes And Appendices* (London, Sweet and Maxwell, 1911), p. 124.

11. Max Rubmann, *Hunger! Effects of Modern War Methods* (Berlin: Verlag von Georg Reimer, 1919), p. 50.

12. Jay Winter, 'Surviving the war: Life Expectation, Illness, and Mortality Rates in Paris, London, and Berlin, 1914–1919' in Jay Winter and Jean-Louis Robert (eds.), *Capital Cities at War. Paris, London, Berlin 1914–1919* (Cambridge: Cambridge University Press, 1997), p. 517.

13. F. Baum, *Deutschlands Gesundheitsverhältnisse unter dem Einfluss des Weltkrieges* (Berlin: Deutsche Verlags-Anstalt, 1928).

14. Roger Chickering, *Imperial Germany and the Great War, 1914 -1918* (3rd edn., Cambridge: Cambridge University Press, 2014), p. 41; Herbert Heaton, *Economic History of Europe* (rev. edn, New York, Harper & Brothers, 1948), pp. 449–50.

15. J. Lee, 'Administration and Agriculture: Aspects of German Agricultural Policy in the First World War', in *War and Economic Development*, ed. Jay Winter (Cambridge: Cambridge University Press, 1975), p. 229.

16. Alice Autumn Weinreb, *Modern Hungers: Food and Power in Twentieth-century Germany* (Oxford: Oxford University Press, 2017), p. 13.

17. Margaret Barnett, *British Food Policy During the First World War* (Boston: Allen & Unwin, 1985), p. xiv.

18. Theo Balderston, 'Industrial Mobilization and War Economies' in John Horne (ed.), *A Companion to World War I* (West Sussex: Wiley-Blackwell, 2012), p. 227. See also *The Food Supply of the United Kingdom* (London: His Majesty's Stationery Office, 1917). Gerd Hardach, *The First World War, 1914–1918* (Berkeley: University of California Press, 1977).

19. Preamble, Declaration of London. International Humanitarian Law Databases. Declaration of London. https://ihl-databases.icrc.org/en/ihl-treaties/london-decl-1909/

20. Eric W. Osborne, *Britain's Economic Blockade of Germany 1914–1919* (Abingdon: Routledge, 2013), p. 26.

21. Article 28, Declaration of London.

22. Article 29, Declaration of London.

23. Article 27, Declaration of London.

286

pp. [188–192]   NOTES

24. Article 23, Declaration of London.
25. Article 22, Declaration of London.
26. Article 25, Declaration of London.
27. Article 33, Declaration of London.
28. Article 34, Declaration of London.
29. Osborne, *Britain's Economic Blockade*, p. 37.
30. Article 1, Declaration of London.
31. Avner Offer, 'The Blockade of Germany and the Strategy of Starvation, 1914–1918: An Agency Perspective', in Roger Chickering and Stig Förster (eds.), *Great War, Total War: Combat and Mobilization on the Western Front, 1914–1918*. (Cambridge: Cambridge University Press, 2000), p. 174.
32. Bentwich, *Declaration of London*.
33. Article 33, Declaration of London.
34. Jürgen Kocka shows how the German military kept out of food rationing and distribution for civilians, which most certainly added to the muted impact of German attempts to increase food supplies for civilians: *Facing Total War: German Society 1914–1918* (Cambridge, Mass.: Harvard University Press, 1984).
35. R. Moeller, 'Dimensions of Social Conflict in the Great War: The View from the German Countryside', *Central European History*, 14, no. 2 (June 1981), p. 152.
36. Benjamin Johnson, *Making Ammonia: Fritz Haber, Walther Nernst, and the Nature of Scientific Discovery* (Cham, Switzerland: Springer, 2022, e-book open access), p. 63.
37. James W. Garner, 'Some Questions of International Law in the European War', *The American Journal of International Law*, Oct., 1915, Vol. 9, No. 4 (Oct. 1915), p. 855.
38. *The Collected Papers of John Westlake on Public International Law*. L. Oppenheim (ed), (Cambridge University Press, 1914), pp. 313–314; Previous versions first published in the *Transactions of the Juridical Society* vol. 1858–1863, pp. 681–721, and in *Commercial Blockades, Considered with Reference to Law and Policy* (London: 1862).
39. Garner, 'Some Questions of International Law', p. 857; See also D. A. Azuni *The Maritime Law of Europe* vol. II, William Johnson (transl.), New York, Riley & Co, 1806, 'It is not allowable to starve or blockade a whole nation… To form a treaty of famine against a whole nation, to attempt to starve women, children, old men, &c; a measure so monstrous was reserved for England first to introduce', p. 98.
40. Ernst Liljedahl, "Tysklands blockadkrig" *Aftonbladet* February 19, 1917, Kungliga Biblioteket. *Aftonbladet* had 33,000–55,000

NOTES   pp. [193–195]

subscribers between 1910–1920; Liljedahl published a similar critique elsewhere. See Ernst Liljedahl, "Englands initiativ till folkrättens sönderbrytande", *Jämtlandsposten*, February 23, 1917, Kungliga Biblioteket. *Jämtlandsposten* had about 4000 subscribers between 1910–1920.

41. Paul G. Halpern, *A Naval History of World War I* (Annapolis, MD: Naval Institute Press, 1994), p. 21.

42. Stephen C. Neff, "Disrupting a Delicate Balance: The Allied Blockade Policy and the Law of Maritime Neutrality during the Great War." *European Journal of International Law*, 29, no. 2 (May 2018), pp. 459–475.

43. Germany avoided this for the first two years of the war, until the Battle of Jutland.

44. Siney, *The Allied Blockade*, p. 22.

45. Osborne, *Britain's Economic Blockade*, p. 22.

46. Bell, *History of the Blockade Against Germany*, p. 37.

47. Ibid., *History of the Blockade Against Germany*, p. 37.

48. Alan Kramer, *Dynamic of Destruction: Culture and Mass Killing in the First World War*. (Oxford: Oxford University Press, 2007), p. 41.

49. Andrea Griffante, 'Food and Nutrition (East Central Europe)', in 1914–1918-online. *International Encyclopedia of the First World War*, ed. by Ute Daniel, Peter Gatrell, Oliver Janz, Heather Jones, Jennifer Keene, Alan Kramer, and Bill Nasson (Freie Universität Berlin, Berlin), https://encyclopedia.1914-1918-online.net/article/food_and_nutrition_east_central_europe, July 29, 2022.

50. Mancur Olson Jr., *The Economics Of The Wartime Shortage. A History of British Food Supplies In The Napoleonic War And In World Wars I And II.* (Durham, North Carolina: Duke University Press, 1963), p. 75. Olson cites Salter. See James Arthur Salter, *Allied Shipping Control.* (Oxford: 1921), p.1.

51. Holder H. Herwig, 'Total Rhetoric, Limited War: Germany's U-Boat Campaign, 1917–1918', in Chickering and Förster (eds.), *Great War, Total War*, p. 191

52. Herwig, 'Total Rhetoric, Limited War', p. 195.

53. Olson, *The Economics Of The Wartime Shortage*, p. 83.

54. Casey MacLean, 'World War I on the Homefront', National Marine Sanctuaries, National Oceanic and Atmospheric Administration. May, 2018.

55. Ute Daniel, *The War from Within: German Women in the First World War* (Oxford: Berg Publishers, 1997), p.173.

pp. [195–198]   NOTES

56. Belinda J. Davis, *Home Fires Burning: Food, Politics, and Everyday Life in World War I Berlin* (Chapel Hill: University of North Carolina Press, 2000), p. 49.

57. A. Taylor, 'A New Sample of the Old German Psychology', *American Relief Administration Bulletin, No. 3 (1 April 1919)*. Hoover Institution Library and Archives. As cited in Mary Elisabeth Cox, *Hunger in War and Peace: Women and Children in Germany, 1914–1924* (New York: Oxford University Press, 2019), p. 262.

58. E. H. Starling, 'The Food Supply of Germany During the War', *Journal of the Royal Statistical Society*, 83, no. 20 (1920), p. 230.

59. Cox, *Hunger in War and Peace*, pp. 85–203.

60. Mary Elisabeth Cox 'Hunger Games: or How the Allied Blockade in the First World War Deprived German Children of Nutrition, and Allied Food Aid Subsequently Saved Them', *The Economic History Review*, 68 (2015), pp. 600–31.

61. Cox, *Hunger in War and Peace*, pp. 111–124.

62. Isabel V. Hull, *A Scrap of Paper: Breaking and Making International Law during the Great War* (Ithaca, NY: Cornell University Press, 2014).

63. Hew Strachan, *The First World War Volume I: To Arms* (Oxford: Oxford University Press, 2001), p. 1139.

64. Kramer, 'Blockade and Economic Warfare', p. 592.

65. Holger Herwig, *The First World War: Germany and Austria-Hungary 1914 –1918* (London: Bloomsbury Academic, 2014), pp. 280–281.

66. Jay Winter, 'Some Paradoxes of the Great War', in Richard Wall and Jay Winter (eds.), *The Upheaval of War: Family, Work, and Welfare in Europe. 1914–1918* (Cambridge: Cambridge University Press, 1988), pp. 38–41.

67. Offer, 'The Blockade of Germany' p. 186.

68. Mark Harrison, 'Myths of the Great War', in Jari Eloranta, Eric Golson, Andrei Markevich and Nikolaus Wolf (eds.), *Economic History of Warfare and State Formation* (Singapore: Springer, 2016) pp. 135–158.

69. N. P. Howard, 'The Social and Political Consequences of the Allied Food Blockade of Germany, 1918–19', *German History*, 11, no. 2, April 1993, p. 161.

70. Cox, *Hunger in War and Peace*, p. 216–219.

71. Frank M. Surface and Raymond L. Bland, *American Food in the World War and Reconstruction Period: Operations of the Organizations Under the Direction of Herbert Hoover 1914–1924* (Stanford, CA: Stanford University Press, 1931), pp. 195, 610–615.

NOTES pp. [198–202]

72. For more on this remarkable story, see Clare Mulley, *The Woman Who Saved the Children: A Biography of Eglantyne Jebb: Founder of Save the Children* (Oxford: Oneworld Publications, 2010).

73. Henry W. Nevinson, 'Woe to the Conquered!', *The Nation* (London), February 15, 1919. As cited in *The Blockade of Germany After the Armistice, 1918–1919. Selected Documents of the Supreme Economic Council, Superior Blockade Council, American Relief Administration, and Other Wartime Organizations*, ed. Suda Bane and Ralph Lutz (Stanford, CA: Stanford University Press, 1942), pp. 717–718.

74. Graham Auman Pitts, '"Make Them Hated in All of the Arab Countries": France, Famine, and the Creation of Lebanon', *Environmental Histories of the First World War* (Cambridge: Cambridge University Press, 2018), p. 175.

75. Weinreb, *Modern Hungers*, p. 14; Charles Paul Vincent, *The Politics of Hunger: The Allied Blockade of Germany, 1915–1919* (Athens: Ohio University Press, 1986).

11. LEGITIMISING VIOLENCE IN THE BRITISH ATTACK ON THE FRENCH FLEET AT MERS-EL-KÉBIR

1. Rachel Chin, *War of Words: Britain, France and Discourses of Empire during the Second World War* (Cambridge: Cambridge University Press, 2022), p. 67.

2. Philippe Lasterle, 'Could Admiral Gensoul Have Averted the Tragedy of Mers el-Kebir?', *Journal of Military History*, 67:3 (2003), p. 840.

3. See, for instance, Adam Sage, 'UK "Must Pay for Shrine to French Dead" at Mers-el-Kebir', *The Times*, 4 July 2020; Pierre Wadoux, 'Marins français tués par les Anglais à Mers-el-Kébir en juillet 1940: crime ou fait de guerre?', *Ouest France*, 13 July 2020.

4. Winston S. Churchill, *The Second World War*: Vol II *Their Finest Hour* (London: Cassel & Co, 1949), p. 206.

5. Archives Diplomatiques (Paris) 10 GMII 473. Note, 5 July 1940; Jean-Baptiste Duroselle, *L'Abime 1939–1944* (Paris: Imprimerie Nationale, 1986), pp. 296–98.

6. 'Italy abuses British Parliament', *The Times*, 6 July 1940, p. 3.

7. Brett C. Bowles, '"La Tragédie de Mers-el-Kebir" and the Politics of Filmed News in France, 1940–1944', *Journal of Modern History*, 76:2 (2004), pp. 372–75; Dominique Rossignol, *Histoire de la propagande en France de 1940 à 1944* (Paris: Presses Universitaires de France, 1991), pp. 306–16.

pp. [203–206]   NOTES

8. Jonathan Steinberg, 'The Copenhagen Complex', *Journal of Contemporary History*, 1:3 (1966), p. 23.

9. Chris Mann, *British Policy and Strategy Towards Norway, 1941–45* (Basingstoke: Palgrave, 2012), pp. 1–4.

10. Graham Rhys-Jones, 'Churchill and the Norwegian Campaign', *The RUSI Journal*, 155:4 (2010), p. 77.

11. Note by the First Lord of the Admiralty, 16 December 1939, cited in Winston S. Churchill, *The Second World War:* Vol I, *The Gathering Storm* (London: Cassell & Co., 1948), p. 431.

12. Ibid.

13. Ibid., p. 432.

14. Ibid., p. 433.

15. Michael Bess, *Choices Under Fire: Moral Dimensions of World War II* (New York: Vintage Books, 2008), p. 12.

16. Michael Walzer, *Just and Unjust Wars: A Moral Argument with Historical Illustrations* (New York: Basic Books, 2000), pp. 229–31, 245.

17. G. H. Quester, 'Two Hundred Years of Preemption', *Naval War College Review*, 60:4 (2007), p. 17.

18. David Reynolds, *Britannia Overruled British Policy and World Power in the Twentieth Century* (London: Routledge, 2000), p. 134.

19. Talbot Imlay, *Facing the Second World War: Strategy, Politics, and Economics in Britain and France 1938–1940* (Oxford: Oxford University Press, 2003), pp. 76–95.

20. The National Archives, UK (hereafter TNA) FO 371/24301, Memorandum emphasising need for France to continue as a belligerent and for the United States to enter as a belligerent, 15 June 1940.

21. Gary Sheffield, 'Introduction', in Emile Chabal and Robert Tombs (eds.), *Britain and France in Two World Wars: Truth, Myth and Memory* (Bloomsbury: London, 2013), p. 19.

22. John Keiger, 'Crossed Wires, 1904–14', in ibid., p. 29.

23. R. T. Thomas, *The Dilemma of Anglo-French Relations 1940–42* (London: Macmillan, 1979), pp. 11–13.

24. Martin S. Alexander, 'Dunkirk in Military Operations, Myths and Memories', in Chabal and Tombs, *Britain and France,* pp. 99–100.

25. Thomas, *Dilemma*, p. 25

26. Churchill, *Finest Hour*, p. 181.

27. TNA FO 371/24301, Memorandum emphasising need for France to continue as a belligerent and for the United States to enter as a belligerent, 15 June 1940; Churchill, *Finest Hour*, p. 187.

28. François Broche and Jean-François Muracciole, *Histoire de la collaboration 1940–1945* (Paris: Tallandier, 2017), p. 87;

Churchill, speech to House of Commons, 4 June 1940, https://winstonchurchill.org/resources/speeches/1940-the-finest-hour/we-shall-fight-on-the-beaches/, accessed 10 January 2023.

29. Churchill, *Finest Hour*, p. 205.

30. Armistice Agreement Between the German High Command of the Armed Forces and French Plenipotentiaries, 22 June 1940, https://avalon.law.yale.edu/wwii/frgearm.asp#art8, accessed 5 December 2022; 'Convention d'armistice entre l'Italie et la France, 24 juin 1940', in Romain Rainero, *La commission italienne d'armistice avec la France. Les rapports entre la France de Vichy et l'Italie de Mussolini (10 juin 1940–8 septembre 1943)* (Paris: Service Historique de l'Armée, 1995), p. 380.

31. Armistice Negotiations at Compiègne, 21–22 June 1940, *Documents on German Foreign Policy 1918–1945* Series D (1937–1945), Vol IX, *The War Years, March 18–June 22, 1940* (London: Her Majesty's Stationary Office: London, 1956), pp. 644–47; Marc Olivier Baruch, *Servir l'Etat français: L'administration en France de 1940 à 1944* (Paris: Fayard, 1997), pp. 77–79; Karine Varley, 'Defending Sovereignty without Collaboration: Vichy and the Italian Fascist Threats of 1940–42', *French History*, 33:3 (2019), pp. 425–27.

32. TNA CAB 65/13/50, War Cabinet, confidential annex, 24 June 1940, 10:30am.

33. Jean-Pierre Azéma and Olivier Wieviorka, *Vichy 1940–1944* (Paris: Perrin, 2000), pp. 54–88; Robert O. Paxton, *Vichy France: Old Guard and New Order, 1940–1944* (New York: Columbia University Press, 1972), pp. 69–92; 109–35.

34. TNA FO 371/24348, Special distribution and War Cabinet from Campbell, 22 June 1940, 3:30pm.

35. TNA FO 371/24348, telegram from Campbell, 22 June 1940, 11:31pm.

36. TNA CAB 65/8/3, War Cabinet, 2 July 1940, 12 noon.

37. Ibid.

38. TNA FO371/24321, message to FO Force H from Admiralty, 2 July 1940.

39. TNA ADM/205/6, 'Narrative of 3 July'.

40. TNA ADM/205/6, Interview with Admiral Gensoul.

41. Ibid.

42. Ibid.

43. Ibid.

44. Baudouin to Cambon, 3 July 1940, Ministère des Affaires Etrangères Commission de Publication des Documents Diplomatiques Français,

pp. [208–212]   NOTES

Documents diplomatiques français 1940, Tome I (1 janvier–10 juillet 1940) (Peter Lang: Brussels, 2004), p. 904.

45. Bernard Costagliola, *Darlan* (Paris: CNRS Editions, 2015), p. 69.
46. 'Un rapport de l'amirauté française sur l'agression britannique', *Le Matin*, 6 July 1940, p. 2.
47. Ibid.
48. 'What France was Told', *The Times,* 6 July 1940, p. 3.
49. TNA CAB 65/13/50, War Cabinet confidential annex, 24 June 1940, 10:30am.
50. TNA PREM 3/197/4, message to CAA from Admiralty, 26 June 1940.
51. TNA FO 371/24321, French ambassador to Foreign Secretary, 3 July 1940; FO 371/24321, note, 3 July 1940.
52. TNA CAB 64/14/1, War Cabinet confidential annex, 1 July 1940, 6pm.
53. TNA CAB 65/8/3, War Cabinet, 2 July 1940, 12 noon.
54. Ibid.
55. Churchill, *Finest Hour*, p. 208.
56. Martin Thomas, 'After Mers-el-Kébir: The Armed Neutrality of the French Vichy Navy, 1940–43', *English Historical Review*, 112:447 (1997), p. 650; Martin Thomas and Richard Toye, *Arguing about Empire: Imperial Rhetoric in Britain and France, 1882–1956* (Oxford: Oxford University Press, 2017), p. 165.
57. Churchill, *Finest Hour*, p. 208.
58. TNA ADM/205/6, 'Narrative of 3 July'.
59. Viscount Cunningham of Hyndhope, *A Sailor's Odyssey* (Hutchingson: London, 1951, p. 244.
60. TNA PREM 3/197/4, Commander-in-Chief Mediterranean to Admiralty, 3 July 1940, 2:31pm.
61. TNA PREM 3/197/4, Commander-in-Chief Mediterranean to Admiralty, 3 July 1940, 3:09pm.
62. Cunningham, *A Sailor's Odyssey*, p. 250.
63. Ibid.
64. Ibid, p. 255.
65. 'Period of Splendid Hope', *The Times,* 5 July 1940, p. 2.
66. Churchill, *Finest Hour*, p. 211.
67. Thomas and Toye, *Arguing about Empire*, p. 163.
68. 'A Tragic Necessity', *The Times*, 6 July 1940, p. 1.
69. 'Britain Up in US Opinion', *Belfast Telegraph*, 6 July 1940, p. 1.
70. 'Lorsque la France a donné sa parole, elle la tient, quoi qu'il puisse arriver', *Le Figaro*, 6 July 1940.

NOTES
pp. [212–214]

71. 'L'odieuse agression de l'Angleterre contre la flotte française a l'ancre soulève l'indignation mondiale', *Le Matin*, 6 July 1940, p. 1.

72. 'Scuttler-in-Chief Gives Order', *The Times,* 5 July 1940, p. 4; 'French Fleet No Longer in Being', *Daily News* (London), 5 July 1940, p. 1; 'London News and Comment', *The Scotsman*, 5 July 1940, p. 4

73. TNA CAB 65/13/53, War Cabinet confidential annex, 27 June 1940, 12 noon.

74. 'A Tragic Necessity', *The Times*, 6 July 1940, p. 1.

75. 'Current Events—A Great Peril Escaped', *Dundee Evening Telegraph*, 5 July 1940, p. 2; 'Lesson for Italy at Oran', *Yorkshire Post and Leeds Intelligencer*, 6 July 1940, p. 4; 'Sea-Power', *Birmingham Daily Post*, 5 July 1940, p. 2

76. 'Norway Lodges a Protest', *The Times*, 19 February 1940, p. 8.

77. 'Raid on Altmark Described', *Belfast Telegraph*, 19 February 1940; 'German Note to Norway', *The Scotsman*, 19 February 1940, p. 5.

78. J. C. Johnstone, 'The Nazi Dreams that were Shattered at Oran', *Belfast Telegraph*, 6 July 1940.

79. Churchill, *Finest Hour*, p. 206.

80. Hansard, vol. 362, House of Commons, French Fleet, debated 4 July 1940, https://hansard.parliament.uk/Commons/1940-07-04/debates/5b3e0cdc-25db-4ee3-bd4c-bc0a26f94395/FrenchFleet, accessed 15 July 2022.

81. Chin, *War of Words*, p. 89.

82. Hansard, vol. 362, House of Commons, French Fleet, debated 4 July 1940, https://hansard.parliament.uk/Commons/1940-07-04/debates/5b3e0cdc-25db-4ee3-bd4c-bc0a26f94395/FrenchFleet, accessed 15 July 2022.

83. 'Period of Splendid Hope', *The Times,* 5 July 1940, p. 2.

84. TNA FO371/24321, Note, 2 July 1940; PREM 3/197/4, letter from Alexander to Churchill, 2 July 1940.

85. Ibid.

86. Ibid.

87. 'Horrible—But Necessary', *Daily News* (London), 5 July 1940, p. 4; Hector Bywater, 'Facts About the French Navy', *Daily News* (London), 5 July 1940, p. 4; 'London News and Comment', *The Scotsman*, 5 July 1940, p. 4; 'Current Events—A Great Peril Escaped', *Dundee Evening Telegraph*, 5 July 1940, p. 2; 'A Tragic Necessity', *The Times*, 6 July 1940, p. 1.

88. 'Churchill in Tears at the End', *Daily News* (London), 5 July 1940, p. 1; 'Let's Talk It Over', *The People*, 7 July 1940; 'As Hanner Swaffer Sees It', *The People*, 7 July 1940; 'Remarkable Demonstration of

294

pp. [214–216] NOTES

Support for Mr Churchill', *The Scotsman*, 5 July 1940, p. 4. For French accusations of British 'rejoicing' at French losses, see 'Pour une diplomatie française', *Le Temps*, 6 July 1940, p. 1.

89. London News and Comment, *The Scotsman*, 5 July 1940, p. 4.
90. 'Let's Talk It Over', *The People*, 7 July 1940.
91. TNA INF 1 264, Daily report on morale, 8 July 1940.
92. TNA INF 1 264, Points from regions, 4 July 1940.
93. TNA INF 1 264, Daily report on morale, 8 July 1940.
94. TNA INF 1 264, Daily report on morale, 7 July 1940.
95. TNA INF 1 264, Daily report on morale, 5 July 1940.
96. TNA FO 371/24311, Note by Campbell, 8 July 1940.
97. TNA FO 371/24321, telegram from Mallett, 6 July 1940; telegram from Knatchbull-Hugessen, 6 July 1940; telegram from Palairet, 9 July; telegram from Campbell, 9 July; telegram from Bentinck, 10 July 1940.
98. Churchill, *Finest Hour*, pp. 211–12.
99. 'Iron Still in British Character', 14 July 1940, Foreign Office United States Correspondence, https://go.gale.com/ps/i.do?p=GDSC&u=ustrath&id=GALE|SC5114141702&v=2.1&it=r&sid=bookmark-GDSC&sPage=381&asid=081d1994, accessed 1 December 2022.
100. John Walters, 'America Feels Happier Now', *Daily Mirror*, 5 July 1940, p. 1; 'US is Relieved by News', *Daily News* (London), 5 July 1940, p. 1; 'The Seizure of the French Fleet', *The Times*, 6 July 1940, p. 4.
101. 'Americans Welcome Churchill's Speech', 14 July 1940, Foreign Office United States Correspondence, https://link.gale.com/apps/doc/SC5114141702/GDSC?u=ustrath&sid=bookmark-GDSC&xid=081d1994&pg=377, accessed 1 December 2022.
102. 'The Navy Does its Job', *The Times*, 6 July 1940, p. 4.
103. Ibid.
104. Ibid.
105. TNA FO 371/24321, French ambassador to Foreign Secretary, 3 July 1940; French ambassador to Foreign Secretary, 4 July 1940.
106. TNA FO 371/24301, Halifax to Campbell, 15 July 1940.
107. TNA FO 371/24301, 'Anglo-French Relations', 7 July 1940.
108. Duroselle, *L'Abime*, pp. 296–98.
109. Walzer, *Just and Unjust Wars*, p. 34.
110. Ibid, p. 46.
111. TNA FO 371/24311, Campbell final dispatch, 27 June 1940.
112. TNA CAB 65/13/50, Confidential annex, 24 June 1940, 10:30am.

NOTES pp. [216–220]

113. P. M. H. Bell, *A Certain Eventuality: Britain and the Fall of France* (Farnborough: Saxon House, 1978), p. 92.

114. Cunningham, *Sailor's Odyssey*, pp. 244–45.

115. TNA CAB 65/13/50, War Cabinet confidential annex, 24 June 1940, 10:30am.

116. TNA FO 371/24348, handwritten note, 24 June; note, 25 June 1940.

117. TNA PREM 3/197/4, message to CAA from Admiralty, 26 June 1940.

118. TNA CAB 65/14/1, War Cabinet, confidential annex, 1 July 1940, 6pm.

119. CAB 65-8-3 – War Cabinet, 2 July 1940, 12 noon. Chin, p. 81.

120. Charles de Gaulle, Appel prononcé à la radio de Londres, 22 June 1940, https://mjp.univ-perp.fr/textes/degaulle22061940.htm, accessed 10 November 2022; Charles de Gaulle, *War Memoirs, Vol. 1, The Call to Honour 1940–1942*, trans. Jonathan Griffin (London: Collins, 1955), p. 97; Julian Jackson, *A Certain Idea of France: The Life of Charles de Gaulle* (London: Allen Lane, 2018), pp. 137–38.

121. '"Tragedy" of Oran', *The Times*, 9 July 1940, p. 3.

122. Ibid.

123. Lucien Bourgues, 'L'inconcevable agression', *Le Petit Parisien*, 5 July 1940, p. 1.

124. Churchill, *Finest Hour*, p. 203.

125. 'A Tragic Necessity', *The Times*, 6 July 1940, p. 1.

12. OPERATION GOMORRAH

1. The National Archives, Kew (hereafter TNA), AIR 14/739A, Harris to chief of air staff Charles Portal, 9 April 1943, encl. 'The United States Contribution to the Bomber Offensive', p. 2.

2. See for example Keith Lowe, *Inferno: The Bombing of Hamburg, 1943* (London: Viking, 2007); Hans Brunswig, *Feuersturm über Hamburg: Die Luftangriffe auf Hamburg im 2. Weltkrieg und ihre Folgen* (Stuttgart: Motorbuch Verlag, 1985); Martin Middlebrook, *The Battle of Hamburg: Allied Bomber Forces against a German City, 1943* (London: Cassell, 2000).

3. TNA, AIR 40/425, Immediate Interpretation Report [on Hamburg], 27 July 1943, p. 2.

4. Ursula Büttner, ' "Gomorrah" und die Folgen' in Hamburg Forschungsstelle für Zeitgeschichte, *Hamburg im "Dritten Reich"* (Göttingen: 2005), pp. 618, 764.

pp. [220–224]   NOTES

5. TNA, AIR 14/249, 'Air Ministry Instructions and Notes on the Rules to be Observed by the Royal Air Force in War', 17 August 1939, pp. 5–7; Joel Hayward, 'Air Power, Ethics and Civilian Immunity during the First World War and its Aftermath', *Global War Studies*, 7 (2010), pp. 127–9; Peter Gray, 'The Gloves Will Have to Come Off: A Reappraisal of the Legitimacy of the RAF Bomber Offensive against Germany', *Air Power Review*, 13 (2010), pp. 15–16.
6. Richard Overy, *The Bombing War: Europe 1939–1945* (London: Allen Lane, 2013), pp. 243–50.
7. Churchill College Archive Centre (hereafter CCAC), Bufton papers, BUFT 3/48, 'Review of the Present Strategical Air Offensive', 5 April 1941, App. C, p. 2.
8. TNA, HO 186/927, 'Report on fire hazard', August 1941.
9. TNA, AIR 40/1814, memorandum by O. Lawrence (MEW), 9 May 1941.
10. See Richard Overy, 'The "Weak Link": Bomber Command and the German Working-Class, 1940-1945', *Labour History Review*, 77 (2012), pp. 11–34.
11. TNA, AIR 20/4768, Air Staff memorandum, 'The Value of Incendiary Weapons in Attacks on Area Targets', 23 September 1941; CCAC, BUFT 3/13, note for Deputy Director, Bombing Ops., 'Area Attack', 19 November 1941.
12. CCAC, BUFT 3/50, Draft for commander-in-chief of Bomber Command [n.d. but January 1942].
13. Charles Webster and Noble Frankland, *The Strategic Air Offensive against Germany: Volume IV* (London: HMSO, 1961), pp. 143–8.
14. CCAC, BUFT 3/24, Bomber Ops to Group Capt. Barnett, 1 November 1941; Draft Appendix B (October 1941).
15. TNA, AIR 20/4768, memorandum from Bomber Operations Directorate, 25 February 1942; 14/276, Harris to Coastal Command, 20 May 1942; Bomber Command Operational Order No 147, 23 May 1942.
16. TNA, AIR 48/33, USSBS, Hamburg Field Report nos. I, 2; Bundesarchiv-Berlin, R3102/10046, 'Zerstörung von Wohnraum in deutschen Städten, 1942–43.'
17. TNA, AIR 40/1271, Target Committee, Report of 87th meeting, 9 April 1943
18. Christ Church, Oxford, Portal papers, Folder 2/File 2, Portal to Churchill, 25 September 1941.
19. TNA, AVIA 18/480, 'Note on trials of Bomb, aircraft incendiary 4 lb on 17.9.1936 and 18.9.1936', 24 September 1936; AAEE Report,

NOTES   pp. [224–227]

'Functioning and Ballistic Trials of Bomb, Incendiary, Aircraft, 4 lb Mark I', 11 May 1937. On numbers of 4 lb bombs dropped during the war TNA, AIR 22/203, Bomber Command War Room Manual of Operations, 1939–1945, p. 54.

20. TNA, AIR 14/763, HQ Bomber Command to all Group Headquarters, 19 January 1942.
21. TNA, PREM 3/75/3, Churchill to Oliver Lyttleton, 28 July 1942; Cherwell (Frederick Lindemann) to Churchill, 24 July 1942; Nuffield College Oxford, Cherwell papers, G189, draft letter Churchill to Minister of Production, 27 July 1942; Archibald Sinclair to Lyttleton, 18 August 1942.
22. TNA, PREM 3/75/4, Cherwell to Churchill, 15 April 1943; Lyttleton to Churchill, 1 April 1943.
23. TNA, AIR 14/763, Bottomley to Harris, 12 May 1942.
24. CCAC, BUFT 3/27, Memorandum from Bombing Ops 1, 'The employment of H. E. bombs in incendiary attack', 18 November 1942.
25. TNA, AIR 14/739A, War Cabinet, chiefs-of-staff paper, 'An Estimate of the Effects of an Anglo-American Bomber Offensive of German towns and Cities', 3 November 1942.
26. CCAC, BUFT 3/26, Minutes of meeting at Ministry of Works, 9 October 1941.
27. University of East Anglia (UEA), Zuckerman Archive, SZ/OEMU/50/7, 9th meeting of RE8 Advisory Group, 16 September 1942; 10th meeting, 24 September 1942; 15th meeting, 29 October 1942; on Middle Ages see CCAC, BUFT 3/26, Director of Bombing Ops, Note on an article in *Die Sirene*, 2 October 1942.
28. Horatio Bond (ed.), *Fire and the Air War: A Symposium of Expert Opinions* (Boston, MA: National Fire Protection Association, 1946), p. 65.
29. The papers and minutes can be found in TNA, 14/1812 and 14/1813. These seem never to have been used in the existing literature on the bombing war.
30. TNA, AIR 14/1812, Minutes of Eighth Meeting on Incendiary Topics, Imperial College, 1 May 1943. On the term 'fire-storm' see University (hereafter UEA), Zuckerman Archive, SZ/OEMU/50/7, 'Note for Advisers Meeting', 12 August 1942.
31. Ibid., SZ/OEMU/52/1, 31st meeting of Air Ministry Bombing Committee, 21 October 1942.
32. RAF Museum, Hendon, London, Peirse papers, AC 71/13/61-2, text of speech to Thirty Club, 25 November 1941.

pp. [228–231] NOTES

33. RAF Museum, Harris papers, H51, Harris to Air Vice Marshal Richard Peck, 4 May 1942.
34. TNA, AIR 8/1109, Harris to Portal, 12 August 1943.
35. TNA, AIR 14/1779, Bomber Command Operational Research Section to Air Ministry, 29 November 1943.
36. TNA, AIR 14/739A, HQ Bomber Command, Intelligence Staff, 'Progress of RAF Bomber Offensive against Germany', 30 November 1943, pp. 1–2.
37. For example, TNA, AIR 9/424, John Slessor to Air Ministry Director of Plans, 17 August 1942. Slessor wrote that while bombing civilians was the policy, 'it is unnecessary and undesirable in any document about our bombing policy to proclaim it'.
38. RAF Museum, Harris papers H47, Harris to Sir Arthur Street (Air Ministry), 25 October 1943.
39. Se Richard Overy, 'Why We Bomb You: Liberal War-making and Moral Relativism in the RAF Bomber Offensive, 1940-45', in Alan Cromartie (ed.), *Liberal Wars: Anglo-American Strategy, Ideology and Practice* (Abingdon: Routledge, 2015), pp. 27–9.
40. RAFM, Harris papers, H51, letter from Harris to Air Vice Marshal Peck, encl. draft leaflet 'Why We Bomb You', 22 July 1942.
41. TNA, AIR 14/585, leaflet translations column 14, November–December 1943.
42. TNA, FO 898/313, memorandum by Ritchie Calder, 'Bombing (military, economic and morale objectives)', March 1942, p.1.
43. Richard Overy, 'Making and Breaking Morale: British Political Warfare and Bomber Command in the Second World War', *20th Century British History*, 26:3 (2015), pp. 391–2.
44. McMaster University, Vera Brittain Collection, Box 101, Alex Wood to Corder Catchpool, 17 January 1944, enclosing correspondence on the firestorm in the *Manchester Guardian*; Friends House, London, Foley papers, MS 448 3/1, BRC leaflet 'Bomb, Burn and Ruthlessly Destroy'.
45. TNA, PREM 3/11/8, Tizard memorandum for Churchill, 22 July 1943; Churchill to Hastings Ismay, 23 July 1943; Portal to Sinclair, 24 July 1943; Churchill, note for Ismay, 30 July 1943.
46. Andrew Brown, *J. D. Bernal: The Sage of Science* (Oxford: Oxford University Press, 2005), pp. 197–201.
47. TNA, AIR 14/1812, Minutes of meeting held at the Ministry of Aircraft Production, 24 June 1942, p. 5.
48. UEA Zuckerman Archive, OEMU/50/7, RE Operational Research Committee, 22 July 1942; Tenth Meeting of RE8 Advisory Group,

24 Sept 1942; RE8 Fifteenth Meeting of Advisory Group, 29 October 1942.

49. Zygmunt Bauman, *Modernity and the Holocaust* (New Haven: Yale University Press, 2001); Erik Markusen, David Kopf, *The Holocaust and Strategic Bombing: Genocide and Total War in the Twentieth Century* (Boulder, CO: Westview Press, 1995). See too their discussion in 'Was It Genocidal?' in Igor Primoratz (ed.), *Terror from the Sky: The Bombing of German Cities in World War II* (New York: Berghahn Books, 2010), pp. 158–174.

50. Freeman Dyson, *Disturbing the Universe* (New York: Harper & Row, 1979), p. 30.

51. Ibid., p. 31.

52. Royal Society Archive, Blackett papers, PB/1/16, Bernard Lovell memoir of Blackett in the *Biographical Memoirs of Fellows of the Royal Society*, p. 65. The C. P. Snow lecture was the 1961 Godkin Lecture at Harvard University.

53. Blackett papers, PB/4/4, 'Notes on effects of bombing on civilian population', 15 August 1941; memorandum for Deputy Director of Plans, Royal Navy, 5 November 1942, p. 3.

54. TNA, AIR 14/1813, Basil Dickens, ORS, to Harris, 23 February 1945.

55. TNA, AIR 14/2165, HQ Bomber Command to BC Groups, 8 March 1944; HQ Bomber Command to Groups, 21 March 1944; AIR 14/764, Operational Use of IB, Vol ii, loose minute.

56. TNA, AIR 14/1812, ORS report '4 lb v 30 lb incendiary', 14 September 1943.

57. TNA, AIR 19/215, minute for the Secretary of State, 15 July 1943; Sinclair to Temple, 17 July 1943; Temple to Sinclair, 20 July 1943.

58. TNA, DEFE 10/390, Chiefs of Staff (JIGSAW Committee), Tenth meeting minutes, 23 February 1960, p. 1; Twenty-Eighth meeting minutes, 2 June 1960; Forty-First meeting minutes, 4 August 1960, p. 2.

ABOUT THE CONTRIBUTORS

Mary Elisabeth Cox is an Assistant Professor of International Relations at Central European University in Vienna, Austria. She is the author of *Hunger in War and Peace: Women and Children in Germany 1914–1924* (Oxford University Press, 2019) and co-editor with Dr Claire Morelon of *Hunger Re-Draws the Map: Food, State, and Society in the era of the First World War* (Cambridge University Press, 2024).

David Edwards is Senior Lecturer in History at University College Cork and series editor of Studies in Early Modern Irish History with Manchester University Press. His publications include *Age of Atrocity: Violence and Political Conflict in Early Modern Ireland* (Four Courts Press, 2007), *Campaign Journals of the Elizabethan Irish Wars* (Irish Manuscripts Commission, 2014), and *The Colonial World of Richard Boyle* (Four Courts Press, 2018).

Charles J. Esdaile was a member of staff in the Department of History of the University of Liverpool for thirty-one years until his retirement in the wake of COVID in 2020. He is the author of numerous works on the Revolutionary and Napoleonic Wars including, most notably, *The Peninsular War: A New History* (Penguin Books, 2002) and *Napoleon's Wars: An International History* (Penguin Books, 2007).

Andrew Lambert FKC FRHistS is Laughton Professor of Naval History at Kings College London. His books include *The Challenge: Britain versus America in the Naval War of 1812* (Faber, 2012, winner of the Anderson Medal of the Society for Nautical Research), *Seapower States* (Yale University Press, 2018, winner of the Gilder Lehrman Book Prize in Military History), and *The British Way of War: Julian Corbett and the Battle for a National Strategy* (Yale University Press, 2021).

Neil Murphy is Professor of Late Medieval and Early Modern History at Northumbria University. He has published five books, including *The Tudor Occupation of Boulogne: Conquest, Colonisation and Imperial Monarchy 1544-50* (Cambridge University Press, 2019), *Henry VIII, the Duke of Albany and the Anglo-Scottish War of 1522-24* (Boydell, 2023), and *Plague, Towns and Monarchy in Early Modern France* (Cambridge University Press, 2024).

Richard Overy is Honorary Research Professor at the University of Exeter and a Fellow of the British Academy. His most recent work, *Blood and Ruins: The Great Imperial War 1931-1945* (Allen Lane, 2021) won the Duke of Wellington Medal for military history and the Distinguished Book Award of the Society for Military History. His next book is titled *Why War?*

Murray Pittock MAE FRSE is Pro Vice-Principal and Bradley Professor at the University of Glasgow. His works include *Scotland: The Global History* (Yale University Press, 2022, Spectator History Book of the Year Choice), *Enlightenment in a Smart City* (Edinburgh University Press, 2019, Association for Scottish Literature Book of the Year), *Culloden* (Oxford University Press, 2016, *History Today* Book of the Year Choice). In 2022 he was Scotland's Knowledge Exchange Champion.

Clifford J. Rogers is Professor of History at the United States Military Academy (West Point). He is the author, editor, or co-editor of a dozen books, including the 71-chapter interactive digital *West Point History of Warfare* and award-winning monographs on English

ABOUT THE CONTRIBUTORS

military strategy from 1327-1360 and on soldiers' lives in the Middle Ages.

Brendan Simms is Professor of the History of European International Relations and Director of the Centre for Geopolitics at the University of Cambridge. His publications include *Europe: The Struggle for Supremacy, 1453 to the Present* (Penguin Press, 2013) and *Hitler: Only the World was Enough* (Penguin Press, 2019).

D. J. B. Trim is Professor of Church History at Andrews University, Michigan, and a Fellow of the Royal Historical Society. He is the author, editor, or co-editor of sixteen books, including *European Warfare* (co-edited with Frank Tallett, Cambridge University Press, 2010) and *Humanitarian Intervention: A History* (co-edited with Brendan Simms, Cambridge University Press, 2011).

Karine Varley is a Lecturer in French and European History at the University of Strathclyde, UK. Her recent publications include *Vichy's Double Bind: French Collaboration between Hitler and Mussolini during the Second World War* (Cambridge University Press, 2023).

INDEX

Åland Islands, 163, 169–72, 179–80, 182
Aberdeen, Lord, 166
Abö (Turku), 172
'absolute contraband', 187, 188, 190, 192
'Act for the Kingdom of Ireland' (1541), 86
Act of Union, 205
Acton, Lord, 157
Acts of Parliament, 148
Adam of Usk, 22
Adam, Agnes, 150
Adam, Margaret, 150
Afghanistan, 160, 183, 184
Africa, 223
Agincourt, battle of, 16, 24, 26, 34–8
Air Ministry Bombing Directorate, 222
Air Ministry Target Committee, 223
Air Ministry, 12, 220–7
committees, 227–34
Alba, Duke of, 63, 64, 65, 66–7
Albemarle, Earl of, 100, 106
Aldeburgh Napes, 194

Alexander II, Czar, 120–1, 161–3, 176–9, 181
Algeçiras, 183
Algeria, 201
Aljubarrota, 37
Allen, William Henry, 131
'Allied Blockade', 185
Alma, Battle of, 167
Almeida, 138
Altmark (German supply ship), 212
Amager, 129
American Colonies, 93
American War of Independence, 116, 117
Amiens, Peace of, 136
Anabaptists, 66
Anglo-French confrontation, 116
Anglo-Dutch force, 63–5
'Anglo-French Blockade', 185, 186
Anglo-French economic war, 161
Anglo-Russian relations, 156, 162
Angosound, 170–1
Annexing Act, 103
Antwerp, 158
Aquitaine, 18, 20
Arbuthnott, Viscount, 107
Ardres, 54

305

INDEX

Armada wrecks, 70
Armed Neutrality, 118–19
Arson, 233
Atholl, 98
Austria, 158, 166, 178–9
Austria-Hungary, 185, 189, 198
Austrian-Hungarian submarines, 195
Axis, 207
  alliance, breakage, 201–2
Ayrshire, 106
Azuni, 192

Bacon, Francis, 123
Badajoz, 135, 143, 146, 152
Bake, 233
Baltic campaigns, 156, 168–77
Baltic port city, 120
Baltic Sea region, 115–17, 158, 161–8, 198
  'Great Armament', 178–81
Barons of Exchequer, 103
Basing House, siege of (Hampshire, 1645), 77
Basque town, 224
Baudouin, Paul, 208
Bauhaus, 226
Bauman, Zygmunt, 231–2
Bavaria, 128
BBC radio broadcast, 217
Beaugé, Jean de, 48
Belgium, 157, 158, 162–3, 184, 190, 193
Berkeley, Maurice, 171
Berkshire, 107
Berlin Decree, 119
Berlin, 127, 174, 207
Bernal, J. D., 226, 231
Bernstorff, Count, 124
Berwick, 52
Bingham, Richard, 69–70

Birmingham, 231
Björko, Treaty of, 183
Black Prince, 27
Black Sea Fleets, 176
Black Sea, 119, 158, 164, 180
Blackett, Patrick, 233
Bland, Humphrey, 94–5, 96, 97, 109, 110, 111–12
Blandy, William, 68
Blitz, 221
Blockade of Germany, British, 185–6
  'English Blockade', 185
  scholars on, 190–1
Bois, Guy, 15–16
Boleyn, Anne, 85
Bomarsund, 163, 168–72, 179, 180
Bomber Command, 219–2
Bombing Restriction Committee, 230
Bonapartist France, 156
Bond, Horatio, 226
Bordeaux, 16–17
Bosch, Carl, 190
Bosphorus, 162, 181
Bottomley, Norman, 225
Boulogne, 47, 48, 49, 53, 95
Boulonnais, 42, 44–5, 47–8, 49, 50, 53, 55
Bourbon, Charles de, duke of Vendôme, 51, 54
Bourbons, 93, 156
Bourchier, George, 81, 82
Bouvet, Honorat, 29
Bremen, 219
Brémule (1119), 34
Brest-Litovsk, Treaty of, 194
Brexit, 3
Bright, John, 166
Britain, 181–4

306

INDEX

Baltic campaigns, 168–77
Baltic Sea region, control, 161–8
Declaration of London (1909), 186–90
drinking, 150–1
economy, 196–200
Franco-British tensions, 205–7
German U-boat campaign, 194–6
'Great Armament', 178–81
honour, 215–17
industrial capacity, 177–8
'Offshore Balancing', 156–60
political justifications, 211–15
ports, 201
post war, 130–3
Royal Navy, 115–19
supreme emergency, 203–5
war and effect, 124–30
British Channel Fleet, 193
British Liberalism, 164
Brittany, 42
Bronowski, Jacob, 226
Browne, Thomas, 129, 141
Bruges, 64
Brunel, Isambard Kingdom, 181
Building Research Station, 226
Bulgaria, 185
Bundesrat, 197
Burghley, Lord, 64
Burgos, 141–2
Bustamente, José, 136
Butler, James, 74

Cádiz, 136
Caernarvon, Earl of, 118
Calais, 26, 27
Caledonian Mercury, 104
Calvinists, 60
Cameron of Fassifern, 103
Campbell, John, 98, 108

Campbell, Ronald, 207
Canadian forest products, 161
Canning, George, 121, 122, 131–2, 134
canon law, 35, 37
Cape Passaro, 123
Cape Santa Maria, battle of (1804), 136
Capitol Hill, 215
Carlow, 80
Carthage, 158–9
Casablanca Conference, 219
Castlereagh, Lord, 121–3, 132, 134, 160
Catapult (Operation), 201, 203–5, 207–11
Franco-British tensions, 205–7
political justifications, 211–15
Cathcart, Lord, 122–3, 125–7, 129
Catherine II, 161
Catherine of Aragon, 85
Catholic Dutch, 68
Caucasus, 181
Central Asia, 162, 181, 182
Central Europe, 119
Chalmers, Charles, 127
Chamberlain, Neville, 221
Channel Fleet, 183
Charles Edward Stuart, Prince, 93
Charles II, 85
Charles the Wise, 20
Charles V, 53, 55
Charles VI, 20, 23
Charleston, 180
Chastise (Operation), 233
Cherbourg Strategy, 159
Cherbourg, 159, 175, 18
Chicago Daily News, The, 211–12
Chichester, Arthur, 84
Chin, Rachel, 213

307

INDEX

China, 180–1
Chizé, battle of (1373), 38
Christianhavn, 129
Church of Notre Dame, 130
Church of Our Lady, 128
churches, 50
Churchill, General, 110, 111
Churchill, Winston, 134, 201, 203–4, 206, 209, 216, 217–18, 230
   political justifications, 211–15
Ciudad Rodrigo, 135, 143, 146
Clement VII, 85
Clerk, Justice, 99, 101, 105, 107
'close blockade', 189
Cobden, Richard, 166
Cockayne, Colonel, 96, 97
'collective responsibility', 97
Cologne, 223, 233
Colt Navy pistol, 177
'conditional contraband', 188, 189
Confederate States, 191
Congress of Vienna, 158
Congreve rockets, 124, 129
Connolly, Richard, 173
Constitution of 1812, 137
Continental System, 161
   forbade, 119
Contraband Proclamations, 186
Copenhagen Roads, 117
Copenhagen, 5, 10, 121, 124, 161, 181, 212–13
   Baltic, control of, 115–19
   post war, 130–3
   war and effect, 124–30
Corn Laws, 166
Coss, Edward, 140–5
Cossack (incident), 167
Costello, Edward, 144
Council of Constance, 28–9
Crawford, Earl of, 106

Crimean War, 7, 9, 155, 162–3
   Baltic campaigns, 168–77
   'Great Armament', 178–81
   industrial capacity, 177–8
Cromwell, Oliver, 59, 84
   Basing House, siege of (Hampshire, 1645), 77
   Drogheda, capture of, 73–6
   English Civil Wars (1642–5, 1648–9), 77, 85
   Ulster massacre, 74, 75
   Wexford, siege and sacking of, 76
Cronstadt, 159–62, 169–74, 176, 178, 180–1
crops, destruction of, 42, 43–5, 49, 51–3, 54, 56
Crown Council, 173
Culloden Moor, 93, 94
Cuningham, Robert, 106
Cunningham, Andrew, 210–11, 216

Dacre, Thomas, 52–3
Dakar, 209
Danish Navy, 132
Danish ships, 202
Danube, 163, 174
Darlan, Admiral, 208, 212, 216, 217–18
Darnley, Earl of, 117, 132
Dauphin, 26–7
de Gaulle, Charles, 217
de León, Fernando González (historian), 64, 67
Declaration of London (1909), 186–91, 199–200
Delagrave, André, 138
Den Brielle (Holland), 63
Denmark, 162–3, 168, 181–3
   Baltic, control of, 115–19

308

INDEX

vs. Britain, 120–4
post war, 130–3
war and effect, 124–30
Deschenes, Parseval, 170
Desmond rebellion (1579–83), 78,
81, 84
Desvres, 45
Dieppe, 60
Disraeli, Benjamin, 166
Donaldson, Joseph, 146–7
Doullens, 46
Dresden, 220, 227
Drogheda, capture of, 73–6
Drummond, Provost, 110
Duisburg, 219
Dundas, Robert, of Arniston, 106
Dundas, Richard, 174–5
Dunkirk evacuation, 206
Dunquerque (battleship), 209
Durston, Gregory, 147
Dutch Revolt, 58, 63–9
Dyson, Freeman, 232–3

Earp, George Butler, 165
East Central Europe, 194
East India Company, 99
'Eastern Crisis', 163
Edinburgh, 46
Edward III, 16, 18–19, 24, 27–8
Edward VI, 86
Eigg, 98
Eighth Air Force (United States),
220
Elbe River, 220
Elbe, 223
Elizabeth I, reign of, 57–72, 82, 86
English troops, disavowals of,
58–9
and the Huguenots, 60–1
wars of religion, 60
Elizabethan soldiers

capture of, 61
disavowals of, 58–9
part of the rebel force, 64
served on the Huguenot side,
60–2
Elsinore, 124
Enfield rifle, 177
Englische Hungerblockade, 186
'English and British violence'
nature of, 5
term, 2–3
English Channel, 175
English Civil Wars (1642–5,
1648–9), 77
'English Park', 169
*English People in the Eighteenth
Century* (Marshal), 149
Entente, 197, 198
Episcopal Church, 102
Essex, Earl of, 70
Étaples, 45
Eure, Henry, 55
Europe, 3, 4, 5, 6, 7, 8, 9, 10, 12,
13, 120, 155

Faroe Islands, 117
Fergusson, Captain, 98
Finland, 168, 169, 182
Fireband, 233
Fisher, Jackie, 134, 183
FitzMaurice's rebellion, 89, 90
Fleming's Regiment, 106–7
Fletcher, Andrew, Lord Milton and
Earl of Saltoun, 99, 107
Flushing, 63, 64–5
food production, destroying, 42,
43–5, 49, 51–3
Forbes, Duncan, of Culloden, 98–9
Force de Rade, 201
Force H (Royal Navy), 208
Fort William, 98

309

INDEX

Four Power alliance, 158
France, 10, 11, 12, 15, 60, 116,
119–20, 134, 158–9, 163, 166,
177–8, 183, 189, 196, 221
Agincourt, battle of, 16, 24, 26,
34–8
alliance, breakage, 201–2
Baltic campaigns, 168–77
vs. Britain, 120–4
Britain's political justifications,
211–15
Catapult (Operation), 203–5,
207–11
Franco-British tensions, 205–7
invasion of (1415), 17
wars of religion, 60, 62
See also Hundred Years' War
Franco-Prussian War, 157
Franco-Russian maritime League,
124
Franco-Scottish alliance, 41
Franco-Scottish ordinance (1385),
24, 25
Frederick the Great, 123
French fleet, 204–5
French Revolution, 150
French Wars of Religion, 62
Friedrich of Hesse-Cassel, 94

Gambier, Admiral James, 122,
124–7, 128–9
Gamla Carleby. *See* Kokkola
Garner, James W., 191–2
Gensoul, Admiral, 201, 207,
216–17
George III, 117, 123
Georgian Britain, 151
Geraldine League conspiracy, 89, 90
German Air Force, 221
German Blitz, 225
German troops, 66

German U-boat campaign, 194–6
Germany, 134, 177, 185–6, 203
Baltic campaigns, 168–77
blockade, scholars on, 190–2
Blockade's effect, 186–7
Bomber Command, 219–27
bombing of, 2, 7, 10
British naval actions, 12
Declaration of London (1909),
186–90
Declaration of London,
consequences, 193
economy, 196–200
Franco-British tensions, 205–7
German U-boat campaign,
194–6
Gernika, 224
Gesta Henrici Quinti, 25
Ghent, 160, 173
Ghent, Peace of, 160
Gibraltar, 208, 210
Gilbert, Humphrey, 64, 70
'gin craze', 150
Gladstone, William, 166, 177,
183–4
Glyndw^r, Owain, 22
Godfroy, Admiral, 210–11, 216
Gomorrah (Operation), 219
Bomber Command, 219–27
committees, 227–34
Gordon, George, 150
Gordon, James Willoughby, 144
Graham, James, 164
Baltic campaigns, 168–77
Grant, William, 118–19
Great and Little Belts, 117
'Great Armament', 178–81
Great Bank of Newfoundland, 123
'Great War'. *See* World War I
Greenland, 117
Gregory XIII, 86

310

INDEX

Grey, Earl, 118
Grey de Wilton, Lord, 69
Groenlo, 71
Gropius, Walter, 226
Gruffydd, Elis, 47, 53
Guesclin, Constable Bertran du, 38
Gulf of Bothnia, 169
Gulf of Finland, 156, 168–70, 178, 180, 182

Haarlem, 65–6, 67
Haber, Fritz, 190
Haber-Bosch-Mittasch synthesis method, 190
Habsburg commanders, 54
Hague Convention II (1907), 187
Halifax, Lord, 213, 215
Hamburg, 2, 219, 222–3, 225
  committees, 227–34
Hango Head, 171, 174
Hanover, 115, 117
Harfleur, siege of (1415), 2, 26, 31–4
Harris, Arthur, 219, 223–4, 228, 229
Harvard, 233
Haslar, 181
Havre de Grace (Le Havre), 60, 61
Hawkesbury, Lord, 117–18
Helsingfors (Helsinki), 175
'hemp crisis', 116
Henderson, Andrew, 93–4
Henry II, 47–8
Henry IV, 22
Henry V, reign of, 11, 15–18, 20–39
  came to the throne, 18
  campaign, 23–31, 38–9
  Harfleur, siege of (1415), 2, 26, 31–4

invasion of Scotland (1400), 21–2
justice and piety, 29–30, 35
killing of prisoners, 38
military experience, 18, 20–3
  1415
prisoners, 37
resumed the war, 20, 23
surrender offer, 32–3
Henry VIII, reign of, 5, 11, 41–56, 78, 80
European and Global contexts, 54–6
exposure, stripping, and sexual violence, 47–9
first invasion of France (1512), 42
Howard's countryside campaigns, 42, 43–5
Ireland during, 85–7
laws of war, 48, 49–51
matrimonial problems, 85
military strategy and scorched earth, 51–4
urban populations, violence against, 46–7
See also Howard, Thomas, duke of Norfolk
Heritable Jurisdictions Act, 102–3
Hesdin, 46
High Middle Ages, 34
Hitler, Adolf, 134, 214
HMS *Cossack*, 174
HMS *Miranda*, 169
HMS *Prometheus*, 127
Holstein, 117, 120–1, 124
'Holy Places' Crisis, 163
honor, 29
Hossack, Provost, 107
House of Commons, 189, 211

311

INDEX

House of Lords, 117, 132, 189, 213
Howard, Edward, 42
Howard, Thomas, duke of Norfolk, 41–56, 87
  campaign in France (1544), 50–1
  death, 42
  first invasion of France (1512), 42
  Henry VIII's congratulation letter, 46
  letter to Henry VIII, 50–1
  military law codes (1544), 50
  scorched earth strategy, 42, 43–5, 49, 51–3, 54, 56
  Scottish campaign (1523), 44, 51–2
  sources of food production, destroying, 45
  urban populations, violence against, 46–7
Howick, Viscount, 120
Huguenots, 60–1, 63
Hull, 231
Hundred Years' War, 10, 15, 17
  Henry V's 1415 campaign, 23–31
  Harfleur, siege of (1415), 2, 26, 31–4
  See also Henry V, reign of; Henry VIII, reign of
Huske, John, 95
Husum, 120
Hydrographic Office, 162

Iberia, 158
Iberian Peninsula, 10, 137
Iceland, 117
Idrone, 80
Imperial College, 226–7, 230
Imperial Russia, 156, 159–60

Incendiary Panel, 232
Independent Highland Companies, 105
India, 119
Inverness, 96, 110–11
Ireland, 1, 4, 5, 10, 15, 57, 58, 73–91, 121, 147–8, 189
  Catholic Church, influence of, 78
  Drogheda's capture (1649), 73–6
  English administration, administrative tasks, 79–8
  English administration, militarized, 79
  English vice-regal rule, 80–3, 87–8
  famine, 84
  Howard's burnings in, 52
  Irish violence (1641–2), 75
  major conflicts, 78
  plantations, 83–5
  population transplantation, 95
  St Peter's Church, taking of, 75
  subjugation of, 78–85
Irish Catholics, 74, 76, 77, 86
Irish Sea, 58
Istanbul, 162, 181
Italians, 69
Italy, 177, 189

Jackson, Francis James, 122, 124–7, 133
Jacobite army, 93, 94, 95, 108, 110–11
Jacobite Rising, 93, 94, 97, 99, 101
Jacobites, 93, 94, 96–7, 98, 101, 110
James IV, 42
James V, 90
Jane of Leith, 100
Japan, 157, 189

312

INDEX

Jean II, 19–20
Jebb, Eglantyne, 198–9
Jedburgh, 46
JIGSAW committee (Joint
Intelligence Group on the Study
of All-Out Warfare), 234–5
Jomini, Baron, 161–2
Juan of Austria, Don, 67
Junot, General, 138–9
Jutland, 120

Kiel, 219
Kildare rebellion (1534–5), 78
Killigrew, Henry, 60, 61, 62
Kinburn, 176, 178
Kokkola, 169–70
Konstam, Angus (historian), 70
Kotlin Island, 160
Kriegsernährungsamt, 197

La Coruña, 145
Lancaster rifled cannon, 175
lands, destruction of, 42, 43–5,
49, 51–3, 54, 56
Lanquet, Thomas, 47
Laois, 83, 89
Lauderdale, Earl of, 110
Law of Arms, 24
law of Deuteronomy, 31
laws of war, 48, 49–51
Layne, Christopher, 157
le Bel, Jean, 16
Leach, Captain, 130
Leach, John, 138
League of Nations Covenant, 204
Leagues of Armed Neutrality, 116,
161
Legion, German, 120
Leiden, siege of (1574), 67
Leipzig, 197
Lewis, George Cornewall, 177–8

'Liberal International Order', 1
liberalism, 166
Liljedahl, Ernst, 192
Limerick, 80, 81, 82
Lines of Torres Vedras, 137, 144–5
Lisbon, 137–40, 152, 158
Lisbon earthquake, 138
Liverpool, Lord, 147, 158, 160
London Naval Conference, 187,
1859
London, 120, 168, 172, 177, 182
Baltic, control of, 115–19
Catapult (Operation), 207–11
Denmark, war and effect,
124–30
Franco-British tensions, 205–7
Germany's economy, 194–200
supreme emergency, 203–5
Louis of Nassau, 63, 65
Louis of Spain, 36
Louis XIV, 128
Low Countries, 63

Maastricht, 67
MacDonald, Clan, 101
MacDonalds of Glynns, 88, 89, 90
MacIntyre, Janet, 150
Mackintosh, Anne, 97
Macpherson, Cluny, 108
Mahan, Alfred Thayer, 134
"malcontents", 68, 69
man-made famine, 42, 43–5, 49,
51–3, 54, 56
Markusen, Eric, 231–2
Marshal, Dorothy, 149
Martinique, 207
Mary I, 62, 86
Masséna, Marshal, 137
McCormack, Anthony, 84
McElroy, James, 226
Mechelen, 68

313

INDEX

Mediterranean Sea, 119
Mellifont, Treaty of, 79
Mers-el-Kébir, 201–3, 210, 212–13, 217–18
Methodism, 149
Middle East, 223
Millennium (Operation), 233
Ministry of Economic Warfare, 222
Ministry of Home Security, 222
Mittasch, Alwin, 190
Montmorency, Constable de, 62
Mons, 63, 65
Montreuil, 46, 47
Moodie, Benjamin, 97, 98
Moore, Graham, 136
Moore, John, 135–7, 143, 152
Morale, 222
Morgan, Hiram (historian), 84
Morlaix, 42, 43, 56, 46
Morley, John, 183–4
Moroccan Crisis I, 183
Morrill, John (historian), 77
Moscow, 181
Mount Lebanon, 199–200
Munster, 82, 83, 84, 89, 90
Murray, George, 125

Napier, Charles, 164–5, 179
    Baltic campaigns, 169–73
Napoleon, 120–1, 158, 202
    Baltic, control of, 115–19
    Denmark, war and effect, 124–8
Nation, The (magazine), 199
National Debt, 183
National Fire Protection Association, 226
Naval Conference, 193
Navigation Acts, 166
Nazism, 204, 218
Nelson, Horatio, 117, 169

the Netherlands, 12, 58, 59, 60, 189
    Dutch Revolt, 58, 63–9
    revolt (1568), 63
    revolt (1572), 63
Nevinson, Henry W., 199
New Model Army, 74, 76
New York Herald Tribune, The, 211
New York Post, The, 215
New York Times, The, 215
Nicholas I, 176, 180
Nicholls, James, 151
Nine Years War (1594–1603), 78, 79, 88
Ninety-Fourth Foot, 146–7
Norfolk, 95
Normandy, 16, 24, 34
Norreys, John, 68
Norris, Thomas, 142
North Africa, 134
North Sea, 117, 120, 193
North, Admiral, 210
Northumberland, 52
Norway, 117, 193
    Franco-British tensions, 205–7
    supreme emergency, 203–5
Nova Scotia, 113

O'Connors, 89, 90
O'Mores, 89, 90
O'Neill, Shane, 88
Odessa, 166
Odin (warship), 169
Offaly, 83, 89
Offer, Avner, 189
'Offshore Balancing', 156–7, 183
One Belt One Road, 158
Operational Research Committee, 231
Oran, 134, 201, 209
Order in Council, 119

314

INDEX

Orkney, 98
Orléans, 61
Orlov, Alexei, 161
Oscar I (Swedish King), 169
Oslo, 212
Ostend, 71
Ottoman Empire, 160, 163, 166, 180, 182, 199

Palmerston, Lord, 179, 163, 164, 183
Paradin, Guillaume, 48
Paris Council of War, 179
Paris, 121, 124, 163, 150, 205
Paris, Treaty of, 188–9
Parker, Geoffrey (historian), 64, 66, 87
Parker, Hyde, 117
Parma, Prince of, 67, 69
Paul IV, Pope, 86
Paul, Czar, 161
Paulet, Amias, 62–3
Peace of Paris, 180
Peirse, Richard, 227
Pelham, Henry, 95, 99, 111
Pelham, William, 80, 81–2, 84
Pelham-Holles, Thomas, 99
Peniche, 137
Peninsular War (1808–14), 8, 11–12, 135, 152
People, The (Newspaper), 214
Percy rebellion, 21, 22
Persia, 162, 181
Pétain, Philippe, 206–7
Peter the Great, 160
Peymann (Danish commander), 128
Philip II, King of Spain, 63, 90
Philip VI, 18
piety, 29–30
pillaging, 42–3, 49

Pitt, William, the Elder, 123
Poland, 12, 168, 182, 221
Political Warfare Executive, 229
Pomerania, 120
Portal, Charles, 223, 225, 230
Porton Down, 226
Portugal, 140, 142, 152, 163, 164
Portuguese army, 37
Pound, Dudley, 209, 216
Prince, Thomas, 93
Prussia, 116–17, 120, 122, 168, 174
    vs. Britain, 120–4

QUADRANT Conference, 228
Quebec, 228
Quinn, D.B. (historian), 88

Radcliffe, Henry, 88
Radcliffe, Thomas, 87–8
RAF Bomber Command, 219–27
rape, 10, 25, 29, 48, 82, 146
Rattray, John, 99
RE8 scientists, 226
Reformation, 59, 71
Requesens, Don Luis de, 67
Reval (Tallinn), 168, 171, 172, 174
Reval harbour, 168–9
Reynaud, Paul, 206
Richard II, 21, 24, 25
Richelieu (battleship), 209
Robert III, 21
Roeulx, 55
Rome, 158–9, 207
Rouen, 60–1
Royal Artillery, 105
Royal Dockyards, 177
Royal Engineers, 176
Royal Marine Artillery, 176
Royal Navy, 115–19, 125, 127, 133–4, 136, 162–3, 166, 208

315

INDEX

Baltic campaign, 7, 9, 12
'British Blockade', 185–6
'Germany's economy, 194–200
'Great Armament', 178–81
Royal Scots (regiment), 94
Roy-Sandby military survey, 100
Ruegen, 120, 122
'rules of engagement', 24
Russell, John, 163
Russell, William Howard, 168
Russia, 120, 174, 181–4, 189, 194
  Baltic campaigns, 168–77
  Baltic coast, control, 161–8
  Baltic, control of, 115–19,
    161–8
  'Great Armament', 178–81
  'Offshore Balancing', 156–60

Saint-Omer, 48
San Sebastian, 135, 143, 140, 146
Sander, Nicholas, 90
Sandys, William, 43, 50
Santander, 152
Save the Children, 198
Saxony, 123
Scapa Flow, 193
Schaumann, Auguste, 145–6
Scheldt (Zeeland), 63, 64
Scheldt Estuary, 156, 158, 181
scorched earth strategy, 42, 43–5,
  49, 51–3, 54, 56, 81, 84, 89,
  137
Scotland, 1, 2, 4, 9, 15, 93–113,
  150
  administration, 98–102
  British high command's view on
    Jacobites, 94
  'Highlands', 102, 103, 104,
    105
  Howard's campaign (1523),
    51–2

Howard's destruction of lands,
  42, 43, 44, 46, 53
Jacobites, 93, 94, 96–7, 98,
  101, 110
livestock raiding, 97
treason trials, 102
Scots Fusiliers (regiment), 94, 104,
  105
Scots Law, 102
Scotsman, The (Newspaper), 214
Sea Beggars, 63
SEAR, 233
Second Armed Neutrality, 116–17
Serra do Buçaco, 138
Sevastopol, 166, 172, 176–9
Seven Years' War, 123
Seventy-First Foot, 147
Seymour, Edward, 46, 54
Sherer, Joseph, 142, 145
Sheridan, Richard Brinsley, 132
Shetlands, 193
Sicily, 123
Sinclair, Archibald, 234
Sinclair, Joseph, 147
Smerwick massacre, 69–70
Smith, Gregory, 148–9
Snow, C. P., 233
Somerville, Admiral, 208, 210
South America, 136
South Asia, 223
South Korea, 157
Spain, 57, 58, 116, 120, 123,
  136–7, 140, 142, 152, 163, 189
  vs. Britain, 120–4
Spaniards, 63, 64, 65–6, 67, 69
Spanish Armada, 158
Spenser, Edmund, 81–2, 89
Spithead, 183
St George's Dragoons Regiment,
  105
St Leger, Anthony, 80

INDEX

St. Crispin's Day, 16
St. George's Day, 156, 180
St. Petersburg, 134, 159–60, 162, 168–70, 174, 178, 180–2
Stevenson, John (historian), 150
Stewart, James, 98
Stralsund, 120
Strasbourg (battleship), 209
Strathbogie, 98
Stuarts, 79, 82, 84, 85, 86
Sulivan, Bartholomew, 169–76
Sussex, 88
Sweaborg, 167, 169–72, 174, 178, 182
Sweden, 116–17, 162–3, 168, 171, 179–82
    German U-boat campaign, 194–6
    German's economy, 196–200
Synod of Moray, 97
Syria, 164

Temple, William, 234
Tennyson, Lord, 168
Teviotdale, 44, 46
Thane of Fife, 100
Thirty-Fourth Foot, 142
Thomas, Martin, 211
'Thousand Bomber Raid', 223
Tilbury hulks (prison ships), 100–1
Tilsit, 120–1
Tilsit, treaty of, 119, 133, 161
Times, 164, 180–1, 212, 218
Tirpitz, Alfred von, 195
Tizard, Henry, 230–1, 233
Totleben, General, 176
Tournai, 47
Toye, Richard, 211
Trans-Siberian Railway, 158
Treatise on Military Discipline (1743), 97

Treaty of Aix-la-Chapelle, 109–10
Treaty of Brétigny, 18, 19
Treaty of Troyes (1564), 61
Tree of Battles, The (Honorat Bouvet), 29
Trent (steamer), 181
Triple Entente Fleet, 200
Tsarist Poland, 194
Tsarist Russia, 122
Tudors, 51, 53–4, 79, 82, 84, 85, 86
Turkey, 159, 183, 185
Turnbull, Stephen (historian), 66
Turpin, Dick, 151
Twenty-Third Foot, 141–2

Ulster massacre, 74, 75
Ulster or Shane O'Neill wars (1557–62, 1565–7), 78
Ulster Plantation, 83
Union warship, 181
United Kingdom of Great Britain
    blockade, scholars on, 190–1
    'British Blockade', 185–6
    Catapult (Operation), 203–5, 207–11
    Declaration of London (1909), 186–90
    economy, 196–200
    Franco-British tensions, 205–7
    German U-boat campaign, 194–6
    'Great Armament', 178–81
    honour, 215–17
    political justifications, 211–15
    supreme emergency, 203–5
United States of America, 116, 159–60, 185, 189
    political justifications, 211–15
US Civil War, 191

INDEX

Valenciennes, 63
Vere, Francis, 71
Versailles, Treaty of, 185
Vesting Act, 102, 103
Vichy French, 134, 202, 207, 217
Vienna, 156, 160, 173, 174
View of the Present State of Ireland, A (1596), 89
Vulture (warship), 169

Walcheren island, 64
Wales, 1, 9
Walpole, Horace, 104
Walpole, Robert, 99
Walsingham, Thomas, 23
Walzer, Michael (historian), 204
War of the Austrian Succession, 105, 109
Washington, John, 168–9
Washington, political justifications, 211–15
Waterloo, 156, 158, 178
Watford, 142
Wellesley, Arthur, Duke of Wellington, 126, 135, 143–4, 152
Wellington, 153
war-crime, 138
Welsh rebellion, 22–3
West Indies, 201, 207
Western Europe, 157
Westlake, John, 191
Westminster, 74–5, 98, 102

Wexford, 82
siege and sacking of, 76
Whatley, Christopher (historian), 111
Whig/Peelite coalition Government, 164
Whitsandbay, 50
Wilhelmine Germany, 197
Wilhelmshaven, 219
William Augustus, Duke of Cumberland, 93, 95, 97, 99–100, 101–2, 104, 105–6, 111, 113
William, Prince of Orange, 63, 65, 66
Williams, Roger, 64–5, 67, 68
Windham, William, 132
Winter War, 203
Wolfe, James, 96
Wolsey, Cardinal, 43, 44
Wood, Thomas à, 75
World War I, 12
World War I, 12, 156, 157, 189
blockade, scholars on, 190–1
'British Blockade', 185–6
Declaration of London (1909), 186–90
World War II, 2, 10, 12, 134, 205–6
Wyndham, Edmund, 49

Yorke, Philip, 99

Zeeland, 63–4, 65, 124
Zuckerman, Solly, 227, 231

318